The Perils OF *Peace*

★ ★ ★ ★ ★

Smithsonian Books

COLLINS
An Imprint of HarperCollins Publishers

THOMAS FLEMING

The Perils OF *Peace*

★ ★ ★ ★ ★

America's Struggle for Survival

After Yorktown

HarperCollins books may be purchased for educational, business, or sales promotional use. For information please write: Special Markets Department, HarperCollins Publishers Inc., 10 East 53rd Street, New York, NY 10022.

First Smithsonian Books paperback edition published 2008

Designed by Kate Nichols

The Library of Congress has catalogued the hardcover edition as follows:

Fleming, Thomas J.
The perils of peace : America's struggle for survival after Yorktown /
by Thomas Fleming.—1st Smithsonian Books ed.
p. cm.
Includes bibliographical references and index.
ISBN 978-0-06-113910-9
1. United States—History—Revolution, 1775-1783—Peace. 2. Yorktown (Va.)—
History—Siege, 1781. 3. United States—Politics and government—1775-1783.
4. United States—Foreign relations—1775-1783. 5. United States—Foreign relations—
Great Britain. 6. Great Britain—Foreign relations—United States. I. Title.

E249.F55 2007
973.3--dc22
2007017221

ISBN 978-0-06-113911-6 (pbk.)

08 09 10 11 ID/RRD 10 9 8 7 6 5 4 3 2 1

Contents

Acknowledgments

I HAVE BEEN THINKING about writing this book for a long time. So my gratitude for help from many people extends far into my past. High on my list is historian and friend Richard Buel, whose highly original research into the economic impact of the Revolution has been an inspiration. The late Richard B. Morris, author of the pathbreaking book, *The Peacemakers,* was another much earlier inspiration. Also important was Robert Cowley, the former editor of *MHQ,* the *Quarterly Journal of Military History,* who kept me writing about the Revolution while I was working on my historical novels. Helpful in myriad ways were the librarians of Yale University, where I spent many summer days doing research. Other librarians were equally helpful in recent years. Lewis Daniels, head of the Westbrook (Conn.) library, had an almost magical ability to conjure needed books by interlibrary loan. That was equally true of Patrick Rayner of the New York Society Library and Gregory H. Gallagher of the Century Association library. At least as important was help I received from my son, Richard Fleming, whose computer expertise enabled me to plumb the growing riches of research on the Internet. Steven Bernstein helped me explore the Library of Congress and other Washington, D.C., collections. My friend Jim Dingeman obtained Internet access to doctoral theses at the Columbia University

Library. Barbara Mitnick, whose books demonstrate her expertise in historical images, gave me illuminating advice in the search for the right pictures. My wife, Alice Fleming, was indefatigable in tracking down the best version of the desired image, no matter how elusive it proved to be. Finally, my special thanks goes to that invisible but essential counselor, my editor, Elisabeth Kallick Dyssegaard, for her invaluable suggestions and encouragement.

Introduction

I HAVE WRITTEN many historical narratives in my career as a historian and historical novelist. While I have the greatest respect for the analytic and intellectual historians who have enriched our understanding of the past, I remain convinced that for most readers, narrative remains crucial to the historical enterprise. A good narrative is a living creature, a flowing river that carries the reader from the questioning first pages through the turbulent tangled middle to the (hopefully) climactic close. Few other reading experiences can approach its rewards.

A historical narrative is more than a good story—although that quality is essential to its success. The word "narrative" comes from the Latin root, *narrare,* which means to know or understand. If the words flow through unexplored territory, so much the better for that wonderfully ambiguous phrase, the reader's interest. Surprise is a much-undervalued ingredient of a good historical narrative. If the historian too is among the surprised, the result is likely to be even more rewarding for all concerned.

All these components are the background for this book. I launched it knowing I was attempting to explore a hitherto-untold story—the struggle for peace and political stability on both sides of the Atlantic Ocean in the two years after the 1781 American victory at Yorktown. Excellent books have been written about the peace negotiations in Europe. Not a few histories of the Revolution have dramatic accounts of the rancid politics that made the precarious union of the thirteen states a dubious bet. But there has been no attempt to see the often-hair-raising interplay of these dramas. I have found the fusion richer than I ever thought possible, not only in political and military twists and turns but also in revelations about the national characters of all the countries in the tangled story—America, Britain, France, Spain, and Holland.

On both sides of the Atlantic, unexpected hitherto-unrecognized heroes emerged. In Britain it was Edmund Burke, a name largely familiar to American readers as the giver of a magnificent speech in 1775, reprobating George III and his followers for plunging into war with America. In 1782 he was the member of Parliament whose courage confronted the intransigent king and uncrowned him. In improbable tandem was a man Burke hated, the immensely wealthy William Petty, The Earl of Shelburne, a tormented mixture of conservative fears and liberal ideals. In France there was the veteran foreign minister Charles Gravier, Comte de Vergennes, a man who saw England as an unrelenting enemy that had to be cut down to size if France were to regain her lost glory. But at a moment of ultimate suspense, he envisioned the possibility of lasting peace with Perfidious Albion. Beside him stands bewildered, uncertain Louis XVI, only twenty when he mounted the throne in 1774, forever yearning to be his own prime minister, an unexpectedly tragic figure.

In America, there was James Madison—not the magisterial author of the Constitution, but the slim, bashful, boyish-looking Continental congressman who fought the forces of parochialism and self interest that were threatening to destroy the fragile union. At the other end of the age range, seventy-six-year-old Benjamin Franklin repeatedly rescued the American alliance with France from the "insatiable" (his phrase) greed of Congress for ever-larger loans. Simultaneously Franklin had to explain away wrongheaded fellow diplomats such as John Adams, who arrogantly informed the French that Americans did not feel an iota of gratitude for their help.

Finally there was—and is—George Washington. In this narrative he is not the conquering battlefield hero. He is a man who has emerged from six years of war with no illusions about the American character. He is still a soldier, but he has also acquired a profound appreciation of the importance of politics. Amazingly, he has also managed to retain his vision of what America could become. His reward, in these two years, is torment and even heartbreak. The tears he weeps in his last days as commander in chief of the Continental Army acquire a new, immensely powerful dimension, far more meaningful for contemporary Americans than they were to the Americans of 1783.

Chapter One

A Potentially Ruinous
Victory

O N OCTOBER 19, 1781, outside the small tobacco port of York-town, Virginia, on the narrow peninsula that jutted into the York River where it joined Chesapeake Bay, soldiers of two nations faced each other on opposite sides of a narrow dirt road. On the left in two ranks, hefting polished muskets, stood the regiments of the French expeditionary force in gleaming white uniforms and black gaiters. Beside them their officers glittered with gold braid; their cocked hats sprouted white, green, and red plumes.

Facing these European professionals on the opposite side of the road stood the regiments of the Continental Army of the United States, wearing improvised uniforms of fringed white hunting shirts and linen pantaloons, buttoned around the calves. Only their officers wore the blue coats with buff facings and the buff breeches that had recently been designated as their official uniform. The Continentals' posture was nonetheless proudly martial, and their French-made muskets had as much shine as elbow grease could lend them. From the elation gleaming on every face, there was no doubt that they considered themselves equal partners in the momentous event that was about to transpire.

Behind the Continentals stood another line of soldiers—militiamen from Maryland and Virginia. These were temporary warriors, summoned to participate in the military drama by their state governors. Uniforms were nowhere to be seen in this rank; officers and men wore rough work clothes and many of the enlisted men were barefoot.

II

At the head of the facing columns of French and American regiments sat two groups of senior officers on horseback. On the right, forty-nine-year-old Lieutenant General George Washington and his aides and subordinate generals were wearing their best blue-and-buff uniforms and their boots gleamed with newly applied polish. Facing them were portly fifty-six-year-old Lieutenant General Jean-Baptiste Donatien de Vimeur, Comte de Rochambeau, commander of the French expeditionary force, and his staff—all in uniforms as resplendent as the officers' in their regiments.

The American commander in chief was unquestionably the dominant figure in this tableau. On horseback, Washington looked even taller and more formidable than on foot. Well over six feet, he had huge hands that gripped his horse's reins with a casual authority. His perfectly cut blue coat was devoid of medals or other decorations; only epaulets and a black cockade pinned to his cocked hat designated his rank.

Beside the French army officers, Admiral Louis Comte de Barras perched uncomfortably on a borrowed horse. The admiral was second in command of the French fleet that had played a crucial part in the drama that was about to reach an improbable climax. The masts of several of the fleet's frigates were visible on nearby waters. Out of sight on the Chesapeake were the massive ships of the line that had fought off the British navy in early September and irretrievably trapped a 7,700-man British army in Yorktown. Including the sailors, there were more than 29,000 Frenchmen at Yorktown and about 9,000 Americans.

This unlikely alliance of American Protestants imbued with defiant ideas about the universal importance of individual liberty and French Catholics loyal to a king who ruled by divine right with the backing of titled aristocrats was about to consummate a victory that none of them would have dared to predict two months ago.[1]

III

Several dozen yards beyond the fighting men, on both sides of the road, hundreds of civilians sat on horses or in carriages, or stood in neighborly groups. Day and night for almost three weeks they had listened to the booming siege cannon and waited breathlessly for scraps of news from talkative soldiers not on duty in Yorktown's trenches. Among the more distinguished of these noncombatants was twenty-six-year-old John Parke Custis, General George Washington's handsome stepson. Jack had sat out the war on his various plantations in Maryland and Virginia, letting other men his age do the fighting and dying. This did not improve his stepfather's already low opinion of him.

Young Custis had inherited an immense estate from his father; with growing distress Washington had watched him mismanage it. Jack sold thousands of prime acres for depreciating American paper dollars and gambled away not a little of these illusory profits. Washington had written him earnest, often stern letters urging him to handle his affairs more prudently—and got nowhere. Meanwhile Washington had never protested Jack's disinterest in military service; he knew his wife, Martha, would be horrified and even traumatized by a demand that her beloved only son risk his life for the glorious cause.

Jack had joined Washington's staff as a volunteer aide as the French and American armies completed their 450-mile march from New York. This flirtation with military glory did not last long. He had contracted camp fever, a form of typhus caused by poor sanitation and lack of soap in eighteenth century armies. It was a potentially fatal disease, especially when combined with dysentery, which had wracked Jack for several days.

A worried Washington had asked his old friend, Dr. James Craik, chief physician of the Continental Army, to care for Jack. But Martha's spoiled son, used to having his own way since birth, insisted he felt well enough to witness the surrender. He promised Dr. Craik he would then retreat to nearby Eltham, a plantation owned by Burwell Bassett, Martha Washington's brother-in-law. Too weak to sit up, Jack reclined on cushions in an open carriage.[2]

IV

Among the civilians were several other improbable visitors to Yorktown. They were members of the Oneida nation of the Iroquois Confederacy. Most wore Indian-style clothing. Their leader, the sachem Great Grasshopper, sported a beautiful blue uniform, thick with gold braid. The

French ambassador to the United States had given it to him when the sachem and more than forty other Oneidas had visited Philadelphia in September.

The Oneidas had been allied with France in the numerous wars the French had fought with the British in the decades before the Revolution. Influenced by a missionary minister from Connecticut, the tribe had joined the American side of the struggle in 1777 and had fought the British and American loyalists and fellow Iroquois in many battles in northern New York. Thus far, the alliance had brought the Oneidas little but pain and suffering. The Mohawks, Senecas, and other nations of the Iroquois had devastated their villages in a series of punitive attacks. Great Grasshopper and other leaders had journeyed to Philadelphia to beg the Continental Congress to save them from starvation in the coming winter. The virtually bankrupt Congress could do little for them, but they encouraged Grasshopper and several warriors to go to Yorktown to see the American and French armies win a badly needed victory. The politicians hoped the experience would persuade the Oneidas to remain loyal to the Revolution.[3]

V

General Washington and his Continentals had been fighting British armies for six and a half years. The goal of independence had grown more and more elusive as war weariness sapped morale and severe financial problems crippled America's ability to feed and clothe the army. Not a little of this disarray could be attributed to the Americans' disappointment in the French alliance, which had electrified the rebellious thirteen colonies when it was announced in the spring of 1778. Swift victory and independence had seemed all but guaranteed.

Alas, the French fleet that arrived off the American coast in June of 1778 had been led by Comte d'Estaing, a cautious general turned admiral who was not inclined to risk his ships or the several thousand marines he could have added to Washington's army. He declined to attack heavily fortified New York City, the main British base in America. An attempt to trap a small British army in Newport, Rhode Island, ended in fiasco when d'Estaing recalled the marines he had put ashore and sailed out to do battle with a British fleet. He never came back, claiming damage from a storm required him to retreat to Boston for repairs.

The abandoned American army was forced to make a humiliating retreat from Newport after fighting a touch-and-go rearguard action against the pursuing British. Admiral d'Estaing headed for the West Indies, where he spent his time assailing the lucrative sugar-growing islands owned by the British. The French committed eight thousand men and d'Estaing's twenty-five-ship fleet to seizing Dominica, St. Vincent, and Grenada from outnumbered British garrisons.

In monetary terms, the West Indies were far more valuable to France—and Great Britain—than the thirteen American colonies. Europeans were insatiable consumers of the islands' chief export, sugar. West Indian trade accounted for 30 percent of France's imports and 35 percent of her exports. On the British islands, sugar exports had risen from 8,176 tons in 1663 to over 25,000 tons in 1775; the trade was now worth more than 3 million pounds, twice the value of imports from the rebellious mainland colonies. Not a few Americans began to suspect that there was some truth in the British contention that France had backed the revolutionists to tie down British troops while the French made conquests elsewhere in the world.[4]

VI

Not until 1780 did the French admit that the Revolution was close to collapse and required more than temporary visits from admirals with separate agendas. France shipped General Rochambeau and his expeditionary force to Newport, Rhode Island, with orders to regard Washington as their commander. But the army was only 5,000 men—too small to make a decisive impact on the war. In spite of pleas from the Marquis de Lafayette and other Frenchmen serving with the Americans, Rochambeau refused to budge from Newport for almost a year. He was hoping—in vain, it became apparent—that a planned second division of his expeditionary force would appear. But these troops had been diverted to other theaters of the worldwide war with Britain.[5]

By 1781, the American army under General Washington's direct command had dwindled to 5,835 men—not much bigger than Rochambeau's half-dozen regiments. Washington ordered that no one was to be discharged from the ranks except men with "visible marks of imbecility." In May, he wrote in his diary: "Instead of having magazines filled with provisions, we have a scant pittance ... Instead of having our arsenals filled with military stores, they are poorly provided . . . Instead of having the regiments [of the Continental Army] filled, scarcely any state has an eighth part of its quota in the field . . . Instead of having the prospect of a glorious offensive campaign before us, [we] have a gloomy defensive one."[6]

The political situation was even worse. Earlier in 1781, after four years of argument, the thirteen states had approved a constitution, the Articles of Confederation. But the supposed federal union had done nothing to revive the country's collapsing finances. American paper money had become totally worthless. Congress had printed 200 million dollars of these "Continentals" backed by nothing but the promise of eventual victory. The federal government had no power to support this staggering mountain of paper with taxes. By 1781, the phrase "not worth a continental" had become a wry cliche. Only hard money, coin of the French, Dutch, English, or Spanish realms, was being accepted by farmers and businessmen. Since the Continental Army had only worthless paper dollars, food was obtained by seizing it from unhappy farmers, paid for by certificates promising hard cash at some future date.[7]

Amazingly, Washington somehow retained his faith in final victory. In June of 1781, he wrote to Congressman John Mathews of South Carolina: "The game is yet in our hands; to play it well is all we have to do . . . A cloud may pass over us; individuals may be ruined; and the country at large, or individual states, undergo temporary distress; but certain I am that it is in our power to bring the war to a happy conclusion."[8]

VII

When Rochambeau's troops met the Americans north of New York for a proposed attack on the city in July of 1781, the French were shocked by the naked reality of the Continental Army. In France they had read books and essays about the Americans being natural-born soldiers, because they had grown up on the frontier and endured danger and hardihood from boyhood. France's intellectuals relied mostly on their imaginations when they wrote about America. They had no idea that the thirteen rebellious colonies had been settled for well over a hundred and fifty years and had evolved a sophisticated civilization, with cities and towns full of artisans and countrysides thick with prosperous farmers, making handsome profits selling a third of their crops to Europe or the West Indies. A frontier existed in the west, of course, but the majority of the people did not live on it, and regarded those who did with not a little condescension. Many thought the frontier attracted mostly misfits and losers who often became shameless degenerates in the wilderness.

In Washington's ranks when the French and Americans met outside New York were a startling percentage of blacks. Not a few of the white soldiers were mere boys and overage men. Their makeshift uniforms, their lean faces, their worn tents in which tree branches covered with blankets served as mattresses, suggested it was an army that "lacked everything at the same time," General Rochambeau thought.

An aide on Rochambeau's staff, Bavarian-born Baron Ludwig von Closen, struggled to retain a positive opinion. In his journal he wrote: "It is really painful to see these brave men almost naked . . . but would you believe it, very cheerful and healthy in appearance." Another aide, Count Axel von Fersen of Sweden, purported to be the lover of Queen Marie Antoinette, had a gloomier view of the American war effort: "The spirit of patriotism resides only with the chief and principal people of the country. The others, who make the majority, think only of their personal interest."[9]

Out of this fog of mutual disillusion and discouragement had emerged an amazing series of coincidences that created the victory at Yorktown. First, the British had veered into a nasty personal quarrel between the army's touchy, neurotic commander in chief, General Sir Henry Clinton, and his second in command, blunt, energetic General Lord Charles Cornwallis. His lordship had been assigned the task of subduing the southern states after Clinton captured Charleston, South Carolina, in 1780. By that time, Georgia seemed totally pacified; a royal governor had been installed in 1779. Without achieving more than a blood-soaked stalemate in the Carolinas, Cornwallis had marched into Virginia—a decision that infuriated Sir Henry. A series of nasty letters ended with Clinton ordering Cornwallis to retreat to the coast, fortify a base, and go on the defensive. Cornwallis had obeyed with the least possible grace, refusing to ship surplus men to Sir Henry and erecting fortifications at Yorktown that presumed an attacking enemy would have only light field artillery.

Meanwhile, Washington and Rochambeau had been pretending to menace the 16,000-man British army in heavily fortified New York with their pathetically inadequate combined force. Not until mid-July did they learn that the French West Indies fleet under a new commander,

Admiral François Joseph Paul de Grasse, was coming to the American coast, thanks to discretionary orders the admiral had received in Paris. Rochambeau, who controlled the correspondence with de Grasse, urged him to sail to the Chesapeake to trap Cornwallis and presented the decision to Washington as a fait accompli.

Not at all certain Cornwallis would be there to capture, Washington had reluctantly agreed to make Yorktown their objective. He used his skills as a spymaster and manipulator of disinformation to deceive Sir Henry Clinton into thinking he was planning to attack New York via Staten Island. Not until the march south was well underway did Clinton learn the truth.

To everyone's amazement, the unlikely concentration took place. Admiral de Grasse's appearance in the Chesapeake surprised and flustered Cornwallis. The outsized French admiral, who was well over six feet (his admirers said he stood six-feet-six on his quarterdeck), easily beat off a halfhearted attempt by the outnumbered Royal Navy to rescue the beleaguered army on September 5. Meanwhile, Washington's and Rochambeau's men closed the trap on the land side of the tobacco port. They battered Yorktown's defenders into submission in a relentless siege during which French heavy artillery, transported from Newport, did fearful damage to the British fortifications.[10]

VIII

Now the moment of ultimate gratification had come. In the brilliant autumn sunshine, the British and their hired German mercenaries emerged from the ravaged Yorktown earthworks and began the half-mile march to the meadow that the allies had designated for the relinquishment of their weapons. The expression on every enemy face was sullen—not only because no soldier enjoys defeat, but because General Washington had decreed that they could not display their regimental or national colors.

General Clinton had imposed these terms on the 5,000-man American army that had surrendered at Charleston in May of 1780. It had been an expression of his scorn for the stubborn rebels, who had rejected his attempts to persuade them to give up without a fight. The testy British commander in chief did not realize he was exposing his own soldiers to similar humiliation little more than a year later.

Both the German and the British troops had labored to make a good appearance. Their muskets glistened, their shoes shone; many were wearing new uniforms. The blue-coated Germans marched with perfect precision; not so the red-coated British. Rank after rank was out of step and here and there a man visibly staggered. They had gotten into the army's supply of rum and many of them were drunk.

Drunk or sober, they were the cream of the British army in America. In the van were the Brigade of Foot Guards, each man chosen with special care. Behind them came the 23rd Royal Welch Fusileers and the 43rd Regiment, who had been in almost every battle fought in America since Bunker Hill in 1775. Two battalions of light infantry had been trained to fight in open formations that enabled them to challenge the Americans in forests and rough terrain.

Traditionally, when an army surrendered after a siege, they were permitted not only to display their colors but their bands were allowed to play a tune from the enemy's musical repertoire. It was another way of saying "we may be defeated but we can still exchange compliments." General Clinton had forbidden this courtesy at Charleston, and Washington insisted on the same musical terms now. So the disappointed British regimental bands chose an especially melancholy air. It was a song which had many versions. One was called "When the King Enjoys His Own Again." More popular were verses titled "The World Turn'd Upside Down."

There is no surviving evidence that anyone in the surrender ceremony recognized the irony of this title. The political world was being turned upside down by those ragged, barely uniformed rebels who had revolted against the most powerful monarch in the world six years ago. One reason may have been a distraction that revealed a great deal about the British attitude toward the surrender. Virtually every British officer and enlisted man in every regiment marched past with his face turned toward the French. They were treating the Americans as if they were invisible.

Near the head of the American column stood twenty-four-year-old Major General Marquis de Lafayette, who had been serving with the Americans since 1777. He had led a small American army that opposed Cornwallis's invasion of Virginia, and many people, unaware of the feud in the British high command, credited him with forcing the British commander to retreat to Yorktown.

Lafayette instantly grasped the meaning of the averted British faces

and did not like it at all. When his splendidly uniformed French compatriots had arrived in 1780, he had insisted they treat the shabby American troops as equals. He was not about to permit the defeated British to
insult them. Whirling, Lafayette snapped an order to his division's band.
Their drums rolled, their fifes shrilled, and the musicians burst into their
favorite song, "Yankee Doodle." Instantly, almost every British head was
jerked in the direction of the music and George III's men stared into the
faces of the king's former subjects.

IX

At the head of the British column, an even stronger inclination to ignore
the Americans prevailed. Leading the surrendered regiments was not
Charles, Lord Cornwallis. The Earl claimed he was too ill—a more pre-
cise word would have been mortified—to participate in the ceremony.
He remained inside the ruined village of Yorktown, handing the task to
his second in command, the leader of the foot guards, Brigadier Charles
O'Hara.

There was an unspoken reason why Cornwallis chose to stay in Yorktown. He may have feared vengeance from angry American Continentals
or militiamen. Since May 1780, his army had rampaged across South and
North Carolina, igniting a sanguinary civil war between rebels and loyalists. The Earl had condoned the loyalists' penchant for hanging rebels,
burning their houses and crops, and slaughtering their cattle. Dozens of
American newspapers had called him a butcher and a monster.

Brigadier O'Hara was a ruddy-faced soldier of forty whose most
distinctive feature was his glittering smile. He was the illegitimate
son of an Anglo-Irish nobleman. The brigadier had proven himself a
courageous soldier on many battlefields, and his self-confidence did not
seem in the least diminished by the embarrassing task assigned to him.
As he emerged from the lane of facing French and American soldiers,
he asked someone to identify General Rochambeau. He (and no doubt
Cornwallis) had decided to mortify the Americans by surrendering to
the French.

There are many differing versions of what happened next. Aide Comte
Mathieu Dumas claimed in his memoirs that he prevented O'Hara from
offering his sword to Rochambeau. The general himself, in a memoir
published after his death, also claimed that O'Hara proffered his sword.

Not a single American account mentions a sword, which the terms of surrender specifically permitted O'Hara—and the rest of the British officer corps—to retain.

This much is certain. Rochambeau gestured to Washington as the commander in chief to whom O'Hara must submit. Without losing his smiling aplomb, the Irishman turned to Washington and explained that Lord Cornwallis was "indisposed." Washington coolly replied that protocol then required Brigadier O'Hara to surrender to the American army's second in command, General Benjamin Lincoln. Not only was this a neat way of avoiding the need to accept a capitulation from a subordinate general, it was exquisite revenge. General Lincoln had been the commander on whom Clinton and Cornwallis inflicted the humiliating surrender terms at Charleston in 1780.

Lincoln, a portly, dignified Massachusetts soldier, was more than equal to the task of accepting O'Hara's capitulation. He pointed to the open meadow in the near distance, where a detachment of French hussars formed a semicircle. That was where O'Hara's men were to deposit their muskets. They would then about-face and march back to Yorktown.

The final scene of the drama began. Regiment after regiment marched to the meadow and in obedience to the growled order "ground arms" from their sergeants, deposited their muskets in a growing pile. As the weapons became a gleaming mountain, a group of captains arrived to surrender the cased colors of the captured regiments. For the British, this was the ultimate moment of mortification. So ended the surrender of Cornwallis's army.[11]

X

On the other side of the York River in the village of Gloucester, the British had stationed a smaller force commanded by the cavalry leader Colonel Banastre Tarleton. Because the post had not been attacked, they were not required to undergo much humiliation. Tarleton led his green-coated horsemen out of their lightly fortified camp with sabres drawn and trumpets blasting defiance. But the infantry, led by the Queens Rangers, the proudest, most aggressive loyalist regiment in America, was forced to march with colors cased, their drums beating an English march.

Tarleton had become infamous throughout the Carolinas for what the Americans called "Tarleton's quarter," his horsemen's tendency to shoot or saber Americans who were trying to surrender. Like most of the accusations of massacre by both sides, there was some exaggeration in the charge. But Tarleton was unquestionably the most hated man in the British army, and it was just as well that he surrendered to two Frenchmen, Brigadier General Marquis de Choisy and the Duc de Lauzun, another flamboyant cavalryman.[12]

XI

On the Yorktown side of the river, as the enemy regiments returned to their tents, the Americans reacted to the way the British had tried to humiliate them. There were not a few contemptuous hoots and insulting names hurled at the "lobsterbacks" as they trudged past. A shocked French officer said the Americans failed to observe "the chivalrous manners" owed to "defeated courage." The jittery British began wondering if they were going to be massacred by their rebel cousins, now that they no longer had guns to defend themselves. They looked anxiously toward the French, silently pleading for help.[13]

The British fears for their safety were groundless. Washington's troops remained under almost perfect discipline. They did not even lose their heads during the chaotic night inside Yorktown that followed the surrender. The British regulars continued to consume immense quantities of rum. Toward dawn, a besotted redcoat seized a musket from an American sentry and sank its bayonet into his chest. The killer undoubtedly became the last casualty of Yorktown seconds later—but the bloodshed did not lead to a massacre.

Among the higher ranks a different atmosphere prevailed. The captured British officers were now gentlemen in distress, and protocol required them to be treated as such. That night, General Washington gave a dinner for the chief officers of all three armies. Lord Cornwallis still pleaded illness and General O'Hara presided on the British side of the table. The Americans were amazed by his composure. A chance visitor might have assumed that he was the conqueror and the French and Americans were his captives.

The Americans did not find O'Hara's self-satisfaction entertaining. But the French were charmed beyond belief. Suddenly all the French officers began vying to be more than polite to their captives. They oozed sympathy for the defeated enemy; they rushed to lend them money, to invite them to private dinners. They conversed companionably about other wars and battles, making the Yorktown defeat seem like a petty sideshow.

On the first night, Rochambeau left Washington's dinner table and went into Yorktown with several aides to pay his respects to Lord Cornwallis. Aide Baron von Closen admired the Earl's "nobility of soul, [his] magnanimity and strength of character." Totally forgotten was the man who had waged war in the Carolinas with ruthless severity. When Cornwallis remarked that his military treasury was virtually empty, leaving himself and his officers "impoverished," Rochambeau loaned him 150 thousand pounds in silver.

Washington and his officers watched the emergence of this Anglo-French mutual admiration society with growing unease. They began to realize that these European soldiers had far more in common with each other than with the Americans and their wholesale rejection of aristocracy and kingship. Was it a sign of trouble to come?

XII

One of Washington's officers, stocky short-tempered Major General Baron Friedrich von Steuben, the German volunteer who had instilled discipline and tactics into the American army at Valley Forge, was especially disturbed by this round of French feasts. With help from American diplomats in Paris, Steuben had passed himself off as a former major general in the Prussian army. His highest rank had been captain. But he had been a staff officer under Frederick the Great, considered the best general of the era, and was keenly aware of the importance of pride in creating an army's esprit de corps.

The Baron was outraged by the way the French were giving their captured enemies splendid dinners which the penniless American officers could not afford. He felt the Continentals were looking like cheapskates. "I will give one grand dinner to our allies, should I eat my soup with a wooden spoon for ever after," he told his aide, William North.

The Baron's problem was the same one that was afflicting almost everyone in Washington's army: no hard money. Steuben had spent the previous year in Virginia, trying to organize a defense force against British incursions. During that time he had drawn $220 thousand in paper dollars from Congress to support himself and his small staff. In hard money, the distressed Steuben remarked in a letter, this staggering sum was barely worth 150 guineas—a little over 750 dollars—and it had long since been spent.

The Baron asked General Washington if he could persuade Congress to give him a month's pay in hard money. Embarrassed, Washington said it was beyond his authority and loaned him twenty guineas out of his own pocket. When Steuben discovered he needed more money for his grand dinner, he sold his favorite white horse and his pocket watch. A Pennsylvania colonel who liked and admired Steuben tried to give him money from his meager purse to preserve the horse and watch. The Baron shook his head and said they were already sold. "I am a major general in the service of the United States, and my private inconvenience must not be put in the scale of the duty my rank calls upon me to perform!" he declared.

The dinner was a notable success but Steuben was broke again. He received Washington's permission to go to Philadelphia to try to collect 8,500 hard dollars that Congress still owed him. He departed on his 300-mile journey with only a single gold piece, a Portuguese "half joe," worth 8 or 9 dollars, in his pocket.[14]

XIII

If General von Steuben was the unhappiest American officer at Yorktown, Lieutenant Colonel Alexander Hamilton was probably the happiest. The siege and his part in it had consummated—and even justified—the riskiest thing he had yet done in his young life. He had quit his job as Washington's aide by picking a quarrel with the commander in chief—and then demanded command of a regiment.

As Hamilton explained it to his father-in-law, Major General Philip Schuyler, he had long disliked the role of an aide "as having in it a kind of personal dependence." Hamilton had accepted Washington's invitation to join his staff in early 1777 with some misgivings; this ambivalence had grown to near-dislike as he discovered the overworked general could be curt and even rude to members of his military "family," as the aides were called. When Washington spoke abruptly to Hamilton one day in February, 1781, the twenty-six-year-old lieutenant colonel had turned the remark into a major insult and huffily declared that they must "part."

A better explanation for this episode can be found in a letter Hamilton had written to General Washington several months before their quarrel: he yearned "to act a conspicuous part in some enterprise that might perhaps raise my character as a soldier above mediocrity." Washington had been "so good as to say" he would be glad to give Hamilton this opportunity. But the general had repeatedly failed to deliver on his promise. The reason was Washington's understandable wish not to lose one of his most valuable aides to an enemy bullet.

For four months in the late winter and spring of 1781, a stalemate ensued. Hamilton, recently married to General Schuyler's daughter, Elizabeth, rented a house in the vicinity of the American camp in the Hudson River Valley and devoted his leisure time to writing melancholy letters to Elizabeth and a series of newspaper articles signed "The Continentalist" calling for a stronger central government. Washington remained opposed to giving Hamilton command of a regiment, claiming it would irritate line officers to find an aide, whose rank of lieutenant colonel was considered more or less honorary, giving them orders.

Only when the ex-aide mailed Washington his lieutenant colonel's commission in July did the general yield and appoint Hamilton to command a newly formed light infantry regiment. Hamilton marched south to Yorktown with the Continental Army and participated in the three-week siege. The struggle reached its climax on October 14, when the French and Americans attacked two key redoubts, numbered 9 and 10, on the flank of the British line. Hamilton persuaded Washington to give him command of the American half of the assault.

Soon after darkness fell, the allied artillery pounded the rest of the British fortifications. At eight o'clock, six mortar shells exploded in rapid succession—the signal for the attack. "Fix bayonets," Hamilton growled to his light infantrymen. "Follow me!" He leaped out of the trench and raced across the shell-hole-pocked battlefield toward redoubt 10. Behind him came his regiment and two other battalions, about four hundred men. Obeying Hamilton's orders to rely on their bayonets and not to fire a shot, they soon sprang into the ditch around the redoubt, while British soldiers on the parapet blazed away at them. Hamilton ordered his men to hoist him to the top, where he dueled sword to bayonet with the cursing British until his men joined him and drove the redcoats off the wall.

Eighty men led by Hamilton's closest friend, Washington aide Lieutenant Colonel John Laurens of South Carolina, swarmed over the redoubt's rear wall. In ten minutes the British major in command of the redoubt surrendered to Laurens. Except for a few men who jumped off the parapets and fled into the British lines, the rest of the redoubt's garrison gave up without further resistance.

A French attack on redoubt 9 was equally successful. Cannon were rushed into both redoubts, and were soon firing into the exposed British line. Three days later, Cornwallis asked for terms. Colonel Hamilton had proven he was a fighting soldier considerably above the military mediocrity of a general's aide. Adding to his happiness were newspaper stories that soon appeared in Philadelphia and other cities describing his role in the climactic charge.[15]

XIV

In his tent, the Marquis de Lafayette, an optimist from birth, wrote to the aged French first (prime) minister, Comte de Maurepas: "The play is over, Monsieur le Comte, the fifth act has just come to an end." He wrote similar letters to each of the king's ministers. Along with General Rochambeau's official report on the siege and surrender, the Marquis' blithe announcements would soon be put aboard a French frigate whose captain had orders to make all possible speed to France.

George Washington's reaction to the victory at Yorktown was a stark and total contrast to the Marquis' cheerful assumption that the war was won. Washington feared the war could still be lost—and the next two years of battles on land and sea and virulent politics in Philadelphia, London, and Paris proved him a far better prophet.

The British still had over 25,000 men on the American continent. The 3,500 French troops Admiral de Grasse had brought from the West Indies were returning there with him, reducing the French and American regulars to an army barely half the size of the British force in New York. Nor was there any reason for assuming that London could not and would not replace Cornwallis's lost regulars.

Far from resting on his Yorktown laurels, Washington wanted to continue the campaign with another hammer blow against the enemy. The obvious targets were Savannah, Georgia, and Charleston, South Carolina, where substantial numbers of loyalists and regulars were entrenched behind strong fortifications, and Wilmington, North Carolina, where a smaller British force was in control. These occupations remained political as well as military threats.

In peace negotiations, the enemy's grip on these thriving ports might become an effective argument for ceding all three states to the king's domain, creating a daunting bloc of royal hegemony on America's southern flank. With Canada firmly in George III's grasp, the British would be nicely positioned to undermine America's independence, if and when they were forced to cede it to the ten other colonies.

Washington was also thinking about how he could persuade Congress to prepare the army and the nation for another campaign in 1782. Even if he succeeded in eliminating the British threat to the southern states, the enemy still had it in their power to wreak havoc in the north. When Admiral de Grasse returned to the West Indies, the Royal Navy could transport their army to attack any place they chose along the coast. Only a well-equipped Continental army large enough to oppose them could maintain the precarious status quo.[16]

XV

The day after the Yorktown surrender, Washington wrote not one but two letters to Admiral de Grasse. The first contained two intercepted letters from General Clinton to Lord Cornwallis, assuring him that Sir Henry was hoping to sail from New York with a fleet and army that would rescue him. Washington naturally wanted de Grasse to be forewarned about the possible appearance of this enemy expedition. He added a further expression of the "grateful acknowledgements, in the name of America, for the glorious event" in which the admiral had played such a central role. Washington's second letter was a plea for a new campaign. He argued that the "unexpected promptness" with which they had captured Cornwallis and his army gave them time to undertake another large accomplishment, one that might well force the British to abandon the war. He pointed to Charleston as the "principal maritime port" in the South and the key to any British hope of sustaining their power in Georgia and the Carolinas.

As long as the admiral and his ships were in American waters, they had "a decisively superior fleet" and a commander "whose talents . . . overawe all the naval force that the most incredible efforts of the enemy have been able to collect." Proposing to seize Charleston in a combined land and sea assault, Washington held out to de Grasse a chance to "terminate the war" in a campaign so potentially glorious, it would guarantee him perpetual fame.[17]

If this operation were not possible, Washington hoped de Grasse might agree to transport two thousand Continentals that Washington planned to send to reinforce the American army in South Carolina. He would ask de Grasse to take these soldiers only as far as Cape Fear, North Carolina, where they could land and free Wilmington from the British grip. The enemy was using the port city to encourage and supply numerous loyalists in North Carolina's interior.[18]

The admiral was immune to Washington's flattery. His answer was a blunt NO to both ideas. He had already stayed too long in American waters. It was time for him to return to the West Indies and continue the war there without another day's delay. There were other lucrative British sugar islands waiting for him to conquer. Once more Washington confronted the indubitable fact that the French had their own agenda in this global conflict.

XVI

Meanwhile, General Washington had myriad other worries. The surrendered British cannon and muskets and the tons of enemy supplies at Yorktown had to be moved inland, lest a marauding British fleet recapture them after de Grasse's departure. The same necessity applied to the captured British enlisted men and officers. Few of the officers were facing captivity. Only a minority of lower ranks would be required to stay with the enlisted men to maintain discipline. The rest would be paroled and permitted to return to New York with Cornwallis. They would be barred from participating in the war until they were exchanged for captured American officers of the same rank.

There was another group of enlisted men in Cornwallis's army who dreaded joining their fellow soldiers in captivity. These were loyalist volunteers and deserters who had switched sides. During the surrender negotiations, Cornwallis's spokesmen had insisted on inserting in the final draft of the agreement an article (numbered 10) which claimed that all Americans who had joined the British army were to be considered no different from the rest of the prisoners.

Washington had rejected this proposal, writing under it: "This article cannot be assented to, being altogether of civil resort." He meant that loyalists would be tried for treason by courts in their home states. Deserters would be tried by army courts martial and if found guilty, hanged.

Cornwallis glumly permitted this veto to stand in the final agreement. But he had inserted into the preliminary negotiations a literal and figurative escape hatch for these men. The Earl insisted that the *Bonetta* sloop of war be left at his disposal after the capitulation was signed to transport one of his aides with dispatches for Sir Henry Clinton. He added that he wanted the ship to sail "without examination."

General Washington was much too shrewd not to discern the real purpose of this good-sized vessel, which had a crew of fifty. Cornwallis knew there was little chance of the Americans agreeing to give loyalists and deserters a free pass. He intended to cram aboard the *Bonetta* all those who might be in danger of a noose. With victory in his grasp, Washington was not hungry for vengeance on these luckless Americans. He silently agreed to this escape clause.

XVII

Another group of captives in Yorktown was briefly mentioned in the surrender agreement—the African-Americans who had fled their masters in Virginia and the Carolinas and attached themselves to Cornwallis's army, hoping for eventual freedom. The articles of capitulation included a clause permitting owners to regain runaway slaves.

When the siege began, the British, to save food, had driven hundreds of blacks outside their lines. A German officer later said he wished he could forget this "cruel happening." The blacks, some of them ill with smallpox, wandered haplessly through the nearby woods, starving and terrified, and died by the hundreds. Joseph Plumb Martin, a Connecticut soldier, recalled in his memoirs seeing their bodies "scattered about in every direction."

After the British surrender, numerous slave owners hurried to Yorktown, hoping to reclaim their runaways. Not a few hired American soldiers to help them, offering a guinea for every fugitive they caught. Some New Englanders were troubled by this work, even though they took the money. Joseph Plumb Martin told how several of his friends refused to return some blacks they had captured for Colonel John Bannister of Petersburg, Virginia, unless he promised not to punish them. Bannister, who was trying to regain eighty-two runaways, said he had no intention of punishing them. They had been seduced from their "duty" by Lord Cornwallis. He considered them innocent of any conscious wrongdoing.

Martin was less than convinced when he saw several runaways brought before Bannister. They were so terrified; they trembled as if they were undergoing a "fit of ague." Bannister, under the eyes of suspicious gun-toting New Englanders, gave a wonderful performance. He told the shaking prisoners they could stay where they were if they chose, and promised not to "injure a hair of their heads" if they returned to his Battersea plantation with him. They reacted, Martin said, as if they had received "a reprieve from the gallows." Among those restored to other masters were seven fugitives from Washington's Mount Vernon and nine from Thomas Jefferson's Monticello.[19]

XVIII

The most important thing on George Washington's mind after the surrender was the preparation of a report of the victory for the Continental Congress in Philadelphia. Washington assigned this task to a new aide, Jonathan Trumbull Jr., the son of his close friend the governor of Connecticut. The forty-year-old Trumbull had become Washington's secretary on June 9, 1781, but had been active in the Revolution since it began, like the rest of his family. While Trumbull did the writing, we may be certain that Washington had a strong influence on shaping this document—as he did with other letters he considered of special importance.[20]

Addressed to Thomas McKean, the president of Congress, the letter began with a matter-of-fact sentence: "Sir: I have the honor to inform Congress, that a reduction of the British Army under the command of Lord Cornwallis is most happily effected." The rest of the letter, as one historian has admiringly noted, was praise of others, from Rochambeau to de Grasse to the negotiators of the surrender terms. Finally came a salute to the "unremitting ardor which actuated every officer and soldier in the combined army."

There was much more than Washington's innate diffidence involved in this low-keyed production. He was determined to avoid even a hint of a triumphal assertion that the war was as good as over. The letter was limited to an account of Cornwallis's capitulation—and no more. Instead of ending on a note of soaring optimism, Washington merely hoped that the president and Congress "will be pleased to accept my congratulations on this happy event."[21]

The letter signed and sealed, Washington now had an important decision to make: who would carry the good news to Congress? Traditionally, a victorious general selected a man whom he wished to honor for distinguished services. Messengers of victory were often further rewarded with promotions and gifts by the delighted recipients, partly a tribute to the special effort they usually made to deliver the news as swiftly as possible.

For Washington, the choice of a messenger was easy. The aide who had won his deepest gratitude was Tench Tilghman. Older than most of the other aides, the thirty-five-year-old Tilghman had been a successful merchant in Philadelphia before the war. His father had been a wealthy lawyer in the same city and knew Washington well enough to spend several nights as a guest at Mount Vernon. The family also had deep roots in Maryland.

Tilghman had joined Washington's staff on August 8, 1776, and for the next five years had served him ably in many capacities, from letter drafter to confidant. Further endearing him was his refusal to accept any pay—a gesture of respect to the commander in chief, who was doing the same thing.

In 1778 Tilghman had used his extensive friendships in Pennsylvania to rally support for Washington during the 1777–78 Valley Forge winter, when there was a serious attempt to combine innuendo and insult into a public outcry that would force him to resign. In his letter to President McKean, Washington wrote that Tilghman's "merits" had gained "my particular attention" and he hoped that Congress would see fit to reward him accordingly.

XIX

Lieutenant Colonel Tilghman accepted the honor with alacrity. But there were problems. He was suffering from a recurrent fever—not the typhus that had felled Jack Custis—but another ague, probably malaria, a common malady along the Virginia coast. The aide had participated in the tension and uncertainty of the negotiations that led to the surrender, followed by the feasting on October 19, leaving him with almost no sleep for two nights.

Weak and flushed, Tilghman nevertheless mounted his horse and rode to the Yorktown waterfront with the leader of the French cavalry, the Duc de Lauzun, whom General Rochambeau had chosen to carry his victory dispatch to Paris. Another Washington aide and a Rochambeau aide were in the party, as well as the Marquis de Lafayette, who could not resist the opportunity to participate, however vicariously, in the delivery of the triumphal news. The Marquis may also have wanted to make sure Lauzun would deliver all his exultant letters to the various members of the French cabinet.

Yorktown was a wreck. Almost every house, especially the one Cornwallis had used as his headquarters, had been smashed into near rubble by the allied cannoneers. Shallow graves covered the bodies of the recently killed. At the water's edge, the bloated bodies of dozens of British army horses bobbed in the incoming tide, beside the ruins of the British frigate *Charon*, which had been set afire by hotshot from the big guns on the night of October 10.

The Duc de Lauzun boarded a French sloop that would take him into Chesapeake Bay to visit Admiral de Grasse aboard his immense 110-gun flagship, *Ville de Paris*, the largest warship afloat. There the cavalryman would receive any messages the admiral might wish to send to Paris, and would transfer to the frigate *Surveillante* for his voyage to France.

Tilghman boarded a much smaller sailing craft and slipped down the York River to the Chesapeake. A brisk wind made for a very satisfying speed, and they soon swung north up the broad bay. Tilghman was heading for Annapolis, where he could catch a packet boat that sailed regularly between the Maryland capital and Rock Hall, on the bay's eastern bank, roughly opposite Baltimore. There he could hire a horse and arrange for relays of fresh mounts to carry him 140 miles to Philadelphia at the fastest possible pace.

Everything seemed to be going smoothly and the exhausted Tilghman decided to get some sleep. Hours later, he was awakened by an unpleasant jolt. He awoke to find boat and bay shrouded in darkness. The embarrassed skipper told him they had run aground on Tangier Shoal, a huge swath of shallow water surrounding Tangier Island. They were still a long way from Annapolis, and they could do nothing but wait for the tide to turn and float them free. Soon after this misfortune, the wind died, leaving them becalmed for twenty-four hours. A superstitious man might have begun to think that the omens for an early peace and independence were not good.

Not until Monday morning did a weary Tilghman reach Annapolis, where he reported to the Council of Safety, the government body that ruled the state when the legislature was not in session. They were gratified to hear the good news he brought—but not nearly as excited as he expected them to be. Governor Thomas Sims Lee had received a letter from Admiral de Grasse, dated October 18, telling him that Cornwallis had asked for terms and the final surrender was only a matter of time. The governor had sent the letter on to Congress in Philadelphia.

This news only added to Tilghman's anxiety. It made his early arrival in Philadelphia of the utmost importance. No one was more aware of how touchy Congress was about the relationship between the Continental Army and the federal government. There were not a few congressmen who were perpetually looking for signs that the army—and Washington, in particular—were not inclined to pay them proper respect.

Alas, Tilghman's luck remained bad. The packet to Rock Hall spent hours loading freight and horses and wagons. Out in the bay, the wind failed again, and they sat becalmed until a breeze stirred at nightfall, costing Tilghman another full day. He mounted the horse that the Maryland Council of Safety had given him and rode for Chestertown, where his father was living. The noted Philadelphia barrister had been exiled from the city because he had stubbornly opposed independence, and insisted on remaining neutral in the great contest.

Along the way, Tilghman shouted his good news to almost everyone he passed on the road. Their reactions made it clear that if Washington thought his carefully muted victory report could dampen the assumption that the war was as good as over, he was in for a large disappointment. One citizen of Newtown on the Chester described the local response. "A large number of worthy citizens assembled to celebrate this signal victory . . . Amidst the roaring of cannon and the exhibitions of bonfires and illuminations, the gentlemen (having repaired to a hall suitable for the purpose) drank the following toasts." Whereupon the narrator listed thirteen toasts, ranging from General Washington and the Allied Army to the King of Spain to the state of Maryland. The next evening, the writer continued, "an elegant ball was given by the gentlemen of the town, that the ladies might participate in the general joy of their country."

At his father's house in Chestertown, Tilghman fell into bed and got a reasonably good night's sleep. Dawn found him on the road to Philadelphia on a fresh horse. Grimly determined now, Tilghman stayed in the saddle all that day and most of the night. He reached Philadelphia at 3 a.m. on October 24. By now his fever had returned; he was shaking and shivering violently as he asked a night watchman to guide him to the house of Congress President Thomas McKean.[22]

XX

The president, who represented Delaware in Congress, also had political connections in Pennsylvania. He was an old Tilghman friend. The weary aide had no hesitation about pounding on his door in the pre-dawn darkness. According to one story, another town watchman almost arrested Tilghman for disturbing the peace. Before the lawman could act, McKean was at the door embracing the exhausted messenger. The president had received de Grasse's letter from Governor Lee on October 22 and had read it to Congress. But everyone decided to wait until official word arrived from General Washington.

It would seem likely that neither McKean nor anyone else in Philadelphia slept well for the next two nights. Tilghman's confirmation of Yorktown's glorious news swept through the city. Watchmen proclaimed the hour as they were required to do and added in a bellow: "All is well and Cornwallis is taken!" The dawn streets were soon swarming with celebrants, while the Liberty Bell in the tower of the Pennsylvania State House (now Independence Hall) clanged its message of freedom. Artillery on the state house grounds and cannon aboard ships in the Delaware River added to the clamor.

Toward the end of the morning, the feverish, exhausted Tilghman was questioned closely by a committee from Congress, consisting of Edmund Randolph of Virginia, Charles Carroll of Maryland, and Elias Boudinot of New Jersey. They wanted a far more complete report than Washington sent in his victory dispatch. They were especially interested in the motives behind the various articles of capitulation. To Tilghman's relief, as he later told Washington, they pronounced themselves "perfectly satisfied" with everything they heard.

After this ordeal, Tilghman was desperately in need of sleep and medicine for his fever. The delegates found him a room in a nearby boarding house. But the messenger of victory did not have a cent in his pocket. There was also not a penny available in the national treasury. Elias Boudinot suggested that each member of Congress contribute a dollar in hard money, and Tilghman was able to collapse without fear of arrest for debt. It was a silent comment on the nation's bankruptcy and the indisputable fact that the victory at Yorktown came just in time.[23]

XXI

That afternoon at two o'clock, Congress, the French ambassador, the Chevalier de la Luzerne, and other hastily assembled dignitaries, including officials from the government of Pennsylvania, who considered themselves the equals if not the superiors of Congress, marched in a procession to the Dutch Lutheran Church. The Reverend Mr. Duffield, a chaplain of Congress, thanked God for Yorktown's near-miraculous outcome. There are prints of Tench Tilghman reading a proclamation of victory from the steps of Independence Hall. This never happened. It would have been the total opposite of the low-keyed tone to the victory celebration that Washington was hoping—in vain—to establish.[24]

Meanwhile, the complete satisfaction expressed by Tench Tilghman's interrogation committee did not prevail in Congress when they read Washington's terse victory report. The South Carolina delegates were enraged to discover that Lord Cornwallis and other high-ranking British officers, such as Colonel Banastre Tarleton, were entitled to depart for New York at their convenience. The Carolinians wanted them arrested and tried as murderers and despoilers of their state. One South Carolina delegate, Arthur Middleton, made a motion that Cornwallis and others be detained "until the further order of Congress."[25]

For a few hours a fierce debate raged. But eventually calmer voices convinced the majority that an attempt to alter Washington's terms would be considered an act of bad faith on the part of the United States, and would only delay what everyone hoped was an imminent treaty of peace. One of the most emphatic speakers on this side of the argument was a slight, earnest young Virginian who had recently arrived in Congress, James Madison. The South Carolina motion was tabled indefinitely.

XXII

That night, in obedience to a proclamation from Pennsylvania's executive council, Philadelphia continued its victory celebration by illuminating (with candles or oil lamps) every window in the city between six and nine o'clock. The proclamation added a plea for "decorum and harmony" on the part of each citizen and a "general discountenance to the least appearance of riot." Those words were evidence of the simmering antagonism between Philadelphia's numerous Quakers, who had stubbornly supported George III throughout the war, and the rest of the city. There was no brotherly love lost between the two groups; in past celebrations of other military victories, the Quakers had declined to illuminate their windows and had gotten them broken by the resentful patriots.

At 6 p.m., when the illumination began, many Quakers refused to participate. It soon became obvious that the appeal for decorum and harmony was little more than pro forma rhetoric. A mob surged into the streets, and the appearance of riot swiftly became a reality, with no attempt by the authorities to restrain the violence prone. Sarah Fisher, whose diary amply demonstrated her loyalist views throughout the war, thought the presence of her husband, Thomas, might deter the rioters. Thomas bolted their front door and refused to open it when angry fists and clubs pounded on it. The rioters broke every downstairs window in the house. Thomas Fisher fled upstairs, where his wife had already taken refuge.

Another non-illuminator, Anna Rawle, had her bolted front door smashed off its hinges. The mob stormed into her house, wrecking furniture and breaking mirrors. Anna, her sister, and her grandmother fled into the backyard and spent most of the night there. Another outspoken Quaker diarist, wealthy Elizabeth Drinker, glumly reported she had seventy panes of smashed glass and a huge crack in her front door, which made it more or less useless.[26]

Not everyone approved of this violence. There was more than political hostility involved in it. Most of the window-breakers were what Philadelphians called "the lower sort"—the city's working poor. They had alarmingly hostile attitudes toward the rich and well-to-do, whether they were Quakers or supposed loyalists or avowed patriots like Robert Morris, the city's wealthiest merchant.

Many people, no doubt including the window-breakers, were exultant when they read the surrender terms in the *Pennsylvania Gazette* the next day and discovered that Washington had refused to agree to Article 10, giving loyalists and deserters immunity from prosecution. John Hanson, a delegate from Maryland who would soon become president of Congress, was especially gleeful. "What will the Tories and refugees [in New York and Charleston] think of their British friends when they find by the answer to the 10th article of capitulation that these of the garrison are . . . given up by Lord Cornwallis to the civil power?"[27]

By the time this letter was written, the sloop *Bonetta* had sailed from Yorktown for New York. Crammed aboard were more than two hundred and fifty loyalists and deserters. With General Washington's prestige at an all-time high, no one made any negative comments on this merciful gesture by the commander in chief.

XXIII

One citizen of Philadelphia who was neither a Quaker nor a loyalist did not join in the city's Yorktown celebration. Nor did he break any windows. Thomas Paine, the author of *Common Sense*, the 1776 book that tilted America toward independence with its savage attack on George III and the idea of kingship, was a forlorn, morose spectator of the tumult in the streets. He sat in his dingy room in a less-than-genteel boarding house on Second Street, penniless and seemingly forgotten.

This was doubly ironic. Paine had just returned from France, where he had served as secretary of the successful mission to Paris led by Lieutenant Colonel John Laurens. Hauled by sixteen teams of oxen and guarded by two Continental regiments, the first fruits of the mission, more than a half-million dollars in borrowed French livres, plus new uniforms and other war materiel, were en route to Philadelphia from Boston at this very moment.

Paine had become an *isolato* in Philadelphia when he plunged into the political brawls that had swirled through the American capital in recent years. He put his facile, often acid pen to work on skewering and even slandering opponents in the style that had worked so effectively against George III. He made enemies by the dozen and they were not three thousand miles away in London. His infuriated foes had called him all sorts of nasty names, including traitor, and forced him to resign from his jobs as secretary of the congressional committee on foreign affairs and clerk of the Pennsylvania Assembly. That meant he lost the salaries that had enabled him to live in modest comfort and turn out occasional essays, all of which he titled *The Crisis*, numbering them IV, V, VI. He was reminding Americans of the first of these Crisis essays, which he had written in the grim autumn of 1776, when the American Revolution seemed on the brink of collapse. It had begun with lines that are still memorable in the twenty-first century: *These are the times that try men's souls.*

Now Paine's soul was being tried by the twists and turns of the politics of the Revolution he had helped to launch. When he first returned to Philadelphia from France, he had written to President McKean, offering to serve as his confidential courier to Washington in Yorktown. McKean did not even bother to answer the letter. Depressed, living on borrowed money, Paine concluded America was "careless of whatever related to my personal interest." A more succinct way of putting it would have been: no one seemed to give a damn what happened to Tom Paine. He decided there was only one thing left for him to do: he would write to General George Washington and reveal the misery of his "situation."[28]

XXIV

In a city ninety miles from Philadelphia, another group of Americans were far more disconsolate than Tom Paine. Behind New York's fortifications, thousands of men and women who remained loyal to George III had lived in anxious suspense for the previous two months, scanning *The New York Royal Gazette* and other newspapers for hopeful reports, and meeting in their houses and favorite taverns to damn the British army and navy for inaction.

Most of the loyalists were refugees from parts of America which the British had seemingly conquered and then abandoned: New Jersey in 1776, Philadelphia in 1777, Rhode Island in 1778. Others came from Connecticut and upstate New York. The wealthy among them lived comfortably in houses from which patriots had fled in 1776. Only about five thousand of the city's twenty thousand residents stayed to greet the conquerors. By 1781 the stay-behinds had been joined by at least twenty-five thousand fugitives from the wrath of their rebel neighbors. The British garrison swelled the population of the city to over forty thousand, most of them crammed onto the southern tip of Manhattan Island. The city of New York did not extend much beyond present-day City Hall.

Historians have long since exploded the myth that most loyalists were rich. By far the majority were middle class and a surprising number were poor. The chief link in their stubborn devotion to the crown seems to have been birth in England rather than America. For the loyalists of modest means, life in New York was grim. They lived in a devastated city. As the American army retreated in 1776, the soldiers had tried to deprive the British of winter quarters by dispatching numerous agents into the city armed with incendiary devices. The ensuing conflagration roared up tree-lined Broadway, consuming Trinity Church and many elegant houses. Before the fire was extinguished by British soldiers and sailors, a fourth of the city, perhaps a thousand houses, had been destroyed.

In 1781, the ruins remained a grisly jumble of charred beams and blackened walls. The British put all available funds into fighting the war, and no private person was likely to invest any money in rebuilding without a guarantee of a royal victory. Instead, the poorest among the refugees stretched sailcloth over cellars and roofless remnants of houses and struggled to survive in this "canvas town." It was not a section of the city where respectable people ventured at night. Many of the residents were accurately described as "very lewd and dissolute persons."[29]

There were also more than three thousand escaped slaves in New York. Most worked as laborers and were paid two and a half pounds a month. A white laborer earned four pounds. Sixty-four black laborers shared one set of five and a half rooms—a manifest impossibility. Most of the time, a majority of them were at work in the countryside, cutting wood or toiling on fortifications. One disgruntled loyalist, Judge Thomas Jones, complained that "a number of houses . . . which would have rented for at least 1,000 pounds a year . . . were occupied by dirty idle thieving Negroes." A study of the provost general's police records shows only a few black thieves, and plenty of white ones.

Many middle-class loyalists who clung to respectability lived a dreary existence, depending on food, fuel, and candles from the military government. Paying jobs were almost nonexistent. The more dexterous attached themselves to various army departments as clerks and factotums. Lawyers and doctors tried to practice their professions with varying degrees of success. So did carpenters, tailors, and other artisans. But life was difficult. The price of food and fuel had grown more astronomical with every passing year.

Many women turned to prostitution to survive. One British soldier who attended a Sunday service at St. Paul's Chapel, in the center of the burned-out area, said he saw "some of the handsomest and best dressed ladies I have ever seen in America. I believe most of them was W[hores]."[30]

Since 1776, New York had been ruled by the military. The loyalists repeatedly asked the army to let them form a civilian government. But they got nowhere. The generals had no intention of surrendering the summary power they enjoyed. They took over almost every church in the city and used them for hospitals, jails, and barracks. The army often ordered an individual or a family to vacate a house to provide a comfortable residence for a newly arrived general or colonel.

A champion in the house-seizure department was the commander in chief, Sir Henry Clinton. He occupied no less than five country houses, as well as a palatial town house at 1 Broadway. Lower-ranking officers were no less greedy. One officer decided to "share" the house of a Brooklyn farmer. He proceeded to occupy every room that had a fireplace, giving his dismayed host the option of freezing to death or moving elsewhere.[31]

This combination of highhanded arrogance and self interest made it difficult, if not impossible, for most loyalists to regard the British army with enthusiasm. They sneeringly called Sir Henry Clinton "the Knight" and deplored his fondness for spending so much time in the Long Island countryside, fox hunting. They took an even dimmer view of the commander in chief's private life. His mistress was the Irish-born wife of a sergeant, by whom he eventually had four children. The private lives of other officers were even less respectable. Aging General James Robertson, who drew a hefty salary as governor of the colony of New York, an utterly meaningless title, spent most of his time, according to one loyalist, "running after little misses" who were young enough to be his granddaughters.

The loyalists formed an association to speak for them and chose William Franklin, Benjamin Franklin's son, as its leader. Franklin had been royal governor of New Jersey and had decided to remain loyal to the king, a decision that deeply distressed and enraged his famous father. The Board of Associated Loyalists obtained a headquarters at 4 Nassau Street and permission from Sir Henry Clinton to launch guerilla forays into New Jersey, southern Connecticut, and New York counties north of the city, which made life harrowing for the more outspoken rebel leaders. After much foot-dragging, Sir Henry provided a brig and a sloop for these operations. The rebel leaders constantly faced kidnapping and if they resisted seizure, sudden death. The loyalists also used these vessels to carry away cattle and other profitable loot. But these quasi-military operations had little impact on the course of the war.

The unhappy loyalists could only hope that in spite of appearances to the contrary, the British army would eventually defeat the obnoxious rebels who had forced them to flee their homes and farms. For most of

1781, loyalists had been optimistic about the progress of the war. "King Cong" as they called the Continental Congress, was bankrupt, their paper money a joke. The British had seemed in control of Georgia and South Carolina. Cornwallis had won an apparent victory in a battle at Guilford Court House, North Carolina, and marched into Virginia. The largest American state offered him only token opposition. Colonel Banastre Tarleton and two hundred and fifty cavalrymen had ridden unchallenged into the heart of the state and came very close to seizing Governor Thomas Jefferson and the entire legislature. Then came the stunning news that Cornwallis had retreated to Yorktown, and a French fleet, soon joined by the French and American armies, was menacing his safety.

XXV

In the midst of this trauma, a royal visitor arrived in New York harbor—Prince William Henry, George III's sixteen-year-old son, the future King George IV. He was serving as a midshipman in the Royal Navy. Loyalist William Smith, former chief justice of New York under the crown, summed up the prevailing reaction. "To our unspeakable joy," Smith wrote to a friend, William Henry had arrived safely aboard the flagship of Admiral Robert Digby. "The presence of the Prince may supply our deficiency."

Smith meant the deficiency of energy and boldness in the commander in chief, General Clinton, and the men around him, whom Smith damned almost daily in his diary. Smith nonetheless remained Sir Henry's legal advisor and confidante, thanks to the judge's numerous contacts with neutrals and secret loyalists in rebel territory. The local commander of the Royal Navy, Admiral Thomas Graves, did not receive much kinder treatment in Smith's diary. But most of the time he stayed on board his flagship, while Smith was in almost daily contact with Clinton.[32]

Smith was not a loyalist by choice—or so he claimed. He had spent the first three years of the war protesting he was a neutral, sympathetic to America's complaints against British greed and arrogance, but unable to support the Declaration of Independence. He was married to Janet L. Livingston, member of a wealthy Hudson River clan, most of whom espoused the Revolution. As a lawyer with deeply traditional instincts—he had written a more-than-passable history of colonial New York—Smith revered Great Britain's balanced constitution, which divided authority between the executive, personified by the king, and the legislature and judiciary. In his opinion "British liberty," with its careful attention to rank and authority, was infinitely superior to wild-eyed unrestrained American liberty.[33]

In 1778, the patriots of New York State grew weary with Smith's neutrality and deported him and his wife and three children to British-occupied New York City. There he continued to play his own kind of double game. He disdained loyalists who breathed fire on rebels and called for hangings by the score when the king's men won the war. Instead, he urged reunion and reconciliation. But he was not loath to urge fire and sword on the rebels who confronted the king's men with guns in their hands. He had played no small part in persuading the British army to launch a preemptive strike on Washington's depleted force in New Jersey in 1780. A combination of luck and desperate courage repelled the attack, which might have ended the war if it had succeeded.[34]

Smith's salute to the Prince was far more than a typical loyalist's semi-mystical allegiance to the idea of kingship. The judge was well aware that William Henry was an affable, unassuming teenager without an iota of experience in fighting a war. For Smith his arrival symbolized Britain's determination to win the long struggle in America. Even if the worst happened, and Cornwallis surrendered, His Royal Highness's presence would signify that they could transcend the defeat. They had overcome earlier losses, such as the surrender of another British army at Saratoga in 1777.

Smith filled pages of his diary with descriptions of the excitement the Prince created in the minds and hearts of the loyalists. On September 27, the day before Washington and Rochambeau began their advance from Williamsburg to Yorktown, Smith reported that "the Prince walk'd thro' a part of the town with Sir H. Clinton and his family." (Smith meant the General's military family—his aides.) Crowds of people followed the Prince. He had previously "gratified . . . their curiosity all the morning" at the window of his residence on Broadway.

The next day, September 28, while Washington and Rochambeau advanced to within a mile of Yorktown's defenses, the Prince was the centerpiece of an elaborate reception for the ranking generals and colonels and prominent loyalists such as William Franklin and William Smith. Later in the day, the Prince strolled down Wall Street while another huge crowd watched him. Everyone thought it was remarkable that he and his escorts walked "uncovered" (with their hats off) in spite of a very hot sun. At 5 p.m., the top generals and other VIPs attended a splendid dinner for the Prince and at 7, "at a nodd from Admiral Digby" the young royal departed to spend the night aboard Digby's flagship. The admiral had warned the excited provincials that they were "bringing the Prince into too much notice for the King's inclination."[35]

Meanwhile, Smith conferred repeatedly with Brigadier Benedict Arnold, who had a plan to attack Philadelphia with five thousand men. Arnold had switched sides in 1780, narrowly escaping a noose when his plan to turn over the key fortress of West Point to the British went awry. General Clinton's intelligence chief, Major John Andre, had been captured in the bungled plot and executed as a spy. Sir Henry blamed General Arnold and regarded him with detestation.

This made General Clinton less than eager to approve General Arnold's plan to seize Philadelphia and threaten to burn it if Washington did not abandon the siege of Lord Cornwallis's army in Yorktown. Clinton played cat and mouse with Arnold, sending him a set of queries that expressed doubt about his ability to take Philadelphia with five thousand men. Brigadier Arnold's answers admitted "no discouragements." But to Smith's disgust, the traitor never got the men.[36]

Smith also raged in his diary at Admiral Graves. He had called a council of his subordinate admirals and captains to discuss whether the fleet should venture to the Chesapeake to try to rescue Cornwallis. Many loyalists were thunderstruck by this apparent indecision. Graves had publicly promised the fleet would sail on October 14. Finally, on October 16, the fleet got under way, the men-of-war crammed with seven thousand soldiers. But a violent storm delayed their progress from the harbor. Not until October 19 did the frantic Smith and his friends learn that the warships had passed Sandy Hook and were on the high seas. In Yorktown, Cornwallis's soldiers were preparing to march from their ruined redoubts to surrender their weapons.

Meanwhile, Smith filled his diary with reports of "1500 Indians and Tories" on New York's western frontier, and a British army of four thousand—some said seven thousand—men descending from Canada. Almost as exciting was a plan to trigger an uprising of 1,500 loyalists in the Hudson River Valley the moment the British attacked the rebel forts guarding the Hudson Highlands. A loyalist named Samuel Hake from Poughkeepsie assured Smith the king's friends were ready and willing to fight.

On October 24 came an entry in Smith's diary that made all these fantasies ten times more painful to contemplate: "A hand bill from Jersey of the surrender of Lord Cornwallis, 17th's inst, shocks the town." The despairing Smith "gave no credit to it." But the next day he glumly reported "the town greatly agitated. General Robertson believes the Rebel news."[37]

The loyalists' agitation multiplied tenfold on November 3, when the *Bonetta* with its cargo of escapees arrived from Yorktown and told their friends about Article X in the surrender agreement. Connecticut and New Jersey had long since passed laws making loyalism a hanging offense, and other states, such as Virginia, imposed long jail sentences and forfeiture of a loyalist's property. The escapees claimed half the loyalists in Cornwallis's army had been abandoned. An outraged William Franklin wrote to a high official in London, telling him how several "respectable" loyalists came alongside the *Bonetta* and begged to be taken aboard, but were refused in "harsh and insulting language." Sir Henry Clinton later wrote that it was "impossible to describe the indignation, horror and dismay" of the loyalists in New York, when the wider implications of Article X became apparent to them.[38]

XXVI

In the darkness before dawn on October 24, the same day New York's loyalists heard the bad news from Yorktown, an array of lights appeared on the heaving seas off the Virginia coast. It was the British fleet and army from New York, still hoping to rescue Cornwallis and his soldiers. A small sloop manned by three men immediately set sail from an island near Cape Charles. At 4 a.m. the soaked, shivering refugees hailed HMS *London,* the flagship of the fleet, and were hauled aboard. They were soon face to face with Major General Sir Henry Clinton and Admiral Thomas Graves. The fugitives told them news they did not want to hear. Cornwallis had almost certainly surrendered; there had not been a single cannon shot heard from Yorktown for the past seven days. They had escaped from the village on October 18, the day after Cornwallis had asked for terms.[39]

The next day, the frigate HMS *Nymphe* hauled alongside HMS *London* and signaled she had an important message for General Clinton and Admiral Graves. It was a letter from Cornwallis, written on October 15 and sent to New York, like previous messages, aboard an armed whale-boat equipped with both oars and sails. The swift craft had slipped by the French fleet in the darkness, as others had done. By the time the vessel reached New York, Clinton and Graves and the combined army and fleet had sailed for Yorktown. The letter had been put aboard *Nymphe* with orders to deliver it to the two commanders as quickly as possible.

The letter reported that on October 14, the Americans and French had captured two key redoubts by storm, outflanking the British lines. After previously assuring Clinton that his defenses were more than adequate, Cornwallis now dolefully reported: "Experience has shown that our fresh earthen works do not resist their powerful artillery, so that we shall soon be exposed to an assault in ruined works in a bad position, and with weakened numbers. The safety of the place is therefore so precarious that I cannot recommend that the fleet and army should run any great risk in endeavoring to save us."

The rescue fleet and army continued to plow south through heavy seas. By October 26, they were close enough to see the looming capes at the mouth of Chesapeake Bay. The admiral sent a whaleboat to the shore, where they discovered some huddled loyalists hoping for rescue. The refugees confirmed the grim news that Cornwallis had surrendered. Admiral Graves ordered two frigates to venture into the great bay to see if the French fleet was still there. In theory, a naval victory was still possible—which could trump the loss of the Earl and his army.

The two frigates returned the next day, Sunday, October 28, to report they had counted forty-five French warships in Hampton Roads. For Graves, this was fatal arithmetic. He had only thirty-six warships in his fleet. The frigates reported they had been pursued and fired on by two enemy men-of-war, which suggested the French were more than willing to fight if the English were so inclined.

Instead of a naval victory, Admiral Graves was thinking of the consequences of a defeat. If Admiral de Grasse came out of the bay with his superior numbers and shattered the British fleet, he would be in position not only to assault Charleston and even New York with the help of Washington and Rochambeau; the outsized admiral could sail south and seize every West Indies island still in British possession. The loss of Cornwallis's army was a heavy blow; the loss of the fleet would be a disaster of epic proportions.

This was typical of Admiral Graves's viewpoint since the Yorktown crisis began. He had not shown a trace of the bulldog aggressiveness that made the British navy famous and frequently triumphant. His "battle" with de Grasse's fleet on September 5 had been a pathetic joke. Ignoring the vital fact that all his ships were copper-bottomed and could easily out-sail the French, he had kept his fleet in a rigid line while de Grasse's ships straggled out of the Chesapeake singly and in small groups, inviting annihilation from a more pugnacious commander.

Graves never allowed his ferociously combative second in command, Admiral Sir Samuel Hood, to get into the battle with his rear echelon men-of-war until the September 5 clash was virtually over. He ignored Hood's advice to take advantage of their coppered ships' greater speed to slip past de Grasse in the darkness and take up a position at the mouth of the Chesapeake. That would have forced the French admiral to decide what to do about this sudden reversal of possession, and incidentally enabled the fleet to rescue Cornwallis's army. Instead, the admiral had decided he had only one choice, retreat to New York.

Where, one may ask, did the British navy find such an inept commander? Admiral Graves was a distant cousin of the British First Minister, Frederick, Lord North. He had suggested the admiral's appointment to the First Lord of the Admiralty, John Montagu, The Earl of Sandwich, and dismissed the doubts that more than a few navy insiders had expressed about Graves's capacity.[40]

Now Admiral Graves was reaping the final fruit of his timidity and incompetence. To Admiral Hood's outrage, the fleet's commander decided to send a letter to London, reporting that Cornwallis was lost beyond recall. He assigned the task of carrying this message to a captured American privateer named *Rattlesnake,* an irony apparently unnoticed by Graves or anyone else. The exasperated Hood called it "the most melancholy news Great Britain ever received" and reiterated his conviction that Cornwallis could have and should have been saved. This opinion, when it became widespread, would make for many sleepless nights for both General Clinton and Admiral Graves.

In Yorktown, Lord Cornwallis had already done his utmost to intensify General Clinton's insomnia. He had written a report of the surrender which blamed the entire disaster on the British commander in chief. His lordship began by declaring that he "never saw this post in a favorable light." When he was attacked in it "by so powerful an army and artillery" only "hopes of relief" persuaded him to attempt its defense. He would have preferred to cross to the Gloucester side of the river and march for New York or attack Washington and Rochambeau "in the open field." But he had been "assured by your Excellency's letters" that the navy and army would relieve him. He therefore did not "think myself at liberty to venture upon either of these desperate attempts."[41]

XXVII

While the British generals played the blame game, General Washington was in more pleasant communication with General Nathanael Greene, his commander in South Carolina. The husky thirty-nine-year old Rhode Islander was an unlikely soldier; he walked with a limp caused by a damaged knee and suffered from asthma. But his leadership gifts had won him rapid promotion to a general's rank.

In 1780, Washington had sent Greene south with orders to rescue the Carolinas from imminent British conquest. Taking charge of a mere remnant of an army, he had combined militia and a handful of Continentals (barely a thousand) to contest the British and loyalists in both states. He eventually forced the king's men to abandon all their interior forts and posts in South Carolina and retreat to Charleston. Greene lost most of his battles ("We fight, get beat, rise and fight again," he remarked at one point.) but managed to inflict heavy damage on the enemy in every encounter.

Greene lacked the men to carry Charleston by storm and the heavy artillery to blast it into submission in a siege. He had other worries. His army was constantly short of food and their uniforms were in rags. The sick and wounded were numerous and his surgeons (doctors) few. But he urged the politicians of South Carolina to return to the state and form a civil government. He issued similar advice to American rebels fighting in Georgia. Like Washington, he was strongly aware that the appearance, if not the complete reality, of American control of both states could be of the utmost importance in future peace negotiations.

To underscore how difficult proving American possession might be, in one of his letters Greene told of considering an attack on Wilmington, North Carolina. He was hoping to confer with Governor Thomas Burke of North Carolina on the possibility of turning out local militia. To his dismay Greene learned that six hundred marauding loyalists led by Colonel David Fannning had captured the governor and a number of his advisors and were holding them prisoner. Greene abandoned the attack.

Washington had done his best to keep Greene informed of the situation at Yorktown. On October 7 the southern commander wrote a letter to Washington congratulating him on "your happy prospects." Greene added a fervent plea for help for his battered army. "The suffering of the Southern states" should claim the attention of their Northern brethren; he hoped that "every exertion will be made for their relief."

Washington wrote Greene he was determined to help the southern army, with or without cooperation from the French. As soon as the Yorktown operation was over, he would send him about two thousand Continentals. This was almost half his field army. Washington added that he had written to the legislatures of Virginia and North Carolina, urging them to "strain every nerve" to support Greene with fresh troops and supplies. He warned the politicians against "relaxing their efforts, from a delusion of a negotiating winter." [42]

Another piece of news in this letter was the decision of Comte de Rochambeau to spend the winter in Virginia, instead of marching to aid Greene or returning north with Washington to menace the British in New York. There was little or nothing Washington could do to change his mind, though it must have seemed foolish to divide their trained soldiers by hundreds of miles of land and water. The commander in chief did his best to improve the situation by arranging for a line of express riders between Yorktown and Philadelphia, which would enable Rochambeau to communicate with Congress and the French minister. Washington also advised General Greene to open a correspondence with Rochambeau in cipher in case an emergency developed with either army. [43]

XXVIII

On November 4th, Lord Cornwallis and his staff and some remaining officers sailed from Yorktown for New York. Washington had taken the time to visit the Earl in the weeks since the surrender and had been politely received. Saying farewell to his adversary was the final task on his list of responsibilities. Admiral de Grasse had already departed with his fleet and the 3,500 men he had brought from the West Indies. Rochambeau and his officers were getting settled in Williamsburg. The general was free to pay a visit to the place he loved most in this world—Mount Vernon.

On the way, he decided to stop at Eltham, the plantation to which the ailing Jack Custis had retreated after witnessing the surrender at

Yorktown. Washington rode at his usual swift pace, accompanied by several aides and a company of his Life Guard. They paused for a light supper at a tavern named Bird's Ordinary, and Washington rode ahead to Eltham, expecting to make no more than a brief visit. To his astonishment and dismay, he was greeted at Eltham's door by a weeping Martha, Jack's wife, Nelly, and her oldest daughter, Eliza, all hysterical with grief. Jack was dying! Martha's sister and her husband, Burwell Basset, had summoned them to Eltham several days ago.

Washington raced upstairs to the sick room. Alas, he arrived only in time to watch the helpless doctors close Jack's staring eyes. Martha's only son was dead, three weeks before his twenty-seventh birthday. Washington tried to calm and console the sobbing women. He sent a hurried note to his aides and guard, advising them to continue to Mount Vernon, explaining that "the deep and solemn distress of the mother and the affliction of the wife of this amiable young man" required him to stay at Eltham and give them "every comfort in my power."

Although she had four children to raise, Nelly Custis was young and beautiful. There was little doubt that she would marry again. For Martha, Jack's death was a desolating blow: she had now outlived all four of her children. For Washington, Jack's death was a blow because it distressed Martha so much. He never expressed any personal grief over his loss. If anything, he probably realized he had done the right thing by carefully avoiding any attempt to involve Jack in the war. If he had been killed by an enemy bullet, Martha would have found it difficult to forgive her husband.[44]

XXIX

The depth of Martha's grief forced Washington to stay six days at Eltham. In that time, Jack was buried in the plantation's private cemetery. Finally, on November 11, Martha said she felt well enough to travel and the family, including Nelly and Eliza, set out for Mount Vernon. There Washington conferred with his manager, his nephew Lund Washington, about the plantation's many financial and physical problems. He made an effort to buy some adjacent land in a long labored letter that suggested he was a very tired man.

The duties and pressures of a commander in chief pursued him. Letters poured in from congressmen, from friends, from the citizens of

Alexandria and Annapolis, from state governors, congratulating him on the Yorktown victory. Invariably, Washington managed, along with his thanks, to include a warning that the war was not over.

On the eve of his departure for Philadelphia, Washington wrote another letter to Nathanael Greene, promising he would use "every means in my power" to stimulate Congress into taking the "most vigorous . . . measures to be ready for an early and effectual campaign next year." A moment later he revealed to this intimate friend his doubts that Congress would listen to him. "If unhappily, we sink into that fatal mistake, no part of the blame shall be mine."[45]

To the Marquis de Lafayette, who was on his way to Boston to board an American frigate to return to France, Washington wrote his most serious and pointed letter. After thanking him for his services to the American cause, and reiterating his deep personal friendship, the general urged the young nobleman to tell King Louis XVI and France's other leaders that ending the war "depend[ed] *absolutely* upon the naval force which is employed in these seas." With a superior fleet to cooperate with the army, the war could be ended "speedily." Without it, "I do not know if it will ever be terminated honorably."[46]

XXX

During these weeks at Mount Vernon, General Washington heard some good news from northern New York. A 700-man British, Indian, and loyalist raiding force had erupted from their base at Fort Niagara, intending to ravage the countryside around Schenectady. The Americans, a mixture of Continentals led by Colonel Marinus Willett and local militia, gathered strength to repel them but it took time. The raiders burned more than a hundred farms, a granary, and three grist mills before news of the oncoming Americans forced them to retreat.

In cold, snowy weather, the king's men made a stand at a stream still called West Canada Creek. More than sixty Oneida warriors had joined the Americans and they played a vital role in the final assault. Captain Walter Butler, a famous loyalist leader, commanded the rear guard. As twilight descended, he stood up to shout defiance at the oncoming rebels. An Oneida shot him in the head. Butler's men fled and another Oneida warrior waded across the icy stream to scalp the dying loyalist. The rest of the British vanished into the darkening woods. Colonel Willett made a point of praising the Oneida in his final report. He called them "the best cavalry for the service of the wilderness."[47]

Most of this good news was reported to Washington by Major General Philip Schuyler, who was in charge of Indian affairs in Northern New York. General Schuyler added some not-so-good news about another worrisome topic in his part of America: Vermont. This self-styled independent republic had been settled by farmers from Connecticut, New Hampshire, and western Massachusetts. They were led by a colorful Connecticutian named Ethan Allen. Unfortunately, most of the land they began tilling in the Green Mountains belonged to people from New York. But the ownership was based on land grants from George III, which gave the Vermonters an excuse to claim they were defending American liberty against imperialist greed. More than once gunfire had broken out over whose claims would prevail.

General Schuyler's letter brought General Washington up to date about growing American fears that the Vermonters might decide to join the British Empire if George III guaranteed the lands they claimed. "I am very sorry to hear the account you give of the governing powers of Vermont," Washington wrote. He had assumed "the terms offered them by Congress would have been readily accepted." The last thing the fragile American nation needed was a civil war.

Adding to General Washington's uneasiness was a gloomy Schuyler prediction that the Yorktown victory would produce military inertia throughout the American union. "My great fear is what you mention," Washington wrote. "All my powers will be exerted this winter to prevent so great an evil."[48]

XXXI

With these disturbing thoughts foremost in his mind, General Washington made sure his arrival in Philadelphia took place with a minimum of excitement. He had heard about the celebration triggered by the November 3rd arrival of the standards of the British and German regiments captured at Yorktown. They had been entrusted to another Washington aide, Lieutenant Colonel David Humphreys. A recuperated Tench Tilghman and the First Troop of the Philadelphia light horsemen had met Humphreys at Chester. The twenty-four standards were handed to "gentlemen privates" (only the best people belonged to the

First Troop) and the cavalrymen and the two aides rode into the city. Down Market Street and along Front Street they proceeded while thousands cheered. At the state house, the captured colors were solemnly presented to Congress.[49]

Washington's arrival on November 26 was totally lacking in such fanfare. Unannounced, without a parade or cheers, he and Martha and the inevitable aides settled into the handsome three-story town house of Benjamin Chew on South Third Street, the most fashionable address in Philadelphia. Today the site is part of the posh Society Hill section. The Washingtons did not go entirely unnoticed, of course. Members of the general's Life Guard were posted at the front door and in the rear of the house. The *Pennsylvania Journal* reported his arrival and called him "the savior of his country."[50]

On November 28 the general went before Congress and got another portent of trouble to come. There were only twenty-four members in attendance. Three states were represented by a single delegate, which meant, according to the rules, they had no vote. Seven other states had only two delegates; if any of these duos disagreed, that state also had no vote.

There was some consolation in the greeting of the new president, John Hanson of Maryland, who assured Washington that it was "their fixed purpose to draw every advantage [from Yorktown] by exhorting the states in the strongest terms to the most vigorous and timely exertions." Washington gazed at the vacant seats and remembered the glory days of 1776, when fifty-six delegates, almost all men of leadership caliber in their home states—Benjamin Franklin, Thomas Jefferson, John and Samuel Adams—had voted for independence. Would this handful of undistinguished politicians have any impact on the states they represented?

Washington also discovered he could not escape celebrations of the Yorktown victory, no matter how hard he tried. As soon as word of his arrival spread through Philadelphia, artists such as Charles Willson Peale began displaying in the windows of their houses illuminated portraits of the general's head crowned with laurel wreaths. One ambitious composition portrayed him wielding a spear as he stamped on a golden royal crown.

When the French ambassador, the Chevalier de la Luzerne, gave a party for the general, the festivities featured an opera, *The Temple of Minerva*, written by the talented Philadelphia composer Francis Hopkinson. It celebrated Washington as a triumphant leader of near mythical proportions. At one point a chorus of young ladies sang:

> *Now that the dreadful conflict's o'er*
> *Now the cannons cease to roar*
> *Spread the joyful tidings round*
> *He comes he comes with conquest crowned*
> *Hail Columbia's warlike son*
> *Hail the glorious Washington!*[51]

Washington could only smile humbly and accept this well-meaning hero worship. It was neither the time nor the place to stand up and tell everyone the dreadful conflict was not "o'er." He could only hope that a letter he had sent to France a few days after Yorktown might prove to be an elixir that would silence the guns and produce peace and independence so swiftly, he would be home in Mount Vernon by spring. But six and a half years of seesaw struggle made it hard for him to believe in this fairy tale ending to what he often called "a long and bloody war."

—————————•—————————

Chapter Two

Diplomats in Distress

WASHINGTON'S LETTER WAS addressed to Benjamin Franklin, John Adams, and John Jay. They were "commissioners"
designated by Congress to negotiate peace with Great Britain. The letter contained a copy of the capitulation signed by Lord Cornwallis on October 19, along with a summary of the number of prisoners
and cannon and muskets captured and a report from General Nathanael
Greene of his victory in the September 6th battle of Eutaw Springs.

Headquarters near York in Virginia, October 22, 1781:

Sirs: As the transmission of the enclosed paper thro the usual channel of
the department of foreign affairs would, on the present occasion, probably be attended with great delay, and recent intelligence of mility [*sic*]
transactions must be important to our ministers in Europe at the present
period of affairs: I have thought it wd be agreeable both to Congress and
yr Excelly. that the matter shd be communicated immediately by a French
frigate dispatched by Admiral de Grasse. I have the honor etc. . . .[1]

Washington considered this letter so important, he ordered his aide
Lieutenant Colonel David Humphreys to commandeer a boat and deliver
it to Admiral de Grasse aboard his flagship. In a covering letter he asked
the admiral to send it to Paris aboard the next departing frigate.[2]

Washington was thinking as an American leader. He wanted the peace negotiators to know he had been the commander in chief at Yorktown, the conductor of the final surrender negotiations, and the man in possession of the captured prisoners and weapons. Although he was ready to acknowledge France's assistance, he wanted the diplomats to know the American army had played a major role. Adding Nathanael Greene's report was a nice way of informing them that the British were being beaten elsewhere in the South without any help from France.

Washington knew he was going out of channels with this letter. He made a point of letting Congress know he had sent it, adding that he would rely on the politicians to understand and forgive "the liberty" he took in dispatching it. He wanted to make sure that Franklin, Jay, and Adams did not think that Yorktown was a mostly French victory. That assumption might make it difficult for them to resist letting the French take charge of peace negotiations, with potentially ruinous results for American independence.[3]

II

Two days before Washington wrote his letter, the new American secretary for foreign affairs, Robert R. Livingston of New York, wrote to Benjamin Franklin. Along with his designation as a peace commissioner, Franklin was also the ambassador to France. Livingston's title represented a new departure for the Continental Congress. After six years of mismanaging the war through a maze of committees that by now numbered in the thousands, Congress had finally taken the advice of numerous critics and decided to delegate specific powers to appointed officials. General Benjamin Lincoln had become secretary of war and Robert Morris superintendent of finance—in effect the secretary of the treasury. Livingston had been put in charge of foreign policy.

Livingston told Franklin that it would be his duty as well as his inclination to maintain an "intimate and regular correspondence with you." He began by reporting that the prospects for winning a victory at Yorktown looked good. Three days later, Livingston wrote another letter, telling Franklin that Cornwallis had surrendered.

The new foreign secretary's tone abruptly shifted from exultation to anxiety. Livingston had been reading Franklin's recent letters and had been transfixed to discover that five months earlier, on May 14, 1781, the ambassador had resigned his post! Congress had promptly answered Franklin, saying they wanted him to stay on the job. Since that time, Congress had not heard a word from him.

"I shall be impatient to hear that you [will] comply wth the wishes of Congress on this subject," the agitated Livingston wrote. He hoped that Franklin would see his additional appointment as a peace negotiator as proof of the "approbation" of Congress for his years of service in France even though the additional powers were an added "burthen." The important thing was "the compleation [*sic*] of the great work in which you so early engaged." [4]

III

Ambassador Franklin's resignation evokes one of the least-known and least-understood chapters in the American Revolution—the hatreds, backstabbings, and slanders that had torn apart the American mission in Paris. It was a clash that embroiled Congress and spilled into the newspapers, endangering the alliance with France and even the survival of the whole revolutionary enterprise. Its aftershocks still threatened the shape and direction of any negotiations for peace.

When Cornwallis surrendered at Yorktown, the seventy-five-year-old Franklin had been in France almost five years. He had arrived in December, 1776, after a harrowing winter crossing of the Atlantic. He did not have the title of ambassador in those dark and desperate days. He was one of three commissioners a harried Congress had appointed to persuade the French to support the collapsing new republic.

In the closing months of 1776, the future of the Revolution was in grave doubt. Washington's troops had suffered repeated defeats in their attempts to defend New York against a British army and fleet. While Franklin was on the Atlantic, the discouraged Americans had abandoned New York to the triumphant British and retreated across New Jersey to Pennsylvania. A panicky Congress had deserted the American capital, Philadelphia, and fled to Baltimore.

Benjamin Franklin was far more than an emergency diplomat. In 1776 he was the most famous American of his era. He had won worldwide fame for his epochal discoveries in electricity, climaxed by the daring experiment of flying a kite in a thunderstorm to prove that lightning and electricity were identical. He had been elected a member of Britain's

Royal Society of London and received honorary doctorates from American and British universities.

For two decades before the Revolution began in 1775, Franklin had lived in England, representing Massachusetts and several other colonies before Parliament. He had become the unofficial spokesman for the Americans, trying again and again to persuade the British to abandon their ruinous determination to tax the colonists without their consent. The experience had convinced him that it was time for America to separate herself from the corruption and greed that characterized so much of British politics under their domineering king, George III.

Franklin's appearance in Paris created a sensation throughout Europe—a badly needed counterbalance to the news of British battlefield victories in America. George III's ministers and their hired writers rushed to fill the newspapers and diplomatic correspondence with the claim that Franklin had fled to escape the imminent collapse of the revolutionary cause. His many friends in England angrily defended him. Among the most outspoken was Edmund Burke, who had repeatedly urged Parliament to rethink its policy toward America. One of the leaders of the opposition in Parliament told Burke he considered Franklin's presence in Paris "much more than a balance for the few additional acres" that the British army had acquired by conquering Manhattan Island. Such was the power of Franklin's name and reputation.[5]

Franklin proceeded to embellish his fame with a performance that was nothing less than masterful. Rather than buying an elaborate wardrobe in the latest Parisian style, like diplomats from other countries, he wore a plain brown suit, a white shirt, and a fur hat which he had acquired on a 1776 mission to Canada and used on shipboard to survive the Atlantic's icy blasts. "Everything about him announces the simplicity and innocence of primitive morals," declared one charmed French writer.[6]

Franklin was playing to the French image of America, that strange compound of myth and wish created by intellectuals such as Voltaire and Jean Jacques Rousseau. Along with being natural-born soldiers, Americans supposedly lived in a world in which private virtue blended with social perfection. Religious toleration, prosperity, and simplicity abounded, thanks to the ubiquity of the farmer's "primitive" life and the proximity of "noble" savages. It added up to an almost total ignorance of America and Americans, but Franklin used these fantasies to win sympathy for the reeling Revolution.

IV

Meanwhile, Franklin was having extremely realistic conversations with three men who were trying to rescue the foundering American cause. The first of this trio was thirty-nine-year-old Silas Deane of Connecticut, who had been sent to France in the spring of 1776 as an agent of the Secret Committee of Congress to purchase weapons and ammunition and clothing for the struggling American army. Franklin had been a member of the committee that chose him. He had given Deane advice and letters of introduction to several influential French friends. When Congress decided a treaty with France had become a necessity, it was logical to make Deane, already in Paris, another commissioner.

Silas Deane's name was not on the list of American diplomats in Europe to whom General Washington mailed his letter from Yorktown. There was a sad, even a tragic reason for this omission. While the Americans were besieging and ultimately capturing Cornwallis at Yorktown, the *New York Royal Gazette,* the voice of Americans loyal to George III, published a series of letters that Deane had written to personal friends, telling them of his total disillusion with the Continental Congress and the American Revolution. Deane urged them to join him in a campaign to reunite Great Britain and America.[7]

In 1776, Silas Deane had been an ebullient, energetic blacksmith's son with a Yale degree and an ambition to become as rich as his hero Robert Morris. Along with his public role as an agent of Congress, Deane had gone to Europe with a secret partnership with Morris in his baggage. Deane was already a successful merchant in his home state; the Morris contract gave him access to a worldwide network of creditworthy merchants, ready to help him take advantage of "the opportunity of improving our fortunes" (as Morris put it) on the private side.[8]

Deane wanted—and expected—to get rich and he did not think there was anything reprehensible about this desire. He was fond of flashy clothes—one critic claimed he owned forty silk suits—and living well. He was willing to work hard to pay for his pleasures; rare was the day when he did not greet the rising sun at his desk.

Mixing private business and public offices was not unusual in the eighteenth century. Robert Morris had been doing it since the Revolution began. Nathanael Greene, for a time quartermaster general of the Continental Army, had private partnerships with several businessmen who supplied the troops. Government salaries were invariably low. Merchants who did business for the government were not expected to live on them. Realistically, the government could not afford to pay a merchant as talented as Robert Morris what he made in an average year.

Silas Deane introduced Franklin to two Frenchmen who seemingly combined access to wealth with a devotion to the American cause. Caron de Beaumarchais was a volatile, mustachioed playwright who had reportedly performed notable deeds as a secret agent for King Louis XV and his grandson, the present king, Louis XVI. Not shy about proclaiming his merits, Beaumarchais told Franklin he had single-handedly persuaded the king to support the rebellion. Louis XVI had given a million livres to a trading company, Hortalez et Cie, created by Beaumarchais, to ship war materiel to America. Louis had persuaded King Charles III of Spain, his Bourbon dynasty cousin, to give Hortalez another million livres—a total of about four hundred thousand American dollars. Both nations insisted on secrecy for this aid. Neither wanted a war with England.

In spite of a diminutive physique, the other Frenchman had a solidity that Franklin found reassuring after listening to the effervescent Beaumarchais. Jacques Donatien Leray de Chaumont had made a fortune in the East India trade and bought the magnificent fifteenth-century chateau of Chaumont, in the Loire Valley. He was commissary of the French army (in charge of supplying uniforms) and overseer of the king's forests. Chaumont was hoping to make another fortune by cornering a major share of France's trade with America when she won her independence. He had advanced Silas Deane a million livres on credit and with Deane's help bought one hundred thousand acres in northern New York. Chaumont began playing the role of middleman, helping Beaumarchais and Deane purchase tons of war materiel to ship to America through Hortalez et Cie.[9]

No longer able to toil long hours, the seventy-year-old Franklin gladly handed over to Deane the business side of the American mission. The older man candidly admitted that he had no head for the complicated deals that eighteenth-century merchants put together. Deane was signing contracts with French merchants, manufacturers, and bankers and talked excitedly of soon shipping thousands of muskets and uniforms and hundreds of cannon to America.

By the time Franklin arrived, Deane and Beaumarchais had spent almost a million dollars—most of it on credit. Deane had been told that

Congress would ship him tobacco and indigo to help fund his mission. Instead, he had not received so much as a single letter. This lack of communication between Congress and its diplomats would torment everyone on both sides of the Atlantic throughout the war. Many letters were captured by blockading British warships or spies. Others were slowed to the point of futility by the length of time—two and often three months—it took letters to cross the Atlantic and be delivered by the barely organized postal services of France, Spain, and war-ravaged America.

Silas Deane did not allow Congress's seeming neglect to dim his entrepreneurial spirit or his passionate patriotism. In December 1776, before Franklin arrived, Deane told his friend, John Jay, "If my letters arrive safe, they will give you some idea of my situation, without intelligence, without orders, without remittances, yet boldly plunging into contracts, engagements and negotiations, hoping that something will arrive from America." Many of Deane's contracts were with professional soldiers from France and other countries who were soon embarking for America to play leading roles in the American army.[10]

Early in 1777, Franklin decided to separate himself from the hurlyburly of Deane's business dealings, which he conducted at the Hotel de Hambourg in the center of Paris. The senior commissioner accepted Leray de Chaumont's invitation to move to the tranquil village of Passy and live in one of the buildings of his spacious villa, the Hotel de Valentinois. About a half hour from the center of Paris, Passy (now a section of the French capital filled with high-rise apartment buildings) was also on the road to the royal palace of Versailles. It was a move that combined practicality and symbolism: Franklin was saying that a man his age needed some peace and quiet—and the diplomatic side of the American mission was his chief concern.

V

This efficient division of labor was disrupted and soon all but destroyed by the presence of the third commissioner that Congress appointed to negotiate a treaty with France. Thirty-six-year-old Arthur Lee was the blond, blue-eyed youngest son of the current generation of Lees, a powerful Virginia family who owned 30 thousand acres of prime farmland and hundreds of slaves. Arthur had endured a lonely childhood. His father, Thomas Lee, died when he was ten; his mother died in the same year.

That left him in the not-so-tender care of his oldest brother, Thomas Ludwell Lee, a cold, domineering man who shipped him off to England at the age of eleven to study at Eton.[11]

Arthur went from Eton to the University of Edinburgh, where he received a medical degree. After a few months of practicing medicine in Williamsburg, Virginia, he decided the law had greater appeal and returned to London where he studied at the Middle Temple and Lincoln's Inn and was admitted to the bar in 1775. Meanwhile he had plunged into politics, writing numerous articles in the newspapers damning British policies toward America and hobnobbing with critics of George III, most of them radical democrats with minuscule followings.[12]

When the Revolution began in 1775, Arthur Lee stayed in close touch with American politics. Two older brothers, Richard Henry Lee and Francis Lightfoot Lee, were elected to the Continental Congress. Richard became head of the Committee on Foreign Affairs and soon formed a close friendship with Samuel Adams of Massachusetts. Arthur's appointment as a commissioner to France was one of the first fruits of this bond between the spokesmen for the two largest states in the American union.[13]

VI

In letters Arthur Lee wrote after Franklin arrived in France, Lee called him our "pater patriae"—the father of the country—years before anyone bestowed the title on George Washington. The two men were already friends. In 1766, Franklin had helped Dr. Lee, as he was often called, become a fellow of the Royal Society of London, a tribute to his Edinburgh medical degree. Franklin had even paid his admission fee. But the friendship had cooled in the early 1770s, when Lee wanted Franklin's job as colonial agent for Massachusetts. Now, the older man's immense popularity in France unhinged Lee. How could the son of a Boston candle-maker receive such adulation while Arthur Lee, scion of the Lees of Virginia, was treated as if he were more or less invisible?

The breadth and depth of Franklin's popularity made him temporarily invulnerable to attack. Lee decided Silas Deane was a better target for his radical zealotry. On the French ships carrying the weapons and clothing Deane had purchased on Congress's credit, the would-be merchant prince sometimes included goods to be sold in Philadelphia or Boston for his personal profit. Deane invested his own money in privateers sailing out of Nantes and other ports. With the help of brokers in Holland or friends in England, he occasionally speculated on the London stock exchange. For Arthur Lee, such transactions were loaded with conflicts of interest and corruption.

Lee shared with his brother Richard Henry Lee and Samuel Adams and their followers a conviction that self interest was incompatible with patriotism. An Adams follower, Dr. Benjamin Rush of Philadelphia, summed up this radical philosophy by dividing whigs (liberals) into six classes. Only one was worthy of respect: the true whig who had not a smidgen of self interest in his patriotic heart. True whigs were the apostles and guardians of public virtue, which Samuel Adams considered America's chief asset in the struggle with Great Britain. This was a noble ideal but when it was used to judge individuals, it could easily become a political weapon.

Lee soon concocted a serious charge against the unsuspecting Deane. Beaumarchais had met Lee in London and boasted to him about the deluge of supplies and weapons he would soon be shipping to America to rescue the faltering Revolution. Lee got the erroneous impression that this war materiel was the gift of King Louis XVI. On the contrary, Americans were expected to pay for the guns and uniforms with tobacco and other products, to begin the process of creating strong commercial ties between France and America. Beaumarchais had persuaded wealthy friends such as Leray de Chaumont to invest money in Hortalez, promising them they would all make millions when the Americans achieved independence and were able to pay their debts.

In his letters to America, Arthur Lee was soon accusing Beaumarchais of being a liar and a crook and Silas Deane of an even worse crime—he was a traitor to his country, using his public role as a diplomat to rob his compatriots of huge amounts of money. At one point he claimed that Deane and his partner, Robert Morris, had spent 3 million livres and another million on credit without the public receiving "a livre's worth." As with all his accusations, Lee offered no proof. Simultaneously Lee accused Deane of being part of a plot "to traduce me here." Along with his perpetual suspicion of everyone's motives, Lee had a paranoid streak winding through his psyche as wide as the River Seine.[14]

While accusing Deane of gross corruption, Arthur Lee decided he might show up Franklin by practicing "militias diplomacy." This was a favorite expression of the Lee-Adams party in Congress—part of their dangerously wrong conviction that militia, part-time soldiers called out in emergencies, were superior to Washington's trained regulars. The militia supposedly had more "spirit."

A militia diplomat did not proceed in the dignified, restrained style of European envoys. Instead he invaded a nation's capital without warning, proffering a treaty of commerce with America if a recognition of independence was forthcoming. Arthur Lee tried this approach in Spain and Prussia and got nowhere. The Spanish did not even let him enter Madrid. In Berlin the British ambassador stole Lee's private papers and made him a laughingstock.

Undiscouraged by his failures, Lee unveiled his solution to the corruption supposedly galloping through the American mission. He told Samuel Adams and Richard Henry Lee to send Benjamin Franklin to Vienna. It was a "respectable and quiet" post (Austria had not shown the slightest interest in recognizing American independence) and thus perfect for a man in his seventies. Silas Deane, if he was not recalled, should be shipped to Holland, which was equally uninterested in helping the Americans. France, "the centre of political activity," should be reserved for Arthur Lee's superior diplomatic gifts. Lee liked to rant about public virtue and his disinterested patriotism, but deep in his troubled soul, he hungered for power.[15]

VII

Another part of this transatlantic drama took place in Nantes, the port from which Deane and Beaumarchais shipped most of their war supplies to America. There Robert Morris had ensconced his much younger half-brother, Thomas, as the commercial agent handling American business in Europe. Thomas soon revealed himself to be a hopeless and often truculent alcoholic, who allowed French merchants with whom he did business to cheat him outrageously. In an attempt at damage control, Franklin persuaded Silas Deane to appoint Ben's grandnephew, Jonathan Williams, who had been working for a London merchant, as a special agent in Nantes to handle both private and public business. A trustworthy trained accountant, Williams was also given the largely impossible task of coping with Thomas Morris.

When Arthur Lee arrived in France, he quickly spotted the disarray in Nantes and raged at Franklin and Deane for not doing something about it. Lee persuaded Congress to send his brother William Lee to France to support him. William was a prosperous London merchant who had been elected an alderman by London voters—a post he declined to resign. Urged by Richard Henry Lee, Congress appointed William commercial agent for Europe, replacing Thomas Morris. But it took months for William's commission to arrive from Philadelphia. Meanwhile Deane and Franklin declined to have anything to do with him.

William Lee was soon warning Congress of "the low dirty intrigue, the selfish views and the wicked arts" of the men Congress had sent to France. Behind this facade of righteousness and slander, William was shipping private goods on government vessels and speculating in the London stock market on a scale far beyond the financial ability of Silas Deane.[16]

VIII

Surrounded by so much acrimony, it was nothing short of a miracle that Franklin was able to achieve an alliance with France. For over a year, he made little practical headway with the cautious foreign minister, Charles Gravier, the Comte de Vergennes. But in their clandestine meetings both men learned to respect and even admire each other as thorough professionals in the art of diplomacy. Having spent the previous twenty years talking politics to the British establishment, Franklin had no illusions that leaders of powerful nations were idealists. He understood that the fifty-five-year-old Vergennes, who had spent his entire life in the French diplomatic service, saw the American Revolution as an opportunity for France to regain the prestige and power she had lost in her previous clash with Great Britain, known as the Seven Years War (1754–61) in Europe and the French and Indian War in America. Vergennes was willing to advance another 3 million livres in secret aid—in many ways a statement of his growing respect for Franklin. But the foreign minister was not going to risk France's public involvement without some evidence that the Americans could hold their own on the battlefield against Britain's professional army.

For most of Franklin's first year in France, this evidence was not forthcoming. George Washington had temporarily reversed the slide toward collapse with his victories at Trenton and Princeton at the end of 1776.

But the British mustered all their military might for a knockout blow in 1777. In the fall of that year, the news that reached the Americans in Paris varied from bad to worse.

Two British armies were on the offensive, one descending from Canada, the other striking at Philadelphia. The Canadian army, led by General John Burgoyne, captured supposedly impregnable Fort Ticonderoga in northern New York and seemed to be advancing irresistibly down the Hudson toward Albany. In Pennsylvania, Sir William Howe, the British army's commander in chief, defeated George Washington in two major battles and the red-coated battalions marched triumphantly into Philadelphia, the nation's largest and wealthiest city. Congress fled ignominiously once more, this time to York, Pennsylvania, a frontier town where most people spoke only German.

In Paris, with the two Lees snarling and sniping from the sidelines, a discouraged Franklin and Deane faced despair—and imminent bankruptcy. Deane and Beaumarchais had spent all the money the French government had advanced them, and bankers and businessmen were demanding interest payments on goods these optimists had bought on credit. All they could do was urge Franklin to borrow more money from Vergennes to pay the interest—and hope for a miracle.

A week later, the miracle arrived on Franklin's doorstep. A messenger carrying dispatches from Congress told them: "General Burgoyne and his whole army are prisoners of war!" The victory at Saratoga in the fall of 1777, won in part with weaponry shipped by Deane and Beaumarchais, transformed Foreign Minister Vergennes's cautious attitude toward the Americans. After two months of intense negotiation the three American commissioners signed treaties of commerce and military alliance with France. The British soon recalled their ambassador from Paris and without bothering to declare war, ordered the Royal Navy to begin attacking French ships around the world. The revolt of the thirteen American colonies became a global confrontation between the eighteenth century's two superpowers, France and England.

IX

Foreign Minister Vergennes piously announced that France sought no territory from the war—King Louis XVI simply wanted to help the Americans achieve independence from England. Political insiders, above all Benjamin Franklin, understood this stance was for popular consumption. Not long after Vergennes became foreign minister in 1774, he had told the twenty-year-old king, "Opinion, they say, is queen of the world. The government that knows how to establish it in its favor doubles . . . consideration and respect" for a "well-directed administration."

At the same time, Vergennes advised one of his assistants in the Department of Foreign Affairs to operate as if he were living in "The Palace of Silence." He should never admit any special knowledge of events, even if the news appeared in the *Gazette de France*. All important conversations should take place behind closed doors.[17]

In Versailles, with its perpetually swirling intrigues, this policy was a vital necessity. Queen Marie Antoinette aspired to be a power player in the tradition of her mother, Empress Maria Theresa of Austria. The queen had her own cadre of followers, few of whom were friendly to Vergennes. In 1776, she had tried to persuade her husband to dismiss Vergennes and had been rebuffed. The foreign minister was in wholehearted agreement with Louis XVI's determination to keep the queen at arm's length, politically.

But Vergennes shrewdly did favors for the volatile former Austrian princess; he helped her courtiers, such as the handsome Swede, Axel von Fersen, find places in Rochambeau's army. He was especially cordial to her closest friend, the beautiful Madame de Polignac, who with equal shrewdness soothed the queen's hostility to Vergennes. When the queen asked if one of her former valets de chambre could join the Department of Foreign Affairs, presto! he was employed.[18]

Vergennes understood that Louis XVI was struggling to be his own man. The king's hero was his father, Louis Ferdinand, who had died when Louis was a boy of eleven. Louis Ferdinand had left memorandums naming men who would be trustworthy ministers. Vergennes had been described as "sagacious and capable." The king's aunt, Princess Adelaide, a woman Louis respected, had added her warm endorsement.[19]

The foreign minister had already demonstrated an ability to bring off risky ventures. In 1772, when he was ambassador to Sweden, he had managed a coup that extracted that troubled country from Russia's sphere of influence by backing an ambitious young king, Gustavus III, against a clique of domineering aristocrats. Ever since King Louis XVI made Vergennes his foreign minister, he had joined the English-hating Minister of Marine, Antoine Raymond de Sartine, in committing France to the immense expense of rebuilding her navy. The navy's unreadiness had been another reason for Vergennes's hesitation to deal with the American commissioners. By happy coincidence, the navy had declared itself ready to challenge the British fleet just as the news of Saratoga reached France. Vergennes saw sea power as the key to winning the global war on which France was embarking.

The foreign minister rationalized this decision by convincing himself that a war with England was inevitable, eventually, to correct the abominable injustices of the peace treaty that ended the ruinous Seven Years War. He knew this new war was a gamble that could have serious consequences if France lost. Ann-Louis Jacques Turgot, the minister of finance from 1774 to 1776, had warned Louis XVI that there was a 20-million-livre shortfall between the nation's income and expenses.

War under these circumstances would be "the greatest of misfortunes, since it would make reforms impossible for a long time, perhaps forever," Turgot said. But Vergennes persuaded Turgot to admit that France could finance a short war—and to support the huge expansion of the French navy. Meanwhile, the foreign minister advised the king that Turgot's brusque confrontational style called for his replacement by the seemingly more cooperative Swiss banker, Jacques Necker.[20]

A short, victorious war that would destroy British hegemony, not only in North America but in the sugar-rich West Indies and the even richer markets of India and China, where the British were reaping a bonanza of profits, and Africa, where Britain dominated the slave trade—this was the vision Vergennes shared with his fellow diplomats in the foreign ministry section of the royal palace of Versailles. To the ambitious young king the foreign minister described the war as his chance to regain the role that his great-grandfather, Louis XIV, had played as the arbiter of Europe, the ruler whose authority could preserve peace among the jockeying powers of the continent. the American Revolution had made this the moment *le plus beau* to revenge the Seven Years War and recapture *la gloire* which rightly belonged to France.[21]

X

One might assume that America's astonishing transformation from faltering revolutionaries to the ally of the greatest power on the continent of Europe would have brought satisfaction and harmony to the diplomats in Paris. But Arthur Lee was still convinced that Silas Deane and Beaumarchais were thieves. Letters denouncing both men continued to flow from Lee's viperish pen to his brother Richard in Congress.

Lee found an ally in another diplomat who arrived in Paris around this time—Ralph Izard of South Carolina. A wealthy planter who had been living in Europe, Izard accepted an appointment as envoy to the Duchy of Tuscany. It was another congressional venture in militia diplomacy. Tuscany made it clear that they had not the slightest interest in recognizing an independent United States. So Izard remained in Paris and soon revealed an arrogance and sour temper that matched and sometimes surpassed Arthur Lee's.

Unfortunately for Silas Deane, Arthur Lee's attacks on him coincided with the arrival in America of a large number of the foreign (mostly French) officers who had wangled commissions in the American army. In Philadelphia they brandished signed contracts entitling them to command regiments and divisions. These hired guns flummoxed Congress and outraged American officers who had achieved similar ranks in battle against the British army. Congress was forced to buy out many of these men and ship them back to Europe. Since Deane's name was on the contracts, he became more and more unpopular with America's politicians.

Franklin did his best to defend Deane. He wrote to The Congressional Committee on Foreign Affairs, telling them that he knew first hand the "infinite difficulty" of resisting the "great men"—mostly prominent French politicians—who had pushed these officers. Franklin assured the committee that Deane had learned from his mistakes and was now "an able, active and extremely useful servant of the publick."

The fuming, overworked Deane remained all too ready to feud with Arthur Lee. Franklin tried to cool him off by assuring him that Lee's paranoid style had many symptoms of incipient insanity. Deane said he was inclined to take Franklin's advice, but he was still convinced that most of Lee's bile "proceed[ed] from the malignity of his heart."

Early in March of 1778, little more than a month after signing the treaties of alliance, a letter from Congress reached Paris informing the commissioners that Deane had been recalled to America. His replacement would be John Adams of Massachusetts, a prominent member of the Lee-Adams party in Congress. John was a distant cousin of Samuel Adams. Not even Franklin could soothe Deane's wrath now. Arthur Lee had triumphed.

Beaumarchais, who raged even more than Deane about Arthur Lee's malevolence, concocted a scenario to help his friend and business partner survive Lee's assault. The playwright went to Foreign Minister Vergennes and arranged for Deane to return to America aboard a warship that would carry Conrad Alexander Gerard, the first French ambassador to America. With them would sail the French fleet commanded by Admiral Comte d'Estaing. The king gave Deane his portrait framed in diamonds and Vergennes wrote a warm letter, portraying Deane as a model patriot. Franklin added an equally warm letter, again defending his fellow commissioner.

Franklin did not tell Arthur Lee about Deane's departure until after he had sailed. Vergennes made equally sure Lee knew nothing about Gerard's appointment as France's first ambassador. When Lee discovered he had been shunted aside, he made Franklin the target of his wrath. "Had you studied to deceive the most distrusted and dangerous enemy of the public, you could not have done it more effectually," he raged.[22]

Henceforth, war was more or less officially declared between Lee and Franklin. Lee's former "pater patriae" became the target of his smear letters to his brother Richard and other members of Congress. He told his correspondents that Franklin spent an unconscionable amount of time tippling and dining in the mansions and salons of Paris. It did not occur to Lee that Franklin was making powerful friends for America at every dinner party.

Lee was even more disturbed by the way the women of Paris swarmed around Franklin at public and private receptions. Soon Arthur was hinting at sexual orgies which were absorbing the supposedly great man—a myth that distorts some American opinions of Franklin to this day. In Lee's puritanical world, immorality loomed in every kiss Franklin exchanged with the ladies of Paris.

XI

On July 14, 1778, Silas Deane arrived in Philadelphia with the French fleet and his glowing endorsements. It would have seemed reasonable, even necessary, for Congress to greet him as one of the men who had made American independence seem assured. Only three short months before, Washington's army had been sitting helplessly in Valley Forge, too weak to attack the entrenched British in Philadelphia. The news of the French alliance had forced the British army to abandon the American capital and retreat ignominiously across New Jersey, where a pursuing Washington mauled them at Monmouth Court House. Everyone talked of victory and imminent peace. None of this explosion of optimism after twelve months of gloom did Silas Deane any good.

Congress was still dominated by the Lee-Adams party and their followers, which some people sourly called "the junto," suggesting they ruled as arbitrarily as any dictator or king. Richard Henry Lee had no intention of letting Silas Deane triumph over his virtuous brothers, Arthur and William. True whig ideology as well as power politics played a role in the bitter scenes that unfolded.

In the suspicion-infested political world of the true whigs, France was now a threat to America's public virtue. Perhaps more of a threat than England had been. Like a fallen woman, America was in France's seductive arms, while the revolutionaries had already discovered England's corruption and thrust that old roué from their bosoms.

First Silas Deane would have to be destroyed. Then the Lee and Adams men would turn their attention to the indolent, pleasure-loving old man behind the public image of the supposedly great scientist and brilliant politician—Benjamin Franklin. Richard Henry Lee summed up the game plan in a letter to Arthur: "Deane, as well as others, shall be attended to here."[23]

XII

The destruction of Silas Deane was a cruel and unrelenting process. First the Lee-Adams party let him sit in Philadelphia for twenty days without bothering to invite him to testify before Congress. Delegate James Lovell of Massachusetts, a Lee-Adams man on the committee on foreign affairs, went around the city bragging about his "subtle" letter which had recalled Deane without any hint that he was to be charged with corruption. Lovell implied that otherwise Deane would have stayed in Europe and enjoyed his ill-gotten millions.

Deane wrote to Congress President Henry Laurens, reminding him of his presence in the city. While he was waiting for a reply, Deane received a letter from General Washington, congratulating him for his contributions to the American cause. This communication was no accident. It was a signal from Washington that he considered Deane's struggle with

Congress part of the ideological war that had erupted between the army and the true whigs during the winter ordeal at Valley Forge. No one had been more harassed by the foreign officers who had signed contracts with Deane than the commander in chief. Yet Washington was still willing to give the recalled commissioner his stamp of approval because he saw him as the symbol of a much larger struggle with the extremists who had tried to browbeat him into resigning at Valley Forge. They had also furiously opposed his realistic solutions to the army's woes—in particular his insistence on guaranteeing Continental Army officers half pay after the war.[24]

When Deane was finally summoned before Congress on August 14, 1778, the recalled commissioner had barely begun his report on his activities in Europe when he was ordered to withdraw while Congress debated whether he should submit a written statement. Not until the following week was Deane asked to resume his verbal report. After a few minutes, he was again ordered to withdraw. Four days later he was recalled, finished his report, and was again dismissed.

For another month, Deane did not hear a word from Congress. Meanwhile they listened to hostile testimony from William Carmichael, who had worked with Deane in Paris as a volunteer assistant. A wealthy egotistic Marylander, Carmichael soon thought he could do a better job than Deane and his initial friendship turned to hostility. His testimony was all nasty hearsay and personal opinion.

When one of Deane's friends tried to defend him, Congress voted that hearsay testimony was acceptable. Next they listened to a letter from Ralph Izard, which echoed Arthur Lee's slanders and suspicions of Deane and Franklin, and was equally devoid of factual proof. When Deane asked for permission to answer Carmichael and Izard, he was ignored. His temper rising, Deane wrote a letter to Congress, asking them to cite "what part of my public conduct" justified the way he was being treated.[25]

The proceedings of Congress were theoretically secret. In fact, as one member remarked to George Washington, "there is as much intrigue in this state house as in the Vatican but as little secrecy as in a boarding school."[26] Everyone in Philadelphia gossiped about what was said and done within Congress's supposedly inviolable chamber. But the secrecy rule enabled delegates to treat men in Deane's position with something close to indifference. During these same weeks, they kept at similar arm's length a representative from Beaumarchais, who was angrily demanding that Congress pay the 4.5 million livres they owed Hortalez et Cie for the guns and ammunition that had helped rescue the Revolution in 1777.

Totally exasperated, Deane decided to take his case to the people because "the ears of Congress are shut against me." On December 5, 1778, the *Pennsylvania Packet* published his address "To the Free and Virtuous Citizens of America." Deane ferociously assaulted both Arthur and William Lee and their two brothers in Congress. He mocked Arthur Lee's militia diplomacy, declaring that he had embarrassed the United States, pestering nations such as Spain and Prussia for aid without the slightest encouragement or hope of success. Arthur and William had both given "universal disgust" to the French and almost fatally compromised the American mission. Deane portrayed Arthur Lee as a reckless critic of the treaty of alliance and a covert enemy of France.[27]

XIII

With this blast, the quarrel between the Lees and Deane and Franklin exploded into a scandal that agitated newspapers and politicians all over America. Richard Henry and Francis Lightfoot Lee reached for their pens to defend their brothers. Henry Laurens, the supposedly neutral president of Congress, denounced Deane for publishing a document that was "dishonorable to Congress." Laurens was a good friend of Ralph Izard, a fellow South Carolinian.[28]

When Laurens discovered that a substantial number of delegates did not agree with him, he resigned so he could participate in the debates about the scandal. The president was supposed to remain aloof from any and all disputes on the floor of Congress. To the surprise of many people, the man elected to replace Laurens was John Jay of New York, who had met and liked Deane when they both served in the Continental Congress in 1775. This was a signal that Deane had serious support in Congress.

New York's delegates, notably the brilliant young orator Gouverneur Morris (a close friend of Jay), had played leading roles in defending an embattled Washington at Valley Forge. They regarded as something close to idiocy Samuel Adams's and Richard Henry Lee's rantings about public virtue and their attempt to inflict their narrow view of patriotism on the nation. Also very much in the political mix was Robert Morris, Deane's secret partner in his private ventures, a man with powerful business allies in the Middle States and the South. Soon many southerners, already alienated by the Lees' moral arrogance, gravitated to the Deane-Franklin camp.[29]

The true whigs considered this alignment nothing less than calamitous for the future of America. Francis Lightfoot Lee called them "Tories" (conservatives) whose sole ambition was to rob the public. Lee darkly predicted that these conspirators had designs of a "much more alarming nature." Samuel Adams claimed their goal was nothing less than getting "the trade, the wealth, the power and the government of America into their own hands."[30]

XIV

The true whigs invited the wielder of the most combative pen in America to join their assault on Silas Deane. Thomas Paine was working as secretary to the Committee on Foreign Affairs, still headed by Richard Henry Lee. Paine entitled his rebuttal "Common Sense," hoping to transfer some of the fame of his best-selling 1776 book, which had persuaded many people to support independence. Claiming to write as a defender of Congress, Paine said he had incontrovertible proof that Arthur Lee was right, the war materiel shipped to America by Hortalez et Cie in 1776–77 was a gift from the French king, not a debt that Congress should pay. This meant both Deane and Beaumarchais were thieves.

In a follow-up article, Paine claimed that "mercantile connections" (aka profit seeking) motivated Deane's supporters. The author of *Common Sense* assailed Robert Morris as the man behind these money-hungry politicians. In blunt language that Paine would soon regret, he accused Morris of giving his own company, Willing & Morris, a half-million dollars worth of contracts to purchase war supplies while he was chairman of the congressional committee in charge of this responsibility. Morris published a curt reply, declaring that becoming a delegate from the state of Pennsylvania did not mean he relinquished his right to function as a businessman—and that included a "mercantile connection" with Silas Deane.[31]

French Ambassador Gerard asked Congress to do something about the way Paine was revealing—and distorting—information about Beaumarchais's contacts with Franklin and other Americans that embarrassed his government. Other critics accused Paine of violating an oath of secrecy that he had signed when he accepted the job as secretary to the foreign affairs committee. Spurred by Gouverneur Morris, who called Paine a "mere adventurer from England ... stuffed with mad assertions," the Deane supporters demanded Paine's dismissal. The pamphleteer, anticipating a majority vote against him, resigned but Congressman Morris still called for a vote. After hours of wrangling, Congress finally voted—only to discover they were evenly split. It was grim evidence of the way the controversy was dividing the country.[32]

Some citizens of Philadelphia decided Tom Paine needed more than a dismissal from Congress to keep him quiet. One night as Paine was leaving a tavern, he encountered a group of well-liquored Deane and Morris supporters on their way home from a private dinner party. They beat and kicked Paine into the muddy gutter and left him there.

Several months later, a pro-Deane writer added insult to these injuries with a poem in the *Philadelphia Evening Post*.

> *Hail Mighty Thomas! in whose works are seen*
> *A mangled Morris and distorted Deane;*
> *Whose splendid periods flash for Lee's defense*
> *Replete with every thing but common sense.*[33]

XV

As the Lee-Adams party brawled with the Deane backers in person and in print, both the Americans and the French were discovering some difficult truths about their alliance. The French fleet that was supposed to rout the British from their bases in New York and Newport, Rhode Island, was not the only disappointment. Ambassador Gerard took a hard look at the American army and was soon telling a shocked Foreign Minister Vergennes what he saw.

Gerard had begun with a glowingly optimistic report in July 1778, describing Washington's Continental soldiers as 16 thousand reliable fighting men, backed by militia who "did not deserve contempt." By September 1778, Gerard was singing a much more melancholy song. There had been a "general cooling of all martial ardor among the people." There was a dismaying "nonchalance" about the way some states maintained their Continental regiments, ignoring Congress's pleas to fill vacancies in their ranks. Gerard worried that "this miserly spirit," combined with a passion for "mercantile cupidity," especially in New England, might induce the Americans to sign a premature separate peace.

Worsening the situation was the galloping inflation that began to afflict Congress's paper currency. Gerard told Vergennes that the cost of maintaining Washington's army for three months in the summer of 1778 would have kept an army of 60 thousand men well supplied in Europe. New recruits for the army were being offered $500 to enlist for three years—and there were few takers. Before the end of 1778, a worried Vergennes was telling close friends, such as the Comte de Montmorin, France's ambassador to Madrid: "I have only a feeble confidence in the energy of the United States."[34]

XVI

None of these developments in America made life simpler or more peaceful for Benjamin Franklin in France. Arthur and William Lee and their South Carolina ally Ralph Izard bombarded him with accusatory letters. They had been joined by the man chosen as Silas Deane's replacement, John Adams. He came to Europe primed to do battle for the public virtue of the new republic and proud of his American celebrity. In 1776 his oratory had persuaded many waverers in Congress to vote for independence. Some admirers had labeled him the "Atlas" behind this historic decision.

From the moment Adams arrived in France, he found himself trying to cope with the same emotion that had tormented Arthur Lee: jealousy. "There was," he complained, "only one American name on everyone's lips: Franklin. His name was familiar to government and people, to foreign courtiers, nobility, clergy and philosophers as well as plebeians to such an extent that there was scarcely a peasant or a citizen . . . who did not consider him a friend."

Franklin greeted Adams with the greatest cordiality and invited him to live at Passy. In their first weeks together, he asked the newcomer to join him at dinners in Paris where Adams met more members of the French establishment than Arthur Lee had met in two years. They included Antoine Raymond de Sartine, the powerful Minister of Marine, and Madame de Maurepas, the influential wife of the French first minister. Like Arthur Lee, true whig Adams completely missed the point. He did not understand that these sophisticated people combined diplomacy, fine wines, and delicious food. "These incessant dinners and dissipations were not the objects of my mission to France," Adams groused.[35]

Ralph Izard informed Adams that Franklin was "one of the most unprincipled men on earth." Arthur Lee spewed even worse venom. To his credit, Adams resisted these inveterate slanderers. In his diary, he described Lee and Izard as "men of honour and integrity." But their prejudices and violent tempers "would raise quarrels in the Elisian Fields if not in heaven."[36]

Jealousy prevented Adams from paying any compensatory compliments to Franklin. On the contrary, Adams found the older man's "love of ease and dissipation" cause for reproach. His "cunning and reserve"— two of the prime talents of a good diplomat—were even more disturbing. In his diary Adams told himself he would need "the patience of Job" to deal with his fellow commissioners.[37]

The new commissioner remained committed to the Lee-Adams party in Congress. When Deane's newspaper attack on Arthur Lee was republished in London newspapers and soon reached Paris, Adams told Franklin that the article was "one of the most wicked and abominable productions that ever sprang from the human heart." The enraged commissioner wrote a letter to Foreign Minister Vergennes in which he accused Franklin of having "attached himself to Mr. Deane." Adams urged the foreign minister to ban the publication of the article in France. To Franklin he added the astonishing statement that if the French sided with Deane, the alliance should be "broke." The foreign minister immediately added Adams to his growing list of France's American enemies and permitted Deane's attack on the Lees to be published with his tacit approval.[38]

Early in February 1779 news reached Paris that made Adams's struggle to deal with his fellow commissioners moot. Congress had decided to abolish the acrimony in the American mission by abandoning the three-headed commission. Henceforth, Benjamin Franklin would be minister plenipotentiary to France, with the title of ambassador.

As a sop to Arthur Lee's vanity, he was named ambassador to Spain, where he had already tried to obtain recognition for the United States and been rebuffed. Adams, the latest diplomatic arrival, got nothing. He was deeply hurt, but he struggled to accept what amounted to a dismissal. Adams grudgingly admitted that putting Franklin in sole charge of

America's relations with France was the right decision and even claimed it gave "the greatest relief to my mind."[39]

Arthur Lee saw Franklin's ascendancy as a sign of America's imminent moral and spiritual collapse. "We shall fall into such a vileness soon that nothing will retrieve our character. The meanest of all mean men, the most corrupt of all corrupt men is assimilating everything."[40]

XVII

In America, the Deane-Lee controversy continued to rage in the newspapers and in Congress. As a result, Congress's reputation went into a steep slide. The solons were so humiliated by the brawl, with its ugly personal accusations and its frequent outbreaks of hostility to the French alliance, they decided at the end of 1779 to suppress all the printed copies of the journals of Congress and reprint them with the nasty debates excised. This only worsened matters; it was impossible to destroy all the old copies, and some remained available to those who still wanted to stoke the controversy.

In this rancid atmosphere, Congress created a committee of thirteen delegates, one from each state, to again try to fix the diplomatic mess in Europe. The formula only produced another round in the Lee-Deane melee. Each side pushed favorite candidates for various jobs, with the Deane backers now controlling a majority of the votes. Out of the brawl emerged a new lineup. Franklin was reconfirmed as ambassador. William Lee and Ralph Izard were sacked; after more wrangling, Arthur Lee was also discarded. John Jay was chosen as ambassador to Spain. To console the Lee-Adams party, Congress found another job for John Adams. They sent him back to Europe as a peace commissioner with the power to negotiate an end to the war.

The reason for this strange appointment was a communication from Ambassador Gerard, revealing the first public evidence of French disillusion with the American alliance. Spain, Gerard informed Congress, was negotiating with English representatives in Madrid, offering to play a mediator's role to achieve an early end to the war. It was time for Congress to state the terms on which they would be willing to sign a peace treaty with England. If the Madrid negotiations failed, Gerard added, Spain was prepared to declare war on England. It was important to state terms that would be satisfactory to this new ally, who had vast possessions in North and South America that Madrid feared the American Revolution might disturb.[41]

XVIII

In the end the terms did not matter very much. By the time Adams reached Paris with his new commission on February 9, 1779, the Madrid negotiations had collapsed and Spain had entered the war as an ally of France—without recognizing American independence. The British were not interested in talking peace with anyone. France's declaration of war had enabled George III to appeal to England's centuries-old antagonism to their ancient enemy; the nation's war fever was sharpened by the American refusal to consider an offer of reconciliation on any terms short of independence.

This outcome had been more than a little predictable. But Congress had not inserted in John Adams's instructions orders to return to the United States if there was no point in his remaining in Europe. Adams found reasons to linger in Paris. There was talk of a French-Spanish fleet invading the English Channel, smashing the outnumbered British fleet and ferrying thousands of French troops across the watery barrier to conquer England.

This ambitious enterprise became another allied fiasco; the French admiral in command was old and timid, the two fleets found cooperation difficult, and disease ravaged their crews. The would-be invaders crept back to their home ports without firing a shot.

The defeat again left Adams with nothing to do. He compounded his dilemma by trying to ignore Franklin. The peace commissioner seemed to think he was entirely independent of the ambassador and had no need to discuss the peace terms he had been told to offer England, much less ask for advice. A puzzled Franklin told one correspondent: "We live on good terms with each other but he [Adams] never communicated anything of his business to me nor have I made inquiries of him, nor have I any letter from Congress explaining it, so that I am in total ignorance."[42]

When Adams consulted Foreign Minister Vergennes about his peace proposals, Vergennes icily informed him that the timing was unpropitious. After the humiliating failure of the French and Spanish fleets in the English Channel, the British navy was counterattacking in the West Indies. In America their army had conquered Georgia and invaded South

Carolina. A less polite man would have told Adams to keep his mouth shut lest he make his country and their French ally look ridiculous.

Still convinced he was a one-man state department, Adams started picking quarrels with Vergennes on other matters. The most serious involved a congressional decision to try to conquer the runaway inflation that was demoralizing America by radically devaluing the Continental dollar. New dollars would be issued, worth forty of the old dollars. This meant, in practical terms, the old dollars were worth 2 1/2 cents. French merchants such as Leray de Chaumont, who had sold tons of goods and weaponry to America and were holding promissory notes for payment in the old money, screamed with rage and pain.

Foreign Minister Vergennes announced he was going to ask Congress to make an exception for France's creditors. John Adams rejected the idea; he said the French merchants were just as guilty as American business-men and consumers, who had created the inflation by paying higher and higher prices for everything. If the French suffered losses, so what? They should be grateful to the Americans, who had given them the opportu-nity to humble England.[43]

Next Adams sent Vergennes an eighteen-page letter telling him that the French navy was not doing a very good job of fighting the war, from an American point of view. When Vergennes tersely informed him that the king and his ministers had already decided to send an expeditionary force and escorting fleet to America, Adams replied that it was about time and reiter-ated his theme song, that France should be grateful to the United States.

Vergennes decided he had no further interest in this burlesque of an envoy and his militia diplomacy. He told Adams that he considered Mr. Franklin "the sole person" who represented the United States in Paris. He therefore desired no more communications from Mr. Adams. The foreign minister gave Adams's letters to Franklin and asked him to send them to Congress.

Franklin, almost as sick of Adams as he had been of Arthur and Wil-liam Lee and Ralph Izard, forwarded the letters with a commentary that summed up the difference between the two men's approach to diplomacy. "He thinks, as he tells me himself, that America has been too free in expressions of gratitude to France; for that she is more oblig'd to us than we to her . . . I apprehend he mistakes his ground and that this court is to be treated with decency and delicacy." Which tactic was preferable was "for Congress to judge."[44]

Franklin told Adams about the dispatch of the letters, and suggested Adams might want to respond in his own defense. Adams ignored him. Almost a year later, when a member of Congress sent Adams a copy of Franklin's letter, he went into a rage and was still ranting about it in his old age.[45]

XIX

Peace Commissioner Adams decided to go to Holland to see if militia diplomacy could persuade the Dutch to recognize American independence and lend the United States 5 million dollars. Franklin told him it was a terrible idea. He did not think Americans should wander around Europe like beggars flourishing tin cups. It was no way to win respect, much less affection. The two men parted with an absolute minimum of cordiality.

Around the same time, Franklin found Silas Deane on his doorstep. Congress had finally dismissed him with permission to return to Europe. The lawmakers had neither approved nor censured his conduct—nor did they pay him the money Deane claimed they owed him. This nondecision left Deane a troubled, bitter man. He had come back to Europe as a private citizen, hoping to make his fortune with the help of Robert Morris. The merchant king backed him with a letter to Franklin, describing Deane as a "martyr to the cause of America," a man who had been "reviled and traduced in the most shameful manner."[46]

Franklin greeted Deane with the warmth of an old friend and gave him a room in his Passy residence. Deane became a nightly guest at dinner, along with the usual half-dozen—sometimes a dozen—visitors who sought the pleasure of Franklin's company. At first, Deane seemed the same lively energetic man Franklin had known and liked in 1776–77. But his conversation began to develop alarming tendencies. He had nothing good to say about Congress and he frequently wondered out loud if American independence was a good idea. It had put a tribe of narrow uncaring politicians ready to listen to the likes of Arthur Lee and Ralph Izard in charge of the country.

Franklin either ignored or offhandedly refuted Deane's diatribes. Most of the time, he may not have paid much attention to him. He had far larger worries on his mind. The military news from America continued to be awful. In the spring of 1780, the British had invaded and apparently conquered South Carolina. The state's governor fled, the legislature disbanded, and the British talked confidently of giving North Carolina the same rough handling if the state did not meekly surrender.

Deepening Franklin's gloom was the way the bankrupt Congress left him at the mercy of every American creditor in Europe. Bills rained down on his balding head, until he grew anxious at the sound of a knock on his door. He struggled to deal with the complications of shipping additional uniforms and guns and ammunition that Leray de Chaumont had bought. Endless delays and a feud between Chaumont and the temperamental Scottish volunteer, Commodore John Paul Jones, drove him almost frantic—followed by news that the largest shipment had been captured by British blockaders.

Thanks to the devaluation of the Continental dollar, Chaumont was only one jump ahead of bankruptcy. Dozens of other French merchants had been ruined or semi-ruined by this measure. Silas Deane, attempting to do business in the optimistic style of 1776, met rebuffs everywhere. He was soon telling his numerous correspondents that the Americans were no longer respected or popular anywhere in Europe. "It is almost as great a disgrace to be known to be American as it was two years since to be an honor," Deane told John Jay.[47]

XX

Back in Philadelphia, another chapter in the transatlantic drama unfolded. Arthur Lee and Ralph Izard returned to America and were invited to testify before Congress. Lee told the politicians that Franklin was not only personally corrupt, so was everyone with whom he worked in France. As usual, Lee offered no proof. Ralph Izard chimed in, intoning: "The political salvation of America depends on the recalling of Dr. Franklin."[48]

Friends told Franklin he was being slandered but there was little he could do about it. Worse news was to come. As 1781 began, Congress was shaken by a huge mutiny in the Pennsylvania Continental troops. The upheaval was contained, largely by giving back pay and discharges to almost all the mutineers, demolishing one of the largest brigades in General Washington's army. Three weeks later, New Jersey's troops mutinied for similar reasons: no pay and atrocious food; this time Washington met force with force, hanging the leaders.

In February, Franklin learned that a panicked Congress had decided to send another diplomat to Europe—Lieutenant Colonel John Laurens, the son of the man who had taken the lead in slandering Silas Deane. Accompanying Laurens was Tom Paine, the man who had smeared Silas Deane and Robert Morris (another close Franklin friend) in Philadelphia's newspapers.

The young lieutenant colonel was ordered to appeal to France for a loan of 25 million livres—a magical number that would supposedly solve the army's woes. The message was all too clear. Congress had lost confidence in Franklin's ability to deal with France. General Washington attempted to soften the implied rebuke by writing a letter to the ambassador explaining that Congress felt the appeal had a better chance if it came from someone with an intimate knowledge of the army's needs. He assured Franklin that Laurens would seek his advice from the moment he arrived in France. Laurens's instructions from Congress omitted this sensible course.

Franklin was much too experienced to see Washington's letter as reassuring. He realized he was on the brink of dismissal, an event that would send belly laughs from Arthur Lee and Ralph Izard resounding across the Atlantic, to be echoed by mordant chuckles from John Adams in Holland and George III in London. Franklin seized his pen and wrote one of the most important letters of his life to Foreign Minister Vergennes. He quoted the Marquis de Lafayette and General Washington as his authorities in his portrayal of an American army on the point of dissolution. With its collapse would go all hope of victory.

Shrewdly playing on his personal relationship with Vergennes, Franklin added: "I am grown old . . . It is probable I shall not have any more concern in these affairs. I take this opportunity to express my opinion to Your Excellency that the present moment is critical." If France refused to come to the army's aid, Congress and "the whole system of the new govern't in America may be . . . shaken." If America collapsed and was forced to rejoin the British Empire, he predicted, in a decade or two, England would be strong enough to "become the *terror of Europe*."[49]

In a few weeks, a pleased ambassador was able to tell Congress that he would do his utmost to help Colonel Laurens—but in the meantime, lest the colonel be captured or lost at sea, Congress did not have to worry about money for a while. Foreign Minister Vergennes had just told him that King Louis XVI had decided to give America another 6 million livres as a free gift—not a loan. This was in addition to the 3 million Vergennes had given the ambassador to pay outstanding bills earlier in 1781.

Whereupon, this canniest of America's founding fathers submitted his resignation to Congress. He told them he had recently celebrated his seventy-fifth birthday. Last year his health had been shaken by several severe attacks of gout and he had yet to regain his normal vigor. He did not think his "mental faculties" had been impaired, but he would probably be "the last to discover" this. He had been in public service for over fifty years. It was time to seek some repose. His decision had nothing to do with any doubts about the ultimate triumph of their "glorious cause," nor with "any disgust" he had contracted in its service. He planned to remain in France—his health did not permit a sea voyage for the time being—and he would be glad to help his successor "with any influence I may be supposed to have."[50]

Franklin told only one man outside Congress about this letter: John Jay, who had been in Madrid for over two years, vainly trying to persuade the Spanish to recognize American independence. Franklin said he wanted Jay to become the next ambassador to France. Jay was one of the earliest opponents of the Lees and the Adamses in Congress. More important, he had impressed Franklin with his astute letters about Spanish foreign policy and Madrid's special relationship with France.

Jay quickly demonstrated he had not lost touch with European—or American—politics. He wrote to Congress, telling them if they accepted Franklin's resignation, they were out of their minds. His reputation throughout Europe had never been higher.

XXI

One can easily imagine how an Arthur Lee or a John Adams would have received Colonel John Laurens when he arrived in France, accompanied by Tom Paine. But Franklin remained Franklin. He was courteous and encouraging. Paine too was cordially received; not a word was said about his attacks on Silas Deane. The agitator and Franklin were old friends. When Paine sailed to Philadelphia in 1774, he had carried a letter of introduction from Franklin that had played a large role in enabling him to prosper as a journalist before he wrote *Common Sense*.[51]

Paine took up residence in Passy and conferred frequently with Franklin on how best to smooth the young colonel's approach to leaders of the French government. Franklin soon found it necessary to do a lot of smoothing of his own. Laurens spoke fluent French but the handsome aide was a man in a hurry and gave a very good imitation of a militia diplomat. After his first meeting with Vergennes, the foreign minister expressed his outrage to Franklin at the way Laurens had insisted on a loan of 25 million livres, dismissing the 6 million that Vergennes had granted Franklin as inadequate.

Laurens also wanted King Louis XVI to guarantee the loan, since Congress's credit was, Laurens candidly admitted, worthless. On top of the cash demand, the young colonel submitted a list of war materiel that included muskets, cannon, uniforms, and medicines. Vergennes warned Franklin that unless Laurens improved his manners, he would not be welcome in Versailles.

No doubt on Franklin's advice, Laurens was soon saying his expectations were "very moderate." But he continued to affront Vergennes with his tactlessness. At one point, when the foreign minister referred to the "favors" which America had received from King Louis XVI, Laurens exclaimed: "Favors! Monsieur Le Comte, the respect I owe my country will not admit the application of such a term." Like John Adams, he was hypersensitive to any hint of French condescension. Franklin simply (and rightly) regarded such terminology as the language of European diplomacy.[52]

Vergennes finally agreed to guarantee an additional loan of 10 million livres and to deliver most of the war supplies that Laurens had requested. Franklin congratulated Colonel Laurens and confided that he had resigned as American ambassador. Perhaps the colonel should stay in France and replace him?

Young Laurens, tacitly admitting how out of his depth he felt, rejected the idea and assured Franklin only orders from General Washington had brought him to Paris. He added that he would never consider succeeding Franklin unless, like a magician, the ambassador "would cast your mantle upon me and give me at the same time abilities to succeed to your reputation."[53]

XXII

Fortunately for the future of both countries, Franklin had a friend who refused to let Congress lose their disenchanted ambassador: the Comte de Vergennes. By this time, the foreign minister had sent a new envoy to

America, plump, affable thirty-six-year-old Chevalier Anne-Cesar de la Luzerne. Ambassador Gerard had resigned, pleading ill health; a more apt description would have been too many doses of anti-French rhetoric emanating from Lee-Adams congressmen. Arriving in mid-1779, Luzerne was determined to find a remedy for this ideological malady. He set himself up in a splendid townhouse not far from the Pennsylvania State House and was soon wielding enormous influence.

Luzerne put several members of Congress, notably John Sullivan of New Hampshire, a former Continental Army major general, on his secret-service payroll. He hired pamphleteers and newspaper editors, as well as one of the most articulate clergymen in America, the Reverend Samuel Cooper of Boston, to write articles praising the French alliance. When Vergennes ordered the ambassador to defend Franklin at all costs, Luzerne's well-lubricated propaganda machine went into high gear.

Soon Luzerne was assuring Vergennes that no one would vote to recall the seventy-five-year-old ambassador except a handful of diehard members of the mostly defunct Lee-Adams clique. When Franklin surprised everyone, including Vergennes, by resigning, it was a foregone conclusion that Congress would refuse to accept his departure.

XXIII

Foreign Minister Vergennes had other things on his mind besides Franklin's mere survival. More and more, he saw the war with England as unwinnable. Alarming cries were emanating from Jacques Necker, France's minister of finance. Necker had assured Vergennes that France could afford the war, but never told him that he planned to finance it by loans from half the bankers of Europe. After four years, Necker was encountering resistance from increasingly wary lenders. He began warning that if the war lasted much longer, France faced bankruptcy.

When Vergennes, concentrating on the planning that led to the victory at Yorktown, ignored Necker, the financier published a revolutionary document, *Le Compte Rendu au Roi* (The Account Rendered to the King), the first-ever revelation of France's bizarre tax structure, in which the wealthiest people in the kingdom paid nothing. This was followed by a Necker-sponsored attempt at a palace revolution aimed at ousting Vergennes. Instead, Necker, a Swiss Protestant who had little or no support inside Versailles, was unceremoniously jettisoned.

Le Compte Rendu became a bestseller in spite of its numerous lies, all favoring Necker, of course. He claimed that he had managed to achieve a surplus of more than 10 million livres in spite of four years of war. To achieve this nonexistent figure, Necker listed the expenditures for 1780 at 254 million livres when they were 677 million; the figures for other years were similarly juggled. France's pretensions to being the first power in Europe were obviously in danger. The seeds of the upheaval that would destroy the monarchy a decade later had been sown. But this was mercifully invisible to Vergennes and his fellow ministers, who lived, like most politicians, in the turbulent present.[54]

Drawing on his decades of diplomatic experience, in mid-1780 Foreign Minister Vergennes ordered French envoys to start talking to the rulers of Austria and Russia, asking if they might be interested in staging a peace conference in Vienna. These neutrals would have the power—and prestige—of proposing a settlement of the war. For America, the diplomats made it clear that France would tolerate an arrangement that might fall far short of independence.

The plan was to let Austria invoke the ancient principle of "uti possidetis" (each side keeps what he possesses) and give the British northern Massachusetts (present-day Maine, which they claimed by virtue of their possession of Fort George, at the mouth of the Penobscot River), North and South Carolina, Georgia, New York, and Long Island, as well as a huge chunk of what is now the Midwest thanks to British forts at Niagara, Oswego, Detroit, and other strategic sites. Once the American problem was settled, the British, French, and Spanish would resolve their differences elsewhere in the world, bargaining over what islands in the Mediterranean and the West Indies and territories in India and Africa would be returned to their prewar owners or retained by the current conquerors.[55]

Although everything was supposed to be totally secret, the proposed Vienna peace conference was soon the talk of Europe, and rumors of it eventually reached America. Some members of Congress expressed concern about the purported terms. If the British were permitted to retain their battalions in so many parts of America, it would not be long before theoretically independent sections of the former colonies were seduced or tricked into their old allegiance to George III.

These critical remarks in Congress made Vergennes even more determined to keep Franklin around; he thought the ambassador would be more flexible about a final settlement. To make sure things went France's way, the foreign minister ordered Ambassador Luzerne to jettison John Adams as a peace negotiator, and request from Congress new instructions for whomever they appointed in his place. Adams, Vergennes wrote, "has a rigidity, an arrogance, and an obstinacy that will cause him to foment a thousand unfortunate incidents and drive his conegotiators to despair."[56]

The true whigs had enough strength left in Congress to resist Adams's outright dismissal. Instead, they broadened the peace commission, appointing Franklin and John Jay to serve with Adams. Thomas Jefferson, sympathetic to the Lee-Adams party, was also appointed but declined to leave Virginia. He was serving as governor and his state had been invaded by the British. As an added gesture of defiance, the Lee-Adams faction threw in another member of their dwindling band, Henry Laurens. This was one of Congress's stranger moves. In 1779, they had appointed Laurens ambassador to Holland; the former president of Congress had been captured at sea and was currently a prisoner in the Tower of London.

When it came to American peace terms—a point as important to Vergennes as the retention of Franklin—Congress succumbed entirely to Ambassador Luzerne's advice. The commissioners were told to "concur" in the mediation by Russia and Austria. In particular, they were to accept the idea of a one-year truce in the shooting war, leaving all the armies in place in America. As for the peace terms themselves, they were advised to be flexible about everything from navigating the Mississippi to the boundaries with Canada. If negotiations began, the instructions continued, "you are to make the most candid and confidential communications upon all subjects to the ministers of our generous ally, the King of France, to undertake nothing . . . without their knowledge and concurrence, and ultimately to govern yourself by their advice and opinion."[57]

XXIV

In the Netherlands, John Adams was still getting nowhere in his struggle to win recognition of American independence and a loan. His letters were a whine of despair and self pity. He called the Dutch people "incomprehensible" and deplored their love of "ease" and "gain"—an odd attitude for a man attempting to persuade them to part with their money. He also bemoaned their bewildering government which had to win agreement from seven semi-independent provinces as well as numerous autonomous cities before it could decide anything.

On August 24, 1781, Franklin informed Adams that his role as solo peace negotiator had been terminated, and he was now one of a group of five commissioners. Obliquely commenting on Adams's refusal to say a word about his activities in Europe, Franklin asked him what he had done thus far as peace negotiator.

Adams replied that he had visited Paris in July to discuss the Vienna mediation with the Comte de Vergennes and had written him four letters, which Franklin could obtain from the foreign minister. The letters were hostile to the idea of a mediated peace and insistent on demanding recognition of American independence before Adams would agree to go to Vienna.

The news of his semi-dismissal hit Adams hard. In an outburst of gloom, he told Franklin that Congress might as well send him and all the other diplomats in Europe home. There would be no peace until every British soldier in America "is killed or captivated." Adams had heard (correctly, it turned out) that the British had responded to the mediation proposal by insisting on two preliminary conditions: France must terminate her alliance with the Americans and withdraw all her forces from North America. This had convinced Adams that "Britain will never think of peace, but for the purposes of chicanery."[58]

On the day he wrote this letter, Adams suffered a breakdown that left him an almost helpless invalid. He called it a "nervous fever" that "seized upon my head." Many historians are inclined to think it was an attack of depression, the worst one Adams had yet suffered in his life. Intermixed with it, in the opinion of some historians, may have been an infectious fever, perhaps malaria. For six days Adams was either unconscious or delirious and for two months he did not write a single letter.

Not until October 22, 1781, did Adams recover—and the first letter he wrote was to Franklin, in a very different tone. Almost humbly, Adams asked Franklin for his "sentiments" about "accepting the mediation of a power or powers." Adams wondered if the mediator was a kind of arbitrator, with the authority to force any nation that participated in a peace conference to accept his decisions. Would this mean that the United States would have to surrender its independence and "come again under the dominion of England?"[59]

XXV

On November 19, 1781, a young American merchant, Elkanah Watson, visited Franklin in Passy. Born in New York, Watson had been doing business in Nantes for several years. On a recent trip to Ghent, Watson had encountered Silas Deane, who filled his ears with a diatribe against the United States and France. The former commissioner now thought America's best hope was reconciliation with England. All Deane's attempts to do business in Europe had failed. He had moved to Ghent to cut his expenses, and was trying to find other ways to raise money in partnership with Dutch and Flemish merchants.

Franklin was distressed to hear Watson's description of Deane's spiritual and political collapse. Deane had written several letters to friends and one to him, expressing similar sentiments. The ambassador was unaware that Deane had arranged to have some of these letters intercepted by the British, apparently in return for a bribe, and they were now appearing in *The New York Royal Gazette.*

Franklin changed the subject by asking Watson if he had any news from America. There had been reports of a clash between the French and British fleets off the capes of Chesapeake Bay. Watson could only add some stray rumors that Washington and Rochambeau were marching to Virginia, hoping to trap Cornwallis's army there. Another story had the British fleet sallying from New York with 10 thousand men to rescue Lord Cornwallis. Still another tale had large reinforcements of men and ships on the way from England.

"Anxiety," Watson wrote in his diary, "was excessive . . . we weighed probabilities—balanc'd vicissitudes—dissected the best maps—and finally it resulted in a disheartening foreboding." The Americans mournfully concluded that the unbeatable British navy would "distroy the French fleet—land their troops and brake up Washington's headquarters. Thus our unhappy country would again bleed at every vein."

A troubled Watson watched as Franklin veered between hope and despair. In the end "his philosophy seem'd to abandon him to gloomy despondency." The young merchant returned to his Paris hotel in a similar mood, "sighing over the distresses of my bleeding country." He fell into a restless sleep—and was awakened at dawn "by a tremendous rapping at my door."

A messenger from Franklin handed Watson a circular featuring a letter from the Comte de Vergennes, which had reached the ambassador only minutes after Watson left Passy. Vergennes reported the Duc de Lauzun had arrived in Paris with the "agreeable news" that Cornwallis had surrendered to the combined armies of France and America. Franklin had stayed up most of the night turning out the circular on a printing press he had installed at Passy. He was now distributing copies all over Paris.

Watson rushed to Passy along with dozens of French and American friends to congratulate Franklin. "He appeared in an ecstasy of joy," Watson said. Pointing out that Cornwallis had surrendered four years to the day after Burgoyne had yielded at Saratoga, the ambassador exulted: "There is no parallel in history of two entire armies being captured from the same enemy in any one war."[60]

XXVI

The good news swept through Paris with the force of an explosion. For three nights the city was illuminated and fireworks displays crisscrossed the darkened sky. On Elkanah Watson's return to Nantes he found every city along his route similarly illuminated and celebrating the victory. Franklin rushed a letter to Vergennes, telling him the news gave him "infinite pleasure." He assured the foreign minister that the "very powerful aid" King Louis XVI had given America in 1781 had "rivetted the affections of that people and made millions happy."[61]

Elkanah Watson told his diary that Yorktown "settles our controversy definitely with England." But Watson was only twenty-three years old. The seventy-five-year-old Franklin knew this was anything but the truth. A great deal—in fact, almost everything—depended on how another king reacted to the news. Franklin was all too aware that George III of England was one of the most stubborn men on the planet. He had brushed aside previous chances to make a reasonably advantageous peace because they involved recognition of American independence. Was he still determined never to surrender an acre of what he liked to call "my dominions"?

Then there was the war France was waging in the West Indies and elsewhere in the world, notably India. In the treaty of alliance, America had promised never to make peace until France too achieved satisfactory terms with England. To this must be added the treaty France had signed

This portrait of a weary George Washington was painted in 1784 by Joseph Wright. After eight and one-half years of war with his mind "always on the stretch," he was a very tired man. *(Credit: Massachusetts Historical Society)*

John Trumbull's painting of the British surrender at Yorktown portrays General Benjamin Lincoln leading the British to the site where they laid down their weapons. The French army is on the left. The Americans, with General Washington on a brown horse, are on the right. *(Credit: Architect of the Capitol)*

General Comte de Rochambeau was the ideal commander for the French expeditionary force. He diplomatically concealed his dismay at the sight of Washington's small army, which "seemed to lack everything at once."
(Credit: Independence National Historic Park)

Immensely wealthy Marquis de Lafayette joined the American army in 1777, at the age of nineteen. Congress made him a major general. A father-son relationship soon developed between him and General Washington.
(Credit: Library of Congress)

Tench Tilghman was General Washington's favorite aide. He was given the choice assignment of carrying the news of the Yorktown victory to the Continental Congress.
(Credit: Library of Congress)

Loyalist William Smith of New York was the confidential advisor of two British commanders in chief. He never stopped hoping—and intriguing—for reconciliation between Britain and America.
(Credit: Emmet Collection, Miriam and Ira D. Wallach Division of Art, Prints and Photographs, The New York Public Library, Astor, Lenox and Tilden Foundations)

Covhin. Pt. 177.

Eng. by H. Wright Smith.

This is the Benjamin Franklin who dazzled Paris by playing the unspoiled American when he arrived in France in late 1776. The fur hat protected him from the freezing winds of the wintry Atlantic. *(Credit: The Granger Collection, New York)*

FACING PAGE: This Benjamin West portrait of the men who negotiated the peace treaty remained unfinished because the chief British envoy, Richard Oswald, refused to pose. Left to right, they are: John Jay, John Adams, Benjamin Franklin, Henry Laurens, and William Temple Franklin, Ben's grandson, who served as the secretary. *(Credit: Library of Congress)*

The ladies of France all but worshipped Ambassador Franklin. Here one crowns him with a laurel wreath. His enjoyment of their company enraged puritans such as Arthur Lee and John Adams, who accused him of gross immorality.

(Credit: Library of Congress)

Louis XVI of France was only twenty years old when he became king in 1774. He yearned to be his own first (prime) minister but needed older advisors to help him deal with his headstrong Austrian queen, Marie Antoinette, who opposed an alliance with the Americans.

(Credit: Library of Congress)

The Marquis of Rockingham was the discouraged leader of the opposition in Parliament during the first six years of the Revolutionary War. After Yorktown he forced George III to agree to accept American independence but died before he could negotiate peace.

(Credit: Emmet Collection, Miriam and Ira D. Wallach Division of Art, Prints and Photographs, The New York Public Library, Astor, Lenox and Tilden Foundations)

RIGHT: Veteran diplomat Charles Gravier, the Comte de Vergennes, was France's foreign minister. He made the decision to sign a treaty of alliance with America, knowing it meant war with Great Britain.
(Credit: Library of Congress)

LEFT: Silas Deane of Connecticut was one of the three commissioners America sent to France in 1776 to persuade France to sign a treaty of alliance. Accused of corruption, Deane returned to America and ignited a huge quarrel within Congress. *(Credit: The Granger Collection, New York)*

RIGHT: Sharp-tongued Virginian Arthur Lee was supposed to help negotiate a treaty with France. Instead he became a violent critic of French influence on America and accused Benjamin Franklin and others of betraying their country.
(Credit: Library of Congress)

John Adams was jealous of Benjamin Franklin and hostile to the French. But he overcame his prejudices and played a major role in the peace negotiations.

(Credit: Library of Congress)

BELOW: George III saw himself as a patriot king with a sacred duty to preserve his "dominions" in America. He mixed patriotism, persuasion, and bribery to create a political juggernaut that dominated Parliament.

(Credit: The Royal Collection)

with Spain to bring her into the war in 1779. By now Franklin knew that the French had promised never to make peace until Spain achieved her goals—the conquest of Gibraltar and Jamaica. Was America also bound by this promise? The latest instructions from Congress to its peace commissioners, to rely completely on the guidance and leadership of France, would seem to leave little room for any other conclusion.

As the illuminations died away in Paris and other cities, independence and peace seemed almost as uncertain as they had been on the night Franklin had pondered the rumors and scraps of facts about Yorktown with young Watson, and feared the worst. Along with George III's unpredictable reaction to Yorktown, there was the possibility that John Adams would revive his militia diplomacy approach to France and turn peace negotiations into a nightmare. As for John Jay in Madrid—Franklin liked and respected him but had no idea how he would react to taking diplomatic orders from France. Back in America, Congress was still wrestling with the problem of keeping an American army in the field, in spite of imminent national bankruptcy.

Unquestionably, General Washington knew what he was doing when he rushed his American version of the Yorktown victory to Paris by the first available French frigate.

·————————·

Chapter Three

An Empire on the Brink

IN THE LAST WEEK of November 1781, London was shrouded in its usual gray haze, a mix of fog and smoke from tens of thousands of coal fires. With over a million inhabitants, the metropolis on the Thames was the largest city in Europe, a gigantic churning sea of humanity, acutely conscious that it was the headquarters of a global empire. In its depths lived colonies of Jews, gypsies, French exiles, Scottish and Irish immigrants, and English men and women of every imaginable religious opinion. They included carefully inconspicuous Catholics, dissenters who called themselves Presbyterians, Methodists, Baptists, or Deists, and members of the established Anglican church, who formed the majority.

The city's politics were equally diverse, ranging from conservative Tories who supported the government no matter who was in charge to ultra-liberal Whigs who suspected all governments. Its guardian river, the Thames, was invariably crowded with ships taking on or discharging cargoes from India, Africa, the West Indies, and the Mediterranean. Into London's banks and merchant houses flowed a stream of cash from around the world—and an equally important stream of credit in the opposite direction.

There were few nations or regions on the globe beyond the reach of the city's merchants. Portugal and its overseas colonies were satellites that shipped tons of gold from Brazil to pay for vast quantities of British products. Even Spain, Britain's frequent enemy in wartime, had a hefty trade in British manufactures through the port of Cadiz, where tons of linens, woolens, cottons, hats, and other products were transhipped to South America. From China came an enormously profitable trade in tea. Captive blacks streamed from Africa to produce the West Indies sugar that sweetened so many British drinks and foods and made slave traders and planters and merchants rich. The semi-public British East India Company paid the government 400 thousand pounds a year and still produced fortunes for its officers, who returned to England to build huge mansions and live like "nabobs." Ultimately the empire was a gigantic corporation that had made Great Britain the richest country in Europe.[1]

II

Around the mansions and town houses of London's West End, where the aristocrats and successful merchants lived, order, cleanliness, and quiet were usually the rule. The streets were reasonably clean and free of noise, except for the clatter of carriage wheels on the cobblestones. But in the East End, where the poor clustered, filth and turmoil were everywhere. Well over half the population made less than 50 pounds a year—about 4 thousand dollars in modern money. Most lived in single rooms in substandard tenements that were so badly built, they frequently collapsed, crushing whole families in their beds. People survived from day to day, dependent on unpredictable employment as laborers on the docks or in the textile mills and other factories. Both men and women were frequently drunk on cheap gin that was available in ubiquitous dram shops for a few pennies a gulp.

In contrast to the paved streets of the West End, mud overflowed the lanes of the East End, while the stench of raw sewage and unwashed human bodies filled the fetid air. Here was where resentment and violence festered, where men and women were robbed and often killed in the night for a few shillings in their pockets or purses. No sane resident of the West End ventured into the East End after dark.

Sixteen months ago, in June of 1780, a gigantic mob had boiled from the East End and terrorized London for a week. Led by a mentally disturbed aristocrat named Lord George Gordon, the rioters were supposedly protesting a law that lifted a civil restriction on Catholics, giving them the right to own land. Behind the howls of "No Popery!" lay rage and frustration at a government that seemed unable to win the war with the American rebels or the war that this needless (as many saw it) conflict had triggered with the country's ancient enemies, France and Spain.

In 1779, when the enemy's combined fleet had invaded the English Channel, outnumbered British men-of-war performed so ineptly, two of the leading admirals had been court-martialed in trials that reeked of politics. Sheer luck had rescued the nation from a ruinous invasion. The admirals had both been acquitted, but rioters had smashed windows in the houses of several government leaders, protesting a humiliation unparalleled in the memory of living Londoners. The far more numerous rioters of 1780 had demolished Newgate Prison, freeing its inmates, looted numerous stores and businesses, including a major distillery, and assaulted or threatened many government officials. The First Lord of the Admiralty, the Earl of Sandwich, was struck by a rock; Chief Justice William Murray, Earl Mansfield, had his house wrecked and burned, as did prominent opposition Parliamentarian Sir George Saville. At one point the mob came perilously close to dragging the king's first minister, Frederick, Lord North, from his carriage. Only a friend brandishing a pistol saved him.

At the height of the mob's fury, twenty grenadiers with loaded muskets had been stationed on the top floor of Lord North's house on Downing Street and friends with pistols and fowling pieces manned the downstairs windows. Charles Watson-Wentworth, the Marquis of Rockingham, the leader of the opposition in Parliament, was equally worried about his house. He obtained a guard of a hundred soldiers to guarantee its survival—and his own. Rockingham—and his right-hand man in the House of Commons, Edmund Burke—played a key role in forcing the benumbed government to bring thousands of troops into the city to restore order.[2]

III

The Gordon riots were not the first social explosion that had shaken London. Rioting was tacitly acknowledged as an expression of political opinion—the sole alternative for the vast majority of England's 7 million men and women. Only 215 thousand males could vote, and this privilege was distributed with an utter disregard for population. The city of London had eight seats in Parliament, while the rural county of Cornwall, with barely 100 thousand tillers of the soil, had forty-four. There were no representatives for good-sized cities, such as Manchester and Birmingham.

Numerous "rotten boroughs" where the number of franchised voters was as few as seven or eight were for sale to the highest bidder, who too often was an agent of George III. Seventy members of Parliament were returned from these parodies of the democratic process. The ruling class justified the system by arguing that every citizen was "virtually" represented by Parliament, even if he did not have an actual spokesman. The Americans had rejected this self-serving rationalization and not a few Englishmen felt the same way.

George III, coming to the throne in 1760 on the death of his grandfather, George II, began as an idealist, determined to purge the nation of political corruption. He saw himself as a "patriot king" destined to break the grip of greedy politicians on royal leadership. But his efforts to control Parliament soon had him working with Henry Fox, the totally corrupt paymaster of the forces, who stole immense sums from the annual budget, aside from the equally huge sums he acquired legally. "We must call in bad men to govern bad men," the king glumly explained to one of his shocked intimates.[3]

It was not long before George III headed a political operation that was as corrupt as the ones he denounced when he was Prince of Wales. In those days of his youth, a first minister and his supporters often spent a million pounds to win an election. George soon saw to it that he had a slush fund which enabled him to play the same game in the major political league he was determined to enter. He insisted on an annual stipend of 800 thousand pounds—40 million dollars—a year to support his "civil list." This gave the king tremendous leverage to "countenance" his supporters in Parliament with government jobs, many of which required little or no work, with invisible pensions for life, or with outright cash bribes. By 1769, he had outspent his legal annual outlay to the tune of 500 thousand pounds, but Parliament paid it off. In 1776, he was awash in 600 thousand pounds of red ink and again, Parliament paid—without demanding the slightest accounting of how the money had been spent.

By this time, Edmund Burke and many other members of Parliament were growing alarmed at the political juggernaut George III had constructed. One expressed his fear that the civil list "would spread corruption through the people to secure a Parliament like an infamous packed jury, ready to acquit the ministers at all adventures." First Minister Lord North reacted with pompous dudgeon. He descanted on how the civil list was "the revenue of the crown," which meant the crown had the right "to dispose of it at will." This masterpiece of circular logic went unchallenged by George III's dutiful majority of the House of Commons.[4]

IV

Lord North was the perfect first minister for a monarch determined to be a patriot king. Short, fat, with a bulbous nose and an apologetic manner, North was the ultimate yes-man. He was the son of wealthy Lord Guilford, who declined to give him enough money to live decently. As a result, North sank ever deeper into debt. In 1777, the king heard that the first minister's recurrent bad health and depressions were caused by money worries, and offered him 20 thousand pounds to free him from this anxiety.

North accepted the king's offer and regretted it almost at once. Four weeks later, the news of General Burgoyne's 1777 surrender at Saratoga reached London. North tried to resign but the king would not even consider it. So North soldiered on, periodically pleading with His Majesty to let him depart, only to be met with another royal negative, often accompanied by a lecture on courage or duty.[5]

From the king's point of view, keeping North around made eminent sense. It guaranteed that George would always have the last word when he conferred with the first minister in the "closet," as private meetings with the king were called. Moreover, when North nerved himself to the task, he was a superb parliamentarian, adept at debate. He often displayed a wry wit that deflated angry opponents. In the cabinet, he provided no leadership whatsoever. Each minister was more or less free to shape his own policy—over which the king, not Lord North, had final approval. That was the way His Majesty wanted it.

V

This government by royal approval created a kind of immunity for the ministers George III appointed with North's compliance. It enabled them to ignore their unpopularity, no matter how much Parliament and the newspapers attacked them. The most egregious example was the secretary of state for American affairs, Lord George Germain. Born a Sackville, one of the oldest and most respected names in the British peerage, Lord George had been court-martialed for cowardice in the Seven Years War for failing to attack a retreating French army, and found guilty. (Strictly speaking, the charge was refusal to obey an explicit order, but cowardice was implied and became the label he wore for the rest of his life.) Lord George was henceforth barred from service in the British army.

As Prince of Wales, George III had become convinced that the verdict was a vicious political plot against Lord George, and was determined to right this wrong when the opportunity arose. In 1775, Sackville, who had changed his name to Germain when a relative by that name left him her large fortune, was Parliament's most vociferous supporter of the king's hard line against America. George made him the American secretary, which put him in charge of the war, ignoring the fact that for most ranking army officers and numerous politicians, he was still the despised coward Sackville.

When the Americans succeeded in winning key battles such as Saratoga that transformed the war, the vituperation against Lord George became public and personal. But George III remained committed to his American secretary, and vice versa, leaving Lord North the thankless task of defending Germain in Parliament.

John Montagu, the Earl of Sandwich, the First Lord of the Admiralty, was another minister who grew more and more unpopular. He was blamed for the royal navy's shocking inadequacies when the war with America began, although Lord North, as First Lord of the Treasury, was more responsible. North had slashed the Navy's budget ruthlessly, in an attempt to reduce the huge national debt Britain had acquired from the Seven Years War. The controversial decision to go to war with America politicized the navy into Lord Sandwich's friends and enemies, which sowed distrust in all ranks. "Discipline in a very great measure is lost . . . officers presume to find fault and think when their duty is implicit obedience," one admiral warned Sandwich in 1780.

Like Germain, Sandwich had a sordid personal past to live down. In his youth he was a founder of "The Hell Fire Club," a group of aristocrats who met at a country estate to enjoy orgies with young women, often with overtones of Satan worshipping. Sandwich's wife went insane, which may have had something to do with the Hell Fire Club. The Earl found a mistress, Martha Ray, a beautiful milliner's apprentice. She had a superb voice and became a popular singer, best known for her rendition of "I Know That My Redeemer Liveth." In 1779, as she was leaving the opera, Ray was murdered by a man whom she may have encouraged because he offered to marry her she had changed her mind and decided to remain with Sandwich.

The opposition in Parliament and numerous newspapers found it easy to attack Sandwich as an incompetent and a disgrace to the navy's honor and its tradition of victory. But George III never wavered in his support of his scandal-stained First Lord of the Admiralty, because Sandwich too was an unshakable supporter of the war with America. One of George's earliest letters, revealing his intentions in the conflict, went to Sandwich in 1775. "I am of the opinion that once these rebels have felt a smart blow, they will submit . . . no situation can ever change my fixed resolution to bring the colonies to due obedience." Since that time, there had been smart blows from both sides, but the situation had yet to change His Majesty's mind—or Lord Sandwich's.[6]

VI

The king's remarkable industry was another factor in this macabre political machine. George III was a prodigious worker. He was at his desk virtually from dawn to dusk, overseeing everything. He read army and navy reports from America, the West Indies, India. He never failed to ponder the often oblique messages from his numerous secret agents, and confidential letters from Britain's ambassadors. He corresponded with cabinet ministers and conferred constantly with two industrious subministers, John Robinson and Charles Jenkinson, who kept him minutely informed about what was happening in Parliament, the cabinet, and other branches of the government.

To this industry the king added a lifestyle that was a model of respectability. In an age when having a mistress was almost a necessity for an aristocrat who wanted to be considered a man of the world, George was faithful to his wife, a homely submissive German princess who presented him with no less than fifteen children. The king hated London and preferred to spend most of his time at his palaces in Kew, in Surrey, or in Windsor—further proof that he was not susceptible to the vices of the great metropolis. This sober lifestyle made him extremely popular with the people. From a political point of view, these traits added up to one word: *formidable.* This bulky, thick-necked, self-righteous, self-confident man was a living force, the embodiment of personal power, determined to see his will prevail, no matter how much the opposition in Parliament and the critics in the newspapers ranted and raved.

VII

The war in America and the West Indies, as well as France and Spain's combined fleet in the English Channel, were not the only crises that Lord North had to defend in the House of Commons, at the behest of his royal master. There was alarming unrest in a country far closer to home—Ireland. The majority of the population were Catholics; they lived in awful poverty, oppressed by a web of legislation known as the penal laws, which denied them the right to vote, own land, or obtain an education.

The Irish Parliament was entirely Protestant; it seldom met and at one point went thirty-three years without an election. All its laws were subject to the English Parliament's veto, while the latter's laws were instantly applicable in both countries. This enabled the British to create a tangle of trade restrictions around Ireland which caused severe hardships to both Catholics and Protestants. Ireland was forbidden to export woolen goods, for instance, and Irish fishermen could not wield their nets on Newfoundland's Grand Banks, giving the British a monopoly in both industries. As a result of these and similar measures, Ireland reeled toward bankruptcy. In 1778, the British had to loan the government 500 thousand pounds to pay its civil servants.[7]

The American war had forced the British government to withdraw most of the troops stationed in Ireland. In 1778, with a French invasion threatening both Ireland and England, Lord North reluctantly permitted the Protestants to raise volunteers to repel it. The Irish Volunteers swiftly multiplied into a formidable army, with estimates ranging from 28 thousand to 42 thousand members. Their ranks were soon infiltrated by Catholics as well as Irish Protestants determined to win a semblance of independence for Ireland. An alarmed Irish parliamentarian warned: "The minds of men are altered with regard to Great Britain . . . there is a dangerous spirit afloat."[8]

Dangerous soon became a mild word. Thousands of Irish Volunteers paraded through Dublin, the second-largest city in the empire, with guns on their shoulders, while tens of thousands cheered them. North dithered and did little or nothing; the opposition, led by Lord Rockingham, who had large estates in Ireland, condemned this inaction. With Edmund Burke at his side, his lordship let it be known that a Rockingham administration would give the Irish, both Catholics and Protestants, a better deal.

These words only encouraged the Irish to move closer to violence. In 1779, mobs roamed the streets of Dublin, their war cry "Free trade for Ireland." Most of the majority who supported Lord North in the London Parliament were adamantly opposed to this seemingly sensible idea, because it threatened England's pocketbook. When North made a few fumbling proposals in this direction, such as permitting the Irish to fish on the Grand Banks, his majority deserted him. Edmund Burke rose in Parliament to mock him. "Why not apply to Ireland the kind of measures [brute force] that were used in America? Ministers dare not . . . America has pointed out to Ireland . . . her just claims upon this country."[9]

The strain of these accumulated crises at times rendered Lord North the equivalent of a basket case. At one point he told John Robinson, the treasury official who was a confidant of both North and George III, that the situation "preyed on his mind so much [it] rendered him incapable of anything . . . he could not bear to be thought the cause of the destruction of His Majesty's power and government and perhaps the ruin of his country." Whereupon the first minister broke down completely, creating, Robinson told a friend, "such a scene of distress, I assure you as made my heart bleed for him."[10]

Not for the first time, North soon surprised his doomsayers. By the end of the year 1779, he had pulled himself together and persuaded Parliament to pass free trade for Ireland. The Irish Volunteers were mollified but they still continued to parade with guns on their shoulders. Ireland remained an unspoken threat.

VIII

In all these political upheavals, with their portents of chaos, Lord North and George III were bolstered by a largely invisible but extremely potent ally: the British government's ability to raise astonishing amounts of money to finance their war machine. One of the historical myths of recent years is the notion that Great Britain had a weak or minimal central government in the eighteenth century. These were the years when England became an empire and a heavy, if not the heaviest, weight in Europe's balance-of-power politics. British armies and the royal navy fought enemies and conquered countries all over the globe.

What was the explanation? During these same years, the British evolved a system of centralized taxation which was more powerful and sophisticated than that of any other nation's in Europe. Not a little of this transformation was achieved by thousands of people who remain faceless, without a history: the innumerable army of clerks who kept voluminous records of every imaginable transaction.

Thanks to this explosion of record keeping, and the will to create a strong centralized state, British government expenditures rose 600 percent in the century between 1688—the "glorious revolution" which brought a Protestant king to the throne—and 1776, the year of the American Revolution, while the population of England and Wales increased only 46 percent. It was Marcus Tullius Cicero, the great Roman orator, who first said that money was "the sinews of war." No other nation in the civilized world had more access to money—and hence superior sinews of war—than Great Britain.[11]

All this money-raising was accomplished with little or no appeal to the will of the people. The executors of the policy were the 2,704 "excise officers" who were supervised by another 300 superiors in the provinces and another 200 in the central office in London. By 1780, the Excise Office was collecting money from 33,000 brewers and suppliers of food to the public, 36,000 tavern keepers, 33,500 tea and coffee merchants, and thousands more businessmen who made candles, soap, cloth, and paper. At least 100,000 private business premises were under the office's supervision, all paying taxes based on their clerk-recorded incomes. No other nation in Europe had access to this kind of guaranteed cash flow.[12]

This remarkable system enabled England to amass huge debts fighting wars with the assurance that they would eventually be paid, either through short-term loans, or funded by the Bank of England as stock paying 4 percent interest, which traded on the London stock exchange. During the American Revolution, the public debt had climbed from 131 million pounds in 1775 to almost 245 million pounds in 1781. By that time, paying the interest on the debt was consuming 66 percent of the public revenue. But the system remained stable; inflation was never more than a minor problem.

In *Common Sense*, Tom Paine's 1776 call for independence, the radical pamphleteer had assured the American people that a war would bankrupt England, guaranteeing an easy victory for America. Having been an exciseman, Paine should have known better. Certainly Lord North knew better. Though he shuddered when he had to borrow more money or raise taxes, he knew the cash would be forthcoming. So did George III. This had not a little to do with his determination to keep fighting.

IX

By one of those strange twists of politics, the Gordon riots created a backlash against the opposition. George III's majority in Parliament blamed them on Edmund Burke and Lord Rockingham, whom Burke had persuaded to support a repeal of the penal law against Catholics owning land in England or Ireland. Burke had a Catholic mother and a father who was a "convert lawyer." That term was a derogatory way of describing an Irish Catholic attorney who had converted to the Protestant faith to escape the weight of the penal laws. Burke had hoped the repeal would be a first step to the removal of all the crippling restrictions against Catholics in England and Ireland.[13]

Long before the Gordon rioters ravaged London, Edmund Burke had been anathema to George III and his followers. The Irishman's ferocious assaults on the king's policy toward America had inspired widespread opposition to the war in and out of Parliament. Four months earlier, Burke had launched an all-out onslaught on the king's civil list and the web of bribery and "countenances" that George had woven through and around Parliament. The speech, which takes up seventy-two columns in the *Parliamentary History,* was awesome in its mastery of detail and its proposals of specific reforms.

Even Lord North called the speech "one of the most able" he had ever heard. But the first minister soon reduced it to babble by breaking up the proposals into separate resolutions and defeating each one over the course of several days. The votes were frequently close; an alarmed George III told Lord North it convinced him "how little dependence can be placed on the momentary whims that strike popular assemblies." It was a nice summary of the king's underlying contempt for Parliament.[14]

Two months later, in April 1780, John Dunning, a Burke admirer who regularly voted with another opposition leader, William Petty, Lord Shelburne, rose in Parliament to propose a resolution: "That the influence of the Crown has increased, is increasing, and ought to be diminished." To everyone's astonishment, Parliament voted 233-215 in favor of the motion. Dunning explicitly linked his words to Burke's speech in the introduction to his resolution.

The support for Dunning's motion was soon revealed as a momentary impulse. When the same gentleman rose to suggest that Parliament should abolish its seasonal meetings and sit in permanent session until the war with America and other crises were resolved, he was voted down by a huge majority. Too many people remembered the "Long Parliament" of the previous century, which led to the English Civil War. Maybe George III was right about the instability of elected assemblies.[15]

X

Scarcely had the buildings set afire by the Gordon mob stopped smoldering when news from America dealt the opposition another devastating blow—the gleeful announcement by the government that the British army had captured Charleston, South Carolina, along with 5 thousand rebel troops. In subsequent weeks, news of more victories in South Carolina reached London. Chortling government supporters were soon predicting the imminent collapse of the American rebellion. Since that time, the opposition had sunk into a discouraged, divided minority, seldom able to muster more than 100 votes in a Parliament with 530 members.

No one was more discouraged than Lord Rockingham. An earnest, affable man with a strong sense of rectitude, he was timid in debate and reluctant to challenge George III's supporters in the House of Lords. Without Edmund Burke, he would have long since retreated to his estate in Yorkshire and enjoyed his racehorses and his numerous worshipful friends and relatives there. Rockingham had brought Burke into politics, first as his secretary and then as a member of Parliament in a district where the Marquis was influential. The gifted Irishman was soon Rockingham's spokesman in the House of Commons and evolved into his political guide. It was Burke who articulated the instinctive commitment to liberty and justice that Rockingham felt in his deepest self, thanks to a family tradition of whiggish resistance to arbitrary power.[16]

The two men had scarcely gotten to know each other when Rockingham became first minister in 1766, summoned by the king when the American colonies had exploded into riots and vituperation against the first attempt to tax them, the Stamp Act. During those tumultuous days Burke had become acquainted with Benjamin Franklin, whose testimony before Parliament criticizing the act had not a little to do with its repeal. Subsequently, friendship with Franklin and other Americans encouraged Burke to give his great 1775 oration, "On Conciliation With America," in which he condemned the punitive laws that the British had inflicted on the rebellious colonists as the essence of tyranny, and called for their repeal.

In 1776, when Burke heard that Franklin had come to France, the Irishman toyed with crossing the channel to see if the American was interested in having Lord Rockingham mediate a reconciliation with England based on the principles Burke outlined in his speech. "At the very least," Burke wrote in a letter to Rockingham, "it would revive the cause of our liberties in England." But several of Rockingham's aristocratic allies talked Burke out of it, fearing that such a foray would damage the already shaky unity of their party.[17]

It would revive the cause of our liberties in England. That was close to the heart of the matter, as far as Edmund Burke was concerned. He was convinced that a revival of individual freedom in England would eventually lead to a new understanding of Britain's proper relationship to America, ending the rebellion, and to the repeal of the odious penal laws that had oppressed the Irish people for 150 years. In time, perhaps even India might be rescued from the grip of The East India Company, which had been looting that hapless country for decades. This rebirth of liberty would never happen as long as George III controlled Parliament through his web of patronage, outright bribery, and appeals to patriotism.

Political oppression was what stirred anger in Burke's heart, from the beginning to the end of his long career. This passionate commitment, rooted in seeing firsthand the pain and misery inflicted on millions in Ireland, was why Burke was willing, as he wryly put it in a letter, to be Lord Rockingham's "flapper." In the eighteenth century the word meant "a person who arouses the attention or jogs the memory." It was, Burke admitted to a friend, a "woeful occupation." But he continued to inundate his too-often supine noble lord with exhortations to stay in the fight for their worthy cause.[18]

XI

On November 25, 1781, this cause looked more and more hopeless. George III had staggered the opposition in the fall of 1780 by dissolving Parliament and calling a general election. The king and his friends won it handily, with the usual combination of bribery, patronage, and royal persuasion. Lord North and his cabinet were in power for another seven years—the legal length a parliament could (and still can) sit without requiring an election.

The victory emboldened Lord North (and George III) to take a step that had been discussed in recent cabinet meetings: early in 1781, they declared war on yet another adversary, the United Provinces, better known as Holland. The Dutch had long been considered England's prime Protestant ally on the continent. They had signed a treaty of alliance in 1678 and England permitted them to recruit Highland volunteers for their famed Scots brigade, the best fighting force in the Dutch army.

Over the decades, the United Provinces had drifted toward neutrality as a more profitable stance. They stayed out of the Seven Years War and made huge amounts of money supplying France with naval stores—timber, cordage, sailcloth—which the primitive French economy did not produce. In the current conflict, they had curtly declined to loan all or part of the Scots brigade to George III and had opened their ports to American privateer captains, such as the "notorious pirate" (as the British called him) John Paul Jones. One of their West Indies' islands, St. Eustatius, became a transfer station for shipping cargoes to the rebellious colonies, a trade so profitable, not a few British merchants joined in.

The British retaliated by seizing a number of Dutch ships on the high seas and began inspecting all their former ally's vessels to make sure they were not violating the British blockade of France and Spain. London listed naval stores and almost every other imaginable commodity as contraband, liable to seizure.

The Dutch retaliated by threatening to join the League of Armed Neutrality, another entity that gave Lord North some restless nights. The League originated in the canny brain of Foreign Minister Comte de Vergennes, but he allowed Empress Catherine the Great of Russia to be the ostensible sponsor. She was eager to assert herself and her huge nation as major players in European politics. Austria, Prussia, Denmark, and Sweden joined and the Dutch decided to join too. The members agreed to escort their merchant ships with men-of-war, forcing the British to fight for their supposed right to inspect them. London, well informed of Dutch intentions, declared war before they announced their decision, making a claim to neutrality invalid.[19]

The British pretext was a draft of a treaty of alliance between Holland and America. They had found it in the baggage of Henry Laurens, when they captured the former president of the Continental Congress while he was en route to Holland as ambassador. The document had never been discussed with officials in the Dutch national government. These gentlemen were much too wary to do anything so likely to enrage the British lion. Nevertheless, the British denounced the treaty as an act of perfidy and declared war.

The treaty was one of William Lee's ventures into militia diplomacy. He had gone to Amsterdam and found a somewhat shady Dutch banker, Jean de Neufville, who was ready and eager to promise anything to promote some business. They had drawn up the treaty without consulting a single respectable Dutch merchant or politician. Neufville had persuaded the pensionary (mayor) of Amsterdam to approve it. The frantic Dutch indicted the city of Amsterdam and the pensionary for criminal behavior in a desperate attempt to appease the British—to no avail.

As the British saw it, a declaration of war punished Holland for the pro-French tilt of her neutrality. But the Royal Navy could spare only six ancient ships of the line to blockade the Dutch coast, under an equally aged admiral, Hyde Parker. After a sanguinary but inconclusive encounter with a Dutch fleet whose ships were as decrepit as his own, Parker returned to England and resigned in disgust. "Sire," he told George III, "you have need of younger men and newer ships."[20]

XII

In spite of an enemies list that now included Holland, Spain, France, and the United States, as well as the North government's alienation of Russia and Austria by spurning their offer to mediate peace, Parliament was virtually comatose throughout the first nine months of 1781. They approved a bill for extraordinary expenses for the army in America and the West Indies that totaled 3 million pounds without a murmur of protest. This fog of complacency—and the opposition's disarray—had enabled Parliament to more or less ignore bad news that had recently reached London from the more distant parts of the empire.

In India, an illiterate adventurer named Hyder Aly, whose military talents had made him the self-appointed Sultan of Mysore, a sizeable state in southern India, destroyed a 3,000-man British army at the battle of Polihur in the fall of 1780. Sixty out of eighty-six British officers were killed, along with two thousand troops. Hyder Aly had been fighting the British off and on for twenty years and Polihur demonstrated that he had learned a great deal about how to make war. His army had cannon and muskets and his cavalry no longer engaged in pointless frontal assaults. Instead they thundered around the British flanks to strike from the rear.

When last heard from, Hyder Aly was about to receive help from the French, who had landed an army and deployed a fleet under one of their most talented admirals, obese, aggressive Bailli de Suffren. They were grimly determined to do to the British what The East India Company's army had done to French merchants and soldiers during the Seven Years War—reduce them to one or two pathetic trading posts. There was a distinct possibility that Britain's 3 million pounds a year in trade with Asia's subcontinent might soon go glimmering.[21]

On the Gulf Coast of America, another charismatic military leader was wreaking similar havoc. Thirty-year-old Bernardo de Galvez, the governor of Louisiana, had organized an army the moment he heard Spain had entered the war in 1779, and headed up the Mississippi to demolish British forts as far north as Natchez. Next he wheeled and invaded West Florida. Backed by a Spanish fleet, he had captured the fortified city of Pensacola, complete with its garrison. Next on his agenda was Jamaica, an island whose capture would demolish British hegemony in the West Indies.[22]

From the Mediterranean came another alarming report. A Spanish army had made a surprise attack on the strategically important island of Minorca, forcing the British garrison to retreat helter-skelter to their fort. They had abandoned tons of supplies and equipment and were facing starvation unless swiftly relieved. At the admiralty, First Lord Sandwich huddled with admirals about how to get ammunition, food, and reinforcements to the panicky defenders.

The dilemma involved the fate of another Mediterranean possession: Gibraltar. This limestone promontory at the southern tip of Spain had given the British control of the inland sea since 1704. It was an affront to Spain's pride that Madrid longed to eliminate. They had launched a siege of the fortress which was still in progress. Thus far, relief ships from Minorca and from England had managed to keep Gibraltar supplied and reinforced. Would the loss of Minorca make the British grip on The Rock untenable?

In spite of these worries, the mood in Parliament and the country at large remained optimistic. As one of Lord North's cabinet ministers remarked, "The opposition is if not dead at least asleep." Edmund Burke reintroduced a bill for civil list reform and Lord North defeated it, 233-190. This comfortable margin made the administration confident that there was nothing to debate. Lord North arranged for Parliament's fall session to open late, on November 27, leaving only twenty-three days before the Christmas recess.

XIII

The opposition was so discouraged, many did not plan to attend this truncated gathering. "You may be anxious to know whether I shall take any part in the House [of Commons]," Charles Pratt, Lord Camden, wrote to a friend. "I protest I do not know. Our opposition is scattered and runs wild in both houses under no leader. God knows how all this will end."[23]

The titular leader of the opposition, Lord Rockingham, was, if possible, even more gloomy. "I go to London with much reluctance," he told the Duke of Portland. Rockingham admitted that he had no idea what his supporters would say during the short session.[24]

The only member of the opposition who was guaranteed to be in Parliament and looking for a fight was Charles James Fox. He was a member from Westminster, the most fashionable part of London, so the metropolis was his natural habitat. But Fox had liabilities that were at least as large as Burke's, with his Irish brogue and convert-lawyer father. Charles was the son of Henry Fox, the first "bad man" that George III had hired to help him rule other bad men.

Henry Fox had bought his son a seat in Parliament when Charles was nineteen, and made him a lord of the Admiralty when he was twenty-one. This attempt to create a statesman was a total failure. Charles spent the first half of the 1770s losing huge chunks of Henry Fox's fortune at Almack's, Brooke's, and White's, three London clubs where the English upper class gambled their nights away, often to their ruin. In 1774, Henry Fox, on his deathbed, raised 140 thousand pounds to pay Charles's gambling debts, which temporarily cured him of that particular vice. But his fondness for loose women, hard drinking, and irregular hours continued unabated.

Fox combined these vices with a personal style that was nothing less than squalid. His clothes were often a mess, his face unshaven. He let it be known that "he never cared what was said about his person." For respectability in style and appearance, he had, one man said, "an infinite contempt." Paradoxically, most of the time, Fox's manner was "mild and pleasing."

Without Edmund Burke, there would have been no Charles James Fox as history knows him. Listening to a Burke speech on the folly of taxing America in 1774 changed Fox from a roué without a cause to a reformer who scorned to reform himself in any personal way. He later said he had learned more from Burke than from all his "books and studies" combined.

For his part, Burke, aware of his Irish liabilities, was more than willing to let Fox take the lead in opposition debate, and back him up with facts and figures and historical analogies that supported Fox's often outrageous rhetoric. Unfortunately, this latest session of Parliament seemed to offer Charles little opportunity for verbal fireworks.[25]

XIV

Around noon on Sunday, November 25, a messenger from a packet boat that sailed between Falmouth and Calais arrived at Lord George Germain's house in Pall Mall with the news that the French were celebrating Lord Cornwallis's surrender at Yorktown. The secretary of state for America immediately sent word of the disaster to George III, who was spending the weekend in the country at Kew House.

Lord George called for his carriage and drove to the house of his fellow secretary of state (for northern affairs), imperious David Murray, Viscount Stormont. As ambassador to France, he had bullied and blustered at the Comte de Vergennes and spied industriously on Benjamin Franklin and Silas Deane to prevent the Americans from achieving the treaty of alliance with France. The two ministers headed for the house of the Lord Chancellor, Edward, Baron Thurlow—another vociferous defender of the war in America. Among the Baron's several motives was the money he made as chancellor—an estimated 20,000 pounds a year.

After a gloomy discussion, the three agreed that there was only one thing to do. They drove to Downing Street and showed the letter to Lord North. He took it, Germain later told a friend, "as he would have taken a ball in the breast." He paced up and down his parlor, throwing up his hands, crying again and again: "Oh God, Oh God! It is all over!"[26]

If there were any doubts about believing the news from France, they were dispelled at midnight on the same Sunday. Another messenger reached Lord George from the good ship *Rattlesnake* with the doleful letter that Admiral Thomas Graves had written off the Virginia coast, after Cornwallis's surrender.[27]

XV

At first, it seemed as if everyone on the government's side agreed with North. A crestfallen Attorney General Alexander Wedderburn told William Eden, an insider who was currently in Dublin trying to keep the lid on that still bubbling pot, that "a change of measures" was considered inevitable. Even Lord George Germain, who had staked his career and reputation on success in America, admitted there seemed to be no enthusiasm for continuing the war "even among the real friends of government." A delegation from the liveried companies of London (tradesmen's guilds) was blunt: "Your armies are captured, your navies . . . annihilated, your dominions are lost," they told George III.[28]

That overstatement was typical of the vituperation Londoners showered on the king and could be safely dismissed. After the first shock, many members of the government realized the opposition was as surprised as they were by the news from Yorktown and had no plan of attack in view, much less the numbers to carry it out. Someone inside the administration, probably Lord George Germain, almost immediately published the letter Lord Cornwallis had written to Sir Henry Clinton on October 20, which began with the savage words *I never saw this post in a favorable light* and went on to blame Clinton for promising relief and reinforcements, inducing Cornwallis to stay in Yorktown until retreat was impossible.

It was a clever way to distract the public. Pro-administration newspapers rushed angry criticisms of Sir Henry into print. The goal was winning sympathy for the king and his ministers, especially Germain, for finding themselves saddled with such an idiot general.[29]

· XVI

The first test of where the politicians stood came on November 27, when George III rode from St. James Palace in his magnificent gold coach to give his speech from the throne, opening the session of Parliament. His Majesty was preceded and followed by the usual escort of brilliantly uniformed horse guards and foot soldiers. In the House of Lords, the visitors gallery was crammed with tense spectators. Peers in their crimson robes packed the benches as the king walked to his throne. Members of the House of Commons crowded into the well of the chamber.

The address had been written by Lord North and other insiders long before the news from Yorktown reached London. Most of it was platitudes about His Majesty's confidence that his subjects supported him in his struggle to preserve the empire. But a ripple of amazement went through the listeners when George III said: "The events of war have been unfortunate to my army in Virginia, having ended in the loss of my forces in that province. But I retain a perfect conviction of the justice of my cause." The king was claiming that Yorktown was merely a local setback. There was not even a hint of an interest in negotiating peace, much less yielding America its independence.[30]

The opposition's spokesmen fulminated. Edmund Burke cried: "Victories gave us hopes, defeats made us desperate, and both [have] instigated us to go on." Charles James Fox claimed the king had told them: "I prohibit you from thinking of peace. My rage for conquest is unquenched, and my revenge unsated." Only "the total subjugation of my revolted American subjects" would satisfy their remorseless ruler.[31]

Lord North ignored these outbursts and told the befuddled House of Commons that in spite of Yorktown, there were still grounds for hoping that America could be persuaded to stay in the empire. Simultaneously, he admitted that the war would have to be fought in a different way. But he staunchly defended the king's view that Yorktown did not mean the war was hopelessly lost.

These vague sentiments became part of the House of Commons's address to the king. In effect, they left the practical question of how to make war in a different way undecided. But the address confirmed Parliament's support of the king's courage and devotion to the nation. Put to a vote, the address carried, 218-129—almost the same numbers by which the members approved His Majesty's speech from the throne in the fall of 1780, when everything seemed to be going well in the American war and elsewhere.

A delighted Lord North rushed a letter to the king with the good news. George III immediately saw it as an authorization to continue the war. He told North that the "considerable majority . . . shows the House retains that spirit for which this nation has always been renowned, and which alone can preserve it in its difficulties."

The king informed his pliant first minister that he had already written to Lord George Germain, asking him to "put on paper the mode that seems [now] most feasible for conducting the war." His Majesty remained convinced that "a good end may yet be made" of the long struggle. "If we despond, certain ruin ensues."[32]

George III was convinced that if America gained its independence, Ireland would instantly demand the same freedom; the lucrative sugar islands of the West Indies would also defect, followed by Nova Scotia, Canada, and even India where British rule consisted of the edicts of The East India Company. England would be reduced to a small impotent island on the edge of Europe, despised by the rest of the world.

Lord North may have also believed in this eighteenth-century version of the domino theory. At any rate, he seemed to have recovered from his initial panic and was more than ready to deal with the outraged roars of the opposition, who grew more and more strident in the ensuing days. North's watchword in the virulent debate was the need to obtain "honorable" peace terms—which would never be won by abandoning the war.

Since the independence of America was, in George III's view, the acme of dishonor for him and Britain, it became evident that peace was not going to be achieved any time soon. On the contrary, the government, in the view of one member of Parliament, still "breathed war." Equally gloomy was another observation made by a student of the political scene: America was no more popular with the British people after Yorktown than she had been before the famous victory. In their imperial hearts, almost everyone, from aristocrats to commoners, still loathed their rebel cousins for signing that traitorous alliance with the empire's deadliest foe, France.[33]

Chapter Four

The Art of Making Something
Out of Nothing

I
N PHILADELPHIA in the second week of December 1781, General Washington wrote a letter to his aide, James McHenry, who had resigned from the army when he was elected to the senate of the Maryland legislature. Washington was sorry to see him leave—he enjoyed the good-humored McHenry's company—but he saw a bright side to his departure. "I am convinced that your transition from the military to the civil life will be attended with good consequences," he wrote. McHenry would be in a position to give Maryland's politicians the kind of information which "they often stand in need of in times like the present."

McHenry had told Washington he hoped to be a conduit for communicating the general's "sentiments on public affairs," and Washington "with great pleasure" was ready to correspond with him on the subject. His overriding sentiment at the moment was an "old and true maxim, to make a good peace, you ought to be well prepared to carry on the war." He was happy to report that he had found "no want of disposition in Congress" to make preparations for "vigorous measures" in the coming year. The legislators had passed resolutions urging each state to fill the depleted ranks of its Continental Army regiments by March 1, 1782.[1]

The general's letter abruptly shifted tone. "It will . . . lay to the states to determine whether we are, early in the next campaign, to take advantage of what we have gained . . . or whether we are as usual to let the enemy bring their reinforcements from Europe." Washington was clearly hoping against hope. He was all too aware that the Continental Congress was a bankrupt, virtually powerless legislative body, with declining influence over the states. Congress had never recovered from the loss of reputation it had suffered during the Arthur Lee–Silas Deane imbroglio.[2]

On December 12, 1781, the new president of Congress, sixty-year-old John Hanson of Maryland, sent a circular letter to the governors of the states. He called upon them "in the most pressing manner to compleat the quota of troops assigned to them." With the letter came a copy of the resolves Congress had passed on December 10, specifying that these new recruits should be enlisted for three years or the duration of the war.

On November 13, 1781, when President Hanson had been in office only eight days, he wrote to his son-in-law, Dr. Philip Thomas, that he was eager to resign. The ceremonial duties were "irksome," his health was "declining," and his family needed him at home. The delegates had convinced him that it would be difficult if not impossible to find a replacement.

Hanson's reluctance to do his job was soon all too visible. A president usually wrote about forty to fifty letters a month to leaders in the various states about issues raised in Congress that required their cooperation or approval. Within three months of taking office, Hanson persuaded Congress to make Charles Thomson, the secretary of Congress, responsible for communicating with the states. This decision transformed what should have been a chance to exercise presidential leadership to a mere bureaucratic process, making Congress even more of a nullity.[3]

II

While Congress went through the motions of governing, the British and their loyalist allies were not entirely quiescent. In November, as President Hanson was trying to find a way to resign, three loyalist spies arrived in Philadelphia on a daring mission. They had been sent by Captain George Beckwith, who had become head of British secret-service operations after the execution of Major John Andre in 1780 for his role in the plot to bribe Benedict Arnold into betraying West Point. The loyalists had persuaded one Thomas Edison, formerly a clerk in Secretary Charles Thomson's office, to lead them to a cache of secret papers full of information about

Congress's troubled relationship with the French ambassador, feuds between the states about western territories, notes on debates about Silas Deane and Arthur Lee, and other explosive matters.

At the last moment, Edison lost his nerve and betrayed the spies. They were seized by the city militia and one of them was executed. The agitated Hanson told his son-in-law that a second spy, John Moody, was also condemned, but was temporarily spared "in hopes of getting something out of him." Moody refused to talk and was hanged on November 23. Hanson praised Edison for revealing the plot; the ex-clerk claimed he had joined the conspiracy planning to reveal it at the right moment.

The third loyalist, Lieutenant James Moody, brother of John, told a very different story in his memoirs. One of the most daring guerilla leaders of the war, James Moody escaped and retreated to New York. He said Edison lost his nerve. But Hanson and the shaken Americans believed the ex-clerk's version. "Something will be done for him as [a] reward," the president wrote."[4]

George Washington was vexed by James Moody's escape. In a letter to Governor William Livingston of New Jersey, who was well acquainted with Moody's exploits, the general regretted that they had not caught the "villain" out of uniform, so he could have been executed as a spy, like his brother and their confederate. "When he was taken before, he was in arms in his proper uniform . . . with his commission in his pocket," Washington ruefully wrote. That time, Moody had also escaped his captors.

Livingston had written to Washington about another loyalist guerilla operation—a plot to capture the federal post office's mail as it passed through New Jersey. Washington told the governor, who was a close friend, that he would warn officials in Philadelphia to be careful about sending "dispatches of consequence" through the regular mail.

Governor Livingston also complained about the large amount of smuggling between British-held New York and loyalists operating along the numerous tidal rivers and in the pine forests of southern New Jersey. Washington told him he could not spare the number of men it would take to stop this traffic. Only a "naval force" would wipe it out—but no such force was available to the bankrupt United States. He grimly remarked that this "pernicious and growing" commerce would never be stopped until the legislatures of the neighboring states made death the penalty for trafficking with the enemy. In states such as New York and New Jersey, where as many as a third of the people were loyalist sympathizers, this was unlikely to happen.[5]

III

Philadelphia was a restless city, almost as divided between the rich and middle class and the "lower sort"—the working poor—as London. Since 1776, the British blockade had badly damaged the American economy; a recent study estimated that business activity declined by a third from its prewar vigor, when Americans had enjoyed the highest per capita income in the civilized world. No one was more vulnerable to this precipitous drop than the citizens of Philadelphia. Much of their prewar prosperity had depended on a massive export trade.[6]

Also roiling the political waters was the depreciation of Congress's continental currency and the rise of inflation. The working poor had more and more trouble paying their rent and buying the necessities of life, such as flour and corn. The price of a bushel of corn went from 3 shillings in 1776 to 180 shillings in 1780. Not surprisingly, wages did not keep pace with these huge price increases.[7]

The working poor were backed by the city militia, which had become politicized as early as 1776, under the leadership of a radical professor from the College of Pennsylvania, Timothy Matlack. He headed a Committee of Privates that applauded his frequent denunciations of the rich and powerful. The militia pressured the Pennsylvania state assembly, which met in the same building as the Continental Congress, into passing price-control legislation and a ban on the export of flour from the city. But the working poor remained unhappy.

One August morning in 1779, numerous copies of a broadside were pinned to doors and trees throughout the city. It claimed the "suffering friends of this country" were being "enslaved, ruined and starved" by wealthy merchants and "an infernal gang of Tories." The diatribe ended with *Rouse, Rouse, Rouse*. COME ON WARMLY.

The militia and the working poor, who often served in their ranks, took this advice literally. They seized four rich men, including Quaker John Drinker, and marched them through the streets with drums beating "The Rogue's March," as if they were criminals. When former Continental Army General Thomas Mifflin, another wealthy man, tried to intervene, a militiaman struck him with a musket. The blow shocked more than a few spectators; in 1776, Mifflin had been a hugely popular leader of the militia.

The march climaxed with an attack on the house of wealthy lawyer James Wilson, a vehement critic of price controls. The assault was answered with gunfire from Wilson and his friends. Six men were killed and fifteen wounded before the president of Pennsylvania, Joseph Reed, appeared with Continental Army cavalrymen and the Philadelphia regiment of light horsemen and arrested many of the militiamen. Reed had previously encouraged the agitators and denounced the rich as furiously as Timothy Matlack. Even more surprising to the demonstrators, Matlack backed the state's chief executive. No doubt by arrangement, the arrested rioters were soon pardoned and released and the defenders of Wilson's house were advised to stay out of Philadelphia for several months while tempers cooled on both sides.[8]

Unfortunately, prices continued to soar and unrest returned. By early 1781, continental money had depreciated to 125-1; by May it had reached 700-1 and became meaningless paper. Merchants and shopkeepers refused to accept it. "The old continental is dying by yards, not inches," Massachusetts Congressman James Lovell told his mentor Samuel Adams, who had retreated to Boston to nurse his political wounds. Outraged mechanics and artisans paraded through the streets declaring they would not allow anyone to work for paper dollars. It was gold or silver or nothing. Hundreds of sailors, armed with clubs, paraded on another day, "cursing ye Continental money and declaring against it."

The Pennsylvania state government insisted that its paper currency was still valid, but this attempt to calm the protestors had little impact; those paper dollars had also depreciated to one-seventh of their nominal value. Militia artillery companies beat their drums furiously in various parts of the city and a mob gathered in front of the state house. No one appeared to assert a leadership role and the protestors went home, confused and angry. For a while, it looked as if a riot as destructive as London's Gordon upheaval was about to shake the American capital.[9]

A panicky President Reed called an emergency session of the state assembly. After days of argument, the legislators repealed all trade restrictions and abandoned all forms of paper money. The free market plus hard money became the only regulator of prices for food and rent. The officers of the militia companies, most of them middle-class men, went along with these new arrangements. The man behind this crushing defeat of radicalism was Philadelphia's leading merchant, Robert Morris.[10]

IV

Born in Liverpool, Morris had joined his merchant father in America at the age of thirteen, in 1747. Seven years later, at the age of twenty, he formed a partnership with Thomas Willing, son of another successful merchant. They soon created a worldwide trading network that made Morris among the richest men in pre-revolutionary America. Neither his wealth nor his English birth prevented him from joining the protest against Britain's oppressive policy toward America. Even austere John Adams, an early advocate of independence, was impressed by the merchant prince. He praised Morris's "masterly understanding . . . open temper . . . and honest heart."[11]

Profiting so hugely from the advantages of the British Empire's web of economic connections, Morris had not been an enthusiast for independence; he voted against the declaration on July 2, 1776. But the merchant prince was sincerely committed to challenging George III's claim to unrestricted power over America and signed the document later in the summer. This hesitation made him less than popular with radical politicians such as Samuel Adams and Richard Henry Lee, who liked to measure a man's patriotism by his early commitment to independence. Their true whig ideology also made it difficult for them to tolerate a patriot who made money out of the war, as Morris insisted on his right to do.

Realists like George Washington had no trouble with Morris's stance. The two men had become close friends in the course of the war. Washington never forgot that in the final days of 1776, when Congress fled to Baltimore, Morris stayed in Philadelphia and supplied him with hard money to pay the spies that helped him pull off the desperately needed victories of Trenton and Princeton. When Washington challenged the true whig extremists during the Continental Army's ordeal at Valley Forge by calling for half pay after the war for the officer corps, it was Morris who cast the decisive vote that carried the measure in Congress, six states to five. On the march to Yorktown, Morris had again rescued Washington by borrowing enough hard money from the French army, pledging his personal credit, to pay the disgruntled Continentals a month's wages.

Only when the Pennsylvania Assembly had passed the free market economic program did Morris agree to become the United States' superintendent of finance. The Continental Congress had already offered him the job. But he did not think he could implement his program in the antibusiness atmosphere created by the radicals who controlled the Pennsylvania government.

In a 1776 letter, Morris told Benjamin Franklin that Congress balked at creating executive departments because they did not want to part with power. They preferred to rule directly through their committees. As superintendent of finance, Morris made sure Congress put a lot of power in his hands. Along with asserting his right to continue to operate as a businessman, Morris insisted on the authority to appoint all the officers in his department and dismiss any officer in any branch of the government who handled public money if the superintendent did not think he was doing his job. "Mr. Morris was inexorable, Congress [was] at his mercy," a disapproving Joseph Reed told a friendly correspondent. The Lee-Adams true whigs had even more violent objections to giving Morris so much power, but they no longer controlled Congress.[12]

V

Superintendent of Finance Morris was the chief reason why George Washington remained in Philadelphia for almost four months after his arrival from Yorktown. He wanted to help his "particular friend" in every possible way. A talented businessman in his own right, Washington was fascinated by the way Morris began exerting all his financial arts to make something out of nothing. The general knew that the final outcome of the Revolution might depend on the financier's success or failure.

In their winter camp at New Windsor, a few miles west of the Hudson River near Newburgh, the main Continental Army was waiting to be paid and clothed and fed. In South Carolina, Nathanael Greene commanded men with the same expectations. On the frontiers Indians and loyalists were still waging a savage guerilla war, which required more soldiers to feed and pay. The British army, regularly paid and well fed, still occupied New York, Charleston, and Savannah. The king's men and their loyalist allies were doing their utmost to use their near-monopoly of consumer goods and their ample secret service funds to seduce Americans into neutrality or renewed loyalty to George III. Everywhere, that ancient root of all evil, money, was a decisive weapon. The United States of America had none. It was up to Robert Morris to create the illusion of solvency.

VI

Morris was well aware that he was not embarking on a pleasant excursion. In a letter to General Washington, he recalled the "unmerited abuse" he had received from the true whigs in Philadelphia and elsewhere in his previous public service in Congress. He told Washington he had vowed never to take a "public station" again. His decision to become superintendent of finance was "contrary to my inclination, to my judgment and to my experience." He had accepted the job for only one reason: "the absolute necessity of a reformation" in America's finances.[13]

Morris saw himself performing the same task as Jacques Necker, the French director general of finances. Necker was considered a miracle worker for his skill in keeping France solvent—an illusion which would prove to be even more total than the one Morris was trying to achieve. In a June 1781 letter to Necker, Morris painted a dark picture of the alternative to America's reformation. "We are likely to become an unruly, ungovernable nation . . . the confidence of the people being destroyed, the credit of the government lost, its vigour is of course gone, and this unhappily at a time when exertion is most wanted."[14]

Superintendent Morris soon proved he was not shy about exercising the powers of his office. There were few parts of the government in which finances did not play a role. He ordered the Marine Department to be placed under his control, and abolished the once potent Board of Admiralty and several other Navy boards. Few argued with these changes. The U.S. Navy had almost ceased to exist. He acquired the right to export or import commodities on the credit of the United States. The proceeds of all foreign loans were placed in Morris's hands, which made him a major player in diplomatic affairs.

Morris swiftly demonstrated that he was ready to act vigorously and decisively to restore the country's credit. One of his first announcements was a refusal to pay the federal government's past debts to individuals. Any debt incurred before January 1, 1782, which he considered the date on which he officially took power as superintendent of finance, would have to wait for a final settlement of all outstanding arrears at the end of the war. He was determined, he said, "to draw some line" between expenditures incurred while he was in office and the huge amount of borrowed money spent before he took office. Otherwise there would be no hope of achieving solvency.

Another bold move was Morris's establishment of the Bank of North America three days after he took office. He capitalized it at $400 thousand in hard money, in shares to be sold for $400 each. A $400-thousand bank—about $6 million in modern dollars—was extremely modest and would in no sense be capable of solving the financial problems of a federal government that owed over $35 million—a half-billion modern dollars. But Morris knew what he was doing. He thought $400 thousand was an attainable figure and would bolster the illusion of solvency. "To ask more than could be obtained would have a fatal effect," he told one correspondent.[15]

In his letters to people he trusted, such as Benjamin Franklin, Morris looked forward to expanding the bank to "ten times" the size of the original subscription. He urged Franklin to persuade French bankers to buy shares. Morris hoped that eventually wealthy Americans would transfer most of their assets to stock in the bank. Federal and state paper money could then be replaced by notes from the bank. This would "unite the several states together in one general money connexion," Morris told another political ally, John Jay. The long-range goal was the creation of an American version of the Bank of England, the linchpin that united Britain's sinews of economic power to create the world's most powerful nation-state.

Ben Franklin applauded this vision. But he warned Morris from his experience with Arthur Lee that he should not expect gratitude from the public for his efforts. "You are sure of being censured by malevolent critics and bug writers, who will abuse you while you are serving them, and wound your character in nameless pamphlets, thereby resembling those dirty little insects that attack us only in the dark . . . molesting and wounding us, while our sweat and blood are contributing to their existence." This prophecy would soon be fulfilled by the appearance in Congress of none other than Arthur Lee.[16]

"Morris notes" were another innovation that was aimed at supplementing notes drawn on the Bank of North America as a currency that merchants could use. These were certificates issued on Morris's large personal fortune—which far exceeded the amount of money in the bank. Morris gave strict orders to government officials to make sure neither the bank's nor his personal notes depreciated in continental dollars. He warned that any federal officeholder found accepting these notes for less than their face value would be fined the full amount of the discount.

One of Morris's most controversial decisions depended heavily on George Washington's friendship and support: the superintendent of finance refused to pay the army. This saved him an estimated $3.5 million a year—a figure that would have wrecked the Bank of North America and the rest of his financial operations. Another innovation probably had not a little to do with winning Washington's approval. Instead of relying on supplies from the individual states—which seldom arrived, forcing the army to live from hand to mouth—Morris signed contracts with individual merchants to feed the soldiers for a set fee. He opened the contracts to competitive bids and signed up those who made the lowest offers. Again, the goal was the illusion of solvency and orderly government. Morris depended on General Washington to assure the soldiers that their back pay would be given to them when the war was won.[17]

VII

The critics foreseen by Franklin were soon all too visible on Morris's Philadelphia horizon. Some noticed that the superintendent was inclined to settle claims that benefited his fellow merchants, especially those who had been his associates. For example, two of his former partners, John Ross and William Bingham, were paid substantial amounts, even though their claims were based on transactions before January 1, 1782.

One hostile observer of the political scene remarked: "The most trifling thing can not be done in any department [of the government] but through Mr. Morris." Joseph Reed went even further, claiming that Morris had become so powerful, Congress had nothing to do except "read despatches, return thanks, receive and return compliments &c".[18]

This was a political exaggeration, of course, but Morris's power, even when he used it to benefit his friends, did not bother the men who were in charge of Congress in 1781. They thought that an authoritative central government was what the United States needed. If Congress's power shrank, the power of the United States government would, they hoped, expand and acquire new vigor in Morris's administration.

One of the leaders of this group of national thinkers was the slim, unimpressive-looking delegate from Virginia, James Madison. Another delegate, Thomas Rodney of Delaware, summed up his first impression of Madison in his diary: "With some little reading from the law [he] is just from the College [of New Jersey] and possesses all the self conceit that is common to youth and inexperience." But Rodney admitted that in Madison's case, he had a "gracefulness and ease" that made "even the impertinence of youth and inexperience agreeable or at least not offensive."

Madison had graduated from college ten years earlier, but his slight 5'6" physique and shy manner still conveyed an impression of extreme youth. It took him over a year to nerve himself to speak in Congress. But his lively wit and his remarkable fund of ribald jokes made him popular after hours. The Virginian was soon making a large impact on Congress by insisting it was time for the United States to act like a nation instead of a collection of accidentally linked states.[19]

Madison was one of the few members of Congress who did not join the cheering when the Articles of Confederation were finally ratified by the last holdout, Maryland, on March 1, 1781, making them the constitutional law of the land. Philadelphia newspapers shouted huzzas. The editors declared the United States "were now ready to grow into greatness and consequence among the nations."

Note the use of the plural verb "were" for the United States, a grammatical confession of minimal unity. Madison, who had spent much of the previous decade on his parents' Virginia plantation, Montpelier, reading and thinking about politics and history, believed the opposite was much more likely to be the case. The United States "were" more likely to disintegrate.

In a 1780 letter he wrote to his friend Thomas Jefferson soon after Madison arrived in Congress, the new delegate pointed out that as long as the national legislature had the ability to print money, it had political power. But once the money depreciated to the status of waste paper, and Congress stopped printing it (in September 1779), its power dwindled. Congress became totally dependent on the states—and the states knew this. Around the same time, a troubled George Washington had reached a similar conclusion. "I see one head turning into thirteen," he told a correspondent.[20]

The Articles of Confederation did not solve this problem; they worsened it. They retained the original congressional policy of one vote per state, but stipulated that nine states had to agree on a resolution concerning even routine business. Since nine states were frequently the total represented at any particular time in Congress, that meant one negative vote could trump a majority of eight. A single state, defending one of its own politicians, or resisting a motion that seemed to be hostile to its interests, could paralyze the will of the majority. On larger issues such as taxation, the Articles required all thirteen states to reach unanimous agreement—a rule that would soon produce a national crisis.

Madison was one of the leaders in trying to restore Congress's political muscle by giving them the right to raise money. He argued that there were implied powers in the Articles of Confederation which gave the national legislature the ability to tax the states and even force them to pay the money they owed. But he hesitated to stretch these implied powers too far at first. He and his friends proposed an "impost"—a 5 percent tax on imports—as the least painful form of obtaining cash for Congress, and persuaded the delegates to approve it early in 1781.

As the year ebbed into 1782, the impost seemed to be going nowhere. Several states had yet to ratify it. Others attached unpalatable amendments to their approval, virtually demanding the right to use the money as they saw fit. In the course of the war, the states had contracted large debts they were struggling to pay. Massachusetts, the biggest spender, owed $5.4 million, Virginia almost $3 million. There was not much enthusiasm beyond the borders of Philadelphia for giving money to Congress to spend on behalf of the nation.[21]

VIII

Robert Morris embraced the impost as part of his program to achieve solvency. Although the tax would only raise an estimated $500 thousand a year, the superintendent of finance saw it as an opening wedge which would eventually include taxes on land and many other likely targets. But for the time being, Morris's main hope of achieving solvency lay in a November 1781 resolution passed by Congress. It declared that the national budget for 1782 would be $8 million, to be paid to the federal government in hard money, from taxes raised specifically for this purpose. Each state was given responsibility for a portion of this sum, depending on its population.

This $8 million would be evidence of America's willingness to assume the role of a unified nation. On February 9, 1782, Morris followed up the proposal with a circular letter to the governors of the states, bluntly explaining why the money was necessary. "The most recent and authentic information from Europe contains the reiterated determination on the part of France to grant us no further pecuniary aid. Spain appears to have neither the inclination nor the ability to afford any, and in Holland it can only be obtained from individuals who will always require security and . . . will not lend to the United States, who as you well know, have no security to give."

Morris inveighed against those who "flatter themselves with the hope of peace." On what was this hope founded? "Has the enemy given the slightest evidence of a desire for it? Instead of suing for peace, they talk only of war." A good example of Britain's truculence was their response to a recent offer from Holland to negotiate a separate peace. "When they might have got rid of one enemy with a word, they disdained it."

In a nasty reference to Tom Paine's prophecy in *Common Sense*, Morris wryly noted: "Years have elapsed since it was pretended that she [Britain] could not find the resources for another campaign, and yet campaigns have succeeded each other with increasing expence and are still like to go on." It was up to the states to furnish the men and money to drive the British out of New York and Charleston as soon as possible. Only then would there be any hope of a successful negotiation for peace.[22]

The influence of Morris's friend George Washington was visible in many parts of this circular letter. In his diary for February 8, 1782, Morris told of asking Washington and Secretary of Foreign Affairs Robert R. Livingston to read the letter, as well as one he was preparing for Congress. Morris said he would "hold them bound to avow" their approval of both letters, and made some changes at their suggestions.[23]

IX

The day after this urgent message was mailed to the governors, Superintendent Morris and General Washington demonstrated how much they recognized that the core of their problem was creating public opinion to support the superintendent of finance's economic program. They signed an agreement with Tom Paine, the man who had written some very nasty things about Morris at the height of the uproar over Arthur Lee's accusations against Silas Deane.

The agreement stated that they recognized Paine's abilities at "informing the people and rousing them into action." They offered him eight hundred dollars a year, to be paid by Robert R. Livingston, the secretary of foreign affairs, out of his secret-service funds. The agreement added that Paine's new job would remain confidential. Public knowledge might "injure the effect of Mr. Paine's publications," as well as "subject him to injurious personal reflections."

In a later memorandum, Morris attributed this unorthodox move to Washington, who said he felt sorry for the penniless Paine and hoped "some provision" could be made for him. We can be fairly certain that a good deal more than pity was involved in Washington's thinking. It was by no means the first time the general demonstrated that he knew the importance of public opinion. In 1780, he had ordered Shepherd Kollock, an artilleryman with peacetime printing experience, to start publishing a newspaper to supply the citizens of eastern New Jersey with pro-American news. The paper counteracted the flood of propaganda emanating from British-held New York.[24]

X

Two days after hiring Paine, Superintendent Morris sent the second letter he had shown to Washington and Livingston to John Hanson, the man who was doing as little work as possible as president of Congress. It was much more irascible than the letter Morris had sent to the governors. One suspects that the superintendent of finance, thanks to his proximity to the doings of the delegates, was aware of how feckless the national legislature was becoming.

Morris began by reporting his "pain" that three states, Maryland, Massachusetts, and Rhode Island, had not approved the impost. This meant it was not yet the law of the land and "our debts ... [were] unfunded and unprovided for." Hence no interest could be paid to Americans who had loaned large sums to Congress or held promissory notes for goods or services contributed to the army. "Those therefore who trusted us in our hour of distress are defrauded." Did anyone in Congress expect that foreigners would trust a government which had no credit with its own citizens? The idea was "madness," Morris all but snarled.

Even tougher talk was to come. Not a single state had levied the taxes to pay their share of the $8-million budget Congress had legislated in November. The first installment was due on April 1, 1782. "There appears to be no solicitude [concern] anywhere" for the support of this measure, "on which the salvation of our country depends," Morris wrote. The superintendent knew the reason for this inertia, of course. The Articles of Confederation had given Congress "the privilege of asking everything" and simultaneously granted each state "the power of granting nothing."

Knowing what was wrong was a very small consolation. It began to look more and more as if the government would have to operate on resources "known only to Him who knoweth all things," Morris mordantly concluded. That meant Europe would continue to gaze with astonishment at a nation which combined unparalleled boldness in begging for more foreign loans and making large claims in its terms for peace with "unparalleled indolence and imbecility of conduct."

Morris has been criticized by some historians for his abrasive style. Only in recent years have we learned that George Washington had given his imprimatur to this ferocious rhetoric. The general's influence was also visible in another section of Morris's lengthy diatribe—Congress's request for men to fill the Continental Army's regiments. Morris informed President Hanson that the states had sent officers but no men. Other officers, experienced men whose services entitled them to "respectful attention," were left without men to command.

Why should the federal government pay the salaries of these officers? If this situation continued, Morris proposed sending the unemployed officers back to their native states, who should then be obligated to pay their salaries. He enclosed an estimate prepared by his office (no doubt with General Washington's assistance) that the federal government would save $60 thousand a month if this was done. Since officers took their servants from the enlisted ranks, the departure of these captains and majors and colonels would give the army a "considerable reinforcement."[25]

Sending the officers home was a very unpleasant threat. The last thing any state wanted was a swarm of disgruntled soldiers in its midst. Probably the term that best describes what Morris (and Washington) were doing here is shock treatment. They were trying to jolt Congress and the nation out of their post-Yorktown self satisfaction before it was too late.

XI

Elsewhere in America, the war continued. Nothing brought this home more vividly than the December 1781 letters from General Nathanael Greene to John Rutledge, the governor of South Carolina. Greene's brilliant campaign had driven the British out of the interior of the state. His final blow was a December 1, 1781, assault on the British outpost at Dorchester, a few miles from Charleston. Greene personally led the attack, which was made by 400 cavalrymen. When the British recognized him, they panicked and thought his whole army was coming at them. After fierce skirmishing in which 30 or 40 loyalists were killed, and a cavalry clash that forced the enemy horsemen to retreat in disorder, the British abandoned the post and retreated into Charleston under cover of darkness.

But the enemy gave no sign of giving up the struggle. Greene told Rutledge that a "gentleman" who had just come from the city estimated there were "not less than 1000 Tories in arms." The enemy was also forming a "Negroe Corps" and some were already on duty. Although the British were now "pent up " in Charleston, "their force is formidable and they can make sudden incursions into the country." It was vital, if Greene's army were to prevent such assaults, that they have adequate food. Greene urged Rutledge to round up at least 2,500 cattle and start "stall feeding" them.[26]

A week later, Greene warned Governor Rutledge that he had heard bad news from Governor Nathan Brownson of Georgia. The British were urging the Cherokee Indians and other tribes to assault the frontiers of Georgia and South Carolina. "A considerable body" of warriors was coming at them; in Georgia, the attacking Indians had forced the Americans to devote most of their strength to defending the capital, Augusta. Greene could only conclude from this news and the way the British were throwing up all but impregnable defenses around Charleston that "the enemy have further designs upon this country."

Even more worrisome was the size of Greene's Continental army. He seldom had more than 1,000 regulars in his ranks. The 3,300-man British army in Charleston heavily outnumbered his soldiers; the 2,000 reinforcements he had received from Washington after Yorktown barely equaled the number of men (most of them Virginians) he lost when their enlistments expired and they had gone home. If the enemy received reinforcements and launched an offensive, that would "oblige us to fall back . . . and once more give the enemy command of the most fertile parts of this country." That could lead to a "change of sentiments" among rebel South Carolinians. In other words, unless the Continental Army protected the citizens of the state, they would switch sides.[27]

In a letter to Robert Morris, Greene reported that the interior of South Carolina was still in turmoil from "parties of disaffected" (also known as loyalists) who "conceal themselves in the thickets and swamps . . . and issue forth from these hidden recesses committing the most horrid murders and plunder and lay waste the country." This was the situation in "a very great part of South Carolina and Georgia." North Carolina was also still "troubled with this kind of banditti."[28]

As long as the British army remained in Charleston and Savannah, desperate loyalists clung to the hope of eventual victory. Yorktown did not eliminate this hope; in some ways the victory nurtured it by suggesting that peace negotiations might soon begin and the British would be able to claim possession of Georgia and South Carolina by virtue of the army's presence in their major ports and the savage guerilla war being waged by George III's adherents in the interior of the states.

The British had withdrawn their small force from North Carolina's chief port, Wilmington, on the approach of the 2,000 reinforcements Washington sent to Greene after Yorktown, but the interior of the state was still in turmoil. Western North Carolina, which had few slaves or large farms, had long been alienated from the coastal eastern section, where huge tobacco and rice plantations like those in Virginia and South Carolina flourished. Before the Revolution, a civil war had exploded when the westerners protested their lack of representation in the state assembly and corruption in the court system. After a pitched battle, seven men were executed and martial law imposed. These bitter memories made some of the "regulators," as the westerners were called, inclined to loyalism.

We have seen how a band of loyalists seized the governor, Thomas Burke, when General Greene was about to confer with him about bringing the southern army into the state to cow the king's men. Governor Burke's captor was loyalist Colonel David Fanning. He frequently commanded as many as 600 men, and was as aggressive and resourceful as the famed South Carolina rebel guerilla leaders, Colonels Thomas Sumter and Francis (The Swamp Fox) Marion.

There was no hope of the Carolinas or Georgia levying taxes to support his army, Greene told Robert Morris. Support must come from "the Northward or we cannot be kept together." His soldiers were virtually naked. "Not a rag of clothing has arrived for our troops." Even more important was money. Greene earnestly disagreed with Morris's decision not to pay the soldiers. "You cannot be insensible that it is impossible to keep an army together for any great length of time without some portion of pay."[29]

XII

Nothing summed up the situation in South Carolina more graphically than the post-Yorktown foray of Irish-born William Cunningham, who held the rank of major in a loyalist provincial regiment. At the beginning of the war, he was a popular young man, with a passion for fine horses. His fiery temper was sometimes a problem, but this did not trouble many people in the heavily Irish backcountry.

At first Cunningham became a rebel, although many cousins of the same name were loyalists. A dispute with the commanding officer of his regiment, who put Cunningham in irons for insubordination, prompted him to switch sides. He soon accumulated other grudges. A rebel had killed his younger brother, who was a cripple and an epileptic, and abused his father. Cunningham reportedly walked all the way from Savannah, Georgia, where he had fled from Whig persecution, and killed the man.

In 1781, Cunningham retreated to Charleston with other loyalists when the British abandoned the interior of South Carolina. He professed to be outraged when Governor Rutledge ordered the wives and children of loyalists who had fled to Charleston to leave their homes and join their husbands behind British lines. Rutledge was retaliating for a loyalist edict, which had forced wives of prominent rebels to leave their homes and join their husbands in exile in West Florida when the British won control of South Carolina in 1780.

Early in November, William Cunningham emerged from Charleston at the head of a regiment of horsemen. They were part of a force of five hundred loyalists under the leadership of a cousin, General Robert Cunningham. They soon split up and William, in command of about three hundred men, began a rampage of murder and destruction through the South Carolina backcountry that became known as "The Bloody Scout."

At Clouds Creek, Cunningham and his men surprised a twenty-man patriot detachment under Captain Stirling Turner. Cunningham had heard they were abusing the families of loyalists in the vicinity. After an exchange of shots, Turner's men realized they were badly outnumbered and tried to surrender. Cunningham killed all but two of them. James Butler, described as a "remarkably active" whig, who had reportedly killed a loyalist friend of Cunningham's, was cruelly tortured. His hands were cut off while he was still alive. His body was so badly mutilated, his wife recognized him only from a Bible in his pocket.

Cunningham and his men stopped at a nearby blacksmith's shop and ordered Oliver Towles to shoe their horses. After he finished, Cunningham killed Towles, his son, and a Negro helper and burned the shop.

Moving down the Saluda River, Cunningham burned mills and barns of prominent rebels. On November 19 (a month after the Yorktown surrender ceremony) he attacked a post commanded by Colonel Joseph Hayes, who had about twenty-four men in a well-built blockhouse. He too had reportedly been abusing loyalists. Hayes refused to surrender, hoping reinforcements would arrive. Cunningham's men set the roof of the blockhouse on fire and Hayes was forced to give up.

Cunningham decided to hang Hayes and one of his captains, Daniel Williams, from the pole of a fodder stack. When the rope broke, Cunningham hacked the two men to death with his sword. He let his men kill anyone else in the garrison against whom they had a grudge. Most of Cunningham's men had come from the district and were massacring former neighbors and friends in a spirit of berserk revenge.

Next, Cunningham turned to individual assassination. He rode up to the home of Lieutenant Governor James Wood, who was the commissioner of sequestered loyalist property. Cunningham dragged Wood out of his house and shot him. As he writhed in agony, his wife begged Cunningham to spare her husband. Bloody Bill, as he was now being called, hanged him from a convenient tree.

Colonel Leroy Hammond, a rebel militia leader, wrote General Nathanael Greene an anguished letter on December 2, 1782, describing Cunningham's swath of terror and death. He lamented that there was a regiment of rebel militia within twenty-five miles of Cunningham throughout his bloody scout but they could do nothing, because they had "not one round" of ammunition. Colonel Hammond managed to obtain some powder and bullets from Georgia, and the rebels set out in pursuit of Cunningham.

Bloody Bill was a canny guerilla. He split his command into small detachments and camped at night in the swamps. The rebels attacked and destroyed one of these detachments but the gunfire alarmed Cunningham and the rest of his command. They escaped their pursuers and reached the safety of the British lines around Charleston, where the local *Royal Gazette* published an article hailing his victories.[30]

XIII

On Nathanael Greene's staff was an officer who had an answer to the mindless violence the British were encouraging, thanks to the weakness of the Southern army. Colonel John Laurens, with his diplomatic triumph (as the Americans saw it) in France and his exemplary conduct at Yorktown, seemed almost divinely equipped to tackle what he saw as the climactic challenge of his military career. If South Carolina could raise another three thousand fighting men, they could attack the British in Charleston and drive them into the sea.

Laurens knew exactly where he could find those missing men. He wanted the state legislature to offer freedom to three thousand slaves if they would enlist in the American army for the duration of the war.

When Washington departed Yorktown for Philadelphia, Laurens headed for South Carolina. The commander in chief knew what his aide was hoping to achieve. In 1778, during the winter at Valley Forge, the colonel had discussed his idea with Washington and with his father, Henry Laurens, who was at the time the president of Congress. Before the war, Henry had been one of the biggest slave traders in America. Along with wealth, he had acquired a repugnance for the ugly business.

Both older men told the idealistic young colonel that they agreed with him in principle, but they doubted that any southern legislator would approve arming slaves. The fear of an insurrection and a race war was already haunting too many minds. In South Carolina, where blacks outnumbered whites, the fear was especially acute. Equally strong was the conviction that without slavery, the southern economy would collapse.

Henry Laurens called himself a "conditional terminator"(of slavery); he was ready to throw his influence into the struggle if and when he thought there was any chance of success. After discussing the idea with southern delegates to the Continental Congress in 1778, the father had glumly concluded that the time for action remained distant. "I will undertake to say there is not a man in America of your opinion," he told his son.

After much discussion but no action, President Laurens finally insisted that John must drop the idea; an individual could not undertake such a radical step; it would require "mature deliberation by the collective wisdom" of all the states in the union. General Washington apparently shared this opinion.[31]

John Laurens had shelved his proposal but he disagreed with both men. In 1778, Washington had approved the creation of a black regiment in Rhode Island. The ex-slaves had fought well in several battles. The following year, when the British invaded and conquered Georgia, John had revived his plan and enlisted his friend Alexander Hamilton as a supporter. Born in the West Indies, Hamilton had seen the slave system close up and loathed it. He composed a passionate letter to his friend John Jay, who was president of the Continental Congress at the time. Laurens, on his way to South Carolina to propose the plan to the state legislature, delivered the letter personally.

In 1776, John Jay had tried to insert a gradual emancipation plan in the New York state constitution, which he wrote almost single-handed. But the state's legislators had rejected the clause. Now he had the satisfaction (as did Laurens) of seeing the Continental Congress pass a resolution urging the states of Georgia and South Carolina to raise a brigade of "three thousand able bodied negroes." Congress would pay the owners of the slaves a thousand dollars for each recruit. If the blacks served honorably to the end of the war, they would be given their freedom and a bounty of fifty dollars. Some historians have called this measure the first emancipation proclamation.[32]

Unfortunately, like many other proposals Congress sent to the states, this 1779 resolution went nowhere. When John Laurens presented it to the South Carolina legislature, it was "received with horror" by the lawmakers, all of whom owned slaves. One outraged member of the state senate proposed an immediate secession from the United States to join Georgia in renewed loyalty to George III.[33]

When the British invaded South Carolina in 1780, John Laurens served in the opposing army that eventually surrendered at Charleston. In a bitter letter to Washington, he condemned his countrymen for their lack of foresight. If they had created his black battalions, Charleston might have been successfully defended. Now, with the South Carolina state government back in business, John was determined to renew his proposal.

This time he had a new ally: General Nathanael Greene. He was from Rhode Island, and had seen that state's black regiment perform in battle. He had discussed Laurens's idea with him many times and was eager to support him. On December 3, after routing the British from Dorchester, he wrote impatiently to his aide, Lewis Morris: "Has Col Laurens got to headquarters?"[34]

By mid-December 1781, Laurens was on his way to Governor Rutledge with a letter from Greene, urging black enlistments. Greene argued that the black soldiers offered South Carolina "double security." They would help defend the state against a British offensive—and they would enable Greene to overwhelm the enemy in an attack on Charleston if the British chose to stay on the defensive. If Governor Rutledge and his council agreed, Greene wanted the men as soon as possible.[35]

Governor Rutledge was familiar with John Laurens and his proposal. He had opposed it in 1779 and he was no more enthusiastic this time. Rutledge's council agreed with him, noting that the previous assembly had "almost unanimously rejected" the idea. However, the governor diplomatically told Laurens he would let the next legislature, scheduled to be chosen later in December 1781, have the last word.[36]

XIV

Colonel Laurens promptly declared himself a candidate for the legislature and was easily elected. While he waited for them to convene, he decided maybe the answer to his problem was some additional military glory. The British, trying to guarantee their supply lines, had put a 400-man garrison on Johns Island, between the estuaries of the North Edisto and Stono Rivers. This enabled them to gather food from the nearby mainland, where many of the population were loyalists. Laurens was ecstatic when Colonel Henry Lee, commander of Greene's cavalry, proposed an attack on the relatively isolated garrison by storming across an inlet called New Cut that was waist deep at low tide. The British guarded this vulnerable point with a galley and two gunboats, but Lee thought their crews were inclined to grow somnolent during the midnight hours.

"No lover was ever so anxious to hear from his mistress when he expected an assignation as I am to receive a letter from you," Laurens told Greene. Because his commission predated Lee's, Laurens was in command of the expedition. At midnight on January 13, 1782, they assembled their attack force. Behind them, General Greene put his whole army in motion to support them, in case the British in Charleston counterattacked. The excited Laurens thought the assault might trigger a "general action"—an all-out battle that would decide who was in control of South Carolina.

Alas, everything went wrong. Laurens divided the attacking force into two columns to guarantee a silent approach. The second column's guide abruptly disappeared in the middle of their march: he may have been a loyalist double agent. The column wandered helplessly in the darkness, floundering through swamps and across rivulets for over an hour while Lee and Laurens waited anxiously at the water's edge for their appearance.

Colonel Lee decided to send his men across the inlet; they reached the island with no difficulty, while the sleepy British lookouts on the galley called "All's safe." Meanwhile, the tide kept rising, and there was no sign of the second column. Lee and Laurens had to recall the men who had already crossed the New Cut. The returnees were forced to wade through chest-deep water and were thoroughly soaked and shivering in the cold January night when they reached the other side.

When Greene arrived with the rest of his army, he decided to take the island in a daylight frontal assault. He brought up artillery to disperse the galleys and gunboat but they briskly returned the fire and refused to budge. That night the British evacuated the island without losing a man. Laurens's glorious general action faded into a large disappointment. "We have got territory," Greene wrote to Governor Rutledge, "but we mist [*sic*] the great object of our enterprise"—the British troops. In a letter to John Hanson, the president of Congress, the general added that "the failure . . . was not a little mortifying to me but much more so to Laurens and Lee."[37]

XV

A week later, a depressed Colonel Laurens headed for Jacksonboro, a small village on the Edisto River, where the newly elected state legislature hoped they could meet in relative safety. General Greene's army was nearby, camped across the probable route British attackers would take from Charleston, thirty-five miles away. Laurens was still determined to press his call for black regiments.

His chief backer, General Greene, wrote another letter to Governor Rutledge, in which he called the situation in Georgia and South Carolina "critical." The British government's "obstinacy," and the unlikelihood of any money or men coming from the Northern states prompted him to repeat his recommendation to raise the black regiments.

Greene told Rutledge he had intelligence reports from Charleston that the British were already arming three thousand blacks who had deserted to their side of the war. (The actual figure was seven hundred.) He raised the specter of the British insisting in peace negotiations that the principle of *uti possidetis* entitled them to claim Georgia and South Carolina. He warned that the Northern states might well be inclined to "giving you up" when they found that the southerners had possessed the means to drive the British out of both states but South Carolina had failed to use their most obvious source of fresh manpower.[38]

Also very much on Laurens's side was George Washington. He wrote to him early in 1782, discussing a report that British reinforcements were on their way to Charleston. "I know of nothing that can be opposed to them with such a prospect of success as the corps you have proposed to be levied in Carolina," he declared.[39]

In the legislature, Colonel Laurens took his seat and quickly introduced his proposal for the black regiments—with a new clause that he hoped would take the opponents by surprise. Governor Rutledge was urging confiscation of the lands and slaves of hundreds of loyalists who had joined the British in the previous two years of carnage. Why not raise the black regiments from the thousands of slaves the state was about to seize from the loyalists?

Laurens's proposal was backed by a number of fellow legislators, including the future historian of the war in the South, David Ramsay. For a while, it looked as if the young colonel was mustering strong support from other South Carolinians outside the legislature. Governor Rutledge described the debate as a "hard battle" which at times made him "very much alarmed."

Perhaps the most significant speech was made by former Continental congressman Aedanus Burke, who claimed that the plan was aimed at the emancipation of all the slaves in South Carolina. Burke implied rather strongly that Greene's Rhode Island birth made him suspect on this point. "The Northern people," Burke wrote to a friend, "regard the condition in which we hold our slaves in a light different from us." Then came a line that aroused one of South Carolinians' deepest fears: Burke recalled being told by a northern delegate to the Continental Congress that it would be a good idea if "our whites and blacks inter-married." The result would be a "hardy excellent race . . . fit to bear our climate."

Colonel Laurens's proposal was put to a vote. A pleased Governor Rutledge was soon reporting: "About 12 or 15 were for it & about 100 against it—I now hope it will rest for ever & a day."[40]

John Laurens was unreconciled to his defeat. In a letter to General Washington, he attributed it to "the howlings of a triple-headed monster in which prejudice, avarice & pusillanimity were united." Washington's reply attempted to console his idealistic young aide with the observations of an older man who had discarded any and all illusions about human nature. In many ways, it is one of the most important letters Washington ever wrote. It cast a piercing light on the later years of the American Revolution. "The spirit of freedom which at the commencement of this contest would have gladly sacrificed every thing to the attainment of its object has long since subsided, and every selfish passion has taken its place. It is not the public but the private interest which influences the generality of mankind nor can the Americans any longer boast of an exception."[41]

Back with Greene's army, Laurens found the general also sympathetic. Colonel Henry Lee, depressed by the failure of the attack on Johns Island, had resigned and gone home to Virginia. Greene offered Laurens his job—commanding the light infantry of the army, which included Lee's "legion," a mixed regiment of cavalry and infantry. Laurens would be constantly on patrol, ready to repel British foragers as well as more serious forays into the countryside. Still hoping military glory would give him the prestige he needed to win support for his black regiments, the unhappy colonel accepted with alacrity.

XVI

The situation in Georgia remained even more uncertain than in the Carolinas. General Nathanael Greene's counteroffensive in South Carolina had sparked a resurgence of rebel attacks in the interior, but British regulars and well-armed loyalists retained a firm grasp on Savannah and its vicinity—with the strength to launch retaliatory assaults whenever it suited them.

As 1782 began, General Greene decided he had acquired an officer who could make something out of almost nothing, thanks to his bravado and daring. It was not an accident that burly, pugnacious Brigadier General Anthony Wayne of Pennsylvania was known as "Mad Anthony." He loved to attack the enemy and often professed indifference to being outnumbered. Wayne had acquired his reputation on many battlefields since 1775. His most notable triumph was his 1779 midnight assault on the British fort at Stony Point on the Hudson River below West Point in which he had killed or captured the entire garrison.

Before the siege of Yorktown, Wayne had served under Lafayette in an uneven struggle to prevent Lord Cornwallis and his army from ravaging Virginia. Lafayette complained their army was so small, they could not even get beaten decently. At one point, hoping to attack the British rear guard as they crossed the James River, Wayne advanced aggressively at the head of his 600-man Pennsylvania brigade. Suddenly out of the trees debouched almost the entire British army. It looked as if Wayne were trapped. Instead of ordering a headlong retreat, Wayne roared "fix bayonets" and led a frontal assault on the startled British. It checked them long enough for Wayne to extricate his men with minor losses.

Wayne would need all his military skills to accomplish anything in Georgia with the army Greene gave him. It consisted of about a hundred Continental cavalry and four hundred and fifty mounted militia from South Carolina and Georgia. Wayne eagerly accepted the assignment. Like many combative generals, he did not perform well as a subordinate. He always wanted an independent command.[42]

General Wayne entered Georgia with his tiny army on January 19, 1782. He had orders from General Greene to do his utmost to end the civil war that continued to rage between rebels and loyalists. Greene particularly urged Wayne "to put a stop as much as possible to that cruel custom of putting people to death after they have surrendered themselves prisoners." Greene also wanted Wayne to check "the practice of plundering" which also had "ruinous consequences" to any hope of peaceful relationships in the countryside.

To bolster Wayne's role, on the same day, Greene wrote to the new governor of Georgia, Alexander Martin, a Rhode Islander who had settled in the state some years before the Revolution. He urged Martin to do his utmost to discourage plundering. It was certain to undermine "all government" if it was permitted to flourish. At least as important, the southern commander urged Martin to "open a door to the disaffected" by offering amnesty and forgiveness to the loyalists. It was "always dangerous to push people to a state of desperation."[43]

Wayne's mere appearance in Georgia badly rattled the British in Savannah. The royal governor, James Wright, rushed a letter to Lord George Germain, the secretary of state for America, claiming that Wayne's army consisted of "3000 Continentals horse & foot together"—

three times the number of men that were in the entire Southern army. Wright was even more upset by Greene's recommendation of amnesty for loyalists. He feared "the great many truly loyal inhabitants here" would "go off and make the best terms they can." It was a graphic glimpse of the psychological impact of the Yorktown victory, and more particularly of Cornwallis's failure to protect the loyalists when Washington rejected Article X of the surrender terms.[44]

Briskly advancing toward Savannah, General Wayne cleared British outposts from the environs of the port city and dared the British army commander, Brigadier Sir Allured Clarke, to come out and fight him. Clarke had two thousand trained British and provincial troops, plus perhaps another thousand loyalist refugees willing and able to fight. Also ready, willing, and able were a hefty portion of the numerous fugitive slaves. The brigadier could have annihilated Wayne but he must have believed the rumor that Mad Anthony had three thousand men; he declined to leave his formidable fortifications.[45]

As the enemy retreated into Savannah, they burned great quantities of rice that Wayne could have used to feed his men. With his army on horseback, Wayne was unable to stop them; cavalry was at a disadvantage on the narrow roads through the woods, from which infantry could decimate them firing on their flanks. He begged Greene to send him some "natural infantry" but the southern commander could not spare a man. Instead, Greene shared with Wayne his profound alarm about a letter General Washington had written to him at the end of December, reporting that three British regiments and a detachment of Hessian grenadiers had sailed from New York, reportedly for Charleston.[46]

Wayne had better luck with a letter to Governor Martin, in which he reiterated Nathanael Greene's proposal to offer amnesty to Georgia loyalists. The governor persuaded the legislature to issue a proclamation, which had a dramatic impact. Swarms of loyalist militiamen accepted the government's forgiveness and laid down their guns, confirming Royal Governor Wright's morose prediction. Wayne declared himself delighted to find a way to win his local war without killing anyone. In a letter to his wife, Polly, he declared: "I am satiate [sic] of this horrid trade of blood & would much rather shame one poor *savage* than destroy twenty."[47]

In a few months, Wayne would demonstrate that he did not take this preference for not destroying savages very seriously. Meanwhile, he continued to beg General Greene and Governor Martin to send him more men. Mad Anthony grew almost strident when his three hundred South Carolina mounted militia went home after two months service. At the end of February he grumbled to Greene that duty in Georgia was "much more difficult than that of the children of Israel, they only had to make bricks out of straw but we [have] had provision, forage and almost every article of war to provide without money; boats, bridges &c to build without materials except what we took from the stump & what is more difficult than all, to make whigs of tories."[48]

Still, Wayne could proudly report that he had "wrested this state out of the hands of the enemy . . . with the help of a few regular dragoons." But that was far from solving the problem of how to keep it "without some additional force." He reported that the British had recently received a reinforcement of Choctaw Indians, brought by boat. Another three hundred Choctaws were coming overland, led by a British commissary, to attack Georgia's western border. Wayne sent a troop of cavalry to confront them and they retreated.

Meanwhile, Wayne and his horsemen captured twenty-three Creek Indians "with every insignia of war upon them." They were planning to meet a pack train bearing gifts for their tribe from the British in Savannah. Wayne's horsemen attacked the pack train, which was guarded by some thirty mounted Indians and loyalists. The guards fled into a nearby swamp and the Americans captured ninety-three horses and packs. Wayne said he was treating the captured Creek warriors "with kindness." He was sending Joseph Cornell, a trader who had dealt with the Creeks for thirty years, to their villages to calm them down.[49]

XVII

In Philadelphia, on February 19, 1782, the *Pennsylvania Packet* printed a copy of George III's speech from the throne to the opening session of Parliament in November. Continental Congressman Oliver Wolcott of Connecticut sent a copy to his daughter Laura with the comment that "the war must be expected to continue." But he complacently added that if the states "exert themselves," the business would "terminate well."[50]

George Washington was far was less confident about the states exerting themselves. In a letter to General Nathanael Greene, the commander in chief said he hoped the speech would convince the states of "the necessity" of producing the men and supplies that Congress had requested. He had done his best to bolster the national legislature with two circular letters to the governors, in which he had used "every argument I could invent."[51]

George III's speech galvanized an associate member of the Morris-Washington partnership, Tom Paine. He rushed a note to Superintendent Morris, informing him that he had requested all the newspapers in Philadelphia for space to comment on the speech the following day. He would not have room or time to "enter into the whole business of revenue" in that article but he planned to include some paragraphs that would create "an animated disposition in the country" to read more on the subject in subsequent articles.[52]

In his opening salvo, Paine lashed out at the "snivelling hypocrisy" of the king's speech. He portrayed George III as an idiot who was driving headlong into a flood of disasters unaware that the waters of woe were "closing over his head." This was vintage Paine, full of the vigor with which he had assailed the king in 1776.

A follow-up article on the federal government's need for revenue was its polar opposite. It was a lugubrious bore, full of vapid generalities before Paine finally got to the point—the states should levy one set of taxes for themselves and another set to raise money for Congress. One biographer has remarked that it was the difference between the spontaneous Paine and Paine the hired hack.[53]

Over the next two months, Paine met Washington and Morris at least once a week. The two leaders even joined the down-at-the-heel journalist for an evening of oysters and conversation in his rented rooms. Not a few critics sneered at Paine's sudden conversion to taxation. But it seems clear that Washington and Morris had convinced him that a strong central government was crucial to the survival of the United States. Whether he could transfer that conviction to the newspaper readers of the nation was a large unanswered question.

XVIII

Behind the scenes, there were hints of growing desperation in the office of the superintendent of finance. The states continued to drag their fiscal feet on raising money for Congress. Morris belabored the hapless president John Hanson, with warnings and exhortations, but the only result was to make this gentleman yearn even more sullenly for retirement.[54]

Like a general attacking another flank hoping to find a weakness, Morris pressed Congress to consider specific taxes on land, a poll tax on voters, and a sales tax on liquor. Congress debated these proposals in the early months of 1782 and referred them to a committee headed by none other than Arthur Lee. The troublemaker had, with his brother Richard Henry's help, won election as a delegate to Congress early in March 1782. When Lee returned from France, Samuel Adams had persuaded Harvard University to confer on him an honorary degree of doctor of laws to polish his tarnished prestige.

Along with Lee, the committee consisted of Samuel Osgood of Massachusetts, who publicly opposed Morris's program like most of the delegates from that state, and Abraham Clark of New Jersey, a self-styled "people's lawyer" who suspected everyone who was rich of corruption and double-dealing. Predictably, they produced a totally negative report, dismissing Morris's proposals because they would supposedly operate "very unequally" on both the states and individuals. Worse, the committee recommended a ban on all federal taxation until Congress settled its financial accounts with the states. Unraveling hundreds of monetary tangles in the poorly kept records of the past six years could easily consume a decade.[55]

Even before he got to Congress, Arthur Lee had been hard at work in Virginia, trying to destroy James Madison because he supported Superintendent Morris's program. Lee tried to get the Virginia legislature to bar Madison from Congress, because he had exceeded a supposed three-year term limit. The lawmakers had voted the limit years earlier and generally ignored it. Madison's friends came to his rescue, repealing the three-year law. But Madison had no illusions that this minor defeat would discourage Lee. "No delegate who refuses to league with him in his war against the financier must expect to be long at ease in his post," he wrote to a Virginia friend.[56]

With Lee and his friends spewing hostility at Morris's program, the superintendent's worst fears were realized on April 1, 1782. That was the day the first quarterly payment on the year's budget was due: the states were supposed to deposit $2 million in the Bank of North America. Instead of that robust sum, there was nothing, not a single dollar. Over the next several weeks, $5,500 trickled in from the state of New Jersey. It was, Morris wryly remarked, about a fourth of what was needed to run the federal government for a single day. "The habitual inattention of the states," the superintendent of finance told Congress, "has reduced us to the brink of ruin."[57]

In New York, Judge William Smith and British intelligence chief Captain George Beckwith read reports of spies and letters of loyalist sympathizers from Philadelphia, looking for signs of the revolution's collapse. The mere hint of such a prospect would be rushed to London to encourage the supporters of stubbornly bellicose George III. How much longer could Robert Morris and Generals Washington, Greene, and Wayne continue to make something out of nothing?

Chapter Five

Uncrowning a King

IF GEORGE III HAD KNOWN the disarray into which the American Revolution was stumbling, he would have been a very happy man. Instead, the weeks after the news of Yorktown reached England on November 25, 1781, were full of worry and anxiety for the patriot king.

Neither His Majesty nor the hardliners in the North ministry were in favor of continuing the American war with the same strategy—invading the continent at crucial points and smashing any and all resistance with masses of infantry and swarms of cavalry. That was the illusory war of 1776, which had produced little except frustration and defeat. With France in the war, supplying the Americans with money and weapons, there was no hope of totally subduing the fractious rebels. Moreover, the French had stunned the English by achieving naval superiority in 1781 and were threatening precious British possessions in the West Indies and India.

George III asked Lord George Germain to come up with a new plan. The American secretary produced a memorandum which proposed retention of Savannah, Charleston, and New York. He argued that in all three ports, the rebel governments would be unable to stop profit-hungry Americans from trading with British merchants—an already widespread practice. Simultaneously, the two southern ports would be invaluable as staging sites from which to wage war in the West Indies. Troops could be transported to them during the hot, unhealthy summer months, when mortality among white men in the islands was high. Meanwhile, the utmost effort would be made to regain naval superiority in North America and the West Indies.

Some ships could be used to blockade or attack rebel-held ports, further crippling the already wounded American economy. Ships could also be used to deliver weapons and ammunition to loyalists and Indians elsewhere in North America, particularly along the Canadian border and in northern Massachusetts around the port of Penobscot. Germain was convinced that a great many Americans had become disillusioned with the Continental Congress and the French alliance, and were ready to fight for the king if they could be assured of strong support.

Extending this idea, the American secretary recommended operations to reoccupy Rhode Island and seize Delaware, which had numerous loyalists, would be easy to defend, and could provide "plenty of provisions for the subsistence of an army." Finally, he argued that the "colonies appear to be under the control of their general" rather than Congress, and Washington was now closely connected to the French, as the Yorktown victory made clear. That meant there was a good chance that the Americans' "natural aversion to the French nation" might eventually incline them to return to their connections with England "if we remain in a situation to receive them."[1]

The memorandum was submitted to the cabinet and sporadically discussed without much enthusiasm during the month of December. Nevertheless, it had considerable influence on Lord North's thinking about the war. This became evident on December 12, 1781, when Sir James Lowther, an independent country gentleman who controlled nine parliamentary seats in the north of England and had long supported the government, introduced a motion that the war in America "has proved ineffectual." Lowther called for a vote on whether further attempts to reduce the Americans to obedience should be abandoned.

Lord North responded to this motion with a combination of combative denunciation and consummate vagueness. If the motion passed, North said it would mean the abandonment of valuable territory held by the British army in America, which would almost certainly be needed as bargaining chips if England hoped to achieve an honorable peace. Abandonment would also make it impossible for His Majesty's army and navy to continue the war against France and Spain in that part of the world. Was that any way to deal with these inveterate enemies, whom Lowther had admitted were powerful foes?

Switching his tone, North launched a rambling discourse on "the future mode of the prosecution of the war." He hinted that the government had plans but asked the members to consider whether it was "either wise or politic for a man in high and responsible office" to say too much about them. He reiterated that he did not think it would be wise to continue the American war "on the same scale" as they had fought it in the past. He hoped this would satisfy gentlemen such as Mr. Lowther who feared continuing it in the previous mode would make England easy prey to France, Spain, and her latest European enemy, Holland.[2]

George III was in complete agreement with this approach. In a letter he wrote around this time, it was obvious that he had read and approved Germain's memorandum. His Majesty insisted that "though internal Continental operations in North America are not advisable," the prosecution of the war was not only still possible, it was a vital necessity to avoid "an ignominious peace."[3]

After three days of furious debate, the opposition, led by Edmund Burke and Charles James Fox, summoned every available vote to support Lowther's motion. The king's supporters were equally energetic. In a roll call taken at 2 a.m., the motion failed, 220 to 179. North had managed a seemingly impossible feat—he had united the three groups into which the king's backers were splitting: those who remained determined to subdue the Americans one way or another, those who wanted to switch Britain's main effort to an offensive against France and Spain, and those who were ready to abandon America eventually, but not for the moment, because it might lead to a humiliating peace.[4]

II

In the debate on the Lowther motion, Lord George Germain was the only member of the government who voiced unqualified determination to subdue the Americans. In fact, when he rose to speak in support of Lord North, his remarks came close to undermining the first minister's artful balancing act. He agreed with North's assurance that the war in America would now be fought in a new, restricted way. But he added: "The moment that the House [of Commons] recognized the independence of America, the British empire was ruined." North had carefully avoided mentioning this explosive topic.

Not a few members decided North's vagueness was little more than a smokescreen for a continuation of an offensive war. Their suspicions were more or less correct. From North's point of view, Germain exacerbated the problem by displays of rhetorical arrogance. At one point the American secretary exclaimed that he "would not be browbeaten or clamoured out of office . . . and he would never be the minister who conceded independence to the Americans." He even dared the opposition to impeach him.

This bluster only aroused Germain's critics to new fury. One of them rose to declaim Edmund Burke's favorite theme, George III's control of Parliament. "Let the noble Lord look around him and he will see the reasons why he is not impeached. He will see a band of hired men ready to support him . . . Give us an honest Parliament and then let us see if the noble Lord would desire to find security in impeachment!"[5]

Not a single member of the cabinet supported the American secretary. Lord North arose from the treasury bench, where the government leaders normally sat during debates, and moved to a seat behind it, leaving Germain in not-so-splendid isolation. This was not cowardice or even timidity on North's part; it was shrewd politics. He was letting Germain appeal to the dwindling numbers that supported a total victory in America, and simultaneously saying he wanted to continue the war in some less aggressive way.

North was emboldened by the knowledge that the opposition was not much more united than George III's forces. One member said he supported the Lowther motion simply because he thought it meant America would no longer be the main theater of the war. On the other hand, Charles James Fox called for the immediate abandonment of New York, Charleston, and Savannah, and the acknowledgment of American independence. Then there was William Petty, Lord Shelburne, and his small but eloquent following. He regularly voted with the opposition but was opposed to granting America independence.

No less than 154 of the House of Commons's 530 members had been absent when the vote on the Lowther motion was taken. As Parliament adjourned for the holidays, George III knew a great deal depended on how these absentees would vote when the legislature reconvened on January 21, 1782. That thought did not make for a restful Christmas season for the patriot king—or his first minister.[6]

III

On December 21, 1781, the day after Parliament adjourned, Lord North informed George III that he had decided it was time to give the Americans independence. The agitated king recounted the conversation in a letter to the secretary of state for northern affairs, Lord Stormont. His Majesty opined that he did not think North believed what he said. The king suspected "he painted his opinion in a stronger light than he felt in hopes of staggering mine."

When North insisted he was speaking with complete sincerity, the king forbade him to "open his mind to the whole cabinet." But he gave North permission to discuss his opinion with Stormont and his colleague, Wills Hill, Lord Hillsborough, the secretary of state for southern affairs. They would be the men in charge of peace negotiations, if and when such an appalling (to the king) transaction took place.[7]

George III's insistence that North remain silent was rooted in signs that support for a continued war in America was weakening in the cabinet as well as in Parliament. But the king's willingness to let North meet with Stormont and Hillsborough was hardly evidence that His Majesty's convictions were also wavering. Both men were the hardest of hard-liners who had staked their political careers on returning rebellious America to obedience. The king obviously expected the two foreign secretaries to talk Lord North out of his latest funk, and restore him to the ranks of royal supporters.

This is more or less what happened when North met with them two days later. North gave them a replay of his performance before the king, expressing his weariness and hopelessness about the seemingly endless war and his trepidations about how to raise more money to support it. But he did not say a word about independence, and he admitted that it would be disastrous to go public with his discouragement. He assured Stormont and Hillsborough that he had no intention of discussing peace terms, in Parliament or out of it. The conference ended with the first minister admitting it might be best to see how things developed in other theaters of the global war.[8]

IV

While Parliament was adjourned for the holidays, the two chief hard-liners, Lord George Germain and First Lord of the Admiralty Sandwich, grimly went ahead with implementing the new tactics. On January 2, Germain sent a letter to Sir Henry Clinton, telling him not to expect any large reinforcements. But the American secretary assured the commander in chief that vacancies in his current regiments caused by disease and desertion would be filled by a shipment of 2,200 new recruits from England. Clinton was also told that all the current bases would be held to enable the fleet and army to raid "ports and towns along the seacoasts." Germain also thought the British-controlled ports could have a potent psychological impact on the loyalists. He urged Clinton to give "all possible encouragement" to them in every province.

Another Germain letter went to Governor General Sir Frederick Haldimand in Quebec, telling him that the king warmly approved his negotiations with the breakaway Americans in Vermont. Germain told Haldimand these talks should be "the primary object of your attention." The American secretary also approved Haldimand's continued encouragement of Indians and loyalists to attack American settlements along the northern and western borders of the colonies.[9]

Meanwhile, Lord Sandwich was reacting to Yorktown and the French seizure of naval superiority with ferocious energy. He was determined to protect the West Indies, in particular Jamaica, which was now the reported target of a combined Spanish-French offensive. Sandwich was pleasantly surprised to find Lord George Germain was giving him all the help in his power. The two men had often quarreled because the first lord had tended to deplete the navy in American waters to bolster the home fleet.

Germain found new military commanders and ordered them to take charge of the islands' defenses. He joined Sandwich in persuading the cabinet to send an order to the admiral now in command in New York, Robert Digby, to dispatch every ship he could spare to the West Indies. Simultaneously the cabinet approved Sandwich's order to Admiral Sir George Rodney to take command of a 12-ship fleet and sail as soon as possible for the precious sugar islands. The aging Rodney had returned to England to recuperate from celebrating the fortune he and his officers had made when he captured the West Indies island of St. Eustatius after London declared war on the Dutch.

Subsequently, Sandwich added another five ships to Rodney's squadron. The desperation in everyone's mind was vividly apparent when the admiral sailed from Plymouth on January 10, 1782, in the teeth of a ferocious westerly gale whose mountainous seas almost drove his ships onto the Breton coast. "The fate of this empire is in your hands," the first lord of the Admiralty wrote to Rodney as he departed. "I have no reason to wish it should be in any other."[10]

V

Lord Sandwich also dispatched reinforcements to India to enable the Far East fleet to deal with French Admiral Bailli de Suffren. With them went four battalions of infantry and a regiment of cavalry. They were virtually sailing off the planet, as far as London was concerned. It would take them at least three months to reach the subcontinent and no one knew whether there would be any British left in India to welcome them. There were alarming rumors that virtually every native in the northern India state of Bengal, the East India Company's largest possession, had turned against the British after fully a third of the population died in a horrendous famine. A confederacy of Indian princes was gathering to "drive the Fringies out." The English, they claimed, "had alienated all hearts." At the southern end of the subcontinent, Sultan Hyder Aly continued to rampage, besieging isolated British forts and menacing Madras, The East India Company's headquarters in the Carnatic region.[11]

Lord North himself was by no means idle during the Christmas holidays. He spent a good part of his time exploring the possibility of a separate peace, either with America or France. With the first minister's approval, David Hartley, member of Parliament and an old friend of Benjamin Franklin's, tried to persuade the ambassador to open secret negotiations with Great Britain.

Hartley pretended to respond to a personal letter Franklin had written to him in December 1781. The ambassador had wondered if there was any way to end this "devilish" war. In his reply, Hartley hoped that America was ready to enter into a separate peace with Great Britain, and that "no formal recognition of independence" would be required. The volunteer negotiator intimated that the alliance with France was the only barrier to ending the war.

Hartley told Franklin he was ready to introduce a bill calling for a ten-year truce between England and America. Lord North had given it his approval. North claimed to want only the assurance that Franklin had the authority to negotiate for Congress to open talks.[12]

Franklin's reply must have stunned Hartley and further discouraged Lord North. The ambassador wondered where Hartley had gotten the idea that the Americans were ready to abandon the French. "I believe there is not a man in America, a few English tories excepted, that would not spurn at the thought of deserting a noble and generous friend for the sake of a truce with an unjust and cruel enemy."

Franklin expressed bewilderment that his expression of a "simple wish for peace" could make Hartley think that Americans would accept a ten-year truce during which they would promise not to assist France while England continued to make war on her. If Congress ever ordered him to accept such terms, he would "instantly renounce" his commission as ambassador and "banish myself for ever from so infamous a country."

The ambassador acidly informed Hartley that he had the authority to negotiate peace, together with fellow Americans John Jay, John Adams, and Henry Laurens. But any negotiation would be carried on "in conjunction with our [French] Allies" as required in the "solemn treaties" they had jointly signed.[13]

Franklin's dudgeon was increased, he later told Hartley, when the ambassador discovered evidence of Lord North's duplicity. While Hartley was piously vowing Lord North only wanted peace with America so he could lead the English people in a renewed war with France, the first minister had another emissary in Versailles, exploring whether the French would consider a separate peace, enhanced by many "very advantageous propositions, in case they would abandon America." Among the propositions was the return of Canada to France—an indication of the sacrifices George III was ready to make to avert American independence.

Foreign Minister Vergennes had rejected the offer as vehemently as Franklin had rebuffed Hartley. The emissary had come from Lord Stormont, suggesting that First Minister North's pretended divorce from Lord George Germain and his fellow hard-liners in Parliament was far from sincere.[14]

VI

The failure of these peace feelers left Lord North with only one option—beyond changing George III's mind, which he considered impossible. The first minister had to jettison one of the government's hard-liners in hopes of appeasing and otherwise dividing some of the opposition. The obvious candidate was Lord George Germain. Lord Sandwich had almost as many critics but he was not so closely linked to the war in America. Throwing him overboard might also disrupt the navy at a time when the sailors were England's last hope of winning an acceptable peace.

Germain soon provided the ammunition Lord North needed for his removal. In New York, Major General Sir Henry Clinton was clamoring for permission to resign and return to England to answer the assault on his reputation being engineered by the backers of Lord Cornwallis. There was an obvious replacement, General Sir Guy Carleton, one of the few British commanders who had not stumbled into disgrace in America. In 1775–76 he had masterfully outfought and outmaneuvered the American attempt to seize Canada. But he got little credit for this achievement because Germain hated him. Carleton had been one of the officers who had found him guilty in the court-martial that had wrecked his career in the Seven Years War. Germain was soon treating Carleton so badly, the general resigned in disgust.

Now North proposed Carleton to replace the demoralized Sir Henry Clinton. Germain refused to consider such an idea. By this time, North had a powerful ally, no less than George III. At first it astonished a number of people to find the king was ready to jettison the one man in the cabinet who supported without reservation His Majesty's refusal to yield on American independence. These puzzlers were underestimating George III's political shrewdness. He was perfectly prepared to sacrifice Germain—as long as it was seen as a quarrel about his unwillingness to appoint Sir Guy Carleton. That would avoid the issue on which the king remained inexorable, the independence of America.[15]

Lord George made it clear that he would only consider a resignation if it was accompanied by "honor"—he wanted a seat in the House of Lords. In his farewell interview with His Majesty, Germain proved himself a tough negotiator. The king offered to make him a baron. Germain demurred. His Majesty distributed this title rather often; Germain wanted a more singular honor to grace his departure. Desperate to get him out the door with a minimum of fuss, George agreed to make him a viscount. Germain crowned his effrontery by telling friends His Majesty had bestowed the elevation on him "without any solicitation on my part."[16]

When the new viscount attempted to take his seat in the House of Lords, he was assailed with a vituperation that was almost unique in the history of the upper chamber. One peer called Germain "the greatest criminal this country has ever known . . . the author of all the calamities of this war." Germain, inured to such abuse from his years in the House of Commons, spoke eloquently in his own defense, and Lord Chancellor Thurlow made a strong defense of his former fellow cabinet member. Germain, now Viscount Sackville, voted in his own favor in the roll call, which accepted him as a member of the House of Lords by a comfortable majority.[17]

VII

Germain was replaced as American secretary by a nonentity named Wellbore Ellis, who agreed to serve only on the promise of a pension. (He was described by one Parliament watcher as having "the vigor of another Methuselah.") But this shift did not mean that Lord Sandwich was safe from the fangs of the opposition. Lord North soon learned there was to be a serious attempt to impeach the first lord of the Admiralty, or at least censure him. In a previous contretemps over Sandwich's performance, Lord North had made it clear that he would consider the censure of any member of the cabinet tantamount to a vote of no confidence in the ministry.

The initial attempt to censure Sandwich came in the House of Lords, three days after Parliament reconvened. The opposition called for an inquiry into "the causes of the want of success of his Majesty's naval forces during the war, and more particularly in the year 1781." The opposition swiftly learned that Sandwich was not Germain, content to dodge their blows by escaping into a peerage. For one thing, Germain was a rich man, while Sandwich was virtually penniless. He frequently remarked that he needed every cent of his salary as first lord and would depend utterly on a pension when he left office. That gift of the king would not be forthcoming if he departed in disgrace.[18]

Sandwich defended himself with considerable skill and force in a speech in the House of Lords, and in a memorandum which summed up his long career as first lord. His defense was more than a little convincing. He had inherited a navy that was the victim of years of peacetime neglect. Hulls made with green timber rotted and disabled dozens of ships because a shortage of seasoned oak had been tolerated to the brink of disaster. Sandwich had reversed this policy and drawn on the latest technology to sheathe the hull of every warship in the fleet with copper—a change that in the opinion of some experts made an English man-of-war the equal of two French warships by increasing its speed and maneuverability. With the skill of a veteran parliamentarian, Sandwich accused his accusers of injecting politics into the Navy's ranks, producing widespread insubordination and indifference to the "good of the service."[19]

The opposition abandoned their attempt to censure Sandwich in the House of Lords. They turned to the House of Commons, where a very different drama unfolded. There, Sandwich could not defend himself personally. He had to rely on North and his associates to muster the government's ranks. Moreover, the leader of the attack was Charles James Fox, by far the most savage of the opposition's orators. To bolster their chances, the opposition invoked a seldom-used device, "the call of the House," which enforced attendance on every member. This move produced unprecedented numbers in the Commons. On some days as many as 468 members were in their seats.[20]

Fox, in his portly disheveled majesty, advanced to the attack in the last week of January 1782, with 443 members present. He focused on whether Sandwich had displayed "wisdom and ability" in deploying his ships, "particularly in the year 1781." Sandwich, in short, was to be eviscerated for Admiral Graves's ineptitude at Yorktown.

Urged on by George III, Lord North and his colleagues resisted vigorously, with Sandwich's eager cooperation. The first lord spent hours briefing government spokesmen on Admiralty affairs so they could defend him intelligently. Meanwhile John Robinson, the treasury official who functioned both as the king's informer and as an assiduous tracker of Parliamentary attendance, worked day and night to turn out a maximum number of government supporters.

On February 7, 1782, Parliament sat as a Committee of the Whole House and Fox assailed Sandwich for his failure to cope with Admiral de Grasse's seizure of naval superiority in the West Indies and on the American coast. He added lesser charges to bolster his claim of glaring incompetence. It all added up to "gross mismanagement of naval affairs in the year 1781," and Fox called for a vote to ratify this verdict.

The motion failed, 205 to 183. Lord North claimed the closeness of the margin made him, in the words of a friend, "horrid sick." North feared the defection of about thirty-five hitherto-dependable government supporters was a bad omen. It was certainly not a hopeful sign, but there was no gainsaying that the attack on Sandwich had fallen short.

Two weeks later, on February 20, Charles James Fox again called for Sandwich's head in almost identical language. This time the opposition invoked not only a call of the whole House but sent emissaries scurrying across England and as far east as Paris to bring wandering defalcators to London for the vote. Lord Sandwich and John Robinson and their numerous staffs worked even harder; Robinson, on the eve of the vote, described himself as "quite spent." This time, the opposition mustered 217 votes. But the government registered 236. Lord Sandwich was clearly going to escape censure and Lord North remained first minister, horrid sick or well.[21]

VIII

Fox and his vituperative friends were by no means the only weapons at the opposition's disposal. Behind the scenes, their master spirit, Edmund Burke, turned to a far more acceptable critic, elderly General Henry Conway. He was regarded as a political moderate; he had served as secretary of state, which suggested he had once enjoyed George III's approval.

On February 22, 1782, Conway proposed a resolution that called for an end to the "further prosecution of offensive war with America." The motion lost by a single vote, 194 to 193. A week later, General Conway proposed a longer version of the same motion, saying many of the same things that Sir James Lowther had declaimed in December—the American war was "weakening the efforts of this country against her European enemies."

Lord North claimed he saw no problem with this contention; he reminded Parliament that he had already repudiated an offensive war with America in the debate on the Lowther motion. A follower of Lord Shelburne, Colonel Isaac Barré, who had gained a somewhat spurious fame (in England) by calling Americans "Sons of Liberty" in 1765, rose to urge Lord North to be less devious. North uncharacteristically lost his temper; his aplomb under attack was usually unshakable. He called Barré "uncivil, brutal and insolent." This gaffe, for which North eventually had to apologize, was evidence that the first minister was losing control of the situation.

North switched from anger to a plea for understanding and patience. He reminded the House of Commons that he was being forced to speak in public—that America, Holland, France, and Spain were all listening to him. Did they really want him to state explicit conditions for peace with America? Warmly pursuing this line, North proposed an amendment to Conway's motion, instructing the government "to treat with America on the footing of independence." The opposition, knowing that the House of Commons was not ready to swallow that indigestible word, furiously accused North of trying to change the subject.

In the ensuing debate, General Conway and other opposition spokesmen declared that the North ministry was too incompetent and divided to make a decent peace with America. They also accused North of hypocrisy; everyone knew the ministry was firmly opposed to American independence. For North, these were menacing sentiments. Behind them lurked his overmastering dread: a vote of no confidence.[22]

Intensifying this fear was a speech by Sir Gilbert Elliott, eldest son of a Scottish nobleman and brother of John Elliott, a distinguished naval officer. Another brother, Andrew, was a prominent crown official in New York. Sir Gilbert had steadfastly supported the North government and the American war for six long years. Elliott now declared he saw for the first time that "the nation, the House of Commons and the Ministers had been for a long time in the wrong" about the war with America.[23]

Again revealing his shaken confidence, a desperate Lord North proposed a postponement of the debate on the Conway motion for two weeks. In that time, he would prepare a bill for peace with America. The House rejected this even more blatant evasion. It reminded the opposition of a recess that North had obtained in April 1780, when the House of Commons was debating the resolution by John Dunning, proposing that Parliament sit in permanent session until the war with America was settled. The recess gave North and George III time to do more than their usual tampering with the House of Commons. When Parliament reconvened, Dunning's motion was decisively defeated.[24]

The opposition was determined not to let North outmaneuver them again. Relentlessly, speaker after speaker pressed for a vote on Conway's resolution. It was past midnight when a weary Lord North finally agreed. By the time the votes were counted, it was almost 2 a.m. The Conway motion carried, 234-215—a decisive defeat for the North ministry. The opposition quickly moved and carried without a vote another motion for an address to the king, informing His Majesty of the changed sentiments of his "loyal commons."

In this second motion we can see the usually invisible hand of Edmund

Burke, bringing to a climax his contest with George III over the patriot king's determination to make Parliament his creature. Everyone knew that Lord North was as much the victim as the agent of this wrongheaded desire for personal rule, not only over Parliament, but over America and the rest of the empire.

Further evidence of Burke's role is a triumphant letter he wrote on February 28, when he had gotten a few hours' sleep after the late-night victory. It went to Benjamin Franklin at Passy, with the following words underlined to emphasize their importance: *"I congratulate you, as the friend of America, I trust, as not the enemy of England, I am sure, as the friend of mankind, on the resolution of the House of Commons carried by a majority of nineteen at two o'clock this morning, in a very full house. It was the declaration of two hundred and thirty four; I think it was the opinion of the whole. I trust it will lead to a speedy peace between the two branches of the English nation."*[25]

On the same morning, the London newspaper, the *General Advertiser,* which supported the opposition, used a large-type headline, rare in the press of this time, to proclaim: PEACE WITH AMERICA.[26]

Edmund Burke and the publisher of the *General Advertiser* would soon ruefully discover that the Conway motion did not mean a speedy peace with America. George III remained determined to bar independence and he thought there was still room for political maneuvers in pursuit of that single-minded goal.

IX

Lord North told his royal master that Parliament had lost confidence in his ministry and "it will be right to see, as soon as possible, what other system can be found." North thought it might be "feasible to divide the opposition, and to take in only a part." The king surprised North by agreeing with him. Instead of a lecture on courage and fortitude, he virtually ordered North to prepare to walk the parliamentary plank.

"I am mortified Lord North thinks he cannot now remain in office," the king told one correspondent. But he seemed to accept North's collapse as a fact to be dealt with, not a faithful servant to be rallied. His Majesty authorized Lord Chancellor Thurlow to explore with two or three noblemen who had followings in Parliament whether they would agree to form an administration on the basis of "keeping what is in our present possession in America."[27]

For the moment, His Majesty needed North and others to prepare his reply to the Commons's address to the throne on the Conway motion. John Robinson and North toiled into the small hours of the morning on a draft, which was rushed to Lord Thurlow for his suggestions and finally submitted to the full cabinet. The ghostwriters put together a response that bore North's trademarks of evasion and vagueness. But George III insisted on certain phrases that gave away the game. He intended to pursue "measures as shall appear to me the most conducive to the restoration of harmony between Great Britain and her revolted colonies."[28]

On Friday, March 1, the king received leaders of the opposition and the speaker of the House of Commons at St. James Palace and delivered his response to their address on General Conway's motion. His Majesty struck a pose of sweet reasonableness in this confrontation. But several members of the opposition were unenthused by the presence of an American standing beside the king: General Benedict Arnold. George III apparently regarded him as evidence that Americans might change their minds about independence. Most Englishman regarded the traitor with distaste because of his role in Major John Andre's death.[29]

On Monday, March 4, with a copy of the text of the king's reply circulating among them, various members of the opposition assailed the response, claiming they saw evidence that the North government was determined to continue an offensive war in America. Charles James Fox declared he was convinced that North and his cabinet were the guilty parties and the king "wished to conclude peace with America, as his faithful Commons had advised him." This outburst of piety toward the king from Fox, of all people, must have stirred more than a few cynical smiles among the opposition. When it came to loathing, only Edmund Burke and Benjamin Franklin ranked higher on His Majesty's hate list.

That same day, March 4, General Henry Conway proposed a far more devastating resolution, one that bespoke the opposition's suspicion and lack of confidence in the government to an unparalleled degree. "The House of Commons would consider as enemies to His Majesty and this country" anyone who "advised or attempted to prosecute an offensive war in America." Charles James Fox backed this expression of total distrust with a savage speech.

North did not even call for a vote on this latest Conway resolution. It passed, in the parlance of Parliament, without a division. But the first minister asked Parliament to give the government more time to prove its sincerity in seeking peace with America. Simultaneously, Lord Chancellor Thurlow was telling the opposition leaders he was trying to seduce into supporting the king that the government's policy was not only "keeping what is in our possession in North America," but also attempting to negotiate with "separate provinces" (individual colonies) and even with districts of these colonies "to detach them from France" and become "separate states."[30]

X

Worsening the government's case was bad news from abroad. In the Mediterranean, the starved, scurvy-ridden garrison of Minorca had surrendered to a Spanish army, imperiling Britain's grip on besieged Gibraltar. The frantic efforts of Lord Sandwich and his admirals to smuggle in provisions had failed. In the West Indies, the French army and navy had captured the sugar island of St. Kitts. This further proof of naval disarray prompted the opposition in the House of Lords to make another attempt to topple Sandwich. An opposition peer called for a vote declaring Cornwallis had been captured at Yorktown because Sandwich had failed to provide him with the protection of the royal navy.

The peers declined to agree, rejecting the proposition 72-37. The vote revealed an aristocratic dislike of the opposition's tactics in the House of Commons, which smacked too much of a determination to humiliate both the North ministry and the king.[31]

Undeterred by this setback, on March 8 Lord John Cavendish, a spokesman for the party led by Lord Rockingham, the largest opposition group in the House of Commons, rose with a proposal for a vote that was an unmistakable declaration of no confidence. Cavendish wanted the Commons to tell the king and the country that "the calamities and expense of the times have proceeded from want of foresight in the ministers." Cavendish's entry into the fray was a clear signal that the Rockinghams were bidding to take over the government.

North and his cabinet saw doom written in capital letters behind Cavendish's words and mustered every vote they could find to defeat it. North claimed, among other things, that the opposition wanted to change the constitution—a negative code for attacking the Rockingham–Edmund Burke determination to end the patriot king's personal rule. Several speakers focused on Charles James Fox and his notorious calls for annually elected parliaments and a redistribution of electoral districts to achieve a more reliable representation of the will of the people.

They also spoke with horror of Burke's desire to reduce the civil list, calling it "a direct violation of national faith." The Cavendish resolution lost, 226 to 216, on a motion by Charles Jenkinson for Parliament to proceed to other business. But Lord North had no illusion that this was more than a temporary escape. He wrote to George III that "after such a division . . . it is totally impossible for the present ministry to conduct His Majesty's business any longer."[32]

XI

Now began the most crucial weeks in the American Revolution—a narrative already replete with enough ups and downs to qualify it as history's most harrowing roller-coaster ride. George III refused to speak with Lord Rockingham about forming a government. The two men had become enemies long ago, when Rockingham headed the government that repealed the Stamp Act in 1766. Rockingham's continued association with Edmund Burke and his reforms were further reason for royal disdain. Instead, George III sent Lord Thurlow to discuss with Rockingham the possibility of forming a "broad bottom" cabinet which the king would select. Simultaneously, George III made sure Lord Shelburne was informed of this negotiation, knowing he was still opposed to American independence.

Lord Rockingham was a nobleman of high principles. That was why he admired and was admired by Edmund Burke, who believed that a purified, truly patriotic aristocracy could lead England to greatness and eventually give tormented Ireland some sort of independence. But Rockingham was also sincerely devoted to the idea of kingship. With his vast estates in Ireland and England, the Marquis was as far from a revolutionary as a politician can get.

At this supremely vital moment in the history of his own country and of America, Lord Rockingham turned to Edmund Burke for advice. What he got was a totally uncompromising statement. Rockingham should become first minister on only one condition: "The king must not give a veto to the independence of America."

Burke insisted on stating it this way—as baldly and bluntly as possible. As a nobleman, Rockingham would have been inclined to a far more orotund and blurry phraseology, which would have permitted the king to evade the issue when and if England's situation changed for the better. The Marquis might even have decided it was better to set no preconditions on his acceptance, lest he be accused of disrespect to his sovereign.

Thanks to Edmund Burke, Rockingham did neither. A glum Lord Thurlow informed the king on March 14 of the ultimatum which Edmund Burke had persuaded Rockingham to deliver. Thurlow added that the Marquis also wanted the power to form an administration of his, not the king's, choosing. Also on the agenda was Edmund Burke's program of economic reform—the purging of the civil list.[33]

The aghast monarch declared his mind was "truly tore to pieces." Almost as if he wanted to prove this cry of self pity, George III announced he was considering abdication. He went so far as to draft a speech to the British people, announcing his decision. "The sudden change of sentiments in one branch of the legislature" had made it impossible for him to conduct the war or obtain peace "but on conditions which would prove destructive to the commerce as well as the essential rights of the British nation." He was therefore "quitting" England forever, and retreating to the German duchy of Hanover, which he also ruled. He was resigning the crown of Great Britain to his "dearly beloved son and lawful successor, George, Prince of Wales." These words would have triggered a political earthquake of very large proportions.[34]

XII

At this point, Lord North reversed a decade of subservience and gave George III a lecture. He told him to put away his abdication speech and accept the brutal fact that "the fate of the present ministry is absolutely and irrevocably decided." That meant, as "Your Majesty is well apprised . . . in this country the prince on the throne, cannot with prudence, oppose the deliberate resolution of the House of Commons." He tried to console the distraught monarch by assuring him that "Your Majesty having persevered, as long as possible, on what you thought right, can lose no honour if you yield at length." Some of George III's "most renowned and most glorious . . . predecessors" had done the same thing.

As for George's frantic clinging to the idea of a "broad bottom" ministry, this too was out of the question. "There are no persons capable and willing to form a new administration except Lord Rockingham and Lord

Shelburne, with their parties." For the king, who knew Shelburne's party was minuscule, this meant submission to the Rockingham phalanx and its hated director, Edmund Burke, and his compatriot, Charles James Fox.

The king replied that he was "hurt" by North's letter, but there was no more talk of abdication. Instead, His Royal Highness warned North: "If you resign before I have decided what I will do, you will certainly forfeit my regard."[35]

The king wrote this letter on March 19, 1782. That same day, North learned from his parliamentary watchdog, John Robinson, that Charles James Fox planned to introduce a motion which declared: "In the present distracted state of the country, it is contrary to the interests of His Majesty to continue the management of public affairs in the hands of the present ministers." It was the ultimate vote of no confidence, and Robinson, still manically counting heads, told Lord North that he was unquestionably going to lose it.

North wrote another letter to George III, telling him what was about to happen and asking him to agree to see Lord Shelburne, at the very least. He begged the king to save his faithful first minister from being "forever stigmatized" on the public record as one of the few leaders removed by a vote of Parliament. In touching terms, Lord North added requests for pensions to some of his most faithful assistants, notably John Robinson, and ended with a special plea for Lord Sandwich, as a "very diligent and very able and a very faithful servant."[36]

On March 20, the king had a long conference with North at St. James Palace. No one knows exactly what was said on either side, but by the time North left the palace, he was a much calmer, almost happy man. At 4:30, he was on the treasury bench when Parliament convened for the day. Lord Surrey, one of Charles James Fox's friends and a fellow member of the Rockingham party, was prepared to announce to a full and tensely expectant House of Commons Fox's motion of no confidence.

Surrey was listed as the first speaker of the day. But Lord North sprang to his feet and asked the Speaker of the House if he might make an announcement that he suspected would lead to an immediate adjournment.

The speaker, in on the secret, recognized North. From the opposition benches rose a roar of protest: "Lord Surrey! Lord Surrey!" North ignored them and tried to speak. Surrey remained on his feet, refusing to yield the floor. By now the opposition had guessed what was coming and revealed their determination to humiliate North, Sandwich, and the rest of the ministers. Charles James Fox lumbered to his feet to introduce a motion affirming that the Earl of Surrey should speak first. A wild debate erupted, lasting over an hour with the Speaker of the House frantically trying to restore order.

Finally Lord North seized a momentary lull in the din to say everyone was wasting his breath, including Lord Surrey. "Those persons who had for some time conducted the public affairs were no longer His Majesty's ministers." The entire North government had resigned. They were merely occupying their official places until other ministers replaced them.

The opposition relapsed into sullen silence. A majority of them still yearned to disgrace North and above all Sandwich. They listened while North thanked the House of Commons for its support during his twelve years as first minister and asked them to forgive his weaknesses. Whereupon he moved for adjournment.

That led to another name-calling wrangle, but the opposition finally had to admit it was pointless to censure men who had already forfeited their jobs. The House of Commons voted to adjourn for five days to enable a new government to form. By now it was about six o'clock. North joined the members surging into the lobby toward the doors of Parliament. There everything came to a sudden stop. It had begun to rain very hard—not untypical weather for London in late March.

A genial smiling North called to several friends to join him for dinner. They accepted and helped him push his way to the head of the crowd. There, waiting in the twilit downpour, was Lord North's carriage. He crowded his friends into the dry interior and turned to the rest of the members, who had expected a midnight session and had left their carriages far away. "Good night, gentlemen," he said. "You see what it is to be in on the secret!"[37]

XIII

The scepter had been struck from George III's hand. But he was thoroughly ungracious in yielding to the men who were trying to establish a genuine parliamentary system, as well as extricate Great Britain from a ruinous war. The king accepted Rockingham as first minister but refused to meet with him face to face. He was only willing to confer with Lord

Shelburne, who still shared his antipathy to American independence. Rockingham accepted this unpleasant proviso, and gave Shelburne a letter, again stating the principles and goals of his administration, with a special emphasis on American independence. He also included the names of the members of his cabinet. Showing their distrust of both the king and Shelburne, Rockingham and Burke specified that the royal consent to these terms would be "confirmed . . . by His Majesty himself."[38]

Exactly how the king confirmed it to Lord Rockingham remains unknown. But Horace Walpole, son of a former first minister and the greatest political gossip of the age, told a friend on March 26, 1782, the day before Rockingham took office, that the Marquis had "triumphed without the shadow of a compromise of any sort." Walpole thought that entitled the Marquis to "all praise and all support."

George III's public dislike of his first minister and his preference for Lord Shelburne made for an uneasy administration, threatened by disunion from the start. Shelburne began taking advantage of the king's favor to compete with Rockingham and Burke on naming his followers to government jobs, even though Rockingham's party outnumbered Shelburne's tiny band ten to one.

Rockingham appointed Edmund Burke paymaster of the forces, the job that had enabled Charles James Fox's father to become one of the wealthiest men in England. But Burke was determined to accept no more than his salary, a handsome 4 thousand pounds a year, and do his utmost to reform this branch of the government. He was equally determined to push his other reforms. Burke's focus was on transforming England, which included drastically altering Parliament's domineering exploitative relationship to Ireland. He apparently hoped the king's semi-public promise to accept American independence would give this part of the Rockingham program enough momentum to reach a swift and satisfactory conclusion without further personal intervention on his part.[39]

This soon proved to be anything but the case. Lord Rockingham had appointed Lord Shelburne secretary of state for home and colonial affairs and Charles James Fox secretary of state for foreign affairs. The American secretaryship was abolished and placed in Shelburne's bailiwick. But Fox, who detested the oblique, uncommunicative Shelburne as much as Edmund Burke did, insisted that he have a share in negotiating peace with America. He remained a proponent of immediate American independence; Shelburne remained secretly opposed, stubbornly hoping for some sort of reconciliation, mostly on British terms. How this tangle would work out was anyone's guess.

Watching this acrimony, George III silently rejoiced and wondered if he might yet get back into the political game. If he had known what was happening in America, His Majesty would have been even more encouraged. On April 1, 1782, as the Rockinghams swept out members of the North administration wholesale, in Philadelphia, Superintendent of Finance Robert Morris was staring national bankruptcy in the face. It was news that would have inflamed His Royal Highness's stubborn hope that the war might end with the submission of some, perhaps most, of his "revolted colonies."[40]

XIV

Two weeks after the Rockinghams took power, a sea battle erupted in the West Indies that had the potential of changing George III from a sullen, defeated politician to a restored monarch of awesome proportions. If it had occurred when the North ministry was reeling from the no-confidence blows of the opposition, and by a device as magical as an undersea cable or a jet plane, the news had reached London in a matter of hours, it would have banished funks and vagueness from First Minister Lord North's psyche for months to come. It would have enabled Lord Sandwich to bellow defiance in the faces of his dismayed critics. It would have unraveled the determination of the opposition for an unimaginable length of time—perhaps forever.

For the first months after Yorktown, the news from the West Indies, if it had reached London promptly, would have done none of these things. Admiral de Grasse returned from Virginia and used his fleet to capture one island after another. The British West Indies fleet under Admiral Hood, with nineteen ships of the line, tried to stop de Grasse but the French admiral's superior numbers forced Hood to retreat. The garrisons of the Leeward Islands had been ravaged by disease and wracked by bad morale. They had no stomach for fighting it out with French soldiers once they got ashore; the inhabitants were even more ready to cut a deal with their conquerors. Soon Nevis, Montserrat, Demerara, and Essequibo capitulated. Only St. Lucia held out—a very important survivor, since it was within thirty miles of the main French base in the West Indies, Fort Royal on Martinique.[41]

On February 25, Admiral Sir George Rodney joined Admiral Hood at sea with the twelve ships of the line he had brought from England. They sailed to St. Lucia, where the five ships that Lord Sandwich had purloined from the home fleet arrived in the next few days. Suddenly, the royal navy had thirty-six ships of the line to Admiral de Grasse's thirty-three, and Rodney, the best fighting admiral on active duty, was in command.

Admiral de Grasse was at Fort Royal, waiting for a huge convoy from France that would bring him the supplies and ammunition he needed to join the Spanish in a massive assault on Jamaica. Rodney was not a man who took advice easily. When Admiral Hood urged him to station cruisers as far north as Guadaloupe to intercept the convoy, Rodney rudely informed him that the supply ships would arrive from the south.

He was wrong. The convoy arrived from the north and anchored in Fort Royal Bay, while Rodney and his cruisers were looking in the other direction. De Grasse began taking troops aboard transports for the assault on Jamaica. Rodney, only thirty miles away at St. Lucia, watched his every movement. On April 7, when de Grasse's fleet raised sails and headed for a rendezvous with the Spanish at San Domingo, Rodney pursued him. It was vital for the British to intercept and defeat the French before they combined forces with the Spanish, which would have raised their firepower to fifty ships of the line.

De Grasse, shepherding a convoy of transports, had to worry about protecting them as well as fending off Rodney. He sailed at a much slower pace; the copper-bottomed British men-of-war soon overtook him. Hood, in the British van, was the first to make contact on April 9. For a while he found himself in a dangerous situation, with only nine ships opposed to de Grasse's whole fleet and Rodney and the rest of the British men-of-war becalmed off the island of Dominica. But the French admiral was not fighting to destroy the enemy fleet, the invariable British doctrine. He was content to duel Hood at long range and give his transports time to escape.

By evening, the British fleet was reunited and resumed the pursuit. Three days later, Rodney attacked de Grasse near the Saints, a group of small islands between Guadaloupe and Martinique. De Grasse had the wind in his favor, a large advantage in the age of sail. But he again declined to attack, and the two fleets sailed past each other in line of battle, bombarding inconclusively.

A shift in the wind disordered De Grasse's rear vessels, and Rodney aboard his flagship, HMS *Formidable*, did the totally unexpected. Followed by five more ships, the *Formidable* burst through the French line. Other British captains imitated his example and a huge melee erupted.

Steering up the weather side of the French line, Rodney created chaos. He delivered a murderous broadside through the stern windows of the *Glorieux* and another through the bows of the *Diademe*. The stunned, confused French captains collided with each other while *Formidable*, followed by the *Duke* and *Namur*, hammered them with broadside after broadside. The British paid special attention to de Grasse's immense 110-gun flagship, the *Ville de Paris*.[42]

Rodney's ships were armed with carronades, a new short-range, extremely destructive cannon which the technologically astute Sandwich had bought in large numbers for the fleet. These guns doubled and redoubled the impact of the British broadsides. "Dreadful must have been the slaughter" aboard the French ships, wrote one British captain.[43]

The French line of battle was torn apart, enabling the British to surround some enemy ships with twice their number. Soon six French men-of-war struck their colors, including the *Ville de Paris*. Around noon, the rest of the French fleet, some twenty-five ships, seized a freshening breeze and fled toward Guadaloupe. Hood expected Rodney to raise the signal for a general chase. "Had he so done," Hood later wrote, "I am confident we should have had twenty sail of the enemy's ships before dark."

But Rodney decided to be content with the large victory he had already won. When Hood went aboard *Formidable* the next day and reproached Rodney for not pursuing the fleeing enemy through the night, the admiral replied: "Come, we have done very handsomely as it is." The seventy-three-year-old commander had had no sleep for the previous four nights, and his health was precarious. He simply lacked the strength for another battle.[44]

Nevertheless, Rodney had won a victory that demolished French and Spanish plans to capture Jamaica. It restored British naval supremacy in the West Indies and on the American coast. He had also captured the man who had made Yorktown possible, Admiral de Grasse, a huge propaganda victory in itself.

Admiral Rodney immediately dispatched a frigate to London with a letter to Lord Sandwich. "You may now despise all your enemies," he wrote. The admiral had no way of knowing that his patron was no longer first lord of the Admiralty. Nor did Sandwich and his royal master, George III, hear anything about Rodney's triumph for the next five weeks. In that time, envoys began talking peace in Paris, political infighting eroded the Rockingham ministry in London, and the Americans confronted an outbreak of anti-French, anti-Franklin mania in the Continental Congress, led by Arthur Lee.[45]

Chapter Six

Men Talk Peace
But There Is No Peace

T PASSY, Benjamin Franklin was not a happy ambassador. Thanks to his numerous correspondents in England and reports in European newspapers, he remained in close touch with the decline and fall of the North ministry. The news was of course pleasing. But Franklin remained extremely wary of what the outcome would be.

In a March letter to Secretary of Foreign Affairs Robert R. Livingston, the ambassador noted the ministry's new policy, that the war in America would only be defensive. "I hope we shall be too prudent to have the least dependence on this declaration. It is only thrown out to lull us. For depend upon it, the king hates us cordially and will be content with nothing short of our extirpation."[1]

A few days later, as North reeled toward collapse, Franklin wrote to Robert Morris: "We must not be lulled by these appearances. That nation [Great Britain] is changeable. And tho somewhat humbled at present, a little success may make them as insolent as ever. I remember when I was a boxing boy, it was allowed after an adversary said he had enough, to give him a rising blow. Let ours be a douser."[2]

In another letter to Morris, Franklin alluded to the chief reason for his unhappiness: "I have been continually in perplexity and uncertainty about our money affairs." Early in 1782, Morris had told the ambassador he needed a loan or gift of 12 million livres from France to balance his books for the year. Simultaneously, bills drawn on Franklin's account still rained down on him.

In Spain, John Jay had gotten nowhere in his struggle for recognition of American independence and a loan. The New Yorker was in constant turmoil over merchants demanding money from him. He feared America's credit would be declared worthless, wrecking all hopes of winning Spain's good will. At times the beleaguered envoy thought he might end in a Spanish debtor's prison. He sent Franklin a stream of letters, begging his help.

In Holland, a discouraged John Adams seemed no closer to a loan or recognition and had become so disillusioned with Dutch bankers, he said that he felt like a swimmer negotiating for his life with a school of sharks. He too depended on the ambassador to pay his expenses. Nevertheless, Adams remained Franklin's enemy, frequently slandering him in letters to friends in America.

Then there were the French creditors. Franklin was involved in a tremendous wrangle with his Passy landlord, Jacques Leray de Chaumont, about money the merchant claimed the United States owed him. Franklin was torn between a determination not to see his country cheated and his sympathy for Chaumont, who had been badly hurt by the devaluation of Congress's continental dollars. Up the line was a staggering payment due to Caron de Beaumarchais in June 1782—2.5 million livres. In a letter summing up his woes, Franklin begged Robert Morris to keep a tight rein on his drafts against the ambassadorial account, so that "our credit in Europe may not be ruined and your friend [Franklin] kill'd with vexation."[3]

Tormenting the ambassador was the plight of American sailors starving in British jails. Captured aboard privateers, their numbers now exceeded a thousand and he had little or no money to buy them decent food. (The rules of war stipulated that the cost of feeding prisoners had to be paid by their home nations.) On the docks in Brest and other ports were tons of purchased war materiel, but Franklin lacked the cash to hire ships. The ambassador asked John Barry, captain of the American frigate *Alliance,* to pick up four hundred tons of these supplies at Brest, but Barry said his orders did not permit him to linger in France. The *Alliance* was needed in America, where the British blockade was still wreaking havoc on the nation's commerce. Barry also feared that too much cargo would endanger his ship; a frigate was not a freighter.

Franklin had been told that Washington's army badly needed gunpowder and weapons. Barry did not think this was the case. In graphic details that revealed the confusion prevailing in the Congress-directed American war effort, the Irish-born captain reported: "When I left Boston there were two hundred tons of [gun]powder drifting about the harbour in a vessel with only one anchor and one cable." The reason: all the magazines on shore were full to bursting with the supposedly scarce commodity. As for weapons, there were twenty thousand muskets in Boston warehouses. No one had the money to pay for "hawling [them] to camp." Perhaps, Barry added, no one wanted them.[4]

II

Franklin shuddered at the thought of asking Foreign Minister Vergennes for another 12 million livres. He told Robert Morris it made Americans look "insatiable." But the ambassador took a deep breath and made the attempt. Franklin's first mention of another loan drew an extremely icy reply from the foreign minister. He informed the discomfited ambassador that thus far in the war, France had advanced the United States 28 million livres—about $150 million in modern money. In 1781 alone, the French had loaned or given Congress 20 million livres. When was the United States going to start helping themselves? Since this was a question that Franklin was also asking, the ambassador was temporarily speechless.

To the rescue came an improbable savior: the Marquis de Lafayette. In the uniform of a Continental Army major general, the Frenchman arrived in Paris on January 20, 1782, and the metropolis exploded with acclaim. The awkward nineteen-year-old who had sailed to America in defiance of the orders of his king in 1777 had become an international hero at twenty-four. Louis XVI and Queen Marie Antoinette received him at Versailles the day after his arrival. In Paris, crowds followed his carriage, cheering and applauding.

Within a few days, the Marquis paid Franklin a visit at Passy to report that Congress had asked him to assist the ambassador in any way he needed or desired. Actually, Congress had passed a resolution, ordering Franklin and the other peace commissioners to work with the Marquis—further evidence of the influence that the French ambassador, the Chevalier de la Luzerne, now possessed in Philadelphia.

Franklin told the Marquis of the financial crisis confronting America. Unless another loan was procured, he would run out of money in February. Vergennes had already told Lafayette he was "not very pleased" with the United States. They were "barely active" and much too demanding. Undaunted, the effervescent Lafayette became Franklin's volunteer intermediary, pleading with the foreign minister and other power brokers around the king for at least a part of the 12 million livres Superintendent of Finance Morris needed.

Soon a relieved Franklin was writing to Robert R. Livingston, telling him the good news. Six million livres would be forthcoming from the French treasury, with a first installment of two million due on April 1. In an understatement, Franklin said the Marquis was "really very serviceable to me." The ambassador praised Lafayette's attachment to the American cause and expressed his pleasure at their "friendly and confidential" relationship. Almost plaintively, Franklin warned the secretary of foreign affairs that the French were saying it was time for the Americans to do more to help themselves. "It is said we are apt to be supine after a little success," the ambassador wrote. "A small increase in industry of every American, male and female, with a small diminution of luxury, would produce a sum far superior to all we can hope to beg or borrow from all our friends in Europe."

This proposal of individual reform was the kind of personal advice Franklin dispensed in his best-selling book, *The Way to Wealth*. In calmer moments, an older, wiser Franklin knew it was "wishing mankind more sense than God has been pleased to give them."[5]

III

Franklin's only consolation during these suspenseful weeks was General Washington's letter from Yorktown, describing Lord Cornwallis's capitulation. He answered it with words that left no doubt about his admiration for the Virginia soldier. The Yorktown triumph would "brighten the glory that surrounds your name and that must accompany it to our latest posterity. No news could possibly make me more happy."

Franklin gave Washington a succinct summary of the English state of mind at present. He called it "making peace by halves." They had foresworn offensive war in America and the North ministry had departed. As yet there was no indication of what they planned to do next. In words that undoubtedly pleased Washington, the ambassador saw no reason "to relax our preparations for a vigorous campaign."

Writing before the news of Rodney's victory reached Europe, Franklin reiterated his fear that "a little success in the West Indies" could easily re-ignite Britain's "natural insolence," and lead to a continuance of the war. He was happy to report he had purchased "great stores . . . for your army" and would ship them to America as soon as possible.[6]

Franklin wrote this letter in his study at Passy. On the wall behind him hung a full-length portrait of General Washington. Anyone who visited the ambassador would instantly grasp that he was representing more than a bankrupt, insatiable Congress.

IV

On March 21, the day after the North government resigned, a messenger brought a letter to Franklin's door at Passy.

> Lord Cholmondely's compliments to Dr. Franklin; he sets out for London tomorrow evening and should be glad to see him for five minutes before he went. Lord C shall call upon him at any time in the morning he shall be pleased to appoint.

The next morning Lord Cholmondely made his bow in Franklin's study and handed him a letter of introduction from his Passy neighbor, Madame Anne-Louise Brillon, who was spending the winter in Nice. She had met Lord Cholmondely there and had been impressed by his earnest desire for peace between England and America. She nervously wondered if he might be a spy. But she was sure Franklin would not allow any secrets to be pried from him.

Lord Cholmondely turned out to be sincere. He was pleased by Parliament's apparent shift toward peace. He happened to be a good friend of Lord Shelburne. Cholmondely wondered if Franklin would like to send a message to his lordship, who would almost certainly occupy a place of power in the new ministry. Franklin accepted the offer and wrote a brief letter to the nobleman, declaring he was pleased by this opportunity to assure him of his "ancient respect for your talents and virtues." He congratulated Shelburne on Parliament's recent resolutions and hoped they would produce a "general peace"—something he fervently wished to see "before I die."[7]

Franklin's and Shelburne's "ancient" acquaintance extended back to

1762, when Shelburne was a member of Parliament and a strong advocate of an early peace with France at the close of the Seven Years War. Franklin had been a player in that victorious finale, using his agile pen to campaign vigorously and successfully for Britain's acquisition of Canada. Over the next several years, Shelburne held various cabinet posts and conferred with Franklin about the deterioration of Britain's relationship with America.

Franklin soon learned Shelburne was now secretary of state for home and colonial affairs and determined to control negotiations with America. Lord Cholmondely's delivery of Franklin's letter gave his lordship an opening to take charge of this issue no matter what First Minister Lord Rockingham or his friend Charles James Fox, secretary of state for foreign affairs, thought about it.

Early in April, Richard Oswald appeared at Franklin's door in Passy with a letter of introduction from Shelburne. Oswald was at first glance a strange choice for a peace negotiator. He was seventy-seven years old, a year older than Franklin, and repulsively ugly, with only one eye in his lined, twisted face. Shelburne had brushed aside two negotiators Rockingham had suggested, adding to his reputation for backstage secretive politics. The trait had earned Shelburne the nickname the Jesuit of Berkeley Square.

Scottish born, Oswald had a very engaging, cheerful manner and was unquestionably a man of the world. He had made a fortune as an army contractor in the Seven Years War and had also prospered in the slave trade. Henry Laurens had been his South Carolina partner for more than thirty years in this traffic in human misery. Oswald had with him a letter from Laurens, assuring Franklin that he could trust this man. Not only was Oswald an old friend, he had put up 50 thousand pounds to bail Laurens out of the Tower of London.

Shelburne's letter was even more emphatic on Oswald's trustworthiness. He assured Franklin that the envoy was "an honest man" whom he had chosen after "consulting some of our common friends." He was alluding to David Hartley and other English liberals who had met and admired Franklin during his twenty prewar years in England. There is no record of Shelburne consulting any of these people about Oswald and it is unlikely that they knew Oswald or if they did, regarded him highly. Like Shelburne, there was more to Oswald than his engaging personality. He was as unfriendly to American independence as the new colonial secretary.

For a while Oswald, posing as an expert on America, had advised Lord North on how to win the war. The Scot repeatedly urged the North government to break up the American confederacy by detaching the southern colonies. His consistent goal was to smash the American rebels with overwhelming military force and ruthless punishments. He even suggested replacing the British garrison in New York with Russian troops, so the British could concentrate most of their army in the South. He called New Englanders a "despicable rabble of rioters" and a "confederacy of smugglers."[8]

Shelburne's letter also assured Franklin that Oswald was "fully apprised of my mind" and added that he (Shelburne) had "few or no secrets." The latter claim was almost laughable. All his life, Shelburne had infuriated fellow politicians by declining to tell them what he was thinking about important issues. It was why he had so few followers in Parliament.

Almost certainly, the new colonial secretary had not told Oswald about a letter he had written on April 4, 1782, to General Sir Guy Carleton, the new British commander in America, and his naval counterpart, Admiral Robert Digby. Shelburne enclosed transcripts of recent sessions of Parliament, in which speakers talked of peace with America. "You must . . . lose no time to avail yourself of the change of measures which has lately taken place, for the purpose of reconciling the minds and affections of His Majesty's subjects," he wrote. He urged the two men to "captivate" the Americans' hearts and "remove every suspicion of insincerity." There was not even a hint, much less the use, of the word independence in this missive. It was a striking example of Shelburne's gift for doubletalk.[9]

Now the colonial secretary reminded Franklin of his role as a peacemaker with France nineteen years ago and insisted he wanted to retain "the same simplicity and good faith" that characterized their friendship in the past. He even hoped that someday they might again discuss "the means of promoting the happiness of mankind." He still thought that was a far more agreeable topic than "plans for spreading misery and devastation" in a war.[10]

V

Franklin found Oswald a likeable man. They talked about peace in general terms, both agreeing it was desirable. Oswald said everyone in England "sincerely wish'd" for an end to the war but he warned that if France insisted on terms that were "too humiliating" to England, the British people would resume the war with renewed fervor. Franklin was unimpressed by this by-now-familiar attempt to split the Americans from their ally. The ambassador told Oswald that America would only negotiate "in concert" with France and asked the envoy if he would like to talk to the Comte de Vergennes.

Oswald soon joined Franklin for a trip to the foreign minister's office in Versailles. Vergennes urged Oswald to abandon his hopes of a separate peace with any of the four nations now in the war against England—France, Spain, Holland, and the United States. Franklin allowed his silent acquiescence to send Oswald the same message. His silence also acquiesced in a warning from the foreign minister that France had "several demands" to make before agreeing to a peace treaty. Oswald all but begged Vergennes to state some of these demands. The foreign minister smoothly pointed out that England, fighting alone, was the logical one to make the first peace proposals. But he assured Oswald that France had no desire to "humiliate" England.[11]

A few days later, Oswald returned to Passy and Franklin gave him a remarkably cordial letter to Shelburne. He assured the colonial secretary that he was completely satisfied with Oswald as a negotiator; he was a "wise and honest man" and he was prepared to talk to him "with all the simplicity and good faith which you do me the honor to expect from me." He expressed the hope that Oswald would return with a commission to negotiate a "general peace" which would "expedite the blessed work our hearts are engaged on." He also thanked Shelburne for a recent act of the Rockingham-led Parliament, which freed American sailors in British jails and provided for their return to America.[12]

When Oswald expressed his delight with Franklin's compliments, the ambassador revealed some private thoughts that he had not shared with Foreign Minister Vergennes. The ambassador said he would like to see more than a "mere peace" achieved between England and America. He hoped Oswald—and Shelburne—would think in terms of a reconciliation between the two nations.

Franklin proceeded to remind Oswald of the enormous damage the war had inflicted on America. Seaports and frontier villages had been torched and their inhabitants often massacred by marauding Indians. There was only one way to reconcile Americans to these injuries; the sufferers had to be compensated in some way. The perfect reparation, in Franklin's opinion, would be the cession of Canada and Nova Scotia to the new United States. Their mostly empty acres could be sold and payment made to the victims of the war. As an afterthought, Franklin added that the thousands of loyalists who had lost their lands to acts of confiscation passed by the various states might also be compensated. A Canada without British troops on the border would also remove a major source of future discord between England and America.

Oswald did not show the slightest hesitation in embracing this proposal to surrender another third of the British empire. He told Franklin "nothing . . . could be clearer, more satisfactory and convincing" than his reasoning. Franklin had prepared some notes for his discourse, which he described at the bottom of the page as "This is mere conversation matter between Mr. O. and Mr. F." Oswald claimed to be so excited by the proposal, he asked if he could take the notes back to London to show Lord Shelburne. Taken by surprise, Franklin agreed.[13]

This desire for a peace of reconciliation did not mean Franklin was even slightly interested in abandoning independence. In his middle years, he had seen America as part of a triumphant empire, whose blend of royal and representative government seemed to embody the best hope of human happiness in a world afflicted by absolutism and tyranny. But this vision had expired during the decade of heartbreak he had spent in London struggling to combat Britain's growing detestation of the defiant Americans. The struggle had ended with Franklin being publicly insulted as a traitor and an incendiary by George III's attorney general, Alexander Wedderburn. He had returned to Philadelphia in 1775 to announce, a full year before most Americans dared to speak the word: "I am for independence."

In a diary Franklin began to keep track of the negotiations with Oswald, the ambassador changed his mind about one point in his Canada proposal. He admitted to himself he was "not pleas'd" by his suggestion that the loyalists should or could be compensated by the United States. The wound that William Franklin's defection had inflicted still tormented Franklin's spirit. He was also supersensitive to any possibility that Arthur Lee and his friends might accuse him of using the peace treaty to help his loyalist son. He was even more uneasy about what the Comte de Vergennes might think of his backstage attempt to acquire Canada and Nova Scotia. Franklin knew that Vergennes did not want to see the Americans obtain Canada. The foreign minister thought an English presence on their northern border would impel an independent United States to stay close to France.

VI

In spite of Franklin's less-than-warm feelings for John Adams, the ambassador immediately informed him of Oswald's visit and summarized the envoy's discussions with him and Vergennes. He urged Adams to join him in Paris for the serious negotiations that seemed imminent. Adams thanked him for the letter and enthusiastically approved Franklin's Canada proposal. If the British agreed, he thought, a swift overall peace agreement would be more than possible. But when he could join Franklin in Paris, "I know not," Adams wrote. There followed a long lamentation that there was no money in Holland for a decent-sized loan to America. All available cash had been drained by loans to every major power in Europe, including England, who still had considerable influence in the country, although they were at war. Adams was determined to keep swimming in the school of sharks, hoping the tide might turn in his favor.[14]

Franklin also wrote to John Jay in Spain, urging him to come to Paris as soon as possible. He knew there was no point in arguing with John Adams, who saw his Dutch loan as his one hope of achieving something outside Franklin's orbit. Already on cordial terms with Jay, the ambassador did not mince words. He had paid all Jay's bills and his "constant residence at Madrid" was no longer necessary. Paris was where he should be henceforth. "Here you are greatly wanted for . . . there is great talk of a treaty proposed but I can neither make or agree to propositions of peace without the assistance of my colleagues." As for Spain, that country "has taken four years to consider whether she should treat with us or not. Give her forty and let us in the meantime mind our own business."[15]

Jay was soon on his way to Paris but it was a journey that would take weeks. Meanwhile, Oswald returned with another letter from Shelburne, oozing hopes for an early end to our "public differences"—a sentiment the envoy enthusiastically echoed. But Franklin soon found that Oswald, though he was supposed to communicate Shelburne's inner thoughts, was "very sparing" on this topic.

There were strong and unpleasant reasons for Oswald's reticence.

Shelburne had rejected Franklin's proposal for a cession of Canada to create a spirit of reconciliation and incidentally compensate the loyalists. Instead, Oswald was ordered to make "early and strict conditions" to restore the loyalists "to the full enjoyment of their rights and privileges" in the rebellious colonies. The indemnification for their losses was also important but it was to be paid by the United States. The colonial secretary also wanted an agreement "to secure all debts whatever due to British subjects."

With a bluntness that was almost breathtaking, Lord Shelburne told Oswald: "No independence [would] be acknowledged" without the loyalists and British creditors "being taken care of." Moreover, "compensation" was expected if the British agreed to evacuate New York, Charleston, and Savannah. Then there was the matter of the United States' relationship to France. To procure their independence, the Americans would have to promise there would never be a "secret, tacit or ostensible connection" with their former ally. Finally, Oswald was to explore with Franklin on a strictly confidential basis the possibility of a federal union between America and Great Britain. If Franklin demurred on any of the "ordered" points, Oswald was to tell him that the British people were "in no way reconciled to independence." If these negotiations failed, they were ready to resume the war "with the greatest vigor."

None of these ideas even approximated the views of the Rockingham party. Shelburne was operating as if he were the king's first minister, and was embarked on a course that Lord George Germain, Lord Sandwich, and the other ousted hard-liners would have approved. The explanation for his conduct was not hard to discover. Along with being known as the Jesuit of Berkeley Square, Shelburne was often called "a thorough courtier" imbued with a reverence for kingship that bordered on awe.

It was no accident that George III had chosen him as the one member of the Rockingham administration with whom he would discuss matters. His Majesty was well aware—and deeply pleased—by these orders to Oswald. So thorough was Shelburne's courtier's role, he even submitted his effusive letter to Franklin for the king's approval. He was rewarded with a terse note from the royal closet that it would be "perfectly safe . . . to send it without any alterations."[16]

VII

In his letter, Shelburne told Franklin something that was far from good news, although it was communicated in an offhand style. Along with Oswald, the Rockingham cabinet was sending another envoy to Paris, supposedly to discuss with Foreign Minister Vergennes the best way to begin negotiations with France. He was an emissary of Charles James Fox, the secretary for foreign affairs, who by this time was infuriated with Lord Shelburne for seizing the initiative in the peace negotiations. Franklin almost certainly did not find this announcement reassuring but he was in no position to object to it.

Meanwhile, Oswald ducked and dodged Franklin's questions about Lord Shelburne's "sentiments" on peace. Instead, the old slave trader talked of the way the "whole ministry" concurred in a desire for peace and all had no hesitation in placing their confidence in Franklin as the man who could help them achieve it. They were sure he still had "some of [his] ancient affection and regard for Old England." As for the cession of Canada, Oswald quoted Shelburne as saying it might be settled "towards the end" of the treaty of peace but he did not think it should be brought up for the time being.

To bolster his bona fides after this lie, Oswald showed Franklin the minutes of a recent cabinet meeting in which it was agreed that American independence would be granted if England could achieve "the same situation" she was in after signing the peace treaty with France in 1763, ending the Seven Years War.

This was tossed off with the same tone of genial confidence that Franklin would cooperate as if he were not aware that the peace of 1763 was considered by France a terrific humiliation. It had included the loss of their hopes for empires in North America and India, their fishing rights off Newfoundland, and an admission that France was no longer a first-class power—a status signified by the British insistence on a commissioner in the port of Dunkirk, with the authority to overrule French officials on a variety of matters. More specifically, as Franklin noted in a letter to John Adams, Oswald implied England expected to regain all the sugar islands in the West Indies that France had captured since 1778.

Franklin again finessed Oswald by suggesting another meeting with the Comte de Vergennes. But it proved to be a waste of time. Lord Shelburne's envoy confined himself to burbling more generalities about how badly everyone in England wanted peace. Back in Passy, Oswald unexpectedly shifted gears and wondered if Franklin was worried about Spanish demands in the forthcoming negotiations. He thought they might be the source of the "greatest obstruction" to a treaty of peace. England had a way of dealing with them. Russia was her secret ally (another lie) and the soldiers and sailors of that nation had recently begun settling "the back part of North America" from their Siberian base, Kamskatka. If the Spanish proved difficult, Russia's ruler, the Empress Catherine, would be glad to launch an army from Kamskatka to assault Mexico. Franklin thought this "a little visionary at present" but pretended to be interested.

Franklin parted from Oswald puzzling over why he had so little to tell him in the way of specifics for a possible peace. In a letter to John Adams, the ambassador was dubious about the way things were going. He thought the offer of independence if France surrendered all her West Indies conquests amounted to "selling us a thing that is already our own" (independence) and "making France pay the price." Obviously, Oswald's nerve had failed him. He had concluded that if he communicated Shelburne's real sentiments, Franklin (and Vergennes) would have told him to board the next packet boat back to England.

Franklin and Vergennes were left waiting for Fox's emissary. They agreed that Oswald's reticence might be due to a power struggle between Shelburne and Fox inside the British cabinet. Maybe this new man would have the proposals they were anxious to hear.[17]

VIII

In England, the Rockingham-Shelburne administration found itself dealing with another country in the empire that had growing ambitions for some sort of independence: Ireland. Henry Grattan, the spokesman for the Irish Volunteers, whose fondness for parading with weapons on their shoulders had so alarmed Lord North, passed a resolution in the Dublin parliament calling for an independent Irish legislature and judiciary. The Rockinghams quickly yielded to the demands. Charles James Fox remarked that "unwilling subjects were no better than enemies."

Edmund Burke thought the Irish reforms did not go far enough. The British retained the right to appoint the lord lieutenant and other members of the executive wing of the government. Catholics were still barred from voting, much less sitting in the Irish parliament. Protestants retained the immense estates their ancestors had seized after the British conquest of Ireland in the previous century. The Church of England remained the official state religion. But the Irish Volunteers and their representatives in the Dublin parliament declared themselves satisfied and voted to raise the quota of Irish seamen for the British navy.

Other Rockingham programs turned out to be modest. In the reform of the civil list, the Marquis displayed a lamentable eagerness to please George III. He guaranteed the king that "not a single article" of the expenses that would be retrenched "touches anything whatsoever which is personal to Your Majesty or Your Majesty's royal family." The Marquis even promised not to fill any government offices with his friends "for what is called strengthening political interest." He refused to make himself "considerable" at George III's expense.[18]

None of this wishy-washy language was promising for those who hoped for a swift resolution of the issue of American independence. This became all too apparent when the negotiator sent by Charles James Fox arrived in Paris early in May.

IX

The new envoy, Thomas Grenville, had a very familiar last name. He was the twenty-six-year-old son of George Grenville, the first minister who had imposed the Stamp Act and other taxes on America in the mid-1760s, beginning the quarrel that led to the Revolution. He arrived with a letter from Charles James Fox, full of effusive compliments to Franklin and the hope that his "liberality of mind" would not prevent him from "esteeming" young Grenville's "excellent qualities of heart and head" in spite of his name.

Franklin assumed Grenville would make Vergennes his chief target. Fox's rationale for sending him was the claim that negotiations with France were in his bailiwick. Instead, Grenville made Franklin his first call—additional evidence that Fox wanted to elbow Shelburne and Oswald out of the negotiations. Franklin invited the young man to dinner and heard little more than the line Oswald had fed him—everyone in England panted for peace. The next morning Franklin accompanied Grenville to Vergennes's office at Versailles, hoping to hear some specific terms. Instead, Grenville repeated Oswald's offer of American independence in return for all the captured sugar islands.

Vergennes gave the young man an indulgent smile and told him America was already independent. Franklin emphatically concurred. Vergennes pointed out how little logic there was in Grenville's assertion that France should restore the sugar islands. The Seven Years War had begun in a dispute over the ownership of "some waste lands" on the Ohio River. In the treaty of peace, was Britain contented with the recovery of these lands? No, they had retained Canada, several West Indies islands, most of the Newfoundland fishing grounds, and conquests in Africa and India. Why wouldn't the British, who had obviously lost the war, concede to France the same right to keep her conquests?

The discomfited Grenville replied that this war was different. It had begun because France had encouraged the Americans to revolt. Vergennes, Franklin noted in his diary, "grew a little warm." He vigorously denied the charge. The Americans had revolted and declared their independence "long before [they] received the least encouragement from France." The foreign minister gestured dramatically to Franklin, and declared the ambassador "would contradict me if I do not speak the truth." Franklin solemnly nodded his agreement, conveniently forgetting that he had conferred with French agents in Philadelphia in 1775, a year before America declared independence. Back in Passy, Franklin wryly noted that young Grenville said he was "not quite satisfy'd" with Vergennes's remarks and was "thoughtful." One historian of the scene has suggested that between these ultimate professionals in the art of diplomacy, the inexperienced Grenville had been treated like a shuttlecock in a championship badminton game.[19]

Five days later, Grenville paid Franklin another visit and unmasked the real purpose of his visit to France: he exhorted Franklin to consider making a separate peace with England. Franklin read him his uncompromising answers to David Hartley's letters and followed these with a lecture on the nature of obligation, which he thought most people did not understand. Perhaps with John Adams in mind, he said too many people felt uneasy in a state of obligation, and came up with all sorts of arguments to prove they had been under "no obligation at all" or had "discharg'd it."

In those personal terms to which Franklin loved to reduce the complexities of national and international politics, the ambassador told Grenville a parable. He imagined that B, a stranger to A, was about to be imprisoned for debt by a merciless creditor. A lends B the money he needs to retain his liberty. If B later repays the money, did that discharge his debt to A? By no means, Franklin insisted. He still owed A a large debt of obligation. This was the way Franklin and his countrymen felt about France. Grenville could only mutter that "this was carrying gratitude very far."

The following day, Grenville reported to Charles James Fox an almost totally different account of this conversation. He claimed that Franklin hinted an immediate grant of independence would make America "infinitely less likely" to support the claims of France and Spain. He added an additional whopper, that Franklin pleaded ignorance of what terms France would ask. This assertion ignored Grenville's conversation with Franklin and Vergennes in which France's position was made very clear. Grenville was trying to help Fox, who advocated an immediate grant of independence. Lord Shelburne and a majority of the Rockingham cabinet disagreed, in spite of George III's promise that he would not veto the concession. With Shelburne as their line of communication to the royal closet, the ministers were aware by this time that the king still loathed the idea. Rockingham, with his perpetual desire to please, was the last man to force the issue with His Majesty.[20]

X

By now over a month had passed since Admiral Rodney had routed the French fleet and captured Admiral de Grasse in the Battle of the Saints Islands. Both sides were still operating in the aftermath of Yorktown and the Spanish capture of Minorca. Looming was the threat that Spain's siege of Gibraltar would succeed there as certainly as they had won Minorca. Nothing had been heard from India, but the British knew that even with the reinforcements sent in early 1782, their Far East fleet was barely equal to the firepower of the talented Admiral Bailli de Suffren. Even more worrisome was the havoc the Sultan of Mysore, Hyder Aly, might be inflicting on land with French support.

The psychological and strategic momentum was still in the hands of Franklin and Vergennes. This was soon apparent in Franklin's treatment of Thomas Grenville. The ambassador learned from the Marquis de Lafayette that Grenville's commission only empowered him to treat with France. Lafayette had been talking to Grenville and the young diplomat had incautiously revealed this to the Marquis, perhaps hoping to ingratiate himself with a man whose chief interest, Grenville assumed, was France.

This revelation was followed by a letter from Vergennes informing Franklin: "They want to treat with us for you. But this the King will not agree to. He thinks it not consistent with the dignity of your state. You will treat for yourselves and every one of the powers at war with England will make its own treaty." All would be secure because the treaties would go "hand and in hand" and would be signed on the same day.

An angry Franklin informed Grenville he would not even talk to him unless he got his commission changed. Grenville vowed to procure the alteration, but the revised document that came from London five or six days later was equally unsatisfactory. It authorized Grenville to treat for peace "with France and her allies." Obviously, the Rockingham cabinet, with George III's brooding presence in the background, could not even write the words, "The United States of America." Franklin informed Grenville that the change left him still dissatisfied.

XI

While Ambassador Franklin was talking in these downright terms, Grenville handed him a copy of a London newspaper containing Admiral Rodney's account of his victory over Admiral de Grasse. Almost as disturbing was a report of British successes in India, which had taken nearly six months to reach London.

Hyder Aly, the sultan who had annihilated a British army at Polihur in 1780, had been challenged by an East India Company army under General Sir Eyre Coote, an Irish-born soldier who had done much to establish the company's supremacy in India during the Seven Years War. Hyder Aly had 65,000 men, Coote an 8,000-man mix of British regulars and Indian mercenaries called sepoys. The two armies met near the town of Porto Novo in a ferocious struggle that lasted for hours. Crucial to the victory were British men-of-war offshore, whose guns broke the final charge of the Mysore cavalry. The triumph badly damaged Hyder Aly's reputation as a military genius. In two more battles, he was again forced to retreat and abandon his dream of driving the British out of Madras and seizing control of the Carnatic region of southern India.[21]

With perfectly staged earnestness, envoy Grenville assured Ambassador Franklin that these triumphs in the West Indies and India "made not the least change in the sincere desires" of the Rockingham cabinet to negotiate peace. Franklin had no trouble translating this seemingly heartfelt language. Grenville was telling Franklin that in the context of England's renewed prowess on sea and land it was time for the Americans to dump France and take the best deal that the British chose to offer.

This confrontation might have become a turning point in the nego-tiations if anyone besides Benjamin Franklin had been America's spokes-man. But Franklin, with twenty years of politicking in London under his belt, knew the Rockinghams and Shelburne could not take credit for Rodney's victory. It was an achievement of Lord Sandwich and the North ministry. Nor did the Rockinghams contribute anything to the Indian victories, which were the result of the East India Company's determina-tion to prevail over Sultan Hyder Aly.

Ambassador Franklin coolly replied that he knew what Grenville was thinking—and it was not going to happen. Grenville vehemently denied he was hoping Franklin would betray France. In a burst of desperation, the neophyte envoy revealed that he had been authorized to acknowledge the independence of America before peace negotiations began. He was telling Franklin this still secret policy to demonstrate his confidence in him. Could there be better proof of his and England's sincerity?

This revelation was followed by another outburst about Franklin's crucial role in reconciling England and America. Franklin remained unimpressed. Unconditional independence had a nice sound but it would take a lot of negotiating to find out what it really meant. In his diary Franklin commented that he had grown too old to be moved by such "flattering language . . . from great men."[22]

Foreign Minister Vergennes backed Franklin's objection to the revised commission and the irritated Grenville promised to obtain yet another revision. When the new commission came back, it was another disap-pointment—Grenville was empowered to deal with France and "other states." There was still no mention of the United States of America.

A few days later, Richard Oswald returned to Paris with a variation on England's supposed desire for peace. "The late victory" in the West Indies was not going to alter a fundamental fact: the empire was on the verge of bankruptcy. If the war lasted much longer, they would be forced to stop payment on stock in the Bank of England, which would ruin their national credit. "Our enemies," he told Franklin in almost lach-rymose terms, "may now do what they please with us." There was only one man who could rescue England from "its present desperate situation"—Benjamin Franklin.

The ambassador was more than a little skeptical about this protestation of imminent financial collapse. He was much more interested in a strange omission in Oswald's discourse. He said nothing about the Rockingham cabinet's supposed decision to offer America unconditional independence before the peace conference began. This suggested a significant division inside the new ministry. "Lord Shelburne," Franklin noted somewhat nervously, "is said to have lately acquired much of the King's confidence."[23]

Several days later, Franklin received some newspapers from England. In one of them, *The London Evening Post*, he read a report that "Mr. Grenville, in his first visit to Mr. Franklin, gained a considerable point of information." America would "enter into a separate treaty with England when she is convinced that England has insured to her *all that she can reasonably ask*."

Franklin was infuriated. He was sure this misinformation, which was aimed at sowing suspicion between America and France, had come from Grenville. The omission of the crucial word, independence, further convinced him that if he had to choose between the two envoys, he preferred Oswald. The ambitious Grenville, son of a first minister, was too eager to prove himself an able negotiator—even if he had to tell outrageous lies about his performance.[24]

For a week, Franklin was unable to do much about his growing conviction that he and Vergennes should try to get rid of Mr. Grenville. The American ambassador was "much indisposed with a sudden and violent cold, attended with feverishness and headach." He rightly concluded he had contracted influenza, which had been raging throughout Europe for several months. In a few days he had recovered. The ambassador had no idea that this epidemic would soon intervene in the peace negotiations in the most dramatic way imaginable.[25]

XII

On June 23, 1782, John Jay arrived in Paris and Franklin cordially welcomed him and his attractive wife, Sarah. Jay told Franklin of a last-minute change in the Spanish attitude toward America. The king's ministers had been "much struck" by the resolutions Parliament had passed, to discontinue offensive war in America. The Spanish foreign minister told Jay they would advise their ambassador in Paris to work out a treaty with him. Instead of waiting forty years, it looked as if the Americans would only have to wait three or four months to achieve Jay's goal of winning another recognition of American independence. The news immensely pleased both him and Franklin.

Franklin took Jay to Versailles to introduce him to Vergennes, who told them he was growing skeptical about the sincerity of the British cabinet—and Mr. Grenville. That encounter inspired Franklin to meet with Oswald the following day and tell him he preferred to negotiate peace with him rather than Grenville—if and when genuine negotiations ever began. Franklin promised to write to Lord Shelburne, suggesting this simplified way to proceed. Oswald was so pleased, he said he was sure that Shelburne would let Franklin write his commission. He virtually promised that the ambassador could spell out THE UNITED STATES OF AMERICA in capital letters if he chose. He too wanted to eliminate the kind of cabinet doubletalk that had confused matters with Grenville. Oswald had already told Franklin he thought some of the cabinet rated Rodney's victory "too high."

The next day, June 28, 1782, Franklin had a visit from Gerard de Rayneval, Vergennes's right-hand man and the secretary to the French council of state. He brought disturbing news. French spies in London had reported that Lord Shelburne with the approval of the British cabinet had dispatched an emissary to New York with orders to officials there to send confidential representatives to the governments of the thirteen colonies. The goal was to tilt them toward a reconciliation with England. They were to offer the same terms the Rockingham ministry had just granted to Ireland—their own parliament and judiciary. Rayneval wanted Franklin and Jay to write to Congress, urging them to counteract these insidious envoys.[26]

XIII

In London, Charles James Fox had become increasingly frustrated and angry at the two-headed peace negotiations in Paris. He was especially enraged at Lord Shelburne for his failure to inform Richard Oswald of the cabinet's decision to offer America independence as soon as formal peace talks began. On June 30, Fox proposed to the cabinet that the government should recognize the United States immediately, with or without peace talks.

This was a typically Foxian overreach, an attempt to settle the clash between him and Shelburne on the spot. Shelburne and his supporters in the cabinet vigorously disagreed; they insisted Britain should get some sort of compensation for this large concession. The cabinet voted with Shelburne—independence should be part of a peace treaty, where it could be used as a bargaining chip to extract concessions from either America or France. No one put the outcome more succinctly than Fox's friend, playwright Richard Brinsley Sheridan: "He was beat."[27]

A disgusted Fox announced he was going to resign as secretary of state for foreign affairs. But he agreed to delay an announcement for the time being, because First Minister Lord Rockingham was not at the cabinet meeting. He was at his town house, suffering from influenza, like thousands of other Londoners. The epidemic had long since crossed the English Channel and was laying low people from all walks of life.

The next day, the cabinet and the rest of London were stunned to learn Lord Rockingham was dead. The first minister's health had been fragile for several years. The struggle to push through his reform program in Parliament and simultaneously make peace with America in the shadow of George III's disapproval—and with Charles James Fox and Lord Shelburne in bitter disagreement within the cabinet—had been an added strain.

Rockingham had been frequently ill during his four months in power. Some people blamed his poor health for his failure to exercise his talent for conciliation and compromise between the two secretaries of state. This had probably been a vain hope from the start: no one could have resolved the mutual loathing that prevailed between Fox and Shelburne, which went far beyond their disagreement over America.[28]

Who was to succeed Lord Rockingham? The obvious chief contender was Charles James Fox. He had a following in Parliament and the oratorical talent to defend his—or any other—government. But George III would have preferred Satan Incarnate to the disheveled self-styled man of the people, who had been abusing him in the House of Commons for years. Knowing he was unacceptable, Fox suggested that another prominent Rockinghamite, the Duke of Portland, become the titular first minister. Everyone—including George III—knew that Fox would be the real leader. The king exploded with rage at Fox's presumption that His Majesty would consent to be a partner to such a deception. His Royal Highness asked Lord Shelburne to form a government.

The thorough courtier managed to recruit enough prominent men from the Rockingham party to create an administration. Charles James Fox and Edmund Burke immediately resigned in protest. The date of the departure of the two strongest voices for American independence was ironically symbolic: July 4, 1782. As the new first minister prepared to take office, he received an even more worrisome letter from George III. The king presumed that Lord Shelburne "must see that the great success of Lord Rodney's engagement has again so far roused the nation, that the peace which would have been acquiesced in three months ago would now be a matter of complaint." As far as His Majesty was concerned, July 4 would never be called Independence Day in America or anywhere else in his empire.[29]

Chapter Seven

Loose Cannons Front
and Center

IN AMERICA, during these same late spring months of 1782, Super-intendent of Finance Robert Morris struggled for ways and means to overcome the universal reluctance to pay taxes to the Continental Congress. One of his boldest moves was the appointment of receivers, specifically assigned to collect federal revenue in each state. Depending on the population of the state, they would be paid a percentage of the money they collected, ranging from one-eighth to one-quarter of the total.

Morris chose these men carefully, at one point riding to Delaware to persuade a prospect. He was looking for political allies as well as efficient government servants. He appointed James Lovell, formerly a key member of the Lee-Adams party, collector for Massachusetts. Morris hoped the difficult Yankee, who had played a large role in the destruction of the superintendent's friend Silas Deane, would become a reluctant but effective ally. Another Lee-Adams follower, William Whipple, was appointed receiver for New Hampshire.

In New York Morris chose Alexander Hamilton as the federal receiver. Having resigned from the army, the twenty-seven-year-old former aide to Washington was studying hard to become a lawyer. Hamilton told Morris that his time was precious and he did not think New York was inclined to pay any tax money whatsoever to the federal government. The governor, George Clinton, was opposed to the idea and had a majority in the legislature.

Morris replied that he hoped the Yorktown hero would go before the legislature and change their narrow minds. He wanted Hamilton on his side so badly, Morris guaranteed the author of *The Continentalist* his full percentage of New York's quota—$940—no matter how little money he collected.[1]

Hamilton accepted and left his law books and his wife and infant son, Philip, to sail down the Hudson from Albany to Poughkeepsie, where the New York legislature was in session. "I will endeavor by every step in my power to second your views," the new collector told Morris. "Though I am sorry to add, without any sanguine expectations." The words evinced the growing tension in the United States between those who wanted a more powerful federal government and those who feared and loathed the idea.

Hamilton got a very cool reception from Governor Clinton. Aside from his dislike of federal taxes, Clinton had recommended his friend Abraham Yates Jr. of Schenectady for the federal receiver's job. Yates had long served as the Continental loan officer for New York. There was one of these officers in each state. They sold bonds to wealthy men who wanted to support the war effort; the certificates guaranteed them annual interest payments and the eventual repayment of the principal. Very little of the money the loan officers raised got to the federal government. The states used it for their own purposes. Morris was determined to eliminate these ineffectual bureaucrats and that was one among several reasons why he refused to name Yates.

Yates was infuriated by his rejection. He claimed to have accepted deferred payment for his services as a loan officer and was now obliged "to shift for the necessarys of life" while this young upstart Hamilton had been granted a "generous and immediate salary." Hamilton told Morris that Yates's "ignorance and perverseness were only equalled by his pertinacity and conceit." The collector's fondness for pandering to the prejudices of the voters had impeded the war effort in New York so seriously, Yates "deserve[d] to be pensioned by the British ministry."[2]

This was not exactly the way to win friends for Morris's views. Hamilton's arrogance revealed one of the liabilities of the superintendent and his supporters. They tended to look with contempt and disdain on those who did not share their economic and political opinions.

In spite of strenuously pushed arguments, Hamilton was able to persuade the state legislature to vote only a modest tax of $18,000 as a first step to paying New York's $375,598 share of the federal budget. Worse, because of the inept way New York collected taxes, Hamilton doubted that the state would raise half the voted sum.

Hamilton succeeded in winning approval for two other proposals. He got both houses of the legislature to recommend a convention of the states "to enlarge the powers of Congress and vest them with funds." But Hamilton gloomily added in his letter to Morris that "he doubted the concurrence of the other states." The legislature also agreed to form a committee to create "a more effectual system of taxation." Neither of these large recommendations cost the legislators a cent, which undoubtedly had much to do with their passage.

Finally, in what may have been a tribute to Hamilton's display of expertise on the thorny subject of government, the lawmakers elected him a delegate to the Continental Congress. The influence of Hamilton's wealthy father-in-law, General Philip Schuyler, who was the leader of the state senate, was another possible reason for this sudden elevation. It might also have been Governor Clinton's way of dismissing Hamilton by giving him the most meaningless job at his disposal.

A gloomy superintendent of finance remarked that Hamilton's description of the halfhearted way New York collected taxes was "an epitome of the follies which prevail from one end of the continent to another." Hamilton replied with an even gloomier analysis of their problems: New York exhibited "the general disease which infects all our constitutions—an excess of popularity . . . The inquiry is constantly what will *please*, not what will *benefit* the people." Worse, after nine months residence in Albany, Hamilton had concluded a third of New York still hoped the British would win the war and the rest "sigh for peace," which he feared they would purchase at a price that would guarantee America a dismal future.[3]

George III and Lord Shelburne would have paid a secret agent a great deal of money to read Hamilton's correspondence with the superintendent of finance. The embryo congressman threw in a series of pen portraits of New York's leading politicians, all etched in acid. Governor Clinton's political principles depended almost entirely on "when a new election approaches." Another man was a good lawyer but his friends "mistook his talents when they made him a statesman." A third "never had judgment and he now has scarcely plausibility."[4]

II

The reaction of Hamilton's friends to his appointment to the Continental Congress was an interesting sample of the conflicts that were dividing Americans in this crucial year. His fellow former aide to Washington, James McHenry, wrote a blunt letter from Baltimore, where "Mac" was prospering as a busy doctor, warning "Ham" that he was making a possibly disastrous mistake.

McHenry told Hamilton the story of two lawyers from Baltimore. During most of the revolutionary struggle, the first neglected his practice and devoted himself to the sacred cause. The other man shunned public service and concentrated on making money. Now, with peace possibly dawning, the fickle public had voted the penniless patriot out of office and replaced him with the rich lawyer. McHenry's moral was: "The good things of this world (including public office) are all to be purchased with money." A man with cash can be "whatever he pleases." Hamilton should concentrate on making enough money to do "justice to your family" and then let the people "persuade" him to be a public servant again.

From John Laurens, still serving as commander of the light infantry in General Nathanael Greene's army besieging Charleston, came a very different letter. He praised Hamilton's decision "to put on the toga" of a legislator. Laurens declared that he did not want Hamilton "even for a moment withdrawn from the public service." Laurens hoped that with Hamilton supporting him in the Continental Congress, he might yet persuade the South Carolina legislature to accept his plan to emancipate three thousand slaves and turn them into fighting soldiers.[5]

Whose advice did Hamilton follow? The answer was in a letter he wrote to Lafayette: "I have been employed . . . in rocking the cradle and studying the art of *fleecing* my neighbors. I am now a grave counselor at law and shall soon be a grave member of Congress." Showing signs that McHenry's advice troubled him, Hamilton added: "I am going to throw away a few months more in public life and then retire a simple citizen and good *paterfamilias*."[6]

Hamilton informed Robert Morris of his resignation as federal tax receiver for New York. Morris tried to be philosophic; he thought Hamilton might be more helpful to his program in Congress. But how was he going to avoid hiring Abraham Yates as the new receiver? The financier did not want to offend Governor Clinton a second time.

Hamilton promised to solve this problem before he left for Philadelphia to don his toga.

The new congressman told Yates he wanted to resolve the enmity between them. He swore he had not sought the receiver's job; it had been forced upon him by Superintendent Morris and his friends. Now he was about to resign the office without having received a cent of pay and implied he was glad to go. Hamilton described the receiver's responsibilities in sweeping terms. Not only did he have to gather taxes, he had to look and think continentally, he should even have "continental eyes" and must always act independently of his state's government. Yates, a declared states-rights man, growled a very reluctant agreement with this job description.

With the greatest solemnity, Hamilton offered Yates the appointment. But he would have to promise never to cease trying to "promote the views of the Financier" (Morris) even if he thought they were "against the interest" of the state of New York. Yates exploded with righteous anger and told Hamilton he was an honest man and the "dictates of my conscience" would not permit him to even consider becoming federal receiver. This enabled Morris and Hamilton to appoint a man who was in harmony with their continental views, without clashing with Governor Clinton.[7]

III

The new receiver, Thomas Tillotson, was soon complaining that there was no hope of getting any money out of New York. The state was by no means the only federal delinquent. Mighty Virginia, with seven times New York's population, had paid nothing. New Hampshire, Delaware, and Rhode Island were in the same dolorous category. Superintendent Morris mixed cajolery and threats, even hinting that he had the power to order the army to collect federal taxes. James Madison, one of his chief backers in Congress, was even more emphatic on this controversial point. Some money trickled into the treasury in July from Pennsylvania and Massachusetts, but it was hardly enough to ease Morris's woes.

In his desperation, Morris took another daring step. He suspended interest on loan-office certificates. Not that the government paid real money; the interest payment consisted of another certificate, which the creditors could look forward to cashing at some distant day. Morris said it was time to stop creating this illusion of revenue and declared he would pay only interest when he could do it in hard money or notes from the Bank of North America.

Soon there was a veritable procession of wealthy Americans parading into the financier's Philadelphia office, or writing him strenuous letters from more distant states, all uttering screams of protest. Morris remained unperturbed. He had expected the decision to produce "much clamor."

Morris hoped that noise from these wealthy men would have an impact in their respective states. "To the public creditors," he wrote, "I say until the states provide revenues they cannot be paid; and to the states I say that they are bound by every principle held sacred among men to make that provision." He urged the creditors to form a committee and lobby Congress and the state legislatures, demanding action. The creditors put together a committee and Morris persuaded Alexander Hamilton to write an appeal for them. Its political impact on the delinquent states was zero minus.[8]

Trying to circumvent Arthur Lee and his circle of critics, Morris's supporters in Congress created a "grand committee" of one member from each of the thirteen states. They reconsidered the direct levies on land and liquor that Morris had proposed and Lee's committee rejected in February. The maneuver worked, on paper. The committee produced a report strongly supporting the taxes. But Congress revealed a dismaying lack of enthusiasm for voting them into life.[9]

The increasingly desperate financier began to think that his only hope of revenue was the 5 percent impost on imports. This had been hanging fire for almost a year. "What a prodigious sum we are losing," groaned Virginia delegate James Madison at one point, as political foot-dragging produced growing fiscal paralysis.[10]

IV

General George Washington decided he had done everything in his power to help Superintendent of Finance Morris and left Philadelphia at the end of March to resume active command of the Continental Army. Accompanied by Martha, his aides, and his Life Guard, he took over a small stone house in Newburgh, New York, near the army's New Windsor encampment. Owned by a widow, Mrs. Jonathan Hasbrouck, the house had an odd layout. The dining room had seven doors and only one window. Washington was to remain at the Hasbrouck house for sixteen and a half months—a longer stay than in any of his previous headquarters.[11]

The financial crisis in Philadelphia was soon creating worries for Washington as well as Morris. The superintendent of finance had signed a contract with a New York merchant, Comfort Sands, to feed the "moving" or main army. Sands was said to live by a novel maxim: "No poor person can be honest." The contractor's performance soon gave a lurid color to this dubious motto. He had promised, Washington pointed out in a letter to Morris, that he would supply every soldier with a daily ration of "one pound of bread made of good merchantable wheat flour, one pound of beef or three quarters of a pound of pork and one gill [four ounces] of whiskey or country rum."

Instead, Mr. Sands, in his determination to avert poverty, shipped the troops spoiled flour, rotten meat, and putrid whiskey. Washington accused Sands of having a "thirst for gain" that was threatening to wreck the army. The "wrongly named" (in Washington's opinion) Comfort had an answer to the general's critique: His contract specified that he would be promptly paid in specie—hard money. The American government had none, theoretically justifying the merchant's persistent nonperformance.[12]

With officers and enlisted men writing letters to their friends and their state legislators describing their awful diet, the Continental Army began growing as unpopular as the Continental Congress. Recruits were few in number and their quality was low. A Massachusetts lieutenant colonel was court-martialed for enlisting in his regiment two deserters from the French army, two deserters from the British, and one George West, "an idiot." American recruiters seemed to have a penchant for the mentally retarded.[13]

A glimpse of Washington's growing desperation was a letter he wrote on April 27, 1782, proposing that Congress enlist German mercenaries in the American army. Thousands of these men, originally hired by George III, had been captured in the course of the war and many of them were apparently eager to serve in the Continental Army and settle in America. The idea had originated with a Polish volunteer, Count Maurice August Beniowski, who thought he could raise 3,500 men.

Congress debated this proposal for the next several months, with great uneasiness manifested by several delegates. "Can we pay them punctually?" asked Arthur Middleton of South Carolina. The answer, of course, was almost certainly no. Middleton also feared it would be considered a sign of weakness that "we can not or will not fill up our armies with our own people." If the idea was adopted, Middleton thought it should be attributed to (or blamed on) General Washington. Congress should have nothing to do with it. After two months of vacillation, the politicians forwarded the proposal to the superintendent of finance and the secretary of war, leaving the final decision to them. To no one's surprise, they did nothing.[14]

Another Washington headache was a quarrel that erupted into mutual demands for courts-martial between two of his best generals, William Heath of Massachusetts and Alexander McDougall of New York. General Heath was the overall commander of the Hudson Highlands; General McDougall commanded at West Point. The two men detested each other over a slur that went back six years. According to General McDougall, when Washington retreated from New York City in 1776, only three men objected to the decision: "a fool, a knave and an obstinate honest man." General Heath was supposedly the knave.

Still fuming over this ancient insult, the portly, usually mild-mannered Heath had put McDougall under arrest for ignoring orders Heath had given him at West Point. General McDougall retaliated by announcing he was ready to prove that General Heath had acted the knave's part in the retreat from New York. It was a stupid dispute and an ironic reminder of another peril of the limbo between peace and war in which America found herself. When soldiers had no enemy to fight, they often fought with each other.[15]

V

General Washington remained grimly determined to act as if he were still fighting a war. He discussed with Secretary of the Army Benjamin Lincoln how many men he needed to capture heavily fortified New York. He glumly concluded that even with all his regiments recruited to their full quotas, and the addition of Rochambeau's 5,000 men in Virginia, he would be able to muster only 13,000 regulars—some 24,000 less than he needed for a successful attack.

The discouraged general turned his attention to a long memorandum in which he analyzed other military alternatives for the campaign of 1782. He pondered the possibility of attacks on Charleston and Savannah, carefully noting the strength of each enemy garrison. He even considered an operation against the British navy base in Halifax, Nova Scotia, in concert with the French fleet. At this point he was unaware that his friend Admiral de Grasse had been captured and his fleet shattered by Admiral Rodney in the Battle of the Saints Islands. Washington closed this wishful meditation by planning a foray into Canada in September. An overland assault by 8,000 men would rout the 5,000 men the British had posted in widely scattered forts and detachments along the border.

In all these plans, Washington included General Rochambeau and his army. He told the Frenchman he had not gone fifteen miles from Newburgh for fear he would miss a message from him. But Rochambeau showed little or no inclination to join the Americans for an assault on New York—or any other objective on Washington's list. Instead, the French commander marched his army from Virginia to Baltimore, where they camped and awaited orders from Paris. This was not good news from Washington's point of view. He saw a strong probability that the expeditionary force might soon depart to join the struggle in the West Indies.[16]

VI

Meanwhile, Washington was coping with an ugly intrusion of the fighting. In mid-April, Brigadier General David Forman of the New Jersey militia arrived in Newburgh, claiming that one of his men had been foully murdered by New York-based loyalists. Forman had long been in charge of posting sentinels along the New Jersey coast; he had often sent Washington important information about British ship and troop movements.

Less well known to Washington and other leaders was Forman's role as head of the Association for Retaliation, an organization he had created in Monmouth County, supposedly to combat raids by loyalists operating from New York. The raids were supervised by the Board of Associated Loyalists, still sanctioned by the British army; the commander was still William Franklin, son of the American ambassador to Paris. The Association for Retaliation had no standing with anyone, for a very good reason. They acted as if law and order did not exist in New Jersey.[17]

Forman told Washington a grisly tale. On March 24, one of his men, Captain Joshua Huddy, had been on duty in a blockhouse at Toms River,

New Jersey, when a midnight assault by well-armed loyalists had overwhelmed the defenders. Huddy and the rest of the garrison had surrendered with little or no resistance. Taken to New York, Huddy and his men were put aboard one of the British prison ships in Wallabout Bay, off the Brooklyn shore. In these vile hulks, almost ten thousand Americans had already died of malnutrition and disease.

On April 12, 1782, men in the service of the Board of Associated Loyalists appeared at the prison ship and demanded that Huddy be surrendered to them. They said he was guilty of murdering one of their group after the man had been captured in New Jersey. Transported to the New Jersey coast near Middletown, Huddy had been hanged and left with a placard on his chest, declaring that the loyalists were going to hang "man for man" as long as the war lasted. Beneath these words in larger letters was daubed: UP GOES HUDDY FOR PHILIP WHITE.

General Forman claimed that captured loyalist Philip White had been killed when he seized a sentry's gun, shot him, and tried to escape. Forman flourished affidavits purporting to prove this assertion. He did not tell Washington that Captain Huddy had been an active member of the Association for Retaliation and had been involved in assaulting and occasionally murdering loyalists and neutrals in Monmouth County.

On the face of it, hanging the captured Huddy was an outrageous act. Washington convened a council of war and asked the assembled generals if the American army should threaten to retaliate against a captured British prisoner. The council voted almost unanimously in favor of this grim policy. Washington wrote a letter to Sir Henry Clinton, demanding that he surrender the officer who had commanded the men who had hanged Huddy. According to General Forman, he was Captain Richard Lippincott, a loyalist who had participated in numerous raids into New Jersey.

Sir Henry replied with outrage, declaring that he would never have tolerated such a barbarous act. He implied that the Board of Associated Loyalists was not a legitimate branch of the British Army and he had no responsibility for its actions. He refused to surrender Captain Lippincott or anyone else, claiming the mess was the result of ongoing outrages committed by both sides in Monmouth County. Washington ordered General Moses Hazen, who was in command of a British prisoner-of-war camp in Lancaster, Pennsylvania, to choose by lot a British captain who was an "unconditional prisoner"—a man captured in battle, not protected by a surrender agreement such as the one signed at Yorktown. Whether through inattention or stupidity, Hazen conducted his deadly lottery among a randomly selected group of British captains, paying no attention to Washington's "unconditional" instructions.

The choice of a victim fell on nineteen-year-old Captain Charles Asgill of the British Guards, who had surrendered at Yorktown. When Washington announced he would be hanged if Clinton did not hand over Captain Lippincott, General Clinton protested with more than justifiable wrath. He grudgingly added that he had decided to try Captain Lippincott by court-martial. If he were found guilty of murdering Huddy, he would be punished by the British code of military justice; that almost certainly meant hanging. In the meantime, an embarrassed Washington agreed to postpone any action on Captain Asgill.[18]

VII

On May 7, 1782, Washington was still waiting to hear the outcome of the Lippincott court-martial when he received a letter from the new British commander in New York, General Sir Guy Carleton. Sir Henry Clinton had gone home. General Carleton smoothly announced he and the new naval commander, Admiral Robert Digby, had received from their government commissions to make peace. He asked Washington to consent to a meeting with him to discuss a local truce between the two armies and requested a passport for his secretary, Maurice Morgann, whom he wanted to send to the Continental Congress with transcripts of recent sessions of Parliament in which speakers called for peace with America. Washington frigidly declined to meet with Carleton and Congress refused to issue a passport for the secretary. The general rightly suspected this was a maneuver aimed at trivializing, if not eliminating, the American peace commissioners in Europe.[19]

Congress passed resolutions affirming the French alliance and warning citizens "against the insidious steps which the Court of London is proposing." They persuaded the Maryland and New Jersey legislatures to pass similar resolutions to discourage Carleton from approaching individual states.[20]

Nevertheless, the well-financed British propaganda machine in New York had ways of getting this message of pseudo peace into circulation. In spite of Washington's attempt to control traffic in and out of New York, loyalists and not a few rebels came and went regularly to and from the city. A dismaying number of Americans greeted Carleton's message with something very close to joy. Soon it was being discussed in the Continental Congress and in the newspapers.[21]

VIII

Washington's—and Congress's—suspicions were more than justified. General Carleton was acting on the orders he had received from Lord Shelburne to do what he could to break up the American confederation and dispose some or all of the states to a compromise peace, short of independence. Maurice Morgann had been Lord Shelburne's secretary before he became General Carleton's—an indication of how seriously His Lordship regarded this diplomacy.

Sir Guy was hoping to draw on a personal aura of trust and friendship for America. He had been the commander in Canada in 1775, when the Americans invaded the province. Carleton smashed a desperate attempt to storm Quebec on January 1, 1776, and captured several hundred prisoners. Instead of hanging them as traitors, he paroled them on the promise that they would no longer participate in the war. They were not really rebels, the general claimed; they were simply deluded victims of demagogues like Samuel Adams. Seven years later, General Carleton was back, eager to persuade the Americans that they had been further deluded by Thomas Paine's *Common Sense* and Thomas Jefferson's Declaration of Independence, with their nasty attacks on the best of kings, George III.

The first thing Carleton did on his arrival in New York was send for Judge William Smith. This canny lawyer was still in touch with loyalists and neutrals throughout New England and the Middle States. Carleton and Smith spent several days discussing "the prospect of succeeding in the reconciliation of the continent." The general said that he would soon be receiving a peace commission that would give him "ample" powers to negotiate. "His object, reunion upon any terms that can be got to wean the continent away from the French," Smith informed his diary.[22]

Carleton told Smith that the Rockingham government was "as firm for the reunion" with America as they would be "generous in the[ir] overtures." Anything said in Parliament could be dismissed as political maneuvers. "Lord Shelburne in particular openly avowed [to Carleton] his principles against the separation."

Smith feared General Carleton was almost too eager to achieve results.

"He is decisive but rapid," Smith wrote in his diary. The ex-chief justice thought the Americans might view Carleton's peace overtures as "weakness." But the judge was tremendously encouraged by the overall plan of attack on the idea of independence.

For the moment, General Carleton was relying on promoting "good humor." He began paroling from New York's various prisons captured soldiers who promised not to do any further fighting against the king. When the first of these parolees reached the Continental Army camp at New Windsor and requested a pass to go home, Washington icily ordered him to report to his regiment—"which disappointed the soldier exceedingly," a New England general worriedly noted.

The morale of the American army, still unpaid and badly fed, was low. If Washington had permitted Carleton to get away with his parole policy, "many soldiers on the outposts . . . might have gone to the enemy, pretended to be taken and have come out under parole and have gone home, to the unspeakable injury of the army," the New England general wrote in his journal. Washington ordered the American commissary of prisoners to credit General Carleton with one exchanged prisoner and told him to stop the practice immediately.[23]

General Carleton also released from jail young Brockholst Livingston, the son of New Jersey's governor, William Livingston. He had been captured by a British frigate while returning from Spain, where he had served as private secretary to his brother-in-law, Ambassador John Jay. Carleton also released John Jay's brother, Dr. James Jay. Like William Smith, he had begun the war as an ardent patriot and grown disillusioned with the Revolution. Dr. Jay had arranged to have himself captured by the British. He was put in jail with Brockholst Livingston to pump him for information about John Jay's mission to Spain. "They [Brockholst and Dr. Jay] came away [from General Carleton's residence] with me to tea," Smith wrote in his diary.

Young Brockholst was soon sent to New Jersey with expressions of cordial friendship for his father, the governor, an old Smith friend. Then Smith conversed with Dr. Jay about "what he got from Livingston in the jail." The young man had talked freely about how little progress Ambassador Jay had made in Spain; Brockholst had come to dislike his dour, discontented brother-in-law; the Madrid mission's official secretary, William Carmichael, was even more "at variance" with the ambassador. Carmichael was giving Jay the same superiority treatment he had given Silas Deane.

Beyond these revelations, Smith found "no intelligence of any moment." This led Smith to suspect that Dr. Jay was a rebel spy. At the very least, Smith sensed, "he thinks better of the rebel cause than when he came in. He certainly has a low opinion of our strength."[24]

IX

The news of Admiral Rodney's victory in the West Indies reached New York on May 11, 1782, six days after General Carleton's arrival. Judge Smith noted it excitedly in his diary and rushed a report to the general from relatives in New Jersey that nineteen out of twenty people in the state were "for peace and reunion." He urged General Carleton to obtain from Sir Henry Clinton before he sailed home his correspondence with the Americans in breakaway Vermont. The Green Mountain colony was considered the place to go if you wanted to remain in the British Empire. "Multitudes flock to it from New England," Smith wrote.[25]

From the British point of view, the timing of Carleton's arrival and the news of Rodney's victory could not have been better. In letter after letter, members of Congress agonized over whether the news was true or only half true. They exchanged rumors of British losses in the battle, trying to make it sound like a draw. But realists such as James Madison concluded that there was "little reason to hope" the bad news was not genuine. Nor was there any likelihood that "the misfortunes of our ally would be repaired" by later victories in the West Indies or elsewhere. It was a shattering defeat for the French navy.[26]

In Newburgh, General Washington and his top officers were equally dismayed by the news of de Grasse's defeat and capture. A glum Major General Henry Knox, commander of the Continental Army's artillery, one of Washington's closest confidants, wrote Alexander Hamilton that the "affair in the West Indies" meant that the American army would be able to do little in 1782 but "eat beef and drink whiskey."

Washington had repeatedly emphasized in his letters to Lafayette and other correspondents that any and all plans for 1782 relied on French naval superiority in American waters. Now this essential ingredient had gone glimmering. The commander in chief fell back on a renewed call to fill the army's depleted ranks. "There is no measure so likely to produce a favorable termination of the war as vigorous preparations for meeting the enemy," the general told Secretary of Foreign Affairs Robert R. Livingston.

Washington knew he was preaching to the converted. But he felt a need to get the message to someone in Philadelphia who dealt with both Congress and America's diplomats in Europe. He wanted to let them know he was not in the least impressed by General Carleton's peace initiatives. Unfortunately, the general's exhortations had become almost too familiar.[27]

X

At this point, the Americans were temporarily rescued from their war weariness and Lord Shelburne's and General Carleton's doubletalk by the Chevalier de La Luzerne, the French ambassador to the United States. No one kept a closer or shrewder eye on the political climate of the embryonic republic than this charming, sophisticated man, who never hesitated to spend money freely to maintain the fragile alliance.

The Chevalier decided Americans needed a public event to demonstrate to themselves and the rest of the world the strength and intensity of their bond with France. Fortunately, there was a perfect pretext. Six months earlier, Queen Marie Antoinette had given birth to a son. The arrival of an heir to the throne was considered by the French people a sign that God was blessing the king and queen. The news was greeted with celebrations and fireworks throughout France. Congress had sent warm congratulations to Louis XVI and his queen.

Luzerne decided the birth of the dauphin was an opportunity for a magnificent celebration. First, the ambassador persuaded Washington to give an elaborate dinner for five hundred officers of the army at New Windsor. This was only a warm-up for the ambassador's Philadelphia festival, one of the most extravagant parties ever seen in America.

More than a thousand invitations went out to army officers, politicians, merchants, and clergymen in and near the American capital. General Washington and General Rochambeau were on the list, as well as John Hanson, still the reluctant president of the Continental Congress, along with Joseph Reed, the president of Pennsylvania. So was Tom Paine, who was on Luzerne's payroll and had written a number of articles extolling the alliance.

A splendid pavilion supported by large painted pillars was erected as a ballroom beside the ambassador's house on Chestnut Street. The ceiling was decorated with elegant paintings and the garden beside the house was cut into walks and divided with cedar and pine branches into artificial groves. Captain Pierre Charles L'Enfant, an engineer serving with the French army, was responsible for these artistic preparations. The talented young man did not know he was launching his career as an American architect and city planner, which would bear fruit in a new capital, Washington D.C., early in the next century.

Newspapers published notices of streets that were closed to traffic in certain directions—a wise precaution. No less than ten thousand gawkers surrounded the invited guests, among whom the plump smiling Luzerne affably circulated. The ladies of Philadelphia already adored him for his suave manners and witty conversation.

At 9 p.m., spellbinding fireworks interrupted the music and dancing. At midnight, the guests sat down to a sumptuous banquet prepared by thirty cooks borrowed from the French army. As champagne flowed, several spectators remarked that the diners looked and behaved "more as if they were worshipping than eating."

By the time the last guest wobbled home in the dawn, there were few if any people in Philadelphia outside Arthur Lee's circle of grumbletonians who had any fault to find with the French alliance. Admiral de Grasse's disaster in the West Indies became a distant disappointment which King Louis XVI's power and wealth would soon repair.[28]

XI

One of the guests at the banquet, Dr. Benjamin Rush, remarked on how strange it was that the birth of a future king should inspire so much joy among republicans. This enthusiasm for monarchy may be the best explanation for an extraordinary letter General Washington received around this time from Colonel Lewis Nicola, suggesting that he dismiss Congress and become America's first king.

An immigrant from Ireland, Nicola had volunteered for the American army, although he was already sixty years of age. He had two decades of military experience in the British army and during the war served with considerable distinction as a recruiter and administrator. In 1782 he was in command of the Invalid Regiment, a group of men who were not healthy enough to fight but were able to perform light duties in the New Windsor camp.

The aging colonel described the army's woes—lack of pay, awful food, inadequate clothing—and blamed Congress. He told the commander in chief that military men were among the first to perceive "the weakness of republicks." Perhaps it was time for Washington to use the "universal esteem and veneration" of the army to become the leader who would conduct America along "the smoother paths of peace." No doubt it would be wise if Washington chose a "more moderate title" than king, lest he rouse the ire of "republican bigots." But Nicola felt a need to communicate his "heterodox" thoughts to Washington, implying that the subject was being discussed throughout the army.

Washington replied to Nicola with "surprise and astonishment." Nothing in the course of the war had given him "more painful sensations" than the colonel's report that "such ideas" existed in the army. He was the last person in the world who would consider such a scheme, which "seems big with the greatest mischiefs that can befall my country." He urged Nicola to "banish these thoughts from your mind and never communicate" them to anyone else.

At the same time, Washington declared that "no man possesses a more sincere wish to see justice done to the army than I do." He promised to exert himself to obtain redress for the soldiers "in a constitutional way." In less than a year, these words would return to haunt General Washington when the army, still unpaid and badly fed, tried to force him to demand justice in a highly unconstitutional way. Meanwhile, the flabbergasted Nicola wrote Washington no less than three cringing letters, begging his forgiveness.[29]

XII

A veritable paradigm of what might befall America at the hands of disgusted soldiers was taking shape outside Charleston, where General Nathanael Greene presided over an army that was getting neither pay nor regular rations—not even the slop that Comfort Sands was feeding the main army at New Windsor. In Georgia, General Anthony Wayne's much smaller force was also suffering from public neglect. Wayne told Greene that "every ounce" of food they procured was "either at the price of blood or the hazard of life."

The superintendent of finance had ordered South Carolina and Georgia to supply the soldiers; they could deduct the cost from their federal taxes. It was one of Morris's vainer hopes. Both states were badly disorganized by two years of rampant violence. Georgia was totally bankrupt. In both states the soldiers had to seize food from recalcitrant farmers to survive.

Early in April, General Greene wrote to Wayne that the "want of cloathing, pay and the irregular supplies of provision . . . has given a very murmuring tone to the army." Among the Pennsylvania troops, whom Wayne had long commanded, the "face of mutiny" was becoming more and more apparent. The generals had not forgotten the January 1781 mutiny of the Pennsylvania Line, which had come close to unraveling the Continental Army.[30]

On April 20, a camp woman named Becky slipped into General Greene's headquarters to tell one of his aides that she had overheard a Pennsylvania sergeant named George Gosnell plotting not only a mutiny but the betrayal of Greene and his top officers to the British. Becky was married to a Maryland sergeant named Richard Peters, who served as General Greene's steward, and was a good friend of Gosnell. The Pennsylvania sergeant was a British deserter who had played a leading role in the January 1781 mutiny.

The plan called for 150 British cavalry to storm the American camp that night. Gosnell and his fellow conspirators would make sure that the sentries on duty gave no alarm. Greene and his staff officers would be seized and dragged to Charleston; Gosnell and other Pennsylvanians would call on the army to quit the war. The Revolution in South Carolina would collapse.

Greene immediately arrested Gosnell and ordered him court-martialed. That night, the 150 British cavalrymen rode to within a mile of the American camp, waiting for the gunshot that would signal them to attack. The shot was never fired but twelve members of the Pennsylvania Line, all presumably members of the plot, deserted to the enemy. On April 22, 1782, Gosnell was found guilty of treason and executed by a firing squad.[31]

An increasingly desperate Greene wrote to Superintendent of Finance Morris and to General Washington, warning that his army might soon "cease to exist." Not even the officers had any money to buy clothes or food from local civilians. Officers and men were in rags and were living on "the poorest of beef and rice" and had not seen a gill of rum for a month. Greene assured Morris that he was "aware of the difficulties under which you labor" but money, hard money, had become a necessity.

"There never was an army more distressed or more discontented," Greene told Washington.[32]

Things got worse, rather than better. By July 1782, Greene was writing bitterly to South Carolina militia general John Barnwell that the state's politicians seemed to think the army "could live on air, or as they do in the kingdom of heaven, without eating and drinking." More than a third of the time, they were "without provisions." He appealed to Governor John Mathews for a more consistent supply system and was told that unless Greene gave him "military aid," it would be impossible to deliver "either regular or effectual supplies to the army." Why? South Carolinians were selling "prodigious" quantities of food to the British in Charleston for hard money. The clink of King George's pounds sterling made them less than enthusiastic about selling food to Greene's army for promissory notes from South Carolina.[33]

Inside Charleston, General Alexander Leslie, taking his cue from General Carleton in New York, proposed a cease-fire. He sent his aide-de-camp, Captain Francis Skelly, to Greene under a flag of truce to tell him of the fall of the North government and show him transcripts of talk of reconciliation in Parliament. Skelly claimed that General Carleton's secretary (Maurice Morgann) was in Philadelphia, talking peace with the Continental Congress. Greene spent over an hour chatting with the affable Skelly, who said he looked forward to soon shaking hands and having a glass of wine with American officers.

General Greene thought Leslie's approach was much too informal to warrant a response. He suspected the British wanted to make it look as if the first overture for a truce came from him. In a tough letter to the president of the Continental Congress, John Hanson, Greene declared that he would not dream of agreeing to Leslie's proposal without the approval of Congress. He also thought it would need the agreement of "our ally"—France.

With remarkable perspicacity for someone fighting a war hundreds of miles away from his political leaders, Greene thought the British goal was to "detach us from our alliance" and "relax our exertions." He dreaded the latter possibility most of all, because of the "temper of the people" in South Carolina. They were too ready to agree with "any thing that promises repose."[34]

Two days later, General Leslie sent Greene a formal proposal for a truce. He said he had "no doubt" that a cease-fire had been arranged "to the northward"—around New York. He felt a duty "to the rights of humanity and the welfare of this country" to end the shooting war in South Carolina as soon as possible. Leslie was ready to send commissioners to discuss terms with any officers Greene might appoint. The Rhode Islander tersely replied that he had received no orders from Congress on the subject of peace, and was not "at liberty" to discuss it.

Greene knew that this meant continued bloodshed. The British needed food for their army and hay for their horses, and the only place to find these necessities was on the farms of South Carolina. General Leslie announced he was going to concentrate his foraging efforts on known rebels, in revenge for South Carolina's policies of seizing the farms and slaves of loyalists. A worried Greene told Anthony Wayne that Leslie planned to "strip the people of all the property he can lay his hands on." But the weakness of Greene's army left him unable to do much about it.[35]

XIII

In Georgia, with a much smaller army—523 men—General Anthony Wayne found himself frequently fighting for survival. A jittery Nathanael Greene, fearing a British push from Charleston, weakened Wayne still further by recalling his 100-man cavalry detachment. The Georgians did their best to bolster Mad Anthony's morale. They voted four thousand guineas to purchase a confiscated rice plantation for the Pennsylvania hero, with a handsome mansion included in the gift. The previous owner was the son of the state's royal governor.[36]

This generosity may have added elan to Wayne's natural aggressiveness. A spy told him that the British commander in Savannah had ordered loyalist Lieutenant Colonel Thomas Browne to take command of some four hundred men to escort a party of Creek Indians who were joining the British garrison. Wayne immediately decided to march by night and attack them. Riding with the advance guard of sixty infantry and forty dragoons, Wayne hoped to seize a causeway across the swamps outside Savannah and block Browne's route of return.

Around midnight, Wayne encountered Browne's entire force on the causeway. A more cautious general would have retreated. Wayne ordered an assault. Howling like maniacs, his forty cavalrymen thundered toward the astonished enemy, while the sixty infantrymen assailed their flanks. Browne's loyalist cavalry fled into the swamp and his infantry, mostly German mercenaries, fired a single volley and followed the horsemen into the muck. The victory was so swift and so total, the rest of Wayne's army never got into the fight. Mad Anthony counted forty enemy dead; he captured eighteen men and thirty horses. It was a tribute, Wayne proudly reported to General Greene, of the virtue of attacking with "vivacity."[37]

Marching his men within gunshot of the British entrenchments around Savannah, Wayne again dared the enemy commander, Brigadier Allured Clarke, to come out and fight. Clarke responded with some black and Indian skirmishers, who did no damage. A few days later, the brigadier and the royal governor of Georgia sent Wayne a proposal for a ceasefire, based on the claim that peace was being negotiated in Europe.

A skeptical Wayne forwarded the proposal to General Greene outside Charleston. Meanwhile Wayne waged a war of nerves on Clarke's garrison, bombarding them with offers of two hundred acres of land to anyone who deserted and agreed to fight in Wayne's army. A satisfying stream of runaways appeared in the American camp, where they were desperately needed. The cavalrymen in Wayne's army were now all Georgia militiamen whose brief terms of enlistment were expiring.

Unfortunately, the elated Wayne had lost track of the Creek Indians whom Colonel Browne had been planning to meet the night Wayne routed him. They had been delayed en route and arrived at their rendezvous point the day after Wayne's victory. The British defeat did not lessen the Creeks' enthusiasm for the royal cause. They were led by one of their fiercest warriors, a six-foot-three-inch giant named Emistisiguo. With them they had 127 packhorses loaded with furs, which they planned to sell to the British in Savannah.

Led by Negro guides, the Creeks had scouted Wayne's position the night before. They planned to overrun his pickets and cut their way through to Savannah. But Wayne had reversed the position of his army on the next night, a precaution he often took to guard against a surprise attack, The main body of his troops were asleep where the pickets had been the previous night, guarded by only one sentry. Emistisiguo killed the sentry, but not before he got off a warning shot.

The howling Indians, a hundred and fifty strong, poured into the American camp, shooting and stabbing the stunned Americans. Wayne found himself fighting hand to hand. But the Americans rallied when Chief Emistisiguo halted his attack to try to load and fire some captured

cannon. Wayne ordered a bayonet assault and the great chief went down
with four wounds in his huge body. Wayne led a cavalry charge past
the dying Emistisiguo. "With his last breath," Wayne told Nathanael
Greene, the chief pulled the trigger of his musket and "killed my horse
under me." The rest of the Creeks fled into Savannah, abandoning their
pack train.

In the morning, General Wayne discovered that twelve of the Creeks
had surrendered to pursuing Americans under Colonel Thomas Posey,
commander of his cavalry. Although Wayne later spoke admiringly of
the Indians' "determined bravery," he asked Posey what he was thinking
when he took these warriors captive. Posey said they had surrendered
on the assumption that they would be treated like any other prisoners of
war. Wayne angrily ordered them executed on the spot, dismissing the
dismayed Posey's protests. Already outnumbered, General Wayne was
determined to discourage the Creeks from throwing their numerous warriors into the contest for Georgia.[38]

Many loyalists were outraged by Wayne's ruthless order and threatened to retaliate. They circulated a report that Brigadier Clarke was going
to unleash the Indians on the civilian populace and "put to the sword any
American officer that might be captured." Wayne's reply was as bellicose
as the brigadier's rumored threat, which Clarke energetically denied he
ever made.

Nothing came of this war of words. In little more than two weeks, a
delighted General Wayne was telling Nathanael Greene that the British
army had evacuated Savannah, leaving the town and fortifications not
only intact, but "perfect." Both he and the civilians were "much obligated
to that worthy and humane officer," Brigadier Clarke.[39]

Wayne decided to demonstrate that Americans too could be pacific in
their policies. He worked out an arrangement with British merchants in
Savannah which enabled them to stay in the city for six months after the
army departed and dispose of their goods, or arrange to transport them
elsewhere. American merchants who had cooperated with the British
were forgiven, and Wayne declared all loyalists who had served with the
British army were also pardoned, if they agreed to serve in a Continental
Army regiment that was being organized to keep order when Wayne and
his men returned to South Carolina.

The Georgia legislature went along with Wayne's generosity toward
the merchants but they balked at a blanket pardon for the loyalists. It

would, they said, "subvert justice." That meant they intended to even scores with loyalists whenever and wherever they got their hands on them.⁴⁰

XIV

Inside British-occupied New York, the evacuation of Savannah was seen not as a defeat but part of the wider war still being waged for the West Indies. Brigadier Clarke and his 1,000-man army debarked at Charleston, along with hundreds of runaway slaves and numerous loyalists who placed no confidence in General Wayne's offer of amnesty. Meanwhile, 1,051 men sailed from Charleston to help defend Jamaica.⁴¹

A curious euphoria pervaded the high command in New York. Part of it came from the afterglow of Rodney's victory. More emanated from reports that poured in, describing American disarray. William Smith noted most of them in his voluminous diary. A copy of one of "Morris the Financier's" letters "shows despair about the taxes." In Paris Ambassador Benjamin Franklin was reported to have defaulted on "30 odd thousand pounds sterling" in bills drawn on him by Congress. "This has thrown all the public creditors into a fright."

The Mid-Atlantic and Southern colonies were accusing New England of being in default on the payment of federal taxes. In Massachusetts several county conventions were protesting the already-heavy state taxes. "They are going out by the same door they went in [revolting against taxes]," one loyalist friend told Smith. There were "great clamors" in all New England against half pay for life for Continental Army officers. A Colonel Taylor arrived from Northbury, thirty miles outside Boston, saying people were eager to hear British terms for ending the war.

"The moment is arrived for propositions to America," Smith told his diary. "I discern Sir G. Carleton has proper sentiments of the imbecility of the rebel party. He is anxious to hear from England and fearful that the ministry may shake hands with the Congress agents in Europe under too high an estimate of their powers here." A South Carolina loyalist who had just returned from England told Smith's wife that General Henry Conway had remarked that "all power" would be given to Sir Guy "respecting this country"—America.

As the man whose parliamentary resolutions had toppled the North government, Conway's voice had special authority. Smith speculated that Carleton would soon be appointed a viceroy with power to dispose of the

Americans as he saw fit. Who would be his confidential advisor on the intricate political maneuvers that were about to unfold? Who else but Judge William Smith?[42]

All these fervid hopes had been born in an information vacuum. In mid-July, Smith noted they had heard nothing from England for three months. On August 2, 1782, the day after Smith wrote his almost ecstatic vision of Sir Guy Carleton as viceroy of America, the general called on Smith with news that deflated this soaring balloon of hope. Carleton had just learned that diplomat Thomas Grenville had gone to Paris with the authority of the Rockingham cabinet behind him and announced to the American peace negotiators that the British were ready to concede the independence of the United States. The news came in a letter from Lord Shelburne, who seemed to approve the concession—or at least accept it as an unalterable decision. Carleton was told to communicate this news to Congress and General Washington immediately.[43]

Smith could not believe his ears. All the letters he had received from England had assured him that the vast majority of the populace was determined never to surrender the colonies. Only a few days earlier, General Benedict Arnold had written to him about the "great change in temper" among the English people and politicians wrought by Admiral Rodney's victory. Smith thought Grenville's offer might well trigger a civil war in England. He even wondered if the ministers who authorized it might be assassinated on London's streets.

If Shelburne was telling the truth, it would "transfer the affection of all America" to France. With tears in his voice, Smith told Carleton that most loyalists thought his appointment as commander in chief had guaranteed the government's good intentions toward the Americans. Now, Smith wailed, came news that meant "the loss of all I had in the world."

The enraged Carleton paced Smith's parlor, denouncing the move. There was no necessity for it. Great Britain was not even close to bankruptcy. She could raise 30 million pounds in loans at the snap of the First Lord of the Treasury's fingers. After Admiral Rodney's victory, their European enemies, France, Holland, and Spain, were no longer threats. The rest of Europe was on Britain's side—or reduced to humbled neutrality.

He would never have left England, Carleton stormed, if he had not been assured he would be given the power to make a liberal settlement with the Americans and "aid to force [its] acceptance" if some colonies proved recalcitrant. Everything he had seen and heard since he arrived in May convinced him that a reunion was more than practicable. The prospects for peace on Britain's generous terms could not have been more "flattering." In an understatement, Smith told his journal that the general "appeared much affected.[44]

XV

Not being a mind reader, especially at a distance of three thousand miles, General Carleton had no idea that Shelburne's letter was another example of his devious style. He had sent it while he was still colonial secretary, as part of his ongoing scheme to trump Charles James Fox by negotiating a reunion with the Americans using Carleton as his envoy to Congress. He apparently thought the general could use the offer of independence as further proof of British readiness to give Americans liberal terms if they agreed to abandon their alliance with France.

General Carleton's response was a disgusted letter of resignation. He told Shelburne he thought he had been sent to America to negotiate a reconciliation with the colonies. Conceding independence left him with nothing to do but preside over embarkations. The letter underscored the painful gap between events in Europe and perceptions in America. Neither General Carleton nor William Smith was aware that by the time they heard this news, the men who offered immediate independence, Thomas Grenville and Charles James Fox, were in political oblivion and Lord Shelburne was the new first minister.[45]

During the next week, Carleton and Smith calmed down and began to think there was another explanation for the Grenville offer. Rereading Shelburne's letter, Carleton became morally certain he had nothing to do with the gesture. The general was sure Shelburne remained profoundly opposed to granting America independence. He paid more attention to the sentence (underlined in the letter) that the offer meant America's treaty of alliance with France was terminated. Shelburne claimed Ambassador Franklin had said as much; he even asserted it was Franklin's "own idea." Shelburne hoped that if the Americans realized that peace was being delayed by French demands, they might even look upon the French troops in their midst as "dangerous enemies."[46]

Judge Smith decided that the offer of independence was "a state artifice" to discover the enemy's bargaining positions or to gain time. He was further reassured by a report that General Conway had made a speech in Parliament, offering the colonies independence on the same basis as Ireland—a separate legislature, with the king presiding over the whole arrangement. General Carleton told Smith he too thought the offer of independence was a "project to get rid of the French and reunite America with Great Britain upon the Irish plan."[47]

XVI

In South Carolina, Nathanael Greene's army had moved to lowlands on the Ashley River outside of Charleston, where drinking water was more abundant. Alas, so were mosquitoes. During the summer, as many as two hundred of Greene's men died of malaria, and hundreds more were stricken. The outbreak left the Americans all but impotent when it came to stopping the British from raiding the countryside for provisions. This was especially trying for Colonel John Laurens, the commander of the light infantry, who was largely responsible for defending the coastline.

Sometimes the British overreached themselves. Assuming the Americans were no longer a threat, they maintained a galley on the Ashley River. The ship regularly sent its crew ashore "to plunder and distress the inhabitants." The crew was also undoubtedly gathering intelligence from loyalist spies. One dark night, Laurens ordered a captain and fourteen infantry to make a surprise attack. They captured most of the forty-man crew and sank the galley. General Greene was delighted with the daring exploit. "No enterprise this war has exceeded it," he told Henry Lee.[48]

But Laurens had few opportunities for similar coups. "The present is an idle insipid time," he told Greene. Laurens had other reasons for being depressed. In the spring of 1782, he had received heartbreaking news from Europe. Before the Revolution, he had been studying law in London and had an affair with Martha Manning, the attractive daughter of his father's business agent. The young woman had become pregnant and John married her to protect her "honor," he had explained to Henry Laurens. A few months later, before the child was born, Laurens sailed to America to join Washington's army. Now he learned that Martha had heard about his 1781 trip to Paris and had rushed to France, hoping to see him. By the time she arrived, John was on his way back to America. The distressed young woman had fallen ill and died in Lisle.[49]

The British army in Charleston, following orders from London, tried to avoid taking the offensive, even when the Americans were within striking distance. Laurens complained to a friend that the commander of the British cavalry in Charleston invariably kept "a navigable river" between his troops and Laurens's men when he was on a foraging raid. His only object, Laurens wrote sourly, was "stealing Negroes or poultry."

Worsening Laurens's mood was General Greene's decision to send the light infantry to the rear of the army for several weeks, so they could obtain forage for their horses. Some of Laurens's officers ignored a recent law barring soldiers from taking food from civilians. This had drawn a public rebuke from the South Carolina government. Laurens thought the civilians were showing egregious lack of sympathy for the soldiers, adding to his already gloomy view of his native state's patriotism.

General Greene grew worried about the colonel's state of mind. Laurens, the general told Henry Lee, acted as if the withdrawal of his troops to the rear of the army was a punishment. He "wishes to fight much more than I wish he should," Greene wrote. The general may have already sensed a tragedy was in the making.[50]

The campaign, Laurens told a friend, "has become perfectly insipid." The word apparently summed up a great deal of his life in 1782. His dream of black emancipation was receding into the mists of the impossible. While his friend Hamilton was on his way to the Continental Congress, Laurens was trapped in South Carolina, bickering over whether his troops were taking too much food from local farmers. His soldiers, who considered themselves an elite corps, declared "they will not live as [the rest of] the army does," on spoiled rice and rotten meat. General Greene issued a stern rebuke to Laurens, telling him the light infantry "will and shall live as the army does."[51]

Even more troubling to Laurens was his failure to win the respect and affection of the officers of Henry Lee's Legion. They disliked the idea of an officer with no cavalry experience commanding them. "I am sorry to inform you that Col. Laurens is by no means popular with the Legion," General Greene told Lee. In June, Greene decided to reorganize the light troops. He made Brigadier General Mordecai Gist of Maryland the overall commander and Lieutenant Colonel George Baylor of Virginia the cavalry commander.

Lieutenant Colonel Laurens was left in command of the Lee's Legion infantry and a few hundred other foot soldiers. The Legion's officers pro-

tested to General Greene against dividing the regiment, implying that
Laurens was unworthy to command even their infantry. Greene dealt
briskly with this challenge to his authority. For Laurens, it was another
humiliation.[52]

XVII

General Greene decided to make Laurens his intelligence officer. With
about a dozen men as a guard, the colonel took a post midway between
the two armies and was soon sending Greene a stream of valuable information. The job was only moderately dangerous. The lines between the
two armies were porous and Laurens had so many personal connections
on both sides of the fortifications, information virtually fell into his lap.

Gathering intelligence bored Laurens, perhaps because it was so easy.
At one point, he became personally irritated with one of his best sources,
the wife of a loyalist doctor, who gave him juicy accounts of what the British were thinking and doing; he suggested she be dropped as an informant. Other loyalists fed him information about the British preparing to
arm escaped slaves and asked his advice on how to win pardons from the
South Carolina state government, rather than go into exile. He was sympathetic to these people, many of whom were friends of his family.[53]

From Albany, Hamilton wrote a letter which did little to raise Laurens's spirits. He reported the latest rumors from Paris, two or three
months late, of course. The British were negotiating a peace treaty.
Though there were "obstacles," Hamilton was inclined to believe the war
was ending. "A new scene opens," he wrote. The new challenge was to
"make independence a blessing." That would require the creation of "solid
foundations" for the federal union, a task that called for leveling "mountains of prejudice" against a strong federal government.

Hamilton urged Laurens to "quit your sword . . . put on the toga, and
come to Congress . . . We have fought side by side to make America free,
let us hand in hand struggle to make her happy." Hamilton signed this
appeal: "Yrs for ever." He had no idea it was the last letter he would write
to his best friend.[54]

XVIII

Laurens soon established from his many sources that the British were

planning to evacuate Charleston. Only a lack of ships prevented an immediate withdrawal. This was extremely valuable information. It relieved
General Greene of his constant fear that General Leslie was planning a
surprise attack. But the war, such as it was, continued. The British still
needed food for their men and hay for their horses.

On August 21, General Leslie launched a major foraging expedition,
supported by over a dozen ships. Laurens's spies told him exactly where
they were going. Greene ordered his new light infantry commander,
General Mordecai Gist, to "strike at them wherever you may meet them."
Laurens learned of Greene's orders and decided to join the prospective
battle, ignoring a bout of malaria which had laid him low for several
days.

Five days later, Laurens joined Gist's men on the north side of the
Combahee River. Some three hundred British regulars were foraging on
the plantations along the river. Gist had arrived the previous day and
worked out a plan of attack. He was going to hit the British at daybreak
on August 27 and drive them into their boats. As they retreated down the
river, he hoped to bombard them with a howitzer from a bluff on a neck
of land at the river's mouth.

Laurens asked to command the fifty men assigned to throw up a
breastwork to defend the howitzer, which the British were likely to attack
by land. Gist agreed and everyone adjourned to nearby houses to get some
rest. Laurens led his men to the Stock plantation, where he was the life of
a party that the Stocks, no doubt grateful for his protective presence, gave
for him and the captain who was in command of the howitzer. Laurens
was in an ebullient mood at the prospect of action the next day. He urged
Mrs. Stock and her daughters to watch the show from a scaffold with a
view of the river.

At dawn, Gist's men surged across the Combahee River to attack
the redcoats—and found nothing but stripped houses and cold campfires.
The British had a very good network of spies giving them information
and they apparently knew exactly what the Americans were planning to
do. They had boarded their ships not long after midnight and headed
down the river toward the sea. General Gist instantly realized that the
enemy probably knew about the plan to bombard them from the bluff.
They would send some men ashore to make sure the howitzer was not in
position to do them any damage.

The general sent a horseman pounding down the road to warn Laurens, and followed him with a hundred and fifty light infantrymen and dragoons. Gist was much too late to avert the unfolding tragedy. When Laurens arrived at the neck of land leading to the bluff, there were a hundred and fifty British infantrymen deployed in the underbrush along the road. They started shooting the moment the Americans appeared dragging their howitzer.

Laurens fell back and considered his options. He did not know General Gist was on the road with reinforcements; one suspects that would not have made much difference to this deeply depressed idealist, who still hoped fresh military glory would help him sell his proposal to arm—and free—slaves. A captain in Laurens's detachment said the colonel was "anxious to attack the enemy previous to the main body coming up."

Laurens ordered a bayonet charge. He put himself at the head of his fifty-man column. The hundred and fifty British soldiers in the underbrush waited until the Americans were at point-blank range and opened fire. There was a huge crash and a billow of musket smoke into the dawn sky. When the smoke cleared, Colonel John Laurens was lying on his back, dead with a bullet in his heart. An officer and several enlisted men lay near him, badly wounded. The rest of the Americans fled, abandoning their howitzer.

General Gist arrived not long after the disaster. An assault cost him a dozen men; he decided the British position was too strong to attack and allowed the redcoats to withdraw to their waiting ships, taking the captured howitzer with them. Glumly Gist reported to General Greene that he had retreated with nineteen wounded to the Stock plantation "where the corpse of Colo Laurens shall be inter'd with every mark of distinction due to his rank and merit."[55]

XIX

In Philadelphia Congressman Arthur Lee was working overtime to ruin Superintendent of Finance Morris, impeach Benjamin Franklin, and dismantle the alliance with France. His favorite weapon was the "treason"—as he called it—of Silas Deane. The ex-envoy's intercepted letters expressing his disillusionment with the Continental Congress and the Revolution had been printed throughout America. Ignoring his own and his brother Richard's role in destroying Deane, Lee bragged about his "detection" of the ex-envoy's perfidy and wondered why it had not "drawn any punishment nor even odium on those who countenanced & profited by his wickedness. Among these Dr. Franklin & Mr. Morris are the most conspicuous."

Lee gleefully pointed out that Morris had been forced to admit in the newspapers that he had been in partnership with Mr. Deane "but pretended he thought him a man of honor." Franklin had tried to "deceive Congress into a renewal of their confidence" in Deane. Lee claimed a recent visitor to Passy had heard Deane "utter the abuse against America" that later appeared in his letters without a word of rebuke from Franklin. Yet the treacherous ambassador had been appointed a commissioner to negotiate peace, "because France wills it."[56]

A worried Congressman James Madison told his Virginian friend, Edmund Randolph, that all Lee's hostile movements "are pointed directly or circuitously" either at Morris or Franklin. One of Lee's favorite gibes at Morris was "tory." Because he had been slow to sign the Declaration of Independence, he was a traitor at heart. Morris and his friends had only changed their "professions" but they had never abandoned their principles. "These are what a tory never changes," Lee averred. They were all still enemies to "public liberty" and ready to "deliver us up tied and bound to the enemy."

Lee soon broadened these personal slurs to include the entire city of Philadelphia. Thanks to Morris's Bank of North America and Philadelphia's "prosperous commerce . . . this tory city had accumulated all the money" in the country. That has "disenabled the other states from paying taxes to support the war." It had been a terrible mistake to seat Congress in this "bosom of toryism." Lee declaimed against the "extravagance, ostentation and dissipation" that characterized too many wealthy Philadelphia women.[57]

Recently, when the British sent supplies to feed their prisoners of war under a flag of truce, inspectors found several thousand pounds worth of goods concealed in the shipment, intended for certain merchants in Philadelphia. Lee was ecstatic; here was proof that the city was a hotbed of toryism. Madison told one of his correspondents "the affair of the flags" was certain to increase Lee's "venom against the minister." He meant Morris, of course.[58]

Backed by his friend Ralph Izard, who had been elected to Congress from South Carolina, Arthur Lee called for an investigation into all the contracts Superintendent Morris had signed with merchants to feed the army and provide other services to the government. He also urged the necessity of investigating any and all financial dealings in Europe that Ambassador Franklin had overseen. A committee under Lee's guidance drafted a report calling for "clear, minute and satisfactory proofs" of every dollar (or livre) spent; they also wanted to know who authorized each expenditure and why. They demanded to see the original vouchers as well as detailed records of the contents of the chests, bales, and trunks in which the purchases were shipped.[59]

Even more destabilizing, Lee renewed debate on the instructions Congress had given the peace commissioners in June of 1781 to rely on French guidance in the peace negotiations. "The yoke is riveted upon us," Lee shrilled. He expressed horror that Franklin, "the man who sold us" in the original treaty with France, was now in charge of negotiating "everything that is dear and honorable to us."[60]

Furiously, Lee insisted that both Franklin and John Jay, erstwhile backers of Silas Deane, should be excluded from the peace negotiations. Lee also ranted against Secretary of Foreign Affairs Robert R. Livingston. He was an ally of Franklin, hence totally untrustworthy. Lee's supporters in Congress began talking him up as the man who should replace Livingston. An anxious James Madison warned that it looked as if Congress would soon be divided by "party heats"—the quarreling factions that had torn the American government apart during the Deane imbroglio.[61]

The disgusted French ambassador, the Chevalier La Luzerne, watched Lee's performance with growing apprehension. He told Foreign Minister Vergennes in an August 1782 letter that Lee's goal was "to stop all the motions of the administration." In the resulting chaos, Lee hoped to emerge as the controlling voice in America's foreign affairs. If he failed, Luzerne suspected, "the opposition he has shown to us [France] in all circumstances" would entitle him to "capitalize" his performance with a handsome reward from the British government.[62]

If First Minister Lord Shelburne had seen this letter, he might well have decided his strategy of splitting the French-American alliance was alive and well. Instead of negotiating with the Americans in Paris, the first minister might have redoubled his efforts to launch direct talks with the bankrupt, quarreling Congress and individual states through General Carleton. Such delays would have been fatal to the chance for peace, which was growing more fragile every day. But the Atlantic Ocean was a barrier protecting the Americans from the worst effects of their folly.

Chapter Eight

A Peace That Surpasses
Understanding

LORD SHELBURNE had been first minister only a few days when he was attacked by Charles James Fox and Edmund Burke as an utterly untrustworthy man. They claimed that the thorough courtier was determined to help George III evade the promise the king had given Lord Rockingham not to exercise a veto over American independence.

Fox called Shelburne's administration "a den of thieves" and did everything in his power to torpedo the ongoing peace negotiations. His representative in Paris, Thomas Grenville, told Foreign Minister Vergennes that the peace parley had received a "fatal" wound with Fox's resignation. Whereupon Grenville resigned as a negotiator and went home to commiserate with his irate, disgusted mentor.

In Burke's speech, the obviously heartbroken Irishman praised "the clearness" of Rockingham's head and "the purity of his heart." To replace him, George III had "pitched on a man of all others the most unlike" Rockingham. Burke predicted that the Shelburne administration would be "fifty times worse" than the government of Lord North, which Parliament had "reprobated and removed."[1]

There was a personal dimension to Fox's and Burke's dislike of Shelburne. Burke claimed "he wants what I call *principles*." By this Burke said he meant "a uniform rule and scheme of life." There was some truth to this statement. Shelburne seems to have spent much of his life searching for religious and political truths without finding any. As a young man he was deeply unhappy. A domineering father and an overemotional mother made home life "detestible"—and left him with little aptitude for friendship. This defect had a great deal to do with souring his relationship with Fox. Also in the mix was Shelburne's immense wealth—his income was estimated at 35 thousand pounds a year. He seems to have felt this staggering sum entitled him to be a leader—but he never mastered the art of political fellowship.[2]

Lord Shelburne's response to the attacks by Burke and Fox was anything but reassuring to them and their followers—or to the Americans. The new first minister said the independence of America would be "a dreadful blow" to the greatness of England. If and when it was granted, "the sun of England might be said to have set." If he ever agreed to renounce America, it would only be out of desperate necessity. For the time being, he was concentrating on making "the most vigorous exertions" to prevent the French from achieving a position that enabled them "to dictate the terms of peace." His ultimate goal, he declared, was to "improve the twilight" darkening England's fortunes at the moment so their sun would rise again.[3]

This was classic Shelburne. No one knew exactly what he meant. For the moment, he benefited from the widespread conviction that he and George III were in agreement on the most advantageous path to peace. Charles James Fox's attempt to give America independence unconditionally was unpopular not only with the king but also with the members of the Rockingham administration who had decided to support Shelburne—and with Parliament as a whole. As one member of Shelburne's cabinet put it, granting American independence could be tolerated only if it was "the price" of a peace that would keep America's ally, France, in a subordinate if not humiliating position in the ongoing struggle for global supremacy.[4]

On July 8, two days before Shelburne spoke in Parliament, he wrote another letter to General Carleton and Admiral Digby in New York, urging them to do everything in their power to persuade the commissioners whom he hoped Congress would appoint for "the revolted provinces" to consider Britain's offer of peace. The implication was clear: the terms might be less than unconditional independence. At this point, Shelburne, operating under the baleful eye of George III, was obviously undecided whether independence for all thirteen rebellious colonies was either necessary or inevitable.[5]

II

In Paris, Benjamin Franklin's reaction to Shelburne's speech was surprising. Two weeks earlier, the ambassador had written to Secretary of Foreign Affairs Robert R. Livingston, reiterating his conviction that absolute and total independence was the only safeguard against George III. In spite of these fire-breathing sentiments, the ambassador decided that there was only one way to find out what Shelburne was really thinking: start negotiating with him. The new first minister's handpicked envoy, Richard Oswald, was still in Paris, eager to talk to his fellow septuagenarian.[6]

Although John Jay had arrived in Paris on June 23, he played only a minor role in this large decision. Almost immediately, Jay and his wife had been flattened by the influenza that was sweeping Europe. Jay would not emerge from his sickroom for over a month. Franklin also did not bother to inform Foreign Minister Vergennes of this initiative.

Here is how Oswald reported Franklin's opening gambit to First Minister Shelburne.

> He took out a minute, & from it read a few hints or articles. Some he said as necessary for them to insist on, others which he could not say he had any orders about, or were not absolutely demanded, & yet such as it would be advisable for England to offer for the sake of reconciliation and her future interest.

Franklin said there were four necessary articles. At the top of the list was "independence, full and complete" with all British troops withdrawn from the thirteen states. The second condition was settlement of the boundaries of the United States with still loyal colonies such as Nova Scotia, which seemed to be claiming a large chunk of northern Massachusetts. The border between West and East Florida and Georgia also needed definition. Most important of all was America's western boundary. Was it to be the Appalachian Mountains or the Mississippi? Franklin wanted the Mississippi. Perhaps because he assumed it was the only boundary that made sense, he did not mention it in his notes. The third article was a drastic revision of the boundaries of Canada. In

1774 Parliament had passed the Quebec Act, which included in Canada a large swath of what is now the American Midwest. Franklin insisted these "back lands," as Oswald called them, belonged to the United States. Fourth was the right to fish on the Grand Banks of Newfoundland—vital to New England's prosperity.

In addition, there were four advisable articles. The first was a grant of 5 or 6 hundred thousand pounds from Parliament to indemnify the people whose towns and farms had been looted, burned, or otherwise destroyed by the British army and navy and their marauding Indian allies. Without this gesture, Franklin predicted a spirit of "secret revenge and animosity" against England would prevail in America for "a long time to come." Another proposal was a "public acknowledgment" by Parliament that Britain had been wrong to start the war. "A few words of that kind," Franklin said, "would do more good than people could imagine." Third was a commercial treaty giving American ships the right to trade freely in English and Irish ports and in the West Indies. Fourth was a reiteration of Franklin's favorite idea: "Giving up every part of Canada."

Franklin also told Oswald to forget the idea that America might accept a semi-independence similar to the one the British recently granted Ireland. The ambassador also made it clear that he had changed his mind about reimbursing the loyalists for their losses. Nor would he approve giving them money from the sale of land in the west, presuming it was conceded to the United States. He told Oswald that he was "correcting the mistakes" he had made in April, at their initial talk. He also corrected another mistake: this time he declined to give Oswald a copy of his notes. That would enable him to deny he said certain things if they were leaked to Vergennes or the press.[7]

Unknown to Oswald, the ambassador was also talking to Lord Shelburne through another channel, a young English intellectual named Benjamin Vaughan, who all but worshipped the ground on which Franklin walked. In 1779, no doubt to George III's outrage, Vaughan had published an edition of Franklin's writings in London. The thirty-one-year-old Vaughan regularly signed his letters to Franklin "Your ever devoted, affectionate and obliged [friend]." Vaughan, whose mother was from Boston, had been born in the West Indies; he was also a worshipper of Lord Shelburne, which made him a member of a very small group. He lived in Shelburne's household and had frequent access to him.

The day after Franklin talked to Oswald, the ambassador wrote to

Vaughan. In a previous letter, Vaughan had warned him that Oswald might speak of peace terms based on "a dependant state of America"—the Irish solution. Franklin blandly claimed to have "heard nothing of it," though he and Oswald had discussed the idea without using that negative term. Instead, Franklin broadened the problem by claiming the rumor of Oswald's (and Shelburne's) intentions was already widespread.

"It is . . . intimated to me from several quarters that Lord Shelburne's plan is to retain sovereignty for the king . . . If this really be his project, our negotiation for peace will not go very far; the thing is impracticable and impossible." At first Franklin had been inclined to believe Lord Shelburne had "once entertained such an idea" but had "probably dropped it." Now Vaughan's words and these intimations from other quarters had thrown "a little doubt into my mind." He had decided not to be so free in his communications to his Lordship, though he still "esteem[ed] and honor[ed]" him. He would pursue this policy until Vaughan gave him some *"eclaircissment."*[8]

This was diplomacy at its most artful. To emphasize his seriousness, Franklin informed the dismayed Oswald that it might be better to suspend their conversations for a few days.

III

In response, Oswald revealed a split personality that would have daunted almost anyone but Lord Shelburne, a man whose inner thoughts were often out of sync with what he said for popular consumption. In a letter to the first minister written after his conversation with Franklin, Oswald denied he ever had any intention of proposing a dependent relationship for America. The Scot claimed he had guaranteed Franklin total independence. Did Lord Shelburne agree? Oswald's aggrieved tone made it sound as if Shelburne might have deceived him. Peace suddenly seemed to be "obstructed," Oswald all but wailed. Any progress toward a comprehensive treaty with the warring powers was "suspended." The Scot feared the blame would be thrown on the new administration, in particular on Shelburne and, though he did not say so, on Richard Oswald.[9]

On the same day, Oswald sent Lord Shelburne another letter that might, in the words of one historian, have been written by an undersecretary for Lord George Germain before Saratoga. It was an explosion of the Scot's secret hatred of American independence. The war was not—and should not be—ending, Oswald declared. The British should keep fight-ing until they had the power to impose a draconian settlement on Amer-ica: a viceroy or lord lieutenant and a privy council of loyalists to preside over the continent. Colleges, especially Harvard, would be supervised, town meetings restricted, oaths taken to guarantee "true and full obedi-ence" to Parliament. It was a frightening glimpse of what Oswald—and a great many other Englishmen—were feeling. Quite possibly, Oswald sensed that Shelburne felt the same rage and frustration over the way England had been humiliated in America.[10]

IV

Nothing was heard from Lord Shelburne for the next two weeks. Then he sent Oswald a letter which he gave his negotiator the freedom to show to Franklin. In it he said he had "reluctantly" decided that Britain had to grant America total independence. Shelburne also enclosed a copy of his June 5 dispatch to General Carleton reporting Grenville's offer of uncon-ditional independence. The letter proved, Shelburne piously asserted, that "there never have been two opinions" about conceding Americans independence.

This was an almost blatant lie; Shelburne's earlier statements to Car-leton and the anti-independence vote he had forced on the Rockingham cabinet, which prompted Charles James Fox to resign, make this fact incontrovertible. Shelburne had now apparently decided that the Fox offer of unconditional independence, once made, could not be withdrawn. But he was determined to use it to turn the Americans against the French. If the attempt failed, he could always blame the breakdown of negotiations on his two most outspoken enemies, Charles James Fox and Edmund Burke.

Shelburne had no intention of making Benjamin Franklin totally contented; the first minister wanted the ambassador's advisable articles, especially his dream of obtaining Canada, "dropp'd" once and for all. As for the possibility of French intransigence delaying a peace treaty, Shel-burne told Oswald that his ministry was "united, in full possession of the King's confidence and thoroughly disposed to peace with France and Spain if it can be obtained on reasonable terms." If that were not possible, the Shelburne administration would "have recourse to every means of rousing the kingdom to the most determined efforts." Shelburne mentioned plans to expand the navy and warned that England's enemies "had large and distant dominions as well as ourselves to play for."[11]

Shelburne expected Franklin to pass this threat on to Vergennes. He also wanted the Americans to have second thoughts about clinging to a France that might soon suffer more defeats in the West Indies and India. Against this push stood Franklin's conviction that if the Americans abandoned France, they would never find another ally who would trust or support them.

V

In Paris, the emergence of John Jay from his sickroom soon gave Lord Shelburne's hopes new vigor—as well as unforeseen complications. Jay had gone to Europe an outspoken admirer of France and her alliance with America. He had wholeheartedly sided with Silas Deane, Robert Morris, and Benjamin Franklin in their brawl with Arthur and William Lee, and warmly endorsed Franklin's policy of trusting France. In a 1780 letter he told Franklin he would never cease to love France, America's best "and almost only friend." But two years of frustration in Madrid had soured Jay's temper and darkened his view of Europeans.

Jay's mood was not improved by his struggle with influenza, which often leaves a person depressed. His doctor told Jay's wife, Sarah, that he had not seen any of his hundreds of patients as "severely attack'd" as the Jays. Further darkening the envoy's feelings was news that his aged father had died in New York—and his older brother James had defected to the British.

Jay soon made it clear to Franklin that he had no enthusiasm for Congress's instructions to accept French guidance in the peace negotiations. Now he transformed his disagreement into a sort of battle flag. He all but announced that he was going to clash with Foreign Minister Vergennes at the first opportunity.

An opening for a confrontation materialized when Jay was introduced to the Spanish ambassador to France, the Conde de Aranda. They met to explore the possibility of a treaty of alliance, as Spain's foreign minister had suggested when Jay was leaving Madrid. The seventy-year-old Aranda, a former first minister as well as a distinguished general in his youth, was an extremely self-assured aristocrat who lived in a splendid mansion with the best wine cellar in Paris. There was no doubt in his mind—or most other minds—that he spoke for Spain. Jay understood neither Spanish nor French, so Foreign Minister Vergennes's right-hand man, Gerard de Rayneval, who spoke fluent English as well as Spanish, acted as the interpreter.

What Jay heard at this conference only confirmed his already profound disillusion with the Spaniards. Aranda said the first thing they had to settle was America's western boundary. Jay proposed the Mississippi River from its headwaters to the border of Spanish-held Louisiana. Aranda politely demurred and drew a line on a map of North America which gave Spain the future states of Illinois, Indiana, Tennessee, Kentucky, and Mississippi. He claimed that Spain's control of the Mississippi and its nearby rivers and territory was validated by their possession of New Orleans and forays up the river since Madrid entered the war in 1779. As for the American expedition under General George Rogers Clark that had captured British forts and routed the British and their Indian allies in the region—that was a mere "raid" which could and should be dismissed. Rayneval, a diplomat in his own right, agreed with Aranda, warning Jay that the Americans were demanding too much. Here, Jay concluded, was evidence that the French and Spanish both wanted to treat the United States as a second-class country.[12]

The lean acerbic New Yorker, who could be a witty and charming conversationalist in private, also grew suspicious of Lord Shelburne. Jay became convinced that he was still hoping to seduce some American states into returning to their allegiance to George III. Jay's suspicions deepened when he read Richard Oswald's formal commission to negotiate peace, drawn up by Shelburne and signed by George III. The Scot was empowered to treat for peace "with the said colonies or any of them or any parts thereof." Jay immediately rejected this terminology, demanding an explicit recognition of the United States of America. When Oswald tried to reason with him, Jay said he wanted independence recognized by an act of Parliament before he would begin negotiating. When he was told that Parliament was recessed for the summer, Jay said George III could issue the statement in a proclamation—an event so unlikely, a dismayed Oswald told Shelburne that Jay was "alienated" from any and all regard for England.[13]

When Ambassador Franklin invited Jay to join him for a conference with Vergennes, the foreign minister gently rebuked the New Yorker for his legalistic hostility to Oswald. "Names mean little," he said. Vergennes pointed out that when formal negotiations began, the Americans would present the British envoys with their commissions, in which they would be identified as representatives of the United States. When the British accepted them, that would be an implicit recognition of America as a nation. Jay looked inquiringly at Franklin, who said he thought this arrangement "would do." Jay grimly disagreed.

The conversation turned to Jay's discussion of America's western boundary with the Conde de Aranda. Both Franklin and Jay vehemently objected to the "extravagant" Spanish claims. Gerard de Rayneval, also in the conference as an interpreter, again made it clear that he thought it was the Americans who were making extravagant claims. Vergennes did not disagree with him. The foreign minister had decided early in the war that it would be best for all concerned if Spain possessed the Midwest, for the same reason that he wanted Canada to remain British. Potential enemies on their borders would guarantee that America remained allied with France.

Back in Passy, Franklin and Jay sat down in the ambassador's study to discuss the contretemps. Franklin remained calm; Jay packed tobacco into a clay pipe and struggled to match Franklin's dispassionate tone. But the New Yorker lost his temper and claimed that the French wanted to keep America as small and impotent as possible. He also accused Vergennes of trying to prolong the war, hoping bankruptcy would reduce the Americans to a pathetic client state, ready to do France's bidding.

Franklin admitted that there was no doubt that the Spanish wanted "to coop us up within the Allegheny Mountains." But he did not put such an apocalyptic interpretation on France's intentions. As he saw it, Vergennes was a man trying to keep two difficult allies happy. Franklin had seen no evidence that the French foreign minister was trying to prolong the war. If anything, Vergennes's suggestion about exchanging commissions, forcing the British to acknowledge the United States, would speed things up.

Franklin, still searching for a way out of the impasse, reminded Jay of their instructions from Congress, that they were supposed to consult the French and accept their guidance in the peace negotiations. Jay's temper spun completely out of control. He told Franklin those instructions were the product of Ambassador Luzerne's influence in Congress—something Jay had accepted with equanimity when he was its president. Franklin urged Jay to remember France's generosity since 1778—the gifts and loans were now approaching 40 million livres.[14]

Jay was no longer listening. He claimed that if America depended on

France, they would be leaning on a broken reed that would "sooner or later pierce our hands." Franklin asked if he intended to violate Congress's instructions. "If the instructions conflict with America's honor and dignity, I would break them—like this!" Jay shouted. Leaping to his feet, he flung his pipe into Franklin's fireplace, shattering it into dozens of pieces.[15]

VI

Far from trying to prolong the war, Vergennes was desperately searching for an acceptable peace as the looming bankruptcy of France became more and more apparent to him and many other people. Necker's replacement as finance minister, Joly de Fleury, had already told the foreign minister that for 1782 alone, the deficit was likely to be 400 million livres. Worse, France's ability to borrow money was dwindling. In Holland she was paying 6.5 percent interest while England was paying 3.5 percent. War contractors were demanding payment from the navy for long-overdue bills and there was talk of default, a ruinous embarrassment to a great power.[16]

Simultaneously, Vergennes was doing his best to mollify Spain by trying to persuade the Americans to accept a western boundary considerably short of the Mississippi. Vergennes did not see this as immoral, nor did the Conde de Aranda. It was the way Europeans had ended wars for centuries, by compromising the antagonists' claims, which were frequently extreme. Aranda spoke of the immense distances of the interior of North America and the folly of quibbling over "a few hundred leagues." Rayneval said similar things and cited historical evidence that France and Spain as well as England had long had competing claims to this vast unexplored region. At one point Rayneval remarked that if anyone had an unqualified claim to the territory, it was the Indians who already lived there.[17]

VII

Also looming like a creature in a nightmare in the French foreign minister's thoughts was a crisis in Eastern Europe that threatened France's historic role as the arbiter of the continent's stability. Joseph II of Austria, ruler in his own right since the death of his mother, Empress Maria Theresa, in the fall of 1780, and the brother of Marie Antoinette, France's queen, was determined to expand his empire and his prestige. He was also bitterly antagonistic to the Comte de Vergennes for failing to support him in an attempt to seize Bavaria in 1778 when the nation's royal ruler, known as the Elector, died. These angry emotions led Joseph to a dramatic meeting with the Empress Catherine of Russia and an agreement to smash the decrepit Turkish empire and divide the spoils.

In June of 1782, the opportunity to strike the first blow in this grand design arose in the Crimea, which was ruled by a Russian puppet, Khan Shahin Girai. A revolt led by the Khan's own brother easily routed him. In theory the Crimea was an independent state peopled by the Tartar descendants of Genghis Khan. As Moslems, they paid vague obeisance to the Sultan of Turkey. But everyone knew the Russians were the power behind the throne, and the Empress Catherine was soon saying the new khan did not represent "the Tartar nation."

Catherine coolly blockaded all the ports in the Crimea and moved fifteen thousand troops to the border. To her threat to invade, Catherine added a warning to the Turks that if they did not accept her solution, her ally Austria would not regard such a decision "with indifference." Joseph, meanwhile, cynically invited France into the dismemberment game, offering her Egypt as a reward.

Vergennes knew what was transpiring behind the diplomatic facades. Catherine and Joseph were preparing to replace France as the arbiter of Europe's balance of power. Almost as painful would be the loss of Turkey as a political ally and profitable trading partner. Vergennes had been ambassador to Constantinople for eighteen years; he was acutely aware of Turkey's weakness. What could he do to stop the power-hungry Joseph and somehow retain France's alliance with Austria, a link solemnized by Marie Antoinette's presence in Versailles? A break with Austria would trigger an even worse nightmare. "The day the court of Vienna separates from France," Vergennes told Louis XVI, "she will have England for an ally." There was only one answer to this dilemma—a peace treaty with England, signed as soon as possible, which would give France the freedom to play a role in eastern Europe.[18]

VIII

Franklin was not privy to everything that the Comte de Vergennes was thinking and doing, but there are grounds for suspecting he knew a good deal. After almost six years in Paris, he had a circle of influential friends in the upper levels of French society who supplied him with the latest political rumors and gossip. His frequent attendance at salons and dinner parties also gave him access to information about what was happening inside Vergennes's Palace of Silence. No matter how much the ambassador learned, it did not alter his fundamental gratitude to the foreign minister and to France—a gratitude he wanted America to display as long as it was possible. That latter word, however, was crucial.

Franklin also knew a good deal about what was happening in London. Benjamin Vaughan and David Hartley were still among his frequent correspondents. Then there was talkative Richard Oswald, whom Franklin had charmed to an almost magical degree. These gentlemen told him that time was of the essence if the Americans wanted to profit from the momentum Franklin had established with Lord Shelburne. The first minister was under attack in the newspapers that supported Fox and Burke and in the papers that had backed Lord North. More than a few insiders predicted Shelburne's thin majority in Parliament would evaporate when the House of Commons reconvened in November.

A peace that included both Franklin's necessary and advisable proposals depended on the outcome of a military operation that had been in progress for over two years—the siege of Gibraltar. Regaining the fortified rock and its strategic port had been the prime reason why Spain had entered the war. Paris was aswirl with rumors of a massive French-Spanish assault that would soon bring the three-year siege to a climax. A British victory might make Parliament more intransigent about peace terms with all the belligerents, including the Americans.[19]

These factors made Jay's smashed pipe a good deal less than the turning point in the peace negotiations that some historians have considered it. Franklin did not react to his colleague's emotional explosion with horror; he understood Jay's feelings far better than the influenza-drained, embittered envoy himself. He agreed that Jay should request a new commission from Oswald but persuaded him to drop his wild-eyed demand for a proclamation of America's independence from George III. The ambassador also convinced Jay that time was of the essence and it behooved him to be as nice to Oswald as possible.[20]

IX

Unfortunately, at this point Franklin collapsed with an attack of bladder stones, a condition that made walking and riding in carriages difficult and painful. Jay continued negotiating with Oswald on his own—and his hostility to France and Spain soon led him into making extreme— and extremely dangerous—statements. "You have only to cut the knot of independence," he told the Scot, and Americans would "take care" to be independent of other nations. This came perilously close to saying he was ready to violate the treaty with France, something Jay had told Franklin he would never do. At another point, he asked Oswald why the British did not detach several thousand troops from New York and Charleston and recapture West Florida from Spain. Jay opined that Britain would be a better neighbor than Spain, an almost incredibly naive remark, considering Albion's reputation for intrigue and arrogance.[21]

Jay also asked Benjamin Vaughan to act as a secret courier between himself and Shelburne. To the young West Indian, the New Yorker expressed even more hostility to France and declared an unqualified readiness to sign a separate peace. The British decided Jay was their opportunity to rupture the American alliance with France. One of their secret agents leaked to him an intercepted letter written by the secretary of the French embassy in Philadelphia, Francois Barbe-Marbois, arguing against an American boundary on the Mississippi. It was a confidential position paper, not a formal declaration of policy, but it convinced Jay all over again that the French were prepared to betray America's interests. Even more alarming was another leak slipped to Jay via the English secret service: Gerard de Rayneval, Vergennes's right-hand man, was in England under an assumed name conferring with Lord Shelburne.[22]

Rayneval went to England incognito to discuss terms for a peace treaty. Jay became convinced that the purpose of his mission was to deprive America of the Mississippi boundary. Meanwhile Shelburne revised Oswald's commission, giving him the power "to treat with the commissioners appointed by colonys, under the title of the 13 United States of America." The thirteen states were then listed by name. This was still not an explicit recognition of the United States. If anything, it smacked of Shelburne's long-running hope to detach one or more of these "colonys" from the list. The British cabinet, who approved the wording, did not consider it "a final acknowledgement of independence." It merely gave the American commissioners "the title they wished to assume." Nevertheless, John Jay decided to be "very happy" with the terminology and began drafting proposals for a formal treaty, based on Franklin's four necessary articles.[23]

X

In Philadelphia, the Continental Congress was another stage on which the struggle for peace was a central concern. Arthur Lee and his allies continued to attack the French alliance. Fortunately for the United States, James Madison appointed himself a defender of America's reputation. On August 8, 1782, Lee took the floor to announce that "the interest, honor and safety" of the United States were at stake in the peace negotiations. Placing "unlimited confidence" in the French would not make them a more reliable ally; on the contrary, it would make the Americans "despicable" in their eyes. Congressman Jesse Root, a Lee ally from Connecticut, called for a committee to overhaul the instructions to rely on French guidance in the peace negotiations.[24]

The slim intense Madison rose to oppose this ruinous proposal, which all but proclaimed the alliance was on the brink of collapse. Shrewdly, he admitted the instructions seemed to "sacrifice" America's national dignity. "But it was a sacrifice of dignity to policy," Madison insisted. When the instructions were voted for on June 15, 1781, America was desperate, Yorktown was only a name on a map of Virginia, and Congress felt embracing France was the only hope of national survival. The instructions in no way inhibited our envoys from "contending with the utmost earnestness for our rights." Changing the instructions would make America look like a nation ready to give "abject and profuse promises" when in distress and to break her word when circumstances changed.[25]

Instead of a committee dominated by Lee partisans, Madison proposed a committee headed by himself, plus four fellow nationalists. They would prepare a report on adding to the June 15 instructions some American concerns about the peace terms, with a special emphasis on the Mississippi as the western boundary. Madison's motion won overwhelming approval, leaving Lee and his adherents gasping with rage.

Madison's maneuvers also blunted in similar style Lee's attacks on Franklin. Lee became so enraged, he wrote an extremely indiscreet letter to a Virginia friend, full of vituperative hatred of France. The friend even more indiscreetly showed it to several people, hoping to muster support for Lee. Rumors that the letter was "highly injurious to the public interests" prompted the Virginia assembly to consider censuring Lee, which would mean his recall from Congress. Lee rushed to Virginia and tried to persuade Theodorick Bland, his best friend in the state's congressional delegation, to support his claim that a majority of Congress was bribed to vote according to instructions from Ambassador de la Luzerne. Bland, realizing he too might be in danger of censure, would only say he had never taken any money from Luzerne. Lee came within two votes of being censured and recalled. Madison wryly reported that Lee "was not in the best of humor" after this narrow escape.[26]

XI

In Paris, before John Jay could show his draft of the peace treaty to Richard Oswald, news arrived from Gibraltar that drastically altered the balance of power between Britain and her enemies. Spain's blockade of the fortress had been a loose affair, frequently all but abandoned by the need to send ships of the line to other theaters of the war. The French repeatedly sought Spain's cooperation in the English Channel and in the West Indies. The Spanish began demanding some of the French fleet to support the Gibraltar blockade and when they failed to materialize, accused France of bad faith. The British successfully penetrated the blockade with convoys of supply ships in 1780 and 1781, and inflicted not a little collateral damage on the Spanish fleet.

To prevent further deterioration of the crucial relationship with Madrid, Vergennes committed France to a major effort to capture Gibraltar in 1782. A French engineer, the Chevalier d'Arcon, came to Spain with a plan to batter the fortress into submission from a dozen huge floating gun batteries. A French squadron reinforced the Spanish fleet to tighten the blockade and French troops swelled the size of the besieging army to thirty thousand men. (The Gibraltar garrison was seven thousand men.) It took six months to create d'Arcon's floating batteries and train more than four thousand men to operate them. They were fitted with pumps to extinguish fires from enemy hotshot; their massive side timbers made them almost invulnerable to ordinary cannon fire.

The attack was scheduled for late September 1782. But the Spanish received word that a British supply convoy was about to sail for Gibraltar, protected by a formidable fleet under the command of Lord Richard Howe, one of Britain's best admirals. The Spanish browbeat the French into attacking immediately, hoping to win the battle before Howe arrived.

This haste led to disaster. The combined Spanish-French fleet spent several days bombarding the Rock with broadsides that accomplished little. On September 13, d'Arcon's batteries were towed into the battle. Unfortunately, the crews had not had enough time to master the complicated equipment. Nor had the men in command of the siege worked out how best to deploy this weaponry.

From the moment the batteries were towed into position, hotshot rained down on them. The first two batteries in the column had to bear the brunt of the bombardment because the others were so poorly deployed. The crews tried to turn on the fire pumps but no water reached their hoses. Soon flames began to glow in the batteries; the blazes became conflagrations and the tons of ammunition aboard the clumsy craft exploded, killing almost every man in their crews. British warships sortied from Gibraltar's inner harbor, wreaking more havoc on the surviving batteries at point-blank range. In eighteen hours, the grand assault collapsed.

As the dismayed Spanish and French commanders tried to decide what to do next, Admiral Howe's fleet, no less than 35 ships of the line, sailed from Portsmouth escorting more than 50 supply ships. The victuallers were joined by convoys from other ports until they totaled 186. On October 11 this immense armada appeared off Gibraltar.

Howe expertly positioned his 35 men-of-war between the victuallers and the 49-ship French and Spanish fleet. Their numerical superiority should have given the allies the muscle to maul Howe's warships. But their will to fight to the finish had been fatally wounded by the revival of the British navy's reputation after Rodney's victory over Admiral de Grasse—and the failed assault on Gibraltar. The 186 British supply ships swept into Gibraltar's harbor without the loss of a spar, bringing enough food and ammunition to guarantee the garrison's survival for another year. Wry laughter at this humiliation of the Bourbon powers echoed through the chancelleries of Europe. The mirth was especially shrill in Vienna and St. Petersburg. The Comte de Vergennes could only writhe and wonder what else could go wrong?[27]

XII

In Paris, the American negotiators were joined by a man whose hostility to France was already a matter of record: John Adams. This undiplomatic diplomat arrived from Amsterdam in late October, his already large sense of self importance inflated by having obtained Dutch recognition of American independence, a treaty of commerce, and a loan of 5 million guilders—2 million dollars. None of these successes would have been achieved without the victory at Yorktown and Britain's arrogant decision to declare war on Holland, making her a French ally. If Adams was aware of these factors, he never mentioned them—although in a burst of semi-candor he admitted to a friend that the best explanation for his diplomatic success was divine providence.

En route to Paris Adams filled his diary with loathing for Benjamin Franklin and suspicion of John Jay for his 1778 support of Silas Deane. "Between two such subtle spirits . . . the one malicious, the other I think honest, I shall have a . . . critical part to act. Franklin's cunning will be to divide us." When the testy New Englander read a copy of Oswald's peace commission, with its evasion of an explicit mention of the United States of America, he immediately assumed it was Franklin's handiwork. Exploding with rage, Adams wrote to Robert R. Livingston, resigning as a peace commissioner. When he found out that John Jay had accepted the Scot's revised commission, Adams hastily retracted his resignation. Soon even he was appalled by Jay's rampant hatred of the French. "Mr. Jay likes Frenchmen as little as Mr. Lee and Mr. Izard did," Adams informed his diary.[28]

Meanwhile, the new arrival had called in a French tailor to outfit him in the latest style, soaped and soaked his bulky torso in one of the bathhouses on the Seine, settled his two secretaries and himself in comfortable lodgings. He also talked freely with Matthew Ridley, an English-born Baltimore merchant Adams had met in Amsterdam, where Ridley had negotiated a modest loan for Maryland. For three days Adams bustled around Paris without bothering to call on the American ambassador to France, Benjamin Franklin.

Adams claimed he was ranked first on the list of peace commissioners and Franklin should call on him. He orated on his detestation of "the old conjuror" to the talkative Ridley. Fortunately, Ridley was in business with Robert Morris, which made him a friend of Franklin. The Baltimorean told Adams he should be the first to call. Adams agreed but changed his mind on the way out his door, declaring he could not overcome his "abhorrence."

Ridley finally coaxed him into it and Adams spent several hours with Franklin at Passy, telling him he totally agreed with the "wisdom and firmness" with which John Jay had negotiated during Franklin's illness. Adams planned to support Jay "to the utmost" in his distrust of the French and his determination to ignore their advice.[29]

Franklin sat silently throughout this harangue. A few days later, during another Adams visit to Passy, the ambassador remarked that Foreign Minister Vergennes was more than a little annoyed that Adams had not called on him. Now the acknowledged leader of the French government, the Comte should have been the first name on the new arrival's appointment calendar.

Even Adams had to admit this was a gaffe of the first order. The next day he journeyed to Versailles, certain that he was going to be lectured and threatened. Instead, Vergennes congratulated him on his performance in Holland and claimed to look forward to working with him in pursuit of a peaceful world. He even invited Adams to dinner and treated the cranky puritan to a feast of fine wine and succulent food that left him burping contentedly all the way back to Paris. This finesse did not prevent Adams from calling on Richard Oswald to assure him that he and John Jay were united in their opposition to taking any advice or guidance from France.[30]

The next time Adams met with Franklin, he got another surprise. The envoys were about to begin negotiating with Oswald as a trio. The ambassador quietly said to his contentious colleagues: "I am of your opinion and will go on [with the negotiations] without consulting this Court [France]." Ever the realist, Franklin had decided that this shift in his stance was necessary to present a united American front. He did not see it as a betrayal of the treaty of alliance with France. Nor did he think it was a violation of the instructions from Congress. It was an adjustment to the diplomatic situation as it was evolving in Europe and America.[31]

Above all, Franklin's decision rose from his conviction that time was of the essence and his growing fear that America might find itself fighting a revived England for several more years—something the bankrupt republic was manifestly incapable of doing. On his desk were desperate letters from Robert Morris, urging him to borrow another 20 million livres from France to stave off financial collapse. These cries of distress were incidentally an ironic comment on John Adams's Holland loan. Its first installment of 1.6 million guilders had been consumed to pay outstanding American bills in Europe.

XIII

Foreign Minister Vergennes could not afford to quarrel with Adams or Jay for reasons remarkably similar to Franklin's. France was not only reeling toward bankruptcy; the humiliating defeat at Gibraltar had revealed that her navy had lost the initiative that the French had seized when she joined the struggle for America. A crucial factor in every war, the initiative enabled the side who possessed it to decide when and where they should fight and vastly increased their morale and chances of winning.

An anguished Vergennes wrote to his friend and confidante, the young French ambassador to Madrid, the Comte de Montmorin: "The English to some extent have regenerated their navy while ours has been used up." The British Parliament confidently voted for a navy of a hundred and ten thousand sailors for 1783—twice the number at the start of the war. The French navy was running out of men. Ships were being sent to sea with raw crews and officers who exhibited an almost disgraceful "lassitude." Recently a new frigate had fought a British man-of-war off the French coast and surrendered with scarcely a show of resistance.[32]

A wave of war weariness was sweeping France. Vergennes was savagely criticized behind the scenes by other members of the royal council, many of them still resentful of his victory over Jacques Necker and his growing power as the king's most trusted minister. Queen Marie Antoinette, angry at Vergennes's refusal to approve her brother Joseph II's imperial adventures, had supported Necker's attempt to force a premature peace. She was now ready to sponsor a palace revolution to oust Vergennes. The queen had never approved the foreign minister's decision to back the Americans.

Grimly, the embattled foreign minister resolved to match Shelburne's carrot and stick diplomacy. He persuaded the equally cash-short Spanish to make one more huge effort to reverse Admiral Rodney's victory in the West Indies and the Gibraltar disaster. Urging Vergennes to this gamble was the Marquis de Lafayette, who had remained in Europe to act as an intermediary between the Americans and Versailles. The two nations began assembling at Cadiz a huge fleet and a 25,000-man army with orders to seize Jamaica from the English and then sail north to blast the British army out of New York—and regain Canada for France.

Vergennes had apparently changed his mind about who should possess the huge northern colony, probably in deference to Lafayette, who had been given command of the army at Cadiz. The Marquis had tried to talk General Washington into letting him lead an assault on the elusive northern prize several times during the course of the war. This foray from Cadiz was a desperate as well as a daring move that might bankrupt both Spain and France—but might also win the war.[33]

XIV

In London, First Minister Lord Shelburne was also growing desperate for peace. George III was becoming more and more suspicious of his thorough courtier, especially when Shelburne told the king of his long conversations with Gerard de Rayneval. The first minister described the diplomat as a "man of business" who had none of the emotional French mannerisms that the British disliked. He was doing a good job of communicating Vergennes's desire for an early end to the war. George warned Shelburne "not to be deceived" by Rayneval. The king was sure anyone sent by Vergennes would come "well-armed with cunning."

Shelburne persisted in trying to convince the king that the mood of the House of Commons made a quick peace essential. The first minister confided to Rayneval that he hoped to change the royal mind about a compromise peace with France, which would include American independence. Rayneval was deeply impressed with Shelburne. "I have seen few persons of a character as resolute and decisive," Rayneval told Foreign Minister Vergennes.[34]

XV

When the Americans resumed negotiating with Richard Oswald on October 29, 1782, they discovered that the United States as well as France and Spain might have to pay for the defeat at Gibraltar. A new negotiator had joined Oswald—a veteran foreign-office diplomat named Henry Strachey, who had a tough, often hostile attitude toward Americans. Once and for all, Strachey excluded from the negotiations all Franklin's advisory proposals—in particular the cession of Canada. Only the four essential articles were on the table, and Strachey was determined to press and prod the Americans to see if they could be browbeaten into making concessions anywhere and everywhere. John Adams called Strachey "as artful and insinuating a man as they could send." Strachey called Adams and John Jay "the greatest quibblers I ever saw." Matthew Ridley, hovering on the edge of the negotiations, nervously noted in his diary: "All things do not seem to go clever."[35]

Henceforth the Americans were on the defensive. Four issues became major bones of contention: the western and northern boundaries of the United States, the right to fish off Newfoundland, the payment of prewar debts that Americans owed to British merchants, and compensation for the loyalists. To an amazing degree, considering their personal differences and antagonisms, the three envoys not only presented a united front, they often counterattacked with remarkable effectiveness.

In regard to the boundaries, John Jay did a superb job of defending the Mississippi as the western border. John Adams performed brilliantly delineating Massachusetts's northern boundary, thus preserving the future state of Maine. When it came to the fisheries, however, Adams confessed he had little to contribute. Harvard graduates seldom paid much attention to the sailors who braved the freezing Atlantic winds in pursuit of cod.

Franklin sent a courier galloping to Nantes, where his nephew, Jonathan Williams, was still in business. Williams found a Marblehead sailor who gave him detailed descriptions of the rights American fishermen had exercised before the war, especially the vital privilege of drying the caught fish on the shore, which enabled ships to bring home a great deal more cargo. Adams used this eyewitness information to talk Strachey into giving the Americans almost everything they demanded.

As two well-trained lawyers, Jay and Adams had no problem agreeing that British creditors had a right to collect their money from individual American debtors in pounds sterling, with the right to sue in American courts to settle disputed amounts. They added a proviso that American merchants could do the same thing in British courts. Although justice was on the British side, this was still an important concession by the Americans; in Virginia alone individual debts totaled over 1.4 million pounds—$6 million. Both sides agreed that only debts incurred before 1776 were collectable.[36]

By the last week in November 1782, only the loyalists divided the negotiators. The British felt the nation's honor was involved in their fate. London was thronged with American refugees, all clamoring for compensation for their confiscated farms and houses and slaves. Letters were pouring into the city from thousands of other loyalists still hoping against hope in Charleston and New York. The British tried to persuade the American envoys that Lord Shelburne's political survival depended on getting some kind of a deal for these angry people.

Benjamin Franklin took the floor and opposed giving the loyalists a penny. Behind his intransigence lay the wound his son William had inflicted by his adherence to George III. This festering humiliation had been worsened by an event in distant America, the murder of the New Jersey militia captain, Joshua Huddy. By this time Richard Lippincott, the man who had commanded the loyalists who hanged Huddy, had been tried by court-martial in New York and acquitted. Lippincott, the court concluded, had only been obeying orders from the Board of Associated Loyalists. The head of that board was William Franklin.

When General Washington received the Lippincott verdict, he demanded that William be handed over to be tried for murder. Too late, he was told. William had retreated to London. Washington asked Congress to help him decide whether Captain Asgill, the officer chosen by lot to die for Huddy's murder, should be hanged. While the politicians dithered, the captain's mother wrote a tearful letter to Louis XVI asking him to save her only son. The king urged Congress to grant her plea and Ambassador de la Luzerne persuaded the solons to consent. This happy ending did nothing to console Franklin for his son's role in the original crime. If anything, the public discussion of the case in London and Paris further enraged him. It made Franklin's opposition to the loyalists unshakable.

John Jay, also humiliated and infuriated by his brother James's defection, sided emphatically with Franklin, at one point calling loyalists "cutthroats." Jay's attitude was hardened by the unexpected appearance of his brother in Paris, denying that he had defected and asking Jay to help him sell the French some dubious naval weaponry. The two brothers had a bitter confrontation and did not speak to each other again for the rest of their lives.[37]

From a distance of two centuries, the interplay of this personal detestation suggests a bias against the loyalists. It requires a seven-league-boots step back in time to realize why many otherwise generous men such as George Washington felt the same antagonism to these opponents of independence. Too many loyalists had repeatedly made it clear that they expected a British victory to be followed by vengeful prosecutions of leading rebels. In 1777, when the British prepared offensive plans that seemed certain to crush the rebels, these loyalists gleefully predicted a "year of the hangman"—the three sevens looked like a row of gibbets. As the revolutionists saw it, the loyalists, like them, had gambled their lives and fortunes on the outcome of the war—and lost. Compensating them from American funds smacked of an admission of guilt, a dilution of the justice of the struggle for independence.

For several days, the negotiators deadlocked over the loyalists. Matthew Ridley noted in his diary that Henry Strachey was determined to win the argument. Unless fresh instructions came from England, Ridley thought "negotiations will probably break off" and the war would continue.

XVI

While the Americans argued, they were nervously aware that the French were negotiating with Lord Shelburne through Gerard de Rayneval, who had returned to England empowered by Foreign Minister Vergennes to achieve a settlement. On November 25, 1782, Edward Bancroft, the secretary to the American mission in France, came back from a trip to London with alarming news. He claimed to have heard from a reliable source that a courier had recently arrived at Versailles with dispatches from Rayneval. When Vergennes read them, he exclaimed to Louis XVI: "I have the peace in my pocket. I am master of the peace!"

Not only was the remark uncharacteristic of the cautious foreign minister; the opposite was the case. Peace seemed to be eluding the two major powers. It took a century for historians to discover that Bancroft was on the British secret-service payroll and was trying to put pressure on the Americans to accept British demands on behalf of the loyalists.

Another visitor increased the pressure on both negotiating teams. Benjamin Vaughan arrived from London, telling them that Lord Shelburne had to have a treaty with America in his hands when Parliament met in a few days. Without it his ministry would not survive. He had already prorogued (delayed) the fall session twice, hoping to buy time.

Franklin may have sensed a weakening of resolve on the part of his two colleagues at these shrewdly timed intrusions. He stayed up late that night writing a letter that reached deep into his revolutionary past. The next day he read it to Jay and Adams. Even Adams had to admit it was devastatingly effective.

The letter informed Richard Oswald and Henry Strachey that if the British insisted on compensation for the loyalists, the Americans would make a counterclaim for all the damages the British army had inflicted on Americans. Franklin began with the burning of Charlestown, Massachusetts, during the battle of Bunker Hill. He listed other burned towns: Norfolk, Virginia; Falmouth, Massachusetts; New London and Fairfield in Connecticut. He discussed the wrecked and looted houses of New Jersey, Pennsylvania, and the southern states. He even included the plundering of his private library in Philadelphia. The ambassador proposed that both sides total up the cost of the damages inflicted on rebels and loyalists. If American damages were higher, the British would agree to pay the balance due. The Americans would do the same thing if the loyalists' numbers won. Franklin ended this tour de force by declaring that even if the British had won the war, George III would have had a terrible time getting compensation for the loyalists. "And you will please recollect—you have *not* conquered us," he wryly added.[38]

The letter left the British negotiators stunned. They realized that such a public accounting would blacken England's reputation around the world. George III's representatives withdrew to a nearby room, where they briefly conferred. Returning, they said they would "strike"—accept the treaty as it stood, if the Americans would agree to insert a clause promising that Congress would request the states to compensate loyalists who had not made themselves "obnoxious" to their fellow Americans. Jay and Adams agreed; Franklin insisted that loyalists who had borne arms against the United States would be excluded from this plea. He was undoubtedly thinking of William Franklin.

The next day, November 30, 1782, the three American commissioners met in Richard Oswald's rooms and signed a treaty which was described as "preliminary articles." They were joined at the last moment by Henry Laurens; his health, broken from his long confinement in the Tower of London and the news of the death of his son, had prevented him from participating in the negotiations. Franklin, Jay, and Adams welcomed his signature on the treaty; he would reassure southern congressmen that they had had a spokesman in the negotiations. Another cordial greeting came from Laurens's former business partner, Richard Oswald.

Henry Laurens looked over the treaty and found there was no room or necessity for any large changes. But the next day, Laurens asked if anything should be inserted about the "plunders in Carolina of negroes, [silver] plate etc." John Adams recalled that Laurens proposed there should be "a stipulation that the British troops should carry off no negroes or other American property." Everyone agreed, including ex-slave trader Richard Oswald. This addition would cause a great deal of turmoil and anguish when it was implemented in America.[39]

The preliminary terms had to be approved by Congress and Parliament, but both sides were confident that a permanent peace had been achieved. Franklin invited the signers and their staffs to a dinner at Passy. Also present were several French friends. One of them raised his glass to toast an independent United States. He predicted the new nation would become one of the great powers of the world. As he said this, he smiled mockingly at the British negotiators. Caleb Whitefoord, Richard Oswald's hardworking secretary, replied: "Yes sir, and they will all speak English. Every one of them!"[40]

It was a revealing glimpse of what the English were thinking in the final days of the negotiations. They had abandoned all hope of seducing America back into the empire and consoled themselves that Britain would have an inside track to commerce with the ex-rebels because of their common language. Some of them, notably Oswald, believed that a warm friendship would do almost as much for trade as the old fealty to king and parliament. Trade would resume but it would take another hundred years to heal the wounds of the war and achieve friendship.

XVII

For the Americans, a large problem remained to be solved: how Foreign Minister Vergennes and Louis XVI would react when they learned that this agreement had been signed without consulting them. By way of mollifying their ally, the preface to the treaty stated that it would not become effective "until terms of peace shall be agreed on between Great Britain and France." But there was still little doubt that the Americans had ignored Congress's instructions to make peace with the guidance of France.

For Jay and Adams, this was not a problem. They had made their hostility to France evident for months. For Ambassador Franklin, it was a public as well as a private quandary. He must inform his friend the Comte de Vergennes of the treaty and explain why the Americans had not consulted him. The ambassador also had to ask for yet another loan to rescue the United States of America from bankruptcy.

Franklin sent a copy of the treaty to Vergennes the day it was signed. For several days, nothing but a frigid silence emanated from Versailles. The foreign minister was astonished by the breadth of the British concessions—the Mississippi boundary, access to the fisheries, the abandonment of the loyalists. The American gains, Vergennes said, "exceed all that I could have thought possible." His chief lieutenant in the foreign office, Gerard de Rayneval, immediately feared the worst. The treaty was a British attempt to buy "the defection of the Americans."[41]

This was the atmosphere in which Ambassador Franklin visited the man who had become his friend as well as his ally and supporter for the previous six trying years. Vergennes stiffly informed the ambassador that the "abrupt signature" of the treaty had "little in it which could be agreeable to the king." Franklin urged Vergennes to note that the Americans had no intention of signing a final peace treaty without France. He also undoubtedly told Vergennes about Benjamin Vaughan's visit, in which he described the precarious state of the Shelburne ministry. Then Franklin asked for another loan of 6 million livres.

Vergennes pretended he had not heard this request; instead, he urged Franklin not to send a copy of the treaty to Congress for the time being. Franklin pretended he had not heard this suggestion and the two men parted amicably.

Not another word was heard from the Comte de Vergennes until December 15, when Franklin wrote him a delicate letter. The ambassador reported that an American ship, appropriately named *Washington*, was about to sail to the United States with a British passport; it would carry a copy of the treaty with Great Britain. Would it be possible for it to also carry the first installment on the 6-million-livre loan? "I fear Congress will be reduced to despair when they find that nothing is yet obtained," he wrote. This was an implied threat that an exhausted America might drop out of the war.

Vergennes lost his famously unflappable diplomatic composure, a persona he had spent thirty years perfecting. He fired off a furious letter

saying he was "at a loss . . . to explain your conduct and that of your colleagues." He reminded Franklin of the failure to consult him and Louis
XVI before signing the treaty. Now they were holding out "a certain hope
of peace in America without even informing yourself on the state of the
negotiation on our part." He asked Franklin to reconcile this behavior
with the respect the ambassador owed to Louis XVI. Only then would he
consider asking the king "to enable me to respond to your requests."[42]

Franklin thought about this challenge for a day and a half—and
answered it with a diplomatic masterpiece, a reply that balanced all
aspects of the situation, from Vergennes's feelings to Congress's instructions to the obligation the ambassador owed his country. He began by
assuring Vergennes he had not asked for a British passport for the *Washington*. The British had volunteered it. The Americans would make sure
that the enemy did not use the ship to send letters or news stories that
might "convey inconvenient expectations into America."

Franklin insisted that "nothing has been agreed in the preliminaries
contrary to the interests of France." This was true enough on the surface.
But the ambassador was well aware that Vergennes had hoped to use the
Americans to extract concessions from the British. Franklin dealt with
this point in a smooth admission of guilt. Vergennes was right—in failing to consult him before signing the treaty, Americans had neglected "a
point of *biensance*" (propriety).

But the omission was not from want of respect for Louis XVI, "whom
we all love and honor." Franklin hoped that this "single indiscretion"
would not be permitted to ruin "the great work which . . . is so nearly
brought to perfection and is so glorious to his reign." If Vergennes refused
to give the Americans any further assistance, "the whole edifice sinks to
the ground immediately."

They would hold the *Washington* until Friday, when Franklin would
visit Versailles to hear Vergennes's answer. Franklin closed with another
reiteration of the gratitude which he and every American felt for the
"great benefits and favors" that Louis XVI had bestowed on them. Then
came a threat, delivered in the same smooth style, and underlined: "*The
English, I just now learn, flatter themselves that they have already divided us.*"
That was all the more reason to hope that this "little misunderstanding"
would be kept secret and George III and his followers would find themselves "totally mistaken."[43]

A few days later, the *Washington* sailed for America with 600 thousand

livres in her hold. Franklin serenely assured his good friend, Superintendent of Finance Robert Morris, that the rest of the promised 6 million-
livre loan would arrive in quarterly installments in 1783. There had been
a "little misunderstanding" with the French about the treaty but it had
been "got over" and all was well on their side of the Atlantic. For a final
touch, the *Washington*'s passport was made out to the United States of
America and signed by George III—his first written acknowledgment of
American independence.[44]

XVIII

In London, it soon became apparent that the peacemaking drama was
far from over. The city was rife with rumors about the preliminary treaty
with America. But First Minister Lord Shelburne kept the terms a secret,
not only from the opposition but from his cabinet. He feared, he later
admitted, that the cabinet would discuss and possibly disapprove of the
agreement.

Shelburne's chief concern was George III. He had to persuade the king
to accept American independence. By this time His Majesty had begun to
think the concession was more or less inevitable. But his resistance to it was
no less stubborn. In a letter to Shelburne, after the preliminaries were signed,
he displayed both these contradictory emotions along with a breathtaking
self righteousness, which comes naturally to kings. "I cannot conclude without mentioning how sensibly I feel the dismemberment of America from
this empire, and that I should be miserable indeed if I did not feel no blame
on that account can be laid at my door, and I did not know that knavery
seems to be so much the striking feature of its inhabitants that it may not in
the end be an evil that they become aliens to this kingdom."[45]

XIX

On December 5, 1782, George III was the central figure in a dramatic
scene which should be required reading in every American—and British—school. It was the day Parliament finally reconvened, after numerous
delays by jittery First Minister Lord Shelburne. George III was required
to make a speech from the throne in the House of Lords, reporting on the
state of the empire. Everyone knew that he was going to say something
important about the negotiations with the Americans.

Pudgy Frederick, Lord North, was George III's subservient first minister. As the war dragged on, he frequently begged permission to resign. In Parliament he could be witty and shrewd.
(Credit: The Granger Collection, New York)

Disheveled Charles James Fox was one of George III's most vociferous parliamentary enemies. He regularly condemned Britain's attempt to subdue America. To the king's horror, he was forced to accept Fox as first minister.
(Credit: The Granger Collection, New York)

ABOVE: Former Congress president Henry Laurens of South Carolina was captured by the British on the way to become ambassador to Holland. He was imprisoned in the Tower of London and threatened with execution. *(Credit: Library of Congress)*

Oblique, quixotic First Minister William Petty, Lord Shelburne, negotiated treaties of peace with America and France. Parliament censured him for giving too-liberal terms and he resigned in disgust. *(Credit: The Granger Collection, New York)*

Merchant prince Robert Morris became America's superintendent of finance in 1782. He tried to avert looming bankruptcy by using blunt language to raise money from the states. In spite of General Washington's backing, he failed.
(Credit: Library of Congress)

RIGHT: General Nathanael Greene of Rhode Island rescued the South from British domination in a brilliant counteroffensive in 1781. After Yorktown he faced mutiny in his army and gross ingratitude from South Carolina.
(Credit: Independence National Historic Park)

"Mad Anthony" Wayne was one of America's most combative generals. In 1782, he invaded British-held Georgia with barely five hundred men and forced an enemy army four times that size to evacuate the state.
(Credit: Independence National Historical Park)

LEFT: Idealistic Washington aide Colonel John Laurens tried to persuade South Carolina to free three thousand blacks and enlist them in the Continental Army. General Washington supported the proposal. But South Carolina voted no.
(Credit: Independence National Historical Park)

RIGHT: In 1783, headstrong continental congressman Alexander Hamilton encouraged the American army to threaten revolt to win Congress the power to raise money by direct taxes. General Washington warned him that an army was "a dangerous thing to play with."
(Credit: Independence National Historical Park)

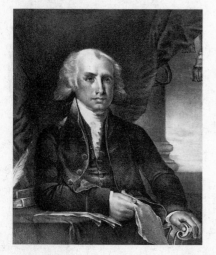

LEFT: Shy, slim James Madison of Virginia became one of the leading voices for a strong federal government in Congress after Yorktown. He also defended Benjamin Franklin and the French alliance from numerous critics.
(Credit: Library of Congress)

RIGHT: General Sir Guy Carleton was the last British commander in chief in America. He took the job hoping to negotiate reconciliation between Britain and America. He found he had nothing to do but "preside over embarkations." *(Credit: Library of Congress)*

LEFT: John Jay spent thirty frustrating months in Spain, trying to win a loan and recognition of American independence. The experience made him suspicious that Europeans wanted to keep America weak and dependent. *(Credit: Library of Congress)*

Engraved for RAYMOND's *History of England.*

ABOVE: The Chevalier de la Luzerne was France's affable ambassador to the United States. He used secret-service money to persuade members of Congress and other prominent patriots, such as Tom Paine, to support France. *(Credit: Independence National Historical Park)*

LEFT: The Comte de Grasse was the outsized commander of the French fleet that helped trap the British in Yorktown. Five months later, a British fleet defeated and captured him in the Caribbean. *(Credit: Library of Congress)*

Spain's chief reason for entering the war was the hope of capturing Gibraltar. But "The Rock" survived a three-year siege, climaxed by the brutal repulse of an all-out naval assault. This painting portrays burning French ships in the distance, while the British defenders exchange congratulations. *(Credit: National Portrait Gallery, London)*

On November 25, 1783, the British finally evacuated New York City. General Washington led eight hundred troops—all that was left of his army—into the city to maintain order. *(Credit: Library of Congress)*

At New York's Fraunces Tavern, Washington said goodbye to a small group of his officers after the British departed. His tears testified to his regret that he had been unable to win the money owed to them by the bankrupt Congress.

(Credit: National Archives [148-GW–179])

On December 23, 1783, General George Washington resigned his commission as commander in chief of the Continental Army. This peaceful surrender of power amazed Europeans and bolstered bankrupt America's prestige.

(Credit: Architect of the Capitol)

This political cartoon criticizes George III and Lord Shelburne for signing such a generous peace treaty. Two men representing France and Spain are leading them with a rope, while another man, labeled America, scourges them with a whip. *(Credit: Library of Congress)*

Irish-born Edmund Burke was the largely invisible hero in Parliament's tormented decision to grant America independence. Burke also fought for civil liberty in Ireland and tried to prevent the British from looting India.

(Credit: The Granger Collection, New York)

Among those present in the crowded House of Lords was Foreign Minister Vergennes's envoy, Gerard de Rayneval, who was deep in parleys with Lord Shelburne, and the young American merchant, Elkanah Watson, who had celebrated the news of Yorktown with Franklin. Watson seemed to have had a gift for being a spectator at history's turning points—and recording them in his voluminous diary.

According to Watson, it was a perfectly miserable—one might also say typical—December day in London. The great city was shrouded in dense fog, which as usual was one-half moisture and the rest coal dust, constricting both breath and visibility. For two hours, the lords and visitors lucky enough to gain admittance waited with growing impatience for the king's appearance. Finally, the crash of welcoming cannon outside signaled the imminent arrival of His Majesty. In royal red robes, he entered the chamber from a small door behind the throne and sat down in his accustomed seat.

It took only a moment for the spectators to perceive that George III was a deeply troubled man. He unrolled the speech that Lord Shelburne had written for him and announced in a toneless voice that the war with the rebel colonies was over. He had directed his representatives in America to end any and all attacks—part of his plan to achieve "an entire and cordial reconciliation" with his former subjects. These words should be contrasted with what His Majesty had said to Shelburne confidentially about American knavery a few days earlier. George was echoing Shelburne's hopes, not his own.

"Finding it indispensable to the attainment of this object, I did not hesitate to go to the full length of the powers vested in me, and offer to declare them—"

His Majesty's voice dwindled to a strangled whisper, and ceased. The appalled spectators watched him struggle for self control. Finally he spoke the fateful, hitherto impossible words: "and offer to declare them free and independent states by an article inserted in the treaty of peace." Gerard de Rayneval reported to Foreign Minister Vergennes that when the king spoke the word independent, his voice was "constrained." The less polite Watson said he "hesitated, choked" and otherwise performed with "an ill grace."

George struggled through the closing sentences of his speech to a totally hypocritical prayer to Almighty God that America might escape the "calamities" England had undergone before she realized a monarchy was essential to "constitutional liberty." He was referring to the English civil war of the seventeenth century, which put Oliver Cromwell in power for thirty years. His Majesty ended by hoping a common language and religion would somehow create "a bond of permanent union between the two countries." Once more, the king was mouthing Shelburne's hopes—virtually the opposite of his own. But the thorough courtier had done a remarkable job of persuading His Majesty to swallow his indigestible advice.[46]

XX

In the House of Lords and House of Commons over the next few days, Lord Shelburne did not fare nearly as well. The Rockingham followers of Burke and Fox were so absorbed in their personal detestation of Shelburne, they instinctively opposed his peace treaty, even though it granted the Americans far more than they would have offered them. Lord North still had a conservative following in Parliament and they had no difficulty concluding from George III's performance in his speech from the throne that His Majesty's enthusiasm for the peace treaty was minimal.[47]

In the House of Lords Viscount Stormont, a hardliner to the bitter end of North's tenure, rose to assail the treaty and Shelburne; he called the first minister's conduct "preposterous" and verging on "imbecility." Stormont asked the lords if they could accept a treaty that says American independence shall be an unconditional fact "whenever France chooses to make peace with us." What could Lord Shelburne have been thinking, to put Great Britain in such a humiliating position? Calling it a "provisional treaty" was ridiculous. Worst of all, Shelburne had abandoned to beggary "that brave set of men," the American loyalists, who had suffered so much for their support of the king.

Shelburne leaped to his feet and declared in his unctuous, overpolite style that Lord Stormont was wrong. American independence was not unconditional or irrevocable. If France refused to make peace on England's terms, independence would be withdrawn and the war would continue until Great Britain was the incontestable victor. Stormont was, to put it mildly, unconvinced. He sneeringly reminded Shelburne that he had said when he took office that Britain's sun would set if America was granted independence in any shape or form. Now his lordship had granted it in writing. Did this mean they were all groping into the future in eternal darkness?

In the House of Commons an even worse scenario transpired. Shelburne still declined to make the treaty public. Charles James Fox and Edmund Burke decided to force the first minister's hand; they both made speeches, maintaining that independence was (and should be) irrevocable and unconditional, no matter what Shelburne said in the House of Lords.

Shelburne's spokesman in the House of Commons was twenty-three-year-old William Pitt, just beginning his rise to power and fame. The son of the first minister who had won the Seven Years War and established England as a global power, Pitt decided Lord Shelburne's position was indefensible and ringingly declared that "unqualified recognition" of an independent America was the policy of the administration. General Conway, the man who had made so many waves calling for an end to an offensive war, said the same thing. Here was stuff for the newspapers to chew on and spit out as acid commentaries.[48]

Parliament was in turmoil and with it a good portion of London. Everyone began advancing his own interpretation of the king's speech, not a few of which explained away American independence. In both the Lords and Commons, Shelburne's men were derided and ridiculed.[49]

As this uproar echoed across the English Channel, the four American commissioners in Paris wondered if they had been deceived and perhaps made to look ridiculous. A panicky Benjamin Vaughan urged Shelburne to send a message to Richard Oswald, ordering him to reassure the Americans. Shelburne did so, but having heard so much doubletalk from the Jesuit of Berkeley Square, it did little to calm their nerves.

XXI

Behind the scenes, another drama was unfolding, one that remains unknown to most Americans, even though without its successful denouement, the United States might not be independent today. While brawling in Parliament with his enemies, First Minister Lord Shelburne was negotiating with France in an attempt to reach a peace treaty before Parliament's wrath at the generous terms he had given the Americans destroyed his administration. Looming over the talks as a threat of a different order was the combined French and Spanish armada being assembled at Cadiz, with its Lafayette-led army of twenty-five thousand men and plans to seize Jamaica and then attack the British army in America. Once it sailed, this expedition would be beyond recall and the war would be almost certain to continue throughout 1783 and perhaps 1784.

The French were operating in the shadow of the disaster at Gibraltar, which had paradoxically made Spain less enthusiastic about an early peace. She still wanted The Rock—at least her foreign minister, the Conde de Floridablanca, wanted it, as a badly needed achievement to maintain his standing with King Charles III. But Floridablanca, who had a habit of flying into hysterical rages at the young French ambassador, Comte de Montmorin, was by now so discouraged with the way the war had gone, he was almost incapable of rational discussion.

At the heart of the drama were the enigmatic Shelburne, who sometimes seemed to be two or three personalities in one body, and Vergennes's agent and spokesman, Gerard de Rayneval. Early in their negotiations, Shelburne startled the Frenchman by announcing that Gibraltar, which the British had so stubbornly and brilliantly defended for three years, was on the negotiating table. If France and Spain were prepared to make appropriate exchanges of territory elsewhere in the world, preferably one or two of the West Indies sugar islands, England would return the fortress to Spain. Shelburne asked for Minorca to replace Gibraltar in the Mediterranean; he also wanted West Florida to give Britain access to the Mississippi River.

Rayneval, amazed by the offer to surrender Gibraltar, agreed and the two men began swapping West Indian islands and territory in Africa and India. The details of a peace agreement were hammered out in intense bargaining, approved by Shelburne's cabinet, and rushed to Paris for Vergennes's approval. "I have put myself at the mercy of France," Shelburne told Rayneval at dinner on November 23, 1782.

At this point, the negotiations with the Americans and with the French were proceeding on parallel tracks and seemingly fortuitous lines. The ability to handle these two dramas simultaneously was a tribute to Shelburne's dexterity and mastery of detail, if nothing else. He was like a man trying to ride two wild horses simultaneously.

Something close to admiration and even a measure of trust had flowered between Rayneval and Shelburne. The young Frenchman had become convinced that Shelburne sincerely desired a peace of reconciliation with America and even more amazing, a treaty that would at least moderate the centuries-old enmity between Great Britain and France. Rayneval managed to communicate his confidence in Shelburne to Vergennes, who summoned the Conde de Aranda to Versailles and in a day-long argument, convinced him to accept Gibraltar and return West Florida to England.[50]

XXII

When a triumphant Rayneval returned to Great Britain with the news of French-Spanish agreement, he was informed that Lord Shelburne had been confronted with a revolt in his cabinet about the surrender of Gibraltar. One of his ministers, the Duke of Richmond, had grown so enraged over it, he told George III that Shelburne was giving away "the greatest jewel of the British Crown." Popular opinion in London, entranced by the repulse of the floating batteries and by Admiral Lord Howe's brilliant relief of The Rock, strongly supported him. Richmond soon persuaded other members of the cabinet to join him in demanding more sugar islands, as well as the virtual abandonment of France's claims in India. An angry Rayneval called these demands "ridiculous" and warned Vergennes the talks were close to collapse.

Nevertheless, Rayneval continued to negotiate. In Paris, Vergennes was working equally hard. The Conde de Aranda had revealed that he had been authorized to find out what Spain might obtain if she abandoned her demand for Gibraltar. Vergennes saw new hope and rushed a courier to Rayneval in London, telling him that if England would offer Minorca and East and West Florida to Spain, the foreign minister would persuade Louis XVI to urge Charles III to forsake Gibraltar.

On December 11, facing renewed attacks in Parliament about the American treaty, Shelburne persuaded his cabinet to offer Minorca and both Floridas to compensate Spain for giving up Gibraltar. Back to Paris went a courier with Rayneval's strong recommendation of acceptance—if Spain would agree.

Now came a moment of truth. Vergennes brought the Conde de Aranda to Versailles again and told him of the latest offer. Would he agree to abandoning Gibraltar? Vergennes expected a storm of argument followed by an insistence on consulting Madrid, a process that would take weeks. During that time, Shelburne might be voted out of office, the expeditionary force and fleet would sail from Cadiz, and the war would resume. Instead, to Vergennes's immense relief and amazement, Aranda accepted the offer instantly.

The Spanish aristocrat knew he was risking his reputation and possibly his life. He later said he had been guided by "the loyalty of a good subject and an awareness of the real situation." He convinced himself that he was "compelled . . . to do what was right." Vergennes, in a similar mood, reluctantly authorized Rayneval to abandon most of France's ambitions in India. Although this concession has not received as much attention from historians, the decision was at least as painful for Vergennes as Aranda's abandonment of Gibraltar. The foreign minister had been hoping to establish a French presence in India that included enough territory to guarantee substantial profits.[51]

In the coming months, news from India would reveal Vergennes had made a wise choice. The French army in India proved ineffective under an old and tired general. Meanwhile, Hyder Aly died suddenly in December of 1782. His son, Tipu, became Sultan of Mysore but he never achieved the power of his father. Although the French fleet remained a threat, without a land force a British victory was more or less inevitable.[52]

In Paris and London, there was more hard bargaining about minor details; additional islands were swapped and the British demanded and got an enlargement of their right to cut wood on the shores of Spanish Honduras, a foothold they would eventually enlarge into a colony. On January 20, 1783, treaties were signed among England and France and Spain. Peace had been achieved two days before Parliament returned from its Christmas recess.

XXIII

Shelburne expected more savage attacks by his enemies in both houses of Parliament. But the overall treaty was too advantageous to Great Britain to be overturned. Essentially, France gained little but American independence and removal of the obnoxious British commissioners at Dunkirk. Although the agreement was called provisional, like the American treaty, few had any doubt that the peace was permanent.

In Cadiz, the Comte d'Estaing, the French admiral in command of the expedition to the West Indies and North America, was preparing to sail on January 16 when he learned that there was more than a chance of peace. He decided to delay his departure by detaching eight ships of the line to escort a fleet of Spanish merchantmen that was arriving from Havana. The warships were still at sea on February 2 when d'Estaing learned that peace had been signed. Until the treaties were confirmed by their government, an armistice between the hostile powers was now in force. Knowing the parlous state of the French and Spanish treasuries, d'Estaing immediately cancelled the expedition, leaving the Marquis de Lafayette the most disappointed man in Europe.[53]

In a letter to his friend and follower, the Comte de Montmorin, the French ambassador to Spain, Vergennes expressed a sense of awed amazement that both sides had overcome so many daunting obstacles to end the global war. The foreign minister's deep religious faith, which he sternly excluded from his professional diplomat's style, came to the fore. Vergennes expressed his gratitude to the "Sovereign Being" who had altered "the heart and spirit" of King Charles III, persuading the monarch to abandon his quest for Gibraltar. Gerard de Rayneval had a similar reaction. He told Vergennes the peace was nothing short of a miracle.[54]

XXIV

Early in the negotiations, Henry Laurens told Benjamin Franklin his achievement would be "called blessed" by every living American. Franklin replied with wry recollections of earlier peace treaties between France and England. In every case the negotiators were vilified and abused. "The blessing promised to peacemakers, I fancy, relates to the next world," the ambassador concluded. "In this they seem to have a greater chance of being cursed."[55]

Franklin was right. There were still several large bumps on the road to a permanent peace. One shock was already looming in London, where First Minister Lord Shelburne's enemies were readying an all-out assault.

On January 27, 1783, Shelburne presented both treaties to Parliament. Still fearful of the public reaction, he rejected a motion in the House of Commons to have them printed. A barrage of nasty comments from Charles James Fox and other Shelburne enemies led to a motion to print them that carried unanimously.

As the details of the treaties swirled through London, Shelburne was attacked from all points of the political compass. The most violent protests came from the loyalists, led by William Franklin and other prominent refugees. They formed a committee and managed to wangle an appointment with the embattled first minister on February 6, 1783. But he was fighting for his political life and could do little for them.

The discouraged Americans wrote to Prince William Henry, on whom they had lavished so much attention in New York; perhaps they were hoping to get George III's ear. The prince's brainless reply was more than a little dismaying: He hoped "your late friends and fellow subjects in the North American colonies" would see the error of their ways and agree to form "a lasting connection with the parent state."[56]

Although the loyalists made a great deal of noise, there was no enthusiasm for continuing the war to help them get better terms. Far more potent were the objections of the planters on several West Indian islands which had been transferred to the French in the final settlement. They had lobbyists in London to state their complaints. The same was true of the Canadian fur traders, many of whom now found themselves operating in American territory in the Midwest.

Other critics assailed the generosity of the American concessions and Shelburne's strategy of settling with the rebels first to put pressure on France and Spain. They chorused that the Americans had outnegotiated Shelburne and his spokesman, Richard Oswald, whom one critic sneeringly described as "that extraordinary geographer and politician."

Admiral Augustus Keppel, first lord of the admiralty in Shelburne's cabinet, had resigned in protest as soon as he read the preliminary treaty with Spain and France. He was joined by another restless member of Shelburne's cabinet, the Duke of Portland. They argued that the British navy had the initiative in the war and was numerically almost equal to the combined French and Spanish fleets. They wanted to continue the struggle until Great Britain won a victorious peace, in which she dictated the terms.

In the House of Lords, Shelburne made considerable headway against these critics. He told the loyalists that England's generosity would make good their losses. He disagreed vehemently with Admiral Keppel and the Duke of Portland about the condition of the British navy, introducing testimony by a high-ranking naval officer that described the fleet as a collection of floating wrecks, their crews undermanned, their dockyards depleted. Shelburne won a narrow thirteen-vote majority from his fellow peers, approving the terms.[57]

The House of Commons was a different story. Edmund Burke and Charles James Fox caught the mood of general dissatisfaction with both treaties and assailed Shelburne as a hopeless bungler. Burke denounced making the Mississippi the western boundary of the United States and spoke piteously of the plight of the loyalists. Joining the chorus was an unexpected voice: Lord North. He had now read the treaties and launched a wide-ranging attack on them. North's support added over a hundred votes to the Fox-Burke wing of the Rockingham party.[58]

While they waited for Shelburne to reveal the texts of the treaties, North and Fox had been secretly conferring, possibly at Edmund Burke's urging—the ex-first minister and the new leader of the Rockinghams were personally friendly, in spite of their many political differences. Between them, Boreas and Reynard, as Burke (and others) wryly called North and Fox, controlled 210 votes—a majority in the House of Commons. The two leaders were united only by their detestation of Shelburne.

Shelburne's spokesmen in the House of Commons argued vehemently in defense of the treaties. The first minister supported their efforts with more than 2,000 pounds in secret-service money slipped to various newspaper editors. But it was a losing fight. On February 21, 1783, after a wild night-long debate, the opposition managed a unique political feat. They accepted the peace treaties as necessary in the light of the nation's reluctance to continue the war. But they condemned the terms of the treaties as much too generous, tacitly accepting Admiral Keppel's argument that the war was winnable, if the British people could be persuaded to keep fighting it. Shelburne's peace "made one sicken at its very name," roared Charles James Fox. In the same manic bellow Fox thundered that the treaties were "more calamitous, more dreadful, more ruinous than war could possibly be."

By a vote of 207-190, the House of Commons voted to censure Shelburne for his peacemaking. The disgusted first minister resigned and told his few friends that the man behind his fall was George III. On the contrary, His Majesty was enormously disturbed and felt that Shelburne had deserted him. It was the final testimony to Shelburne's inability to win—and keep—political trust. He would never hold office again.[59]

A dismayed John Jay wrote to Benjamin Vaughan, asking why Shelburne had resigned simply because he had lost a single vote in the House of Commons. Now what was going to happen? Would a new ministry contrive to junk the preliminary treaties and continue the war? It would soon be apparent that the answer to that question was not clear to anyone, including George III.

Edmund Burke's view of the situation was more than a little satur-
nine. "We have demolished the Earl of Shelburne but in his fall he has
demolished a large piece of the building," he wrote to one of his closest
friends. By this Burke meant that the Rockingham party, with whom he
had hoped to reform Britain, had been badly damaged in the struggle
with Shelburne. "This wicked man . . . no less weak and stupid than
false and hypocritical, has contrived to break to pieces the body of men
whose integrity, wisdom, and union were alone capable of . . . recovering
this kingdom from the miserable state into which it is fallen." To destroy
Shelburne was "a necessary preliminary" but Burke wondered whether
the "proper results"—a resumption of the struggle for reform—would follow it.

"I greatly fear they will not," wrote the doleful Irishman. "For once
I confess I apprehend more from the madness of the people than from
any other cause." Burke's cynicism about the Fox-North coalition and its
seemingly popular support were all too visible in these words. He grimly
concluded: "Things are in great confusion."[60]

If the embittered Burke or the agitated John Jay knew what was happening in the United States of America at this time, they would have been
even more dubious about the outcome of the seemingly endless struggle
that Americans called the Revolutionary War.

Chapter Nine

Will It Be Peace—
Or Civil War?

IN PHILADELPHIA during the last months of 1782, Superintendent of Finance Robert Morris, his assistant New Yorker Gouverneur Morris (no relation), and their backers in Congress sank into frustration and near despair. The attempt to collect taxes through federal receivers appointed by the superintendent had been a disastrous failure. They had raised only about 20 percent of the $8 million budgeted for the federal government. The Morrises, James Madison, and others who believed in strengthening the national government decided to bet the dwindling residue of their hopes on the impost—the 5 percent tax on imports. The revenue would at least pay the interest on the millions owed to France and establish the principle of federal taxation.

The superintendent of finance put all his formidable energy and aggressive vocabulary into this campaign. The mood in Congress was almost totally supportive. Only a few diehard Morris-haters such as Arthur Lee sniped from the sidelines. There were active agents speaking and writing on the impost's behalf in every state. In Rhode Island, former Brigadier General James Varnum, now a member of Congress, wrote a series of trenchant articles extolling the idea as the answer to the needs of the suffering soldiers in the Continental Army and an elixir to restore America's credit in Europe.

For a while the nationalists seemed to be succeeding. State after state

approved the impost, including mighty Virginia, which had been especially averse to paying federal taxes, and New York, where Governor
George Clinton frequently spoke and acted as if he were head of an independent country. In July Massachusetts, where anti-tax feeling always ran
high, voted a reluctant approval, after much debate.

By October, as the British and American negotiators began hard
bargaining in Paris, there was only one state that had not approved the
impost: Rhode Island. One might think this was no more than a passing
blemish on the bright prospects for a financial and political triumph by a
vote of 12-1. But under the provisions of the Articles of Confederation,
any measure involving federal taxes had to be approved by *all* the states
before it became law. Tiny Rhode Island was a roadblock on the path to
national salvation.

The man who seemed to be the creator of this barrier was a Rhode
Island congressman, David Howell. A former mathematics teacher at the
University of Rhode Island, Howell had launched his political career on
his opposition to the tax. He had won election to Congress by attacking
General Varnum in a series of nasty letters to the *Providence Gazette,*
which portrayed the impost as not much different from the 1765 Stamp
Act created by "an infernal junto of British ministers." Howell predicted
the tax would put Congress on the road to absolute power and become
the death knell of American liberty.

This overkill came naturally to Howell, who was a born demagogue.
He adored the limelight and was expert at portraying himself as a spokesman for the average man. He signed his public letters "A Farmer." In fact
he was the hired gun of a clique of Providence merchants, led by wealthy
John Brown, who had decided they were not going to let any government
diminish the handsome profits Rhode Island was making on the high
seas, in spite of the still-troublesome British blockade.

Howell was capable of some very dirty tricks. He got his hands on
several letters from John Adams and by quoting selectively from them,
made it seem that the Netherlands and other European countries were
eager to loan money to the United States, making the impost superfluous. Howell arranged for his tampered version to be published anony-
mously in Rhode Island. Only when a congressional investigation led to
his door did he admit his role in the deception. An angry James Madison
reported "great and universal indignation and astonishment" in Congress
over Howell's conduct.[1]

On November 1, 1782, the Rhode Island assembly spent a full day listening to pro and con statements on the impost from leading politicians, including Superintendent of Finance Morris and Congressman Howell. Far more influential was John Brown's backstairs campaign to line up votes against this federal threat to what he called "the sovereignty and independence" of Rhode Island. As evening shadows filled the hall, the assembly voted unanimously to reject the impost. "Thus ended the long and much talked about five percent duty," John Brown boasted to his son in a triumphant letter. "I wish never to have it introduced into this free state til time shall be no more."[2]

II

Congress decided to send a three-man delegation to Rhode Island to talk to the state's assembly and governor. They were on their way in early December when distressing news reached them. Virginia's legislature had reversed itself and decided it did not support the impost after all. The dismayed politicians returned to Philadelphia, where they soon learned the explanation for this stunning about-face.

In early October, Arthur Lee had hurried from Philadelphia to Richmond, where he took his seat in Virginia's legislature, the House of Burgesses. He was joined by his brother, Richard Henry Lee, a master of legislative maneuver. Together they had changed enough minds about the impost to produce the turnabout. In a clever touch, Arthur voted against the reversal so he could return to Congress and piously claim he had supported the impost. "That we have bad men amongst us is [now] quite clear to me," Virginia's angry governor, Benjamin Harrison, told James Madison.[3]

An increasingly desperate Superintendent Morris asked Tom Paine to change Rhode Island's mind about the impost. Paine arrived in Providence in late December 1782 and began publishing articles in the *Providence Gazette*. At first he concentrated on extolling the good effects that the money from the impost would achieve for the nation. But the more time he spent in the smallest state, the more convinced Paine became that behind the posturing about liberty and independence from Howell and his followers lay an ugly self-interested conspiracy. He began calling the assembly vote an "ambuscade" perpetrated by "about ten or a dozen merchants . . . who with a very profitable trade pay very little taxes."

John Brown's counterattack was savage. The *Gazette* was bombarded with letters denouncing the "mercenary writer" who had been sent by the would-be oligarchs in Congress to destroy tiny Rhode Island's sovereignty. Others noted Paine's fondness for a drink and suggested his arguments emanated from a surplus of "inflammable spirits." A gleeful David Howell was soon telling his friends that Paine was being handled "without mittens." The insult-filled controversy only confirmed the failure of the impost and encouraged more people to speak and write about Congress with contempt. It also left Tom Paine wondering about the future of the country he had helped to found.[4]

III

The only good news that Congress heard from any part of the nation was the British evacuation of Charleston in December 1782. But this happy event mutated into another worry. The city's *Royal Gazette,* in its final edition, summed up the South Carolina loyalists' reaction to the decision: "Every loyal breast" was filled with "terror and dismay." General Alexander Leslie promised General Nathanael Greene that he would not destroy the city if the Americans promised not to attack his troops as they withdrew. Greene readily agreed but this mutual generosity did not lead to any further accords.[5]

An angry quarrel broke out over the British plan to take with them thousands of slaves inside their lines. The Americans claimed most of them had been seized by marauding British and loyalist troops and insisted on their return. They accused one British officer of sequestering as many as eight hundred blacks whom he planned to sell in the British West Indies. Leslie, on orders from General Carleton, balked at returning any blacks whom the Americans considered "obnoxious." Every black in the occupied city soon claimed this label. Short-tempered Governor John Mathews broke off the negotiations and the stalemate persisted until the last ships departed.

A South Carolina eyewitness account included some ugly final scenes. Blacks who had been left behind sometimes "fasten[ed] themselves to the sides of the boats. To prevent this dangerous practice, the fingers of some of them were chopped off." The overcrowded fleet deposited hundreds of other blacks on one of Charleston's outer islands, promising to send ships for them when available. They died by the hundreds of malnutrition and camp fever.[6]

As the British made sail, General Anthony Wayne took over the town at the head of the American light infantry and the cavalry of Lee's legion. Later in the day, General Greene escorted Governor Mathews to the state house, while thousands of people cheered. This was virtually the last vestige of cordiality between the South Carolinians and the Continental Army. When one of Greene's officers strolled through the city, he reported that he "didn't meet with that friendly reception that might reasonably be expected." He would soon find out why.[7]

IV

South Carolina's patriots now considered Greene and his army superfluous. They became extremely reluctant to supply his soldiers with food or clothing. On New Year's Day 1783, Greene remarked to one of his senior officers that they had nothing to eat "either for man or beast." Discontented soldiers added to Greene's woes. The day after the British departed, the general learned that the Maryland regiment in his army was going home. They thought the war was over. The general rushed to their camp and ordered them to remain on duty or face the penalty for desertion—death by hanging.[8]

To feed and clothe his mutinous army, General Greene entered into an agreement with John Banks, a Virginia merchant who combined speculation with government contracting. Greene had given him notes drawn on Robert Morris with which Banks bought clothing from British merchants in Charleston before the evacuation. He sold the clothing to Greene's army after the British left. The same notes were sent to Virginia to buy tobacco and sell it to these same merchants in the West Indies. The governor of Virginia construed this as trading with the enemy and refused to approve it, leaving Banks in a large financial hole.

By this time the merchant was also supplying Greene's army with food. When the general found Banks was teetering on bankruptcy, he pledged his own credit for more than 30 thousand pounds—$150 thousand—to keep him in business. This proved to be only a stopgap—Banks went broke anyway, leaving Greene responsible for this large debt.[9]

Unwisely, Greene yielded to the desperation he felt from these monetary pressures and urged South Carolinians not to follow Virginia's example but to withdraw their approval of the impost. The new governor, Benjamin Guerard, wrote Greene a sneering reply and urged the legislature to ignore the general's unsolicited opinion. The legislators voted to withdraw their approval—and criticized Greene for interfering in the state's politics.

An even more unpleasant dispute erupted when a British officer who had married a Charleston woman arrived by ship from East Florida under a flag of truce to deal with some financial matters in regard to his wife's property. General Greene assured him he was free to go where he pleased in the city. Governor Guerard, obviously eager for a quarrel, announced Greene had committed an affront to the sovereignty of South Carolina, and arrested the officer and the crew of the ship. An enraged Greene threatened to use his troops to free them. The governor backed down but not before many people wondered if civil war was about to erupt.[10]

It is easy to see why General Greene, in letters to Robert Morris and others, began deploring "the great blindness" throughout America to what would promote the nation's happiness. "A rage for the sovereign independence of each state" was at the root of it. He wondered if there was any hope for "national honor or national revenue."[11]

V

Also on Congress's uneasy mind was the problem of Vermont. Many people thought the dilemma could be summed up in two words: Ethan Allen. The tall, loquacious adventurer had captured the imagination of the country by leading a mob of "Green Mountain Boys" to seize the British bastion of Fort Ticonderoga in 1775. Unfortunately, Allen himself was captured in 1776 during the American invasion of Canada and spent two years in British jails, frequently threatened with a noose. Bolstered by his grandiloquent *Narrative of Colonel Allen's Captivity*, the ordeal only added to Allen's popularity. Even George Washington said there was "an original something in him that commands admiration." But the *Narrative* did not change the minds of prominent New Yorkers who claimed the land which Allen and his followers were farming. Nor did it alter the attitude of Governor George Clinton of New York, who described Allen and his followers as "revolted subjects of the state" and Vermont as "rebellious northeastern districts."[12]

Congress did not know what to do with this hot potato. Vermont had adopted a constitution and elected a governor, an Allen ally named Thomas Chittenden. They had even erected a court system, though there were seldom more than one or two trained lawyers in or near the state.

Their militiamen had fought courageously against General Burgoyne's 1777 invasion. But Congress clung to a resolution declaring Vermont should cease to exist and return to New York's jurisdiction. Vermonters replied that they feared for their rights under a government which tolerated all religions. Obviously they were prepared to say anything, no matter how absurd, to hang on to their stolen property.

Various congressional attempts to negotiate a settlement went nowhere, especially when Vermont began incorporating towns in New Hampshire into its mini-imperium. Soon Massachusetts was also screaming that some of its territory was being co-opted. New York, by far the biggest loser, remained intransigent.

Ethan Allen and his brother Ira and their friend Governor Chittenden became prominent Vermont landowners. Through a front called the Onion River Company, they bought thousands of acres of land from settlers discouraged by the ongoing political turmoil. The Allens decided they needed a protector and began talking to General Sir Frederick Haldimand, commander of His Majesty's forces in Canada. By early 1781, Haldimand was sufficiently impressed to send a copy of a proposed treaty to Sir Henry Clinton in New York. Under its terms, Vermont would become a separate royal province.

General Clinton asked his legal advisor, Judge William Smith, whether he had the authority to sign such a document, which would have, among other things, ratified the Vermonters' claims to their lands. New York patrician Smith owned (or claimed) a hundred thousand acres of land in Vermont, granted by George III. The judge told General Clinton he did not have the authority to approve this deal; the treaty and a history of the negotiations were sent to England for royal and parliamentary approval, a process that would take months and possibly years.

In February 1782, copies of these incriminating documents were suddenly presented to the New York legislature by Governor George Clinton as proof of Vermont's perfidy. He sent copies to New York's delegates in Congress and bellowed that "the public peace and the dignity of Congress" demanded an invasion of Vermont. Who leaked these embarrassing papers? Suspicion points to Judge William Smith, who was trying to protect his hundred thousand acres in this war within the larger war. Congress ignored Governor Clinton's cries of alarm.

Vermonters of course denied any intention of betraying the United States. Ethan Allen and his friends insisted they were only talking to the

British because Congress had threatened them with armed force if they did not obey their dictatorial edicts. General Haldimand, meanwhile, was expressing intense frustration because Allen did a perpetual dance around consenting to sign a treaty. Ethan was manipulating both Congress and the crown, hoping to get Vermont into the union on Green Mountain Boy terms. Then they would thumb their collective noses at everybody.[13]

VI

In Newburgh, Washington and his disgruntled soldiers in the nearby New Windsor cantonment were still mired in difficulties and shortages. Earlier in the fall of 1782, General Comte de Rochambeau's French army had finally marched north, not to fight the British in New York, but to say goodbye to the Continentals. Rochambeau had received orders to sail from Boston to join French and Spanish troops for the assault on Jamaica that Lafayette and Admiral d'Estaing were planning in Cadiz.

The encounter with the French army was an acute embarrassment for Washington and his officers. The brilliantly uniformed French, their pockets overflowing with *livres d'or*, entertained the ragged Americans at elegant feasts. In return, the Americans could serve them nothing but (in Washington's words) "stinking whiskey—and not always that—and a bit of beef without vegetables." Contractor Comfort Sands, who emerges from this tale as a hitherto unrecognized threat to America's survival, had refused to allow the officers any credit for rations not drawn from the common pot. They could not obtain an advance to entertain friends, or build up a backlog by dining elsewhere. Sands was treating the officers like enlisted men—a guaranteed recipe for trouble.[14]

Far from apologizing, Sands still insisted on being paid in hard money. An exasperated Superintendent of Finance Morris fired him and hired another contractor, who charged far more per ration than Sands but accepted long-term credit. The contractor had strong business connections in New England and the army was soon eating well. But a temporarily improved diet did not revive the morale of the officer corps.[15]

VII

As General Rochambeau resumed his march to Boston, he had an experience that summed up almost everything that was right—and wrong—with the American Revolution at this point in its brief existence. Rochambeau's aide, Baron von Closen, called it "an experience unlike any, I believe, since the beginning of the world." The farmer on whose land Rochambeau and his men had camped demanded 1,800 livres for damages the troops had inflicted on his property. They had cut wood for fires and knocked down and probably burned fences to clear space for the camp.

During their stay, General Rochambeau had ordered his men to build an aqueduct from a nearby lake to bring water to the troops. The farmer used it to turn a gristmill near his house. It would have cost him a great deal of time and money to build this watercourse at his own expense. But the farmer did not factor this gift into his claim for damages.

General Rochambeau told his aides to offer 400 livres for the damages. The farmer angrily refused and summoned the local sheriff. This worthy showed up on the morning of the French army's departure. He solemnly informed General Rochambeau that the farmer's claim had been appraised and approved by three jurors of the county, and the general must pay it—or else.

The sheriff drew a parchment from his pocket, confirming his powers. It was signed by Governor George Clinton of New York. As the general and his aides scanned it, the sheriff declared with a nervous stammer that he had no choice but to inform Rochambeau: "YOU ARE MY PRISONER." The general's aides burst into laughter. The general was not so amused at first but finally forced a stiff smile and told von Closen, who spoke English, that "out of his respect for the laws of the country, he would pardon him [the sheriff] for what he had just done." He added that he could have ordered a detachment of grenadiers to escort him to General Washington. Instead, he would just advise him "to go away." The sheriff departed, von Closen said, "like a naughty boy."

As the army formed a line of march, Rochambeau told another aide to settle with the farmer. He accepted 600 livres but he never got the money. When Governor Clinton heard the story, he fired the sheriff and made the farmer pay all the expenses of the case.[16]

VIII

As 1783 began, rumors arrived on ships from Europe that Benjamin Franklin and his fellow negotiators in Paris were close to signing a separate peace with Britain. All that was needed now was a treaty between

England and France and her European allies, Spain and Holland, to end the war. This glimpse of peace just over the horizon aroused in the officer corps a surge of sullen fury. Congress had not paid them for years. As a reward for their services, they had been promised half pay for life. Now Congress no longer needed them and was reportedly going to welch on this agreement—and on their back pay.

Antagonism between the legislators and the officers was not new. The mutual alienation had flared repeatedly during the Valley Forge winter when Samuel Adams and his followers had done everything but threaten secession from the union to block a vote on promising the officers half pay for seven years after the war. At Washington's urging, the bounty had been extended to half pay for life in 1780, but almost immediately, under pressure from New England, the lawmakers got cold feet and rescinded their generosity.

Instead, they recommended the half-pay idea to the individual states, where it got a very mixed reception. When Connecticut agreed to the impost in May 1782, her legislature specified that not a single tax dollar should go to the army's officers for half pay. Small wonder that there was a growing determination on the officers' part to settle matters.

The officers dispatched a three-man delegation to Congress led by Major General Alexander McDougall of New York. Choosing McDougall as a spokesman was a statement in itself. In the early 1770s this abrasive, demagogic Scot had been a leader in staging riots and protests against the British. He had already led another delegation to Philadelphia demanding redress for the army's generals, who were furious at Congress for refusing to raise their pay to keep up with inflation. In that visit, though he spoke with his usual stutter, General McDougall did not mince words: the Revolution had become a war "for empire and liberty to a people whose object is property." The army expected a fair share of that property in return for protecting it.[17]

This time, General McDougall and two colonels, Mathias Ogden of New Jersey and John Brooks of Massachusetts, brought with them a petition from the officers which General Washington assured Congress was written in "respectful terms." While this was true by and large, some of the language was more than a little strident. "We have borne all that men can bear," the petition declared. "Our property is expended—our private resources are at an end, and our friends are wearied out with our incessant applications."

Harsh personal reality supported this rhetoric. Before the Revolution, McDougall had been a fairly wealthy man. After seven years of war, he was penniless and so were the two colonels who accompanied him. It took them almost two weeks to borrow the money they needed for the trip to Philadelphia. There was not much doubt that they subscribed to the petition's closing words. "Any further experiments on their [the Army's] patience may have fatal effects."[18]

IX

In the City of Brotherly Love, a discouraged Robert Morris viewed the arrival of these soldiers as possibly heaven sent. If he could not persuade the states to pay their share of the federal budget with positive arguments about the money's importance to the country's well-being, perhaps he could frighten them into parting with some cash by persuading the army to become the most vociferous of the public creditors. Within twenty-four hours of General McDougall's arrival in Philadelphia on December 29, 1782, the superintendent of finance conferred with him.

Equally pleased by McDougall's arrival was Congressman Alexander Hamilton, who had taken his seat as one of New York's delegates in November 1782. The "Continentalist" essays he had written in 1781 left no doubt that he supported a vigorous, well-financed federal government. Hamilton immediately saw that the "necessity and discontents of the army" were "a powerful engine" to galvanize Congress and the states into passing not simply the impost but a whole new taxation system. Hamilton's close friend and Superintendent Morris's right-hand man, Gouverneur Morris, enthusiastically agreed. On January 1, 1783, Morris confidently predicted: "Good will arise from the situation into which we are hastening."

Congressman James Madison, unaware of how far the Morrises and Hamilton were willing to go, thought the soldier's petition would "furnish new topics in favor of the impost." As the strongest voice for federal power in Congress since 1780, the Virginian was equally ready to back a new federal funding system. This is what Morris wanted, and he soon convinced McDougall that he had to arouse the army's officers to support the idea in unmistakable terms. McDougall promptly wrote to General Henry Knox, commander of the Continental Army's artillery, urging him to help unite "the influence of the army and the public creditors to obtain permanent funds for the United States."[19]

On January 6, General McDougall submitted the officers' petition to Congress. The lawmakers created another "grand committee" of one delegate from each state to consider the demands. Hamilton was chosen for New York and Madison for Virginia. The next day the committee talked to Superintendent of Finance Morris, who displayed a grim intransigence. He had no money for the army and no prospect of getting any. He would not even promise to pay a dollar until "certain funds" were "previously established." Everyone knew he was talking about new taxes. The financial situation was "so alarming," Morris wondered if Congress should create a "confidential committee" to hear the gruesome details without panicking the public.[20]

When General McDougall and the two colonels met with the grand committee on January 13, 1783, James Madison thought the general's language was "very high colored." The petition demanded an advance on the officers' back pay, an assurance that the balance would soon be forthcoming, and reassurance that Congress would make good on the promise of half pay for life. McDougall said an immediate advance was an "absolute necessity." He discoursed on the soldiers' sufferings and deprivations throughout the war and disparaged the on-again–off-again way Congress had dealt with paying them. The "seeming approach of peace" made them fear they were in danger of being "still more neglected."

Colonel Ogden said that unless Congress gave them positive answers, he did not want to return to New Windsor to face his fellow officers. General McDougall said the army was "verging to that state" which would "make a wise man mad." Colonel Brooks warned that a disappointment would throw the army into "extremities." McDougall closed the discussion by claiming the "most intelligent & considerate" part of the army" were "deeply affected" by the bankruptcy of the federal government and feared Congress was on the brink of dissolution. They were sure if the federal union collapsed, there would be wars between the states in which they would almost certainly be forced to fight and possibly die.[21]

James Madison was so moved by what he heard in this meeting, he told his Virginia friend Edmund Randolph that he wished what the soldiers had told them could be "promulgated throughout the U.S." At the very least it would "put to shame" politicians like David Howell and Arthur Lee, who were blocking Congress's attempts to solve the nation's financial crisis. The grand committee appointed Madison, Hamilton, and John Rutledge of South Carolina to prepare a report on the meeting for Congress.[22]

Hamilton wrote the report and submitted it to Congress on January 22, 1783. Two days later, as Congress debated the problem, Superintendent of Finance Morris announced his resignation. This timing was not an accident. He and Hamilton were working closely to put maximum pressure on Congress. Morris wrote a ferocious letter, saying that his financial and moral reputation were "utterly insupportable" in the light of the nation's looming bankruptcy. He would continue to serve as superintendent until the end of May. By that time, if Congress had failed to find "permanent provision for the public debts of every kind," he would retire to private life.

The letter, Madison wrote in the notes he was keeping of the debates in Congress, "made a deep and solemn impression" on the delegates. They realized that if it became known it would be a "source of fresh hopes to the enemy and ruinous to domestic and foreign credit." The stunned legislators ordered the secretary of Congress, Charles Thomson, to keep the letter secret. Thomson omitted all mention of it from the official journal.[23]

Hamilton's report recommended that Congress leave to Superintendent Morris's discretion giving the soldiers an advance on their salaries and settling their accounts for back pay. Congress agreed with scarcely a word of demur and promised to "make every effort in its power" to raise from the states enough money to fund "the whole debt of the United States." The third part of the soldiers' complaints, half pay for life, did not receive the same enthusiastic endorsement. Hamilton suggested giving the officers six years' salary as a reasonable commutation of their claim. A coalition of New England states, joined by New Jersey, blocked the proposal.[24]

The frustrated nationalists turned to persuading Congress to approve a new impost. Much of the debate revolved around how to collect it. The New England–New Jersey bloc favored state-appointed officials and wanted the money to pass through state treasuries. Hamilton and Madison wanted federal appointees who would pay the money directly to Congress. Toward the end of January, in a heated debate on this disagreement, Hamilton proposed using army officers to collect the money. They would be the most reliable supporters of "the power of Congress."[25]

This was a mistake. Madison nervously noted it was "imprudent and injurious to the cause." Arthur Lee and his allies were soon telling every-one that Hamilton had "let out the secret." He and the Morrises were in favor of a military dictatorship to collect federal money. In a letter to Samuel Adams, Arthur Lee accused them of "tory designs" aimed at "subverting the Revolution."[26]

If Lee had seen the letters that General McDougall was writing to Newburgh at this time, he would have been even more convinced that he was right. Superintendent Morris and the men around him were acutely aware that at any moment, the rumor of a signed peace treaty might be confirmed by a ship from France. They feared Congress would instantly lose interest in satisfying the officers. On February 4, Hamilton again tried to persuade Congress to approve the payment of six years' salaries to commute the officers' half-pay claim. He was again rebuffed. Two days later, Colonel Brooks left for New Windsor with explosive mail in his dispatch pouch.

Two letters went to General Knox. One, from General McDougall and Colonel Ogden, painted the chances for half-pay commutation in very gloomy terms. The other was from Gouverneur Morris, who styled himself Knox's "dear friend." Morris urged Knox to see that the army united with the other public creditors to "influence the legislatures" to establish permanent federal taxes. Four days later, McDougall sent Knox another letter in disguised handwriting under the pseudonym "Brutus" telling him that the army might have to declare they would not disband until Congress and the states met their demands.[27]

This was extremely risky business. McDougall, the Morrises, and Hamilton were aware that the whole world—in particular the British army in New York—were watching and waiting to see how the Americans would handle the news of independence and peace. A declaration that the army would not disband was very close to mutiny and opened all sorts of doors to future calamities. It would also announce to the watching world that America's politicians and their constituents refused to deal justly with the demands of the men who had won victory in the long war.

X

Thus far, the conspirators had been relying on General Knox to organize the resistance in New Windsor. But they could not—and did not—dream of ignoring the man who came to the average American's mind when the word "army" was mentioned in a speech or conversation: General Washington. On February 13, 1783, with a boldness that is more than a little breathtaking, Congressman Alexander Hamilton undertook the task of bringing the commander in chief into the conspiracy.

Hamilton was spurred by the arrival in Philadelphia of a copy of George III's December 5th speech to Parliament, conceding American independence. It made the appearance of the preliminary peace treaty even more imminent. Hamilton began by saying he wanted to share with Washington "my ideas on matters of delicacy and importance." The state of America's finances "was perhaps never more critical." Never before in the Revolution had a situation called more for "wisdom and decision in Congress." Alas, Congress was governed "not by reason but by circumstances."

This meant that the army would have to "procure justice to itself" by its own efforts, whether peace or war prevailed in the immediate future. The claims of the army, if "urged with firmness" would influence "the weak minds" in Congress and "add weight" to Congress's demands for cooperation from the "several states." The difficulty was how to keep "a *complaining* and *suffering* army within the bounds of moderation."

This, Hamilton coolly declared, was what Washington's influence must and would achieve. It was vital to "the public tranquillity" that Washington retain "the confidence of the army without losing that of the people."

Hamilton was sure that Washington could "guide the torrent" even if things reached the point of "extremity." But the twenty-eight-year-old congressman confessed a concern that General Washington needed to hear. Not a few of the army's officers thought he did not support their claims "with sufficient warmth." Hamilton knew this was the polar opposite of the truth. But the idea was "not less mischievous for being false." Washington should make sure his words and actions refuted the notion if "commotions unhappily ensue."[28]

In his talks with General McDougall and the two colonels in Philadelphia, Hamilton had learned that many officers no longer felt loyal to Washington. He seemed more concerned with his run-down farms in Virginia than with the army's complaints, and was frequently irritable and distant. Serving without salary at his own request, he seemed aloof from the issue of how much money Congress owed the officers.

Today, a sympathetic psychotherapist would say the commander in chief was suffering from a mild depression—hardly surprising after seven years with his mind "on the stretch," as Washington often described it. His mood was not improved by wintering in what he called "the rugged and dreary mountains" around Newburgh.[29]

XI

Displaying his rare gift for accepting criticism without resentment, General Washington replied on March 4, thanking Hamilton for his candid letter. Rather testily, he added that it would be helpful if Congress shared with the commander in chief of the army the nation's financial situation. Without information, a man can find himself "on the brink of a precipice before he is aware of his danger." That now seemed to be the case. Exactly what he should do about it, as "a citizen and a soldier" was not immediately apparent. He feared the possibility of "civil commotions" that would "end in blood."

Washington inadvertently confirmed what Hamilton had heard from the McDougall committee. The general was aware that a group of malcontents were circulating stories of his indifference to the soldiers' needs. He called them "the old leven [leaven]." This was a shorthand term for General Horatio Gates and his circle. During the winter at Valley Forge, Gates had used his 1777 victory over the British at Saratoga to try to supplant Washington as commander in chief. Gates was still with the army, wearing a mask "of apparent cordiality."

Washington claimed he had "no *great* apprehension " of Gates, or of the army, exceeding "the bounds of reason and moderation." He would continue to support the officers' "just claims" and was confident that every "sensible [state] legislature" would try to satisfy them. He could not believe the states were "so devoid of common sense and common honesty" as to ignore the soldiers. Meanwhile, he assured Hamilton he would keep his letter a secret.[30]

Hamilton did not share Washington's faith in Congress or the state legislatures. On February 14, he wrote to Governor George Clinton of New York, filling him in on the crisis, and bluntly stated his fear that "arrangements" to satisfy the army and other public creditors would not be made. This prompted him to think of New York's "safety." It was one of the largest states geographically but its population was relatively small. Hamilton suggested that Clinton persuade the New York legislature to offer generous parcels of land to every officer and soldier in the Continental Army. Hamilton thought "a large part of the Army would incline to sit down among us." This would guarantee New York a ready-made professional fighting force, should Massachusetts or the rogue state of Vermont grow covetous of its empty acres.[31]

Meanwhile, Colonel John Brooks was conferring with General Knox in New Windsor and possibly with General Washington in nearby Newburgh. Knox had never responded to General McDougall's original letter, asking for his cooperation. The rotund Knox (he weighed 280 pounds) sympathized with the soldiers and with the nationalists' desire to maintain the shaky American union. But he recoiled from a plan that might sully the army's reputation. He told Brooks he would not encourage even the threat of a mutiny, and he restated this opposition in vehement letters to General McDougall and Gouverneur Morris in Philadelphia.[32]

In Congress, the nationalists were floundering under a counterattack from the states' rights men. They defeated Hamilton's attempts to give Congress the power to appoint federal tax collectors for a new impost. Congressmen from Virginia and South Carolina proposed that money from the impost be devoted exclusively to meeting the army's demands— which would unravel the idea of putting a permanent federal revenue at Congress's disposal. When Hamilton and Madison made another try at pushing through a vote in favor of half-pay commutation, they were again rebuffed. The desperate nationalists redoubled their warnings of an upheaval in the army. But their foes scoffed and pointed to the king's speech and the imminent arrival of a peace treaty. Arthur Lee smugly maintained that a majority of the army would remain loyal.[33]

The nationalists around Morris decided their only alternative was a real mutiny, which Washington and Knox would, they hoped, swiftly suppress. For their agent they chose Pennsylvania Colonel Walter Stewart, a former Gates aide, who was returning to the main army from Philadelphia after recuperating from an illness. He had been in contact with McDougall and the two colonels and knew how little progress they had made with their petition.

Either Morris or McDougall or both told Stewart that peace was about to be proclaimed and Congress planned to dissolve the army without paying them a cent. Simultaneously, Superintendent Morris persuaded Congress to make his letter of resignation public. He knew this would be shocking news to the army's officers; they were almost certain to assume it meant the end of their hopes of compensation for their services.

XII

Around General Gates was a group of hotheaded younger officers whom he had converted into critics of Washington. Gates told them of Stewart's warning of the army's imminent dissolution and Morris's public resignation. Possibly, Stewart also told Gates that Morris had promised to back him if it became necessary to overthrow Washington. There are hints of this last extremity in later letters between Gates and his young admirers.[34]

We have Washington's eyewitness account of what happened next. Within hours of the arrival in New Windsor of a "certain gentleman" (Colonel Stewart), the army was swept by rumors that the officers were going to be treated shabbily by Congress and the states. Some members of Congress were actively hoping that the soldiers would compel certain "delinquent states" to do them justice. These rumors "prepared the minds of the officers" for the next step. On March 10, 1783, an anonymous broadside called for a meeting of all the army's field officers (colonels and majors) and company representatives (captains or lieutenants) the following morning (Tuesday) at 11 o'clock.

This "Newburgh Address," as it was later titled, exhorted the officers to abandon "the milk-and-water style" of their petition to Congress. If they did not act now, they were condemned to growing old "in poverty, wretchedness and contempt." Peace would benefit everyone but them. It was time to confront the "coldness and severity of [the] government" and the ingratitude of their fellow citizens, whom the army's courage had made independent. There was only one option left: their swords. They should "suspect the man who would advise [them] to more moderation and longer forbearance." If peace was at hand and Congress refused them, it was time to give the politicians a taste of steel. If the war continued, they should all "retire to some unsettled country" and mock when a frightened Congress confronted a revived enemy without the army's protection.[35]

This blast of rage was written by twenty-four-year-old Major John Armstrong, Horatio Gates's current aide. General Washington was shocked by "the gulph of civil horror" that Armstrong's violent rhetoric opened before the nation. He was also not a little angered by the contemptuous way Armstrong tried to preempt Washington's expected attempt to urge moderation.[36]

Rather than challenge this wild emotion with an address of his own, Washington played the commander in chief. He issued a brisk order, banning the Tuesday meeting as "disorderly" and "irregular." Instead, he ordered a meeting at noon the following Saturday, at which all the officers and the senior general present at Newburgh—Horatio Gates— would discuss General McDougall's report of his meetings with Congress. Washington requested a summary of the meeting—a nice touch. It implied he had enough confidence in the officers to let them consider the army's options without any interference from him.

The Gates men had no intention of letting Washington outflank them. Armstrong promptly produced another anonymous address, in which he claimed a Saturday meeting would be just as effective as a Tuesday gathering. Either way, Washington apparently approved of their course. There was no hint of rebuke from the commander in chief about the substance of the first address. Waiting until Saturday could not "possibly lessen the independence of your sentiments."[37]

XIII

In this atmosphere of supercharged tension, on March 15 generals and field officers and one representative from every company stationed in or near New Windsor gathered in a large vault-roofed building the soldiers had constructed in December. Sometimes called "The Temple" because it was used for religious services, its main purpose was to encourage mingling between officers from different states. Balls and theatrical entertainments were also held in the main room, which had a stage at the far end.

For those with a knowledge of history, the date of the meeting was unnerving. It was the Ides of March, the day on which Brutus assassinated Julius Caesar, beginning the upheaval that led to the collapse of the Roman republic. The officers were soon seated and General Gates mounted the stage to assume his role as chairman. Grim satisfaction was the prevailing expression on the faces of the audience. They knew Gates was on their side. It was an open secret that his aide, John Armstrong, was the author of the anonymous addresses.

The main item on the agenda was supposed to be General McDougall's report. (The general was still in Philadelphia.) Before the slight, gray-haired Gates could say a word, an unexpected visitor stepped onto the stage through a nearby door: General Washington. He strode to the lectern and asked General Gates if he could say a few words. The flustered Gates could hardly refuse him.

General Washington turned to his officers and did not like what he saw: on almost every face there was a forbidding mixture of surprise and resentment. They considered his appearance a doublecross; they thought he had promised to let them discuss the situation independently.

To several observers, General Washington seemed to be in danger of losing his legendary self-control. He spread some prepared remarks on the lectern but he did not read them. Instead of an appeal for moderation, he swept the room with angry eyes and launched a direct attack on the anonymous addresses.

Washington said they were "unmilitary" and "subversive." They appealed to "feelings and passions" rather than "reason and good sense" and had "insidious purposes." More to the point, they seemed to impugn his readiness to be the army's friend and advocate. With not a little resentment in his voice, he reminded them that he had been among the first to step forward to defend "our common country" in 1775 and since that time "had never left your [the army's] side. How could anyone infer after so many years of companionship, in which his own military reputation had become identical with the army's, that he was "indifferent to its interests"?

The faces in the audience remained grim and unconvinced. These men had been disappointed too often to accept Washington as their incontestable friend. Wasn't he at least partly responsible for letting them reach this desperate situation?

His voice rising, Washington assailed the actions the addresses proposed—quitting the war and the country and retreating into the wilderness, or marching on Congress with drawn swords. "My God!" Washington exclaimed. Can this writer "be a friend to the army? Can he be a friend to the country? Rather is he not an insidious foe?" He might even be a "secret emissary" from the British in New York, who never stopped trying to sow discord among the Americans.

Since almost everyone knew Armstrong—and Gates—were behind the addresses, this treason tack probably angered as many men as it impressed. Seeming to sense this, Washington renewed his assault on

Armstrong's addresses. Advising the officers to suspect the man who recommended moderation was, Washington said, a personal insult and "I spurn it." It was an attempt to suppress freedom of speech so he and the army could be led away, "dumb and silent . . . like sheep to the slaughter."

Congress was not the army's enemy, Washington insisted. Most of the delegates had "exalted sentiments" of the army's merits and services. "Deliberative bodies" always acted slowly, but he vowed to do everything in his power to obtain "complete justice" in reward for "all your toils and dangers."

Passionate now, with an emotional intensity that he had never before exhibited, Washington exhorted the officers "in the name of our common country" and "your own sacred honor," to express their "detestation" of any man who wanted "to overturn the liberties of our country" and "open the flood gates of civil discord." Instead, he begged them to retain their dignity and honor. If they did this, he was certain that someday people would praise their "glorious example" and say, "Had this day been wanting, the world had never seen the last stage of perfection to which human nature is capable of attaining."[38]

This surge of emotion stunned most of the officers. But it did not change many minds. The men sat silent, their anger still pervading the 70-by-40-foot room. Washington fumbled in his inner coat pocket and drew out a copy of a letter he had recently received from Virginia Congressman Joseph Jones, telling him some of the positive steps Congress was planning to satisfy the officers.

Washington began reading the first few lines, then stopped and peered at the page. Reluctantly, he reached in his waistcoat pocket and extracted a set of glasses he had recently received from Philadelphia. No one except a few aides had seen him wearing them. "Gentlemen," he said. "You will permit me to put on my spectacles, for I have not only grown grey but almost blind in the service of my country."

A rustle of unease, a murmur of emotion, swept through the audience. A few of the officers wept openly. Others brushed away tears. Washington finished reading Jones's letter and departed. Instantly, General Henry Knox was on his feet with a motion to thank Washington for his speech. There were no objections.

Next, aides read aloud McDougall's report from Philadelphia, which did little more than describe his meeting with the grand committee. Colonel Rufus Putnam of Connecticut rose to recommend appointing General Knox, Colonel John Brooks, and a third officer to prepare resolutions for the officers' approval. These statements were, of course, already written; after no more than a decent interval Knox brought them to the stage and read them. They affirmed the army's unshaken attachment "to the rights and liberties of human nature" and asked Washington to become their public advocate with Congress.

Another resolution declared the officers' "disdain" for the "infamous propositions" advanced in the anonymous addresses and also condemned the attempts of "some unknown persons" to collect the officers together for purposes that were "totally subversive of discipline and good order." Here was the back of Washington's (and Knox's) hand to Gates and his circle.

The resolutions were approved overwhelmingly. Only one man rose to object to this endorsement: lean, acerbic Timothy Pickering of Massachusetts, the army's quartermaster general. He condemned the hypocrisy of heaping infamy on publications that during the four preceding days almost every officer in the army had read with "rapture." Some people later said if one more speaker had followed Pickering with similar sentiments, the officers' rage might have reignited. But no one else said a word. The officers quietly departed to their quarters and the most perilous moment in the brief history of the United States of America ended peacefully.[39]

XIV

The crisis was not over. Four days before the meeting, Washington had sent copies of the Newburgh addresses and a worried letter to Congress. Their impact was severe. In his notes, James Madison called it "alarming intelligence" which "oppressed the minds of Congs. [congressmen] with an anxiety and distress that had been scarcely felt in any period of the Revolution." The news arrived with Congress deadlocked over commutation of half pay for life and the impost to pay for it. The nationalists used a legislative ploy to intimidate the naysayers. They named a committee to prepare a reply to Washington that consisted of men who had been outspoken opponents of both proposals.

Fat, blustering Eliphalet Dyer of Connecticut, a Gates advocate and Washington critic during the Valley Forge winter, was probably the main target of this move. He had been loudly opposed to commutation but he was known to change his mind under pressure. Dyer was soon saying that if commutation would "quiet and pacify the army," he was for it. On March 20, he personally proposed a motion to pass the commutation bill. It was, Madison wryly noted, "extorted from him by the critical state of our affairs." To sweeten the harsh medicine, Hamilton proposed reducing the lump sum from six to five years' pay, and agreement was achieved. Even Arthur Lee was intimidated into voting for it.

Supporting the legislation that would raise the money to pay for commutation and back pay was another matter. Knowing the army was momentarily satisfied, the states' rights men and Morris-haters like Lee and fearers of congressional power like David Howell reemerged and made a hash of the legislation that Congress passed a month later. It called for a new impost but it was limited to twenty-five years and specified the money could only be used to pay debts. Worst of all, the collectors would be appointed by the states, a guaranteed recipe for most of the money never reaching Congress. A disgusted Alexander Hamilton refused to vote for it. Superintendent of Finance Morris was appalled.[40]

XV

Washington's use of the word "precipice" in describing the Newburgh confrontation was not an exaggeration. If he had failed to change the officers' minds, the army would have marched on Congress to dictate terms at the point of a gun. The states, especially large ones like Virginia and Massachusetts, would almost certainly have refused to approve such a deal. If the army had attempted to force the states' compliance, civil war would have erupted. The shaky American confederation would have collapsed and the British, still with a fleet and army in New York, would have been irresistibly tempted to get back in the game. Not surprisingly, British secret agents were keeping General Carleton in close touch with what was happening. In February, one operative reported that the army considered Congress "so very contemptible" it was "ripe for annihilating them."[41]

More of this potential for disaster was visible in a dramatic exchange of private letters between Congressman Hamilton and General Washington. On March 25, 1783, Hamilton told his former commander in chief that he feared there was good reason for the army to distrust Congress. There was a "principle of hostility to an army" loose in the country and too many congressmen shared it.

What could the army do if Congress proved ungrateful? As a realist, Hamilton saw that an unleashed army would soon turn to banditry and "reverse our revolution." But his "chagrin" at Congress and sympathy for the army tempted him to encourage the upheaval. Hamilton confessed he had "an indifferent opinion of the honesty of this country." He could only hope God "would send us more wisdom."[42]

Washington replied that Hamilton's letter stirred "pain" mingled with "astonishment and horror" at the picture it drew of the army on the rampage and an impotent Congress. He insisted that "redress by force" would and could solve nothing. But he admitted that the "suspicions of the officers" were still very much alive. It was absolutely essential to settle their back-pay accounts before the army was disbanded.

Even more worrisome, Washington continued, was a suspicion that men in Philadelphia had been manipulating the army, not out of a desire to do justice to their demands, but as "mere puppets to establish continental funds" to pay the wealthy civilian creditors. Worse, "the financier" was suspected "to be at the bottom of this scheme." If either suspicion were true, Washington had a solemn warning to deliver: "The army . . . is a dangerous instrument to play with." If peace were really at hand, it would be a good idea to "get it [the army] disbanded without delay."[43]

The harassed commander in chief did not realize he was recommending a solution that would make almost every officer in the army infuriated and disgusted with Congress—and with General Washington.

Chapter Ten

A Runaway Congress vs.
A Berserk Parliament

ONGRESS HAD OTHER WORRIES on its collective mind besides the angry Continental Army. On March 12, 1783, the good ship *Washington*, commanded by Captain Joshua Barney, sailed up the Delaware to Philadelphia with a copy of the preliminary peace treaty with Great Britain. James Madison was soon reporting that a great many delegates were deeply concerned by the way Franklin, Jay, and Adams had ignored their instructions and negotiated a separate treaty without informing France. This "variance," as Madison called it, seemed a blatant violation of Congress's instructions to make peace with the guidance of America's ally.[1]

On the whole, Madison found that most congressmen thought the peace terms were "extremely liberal." But many of them objected to the stipulation that Congress had to recommend some sort of restitution for the seizure of the property of loyalists who had not borne arms against the United States. They felt that the envoys had sacrificed "the dignity of Congress to the pride of the British king." No one had the slightest doubt that the states would ignore the recommendation and this would give George III a chance to deplore Congress's lack of authority and imply that America was not a civilized country.[2]

Also troubling to Congress was a secret article about the West Florida boundary that the commissioners had attached to the treaty. It was an outgrowth of John Jay's talks with Richard Oswald about Jay's preference for West Florida again becoming a British colony. If the British ended up with it in the final treaty, the Americans agreed to give them a boundary considerably north of the one they had negotiated with Spain—it would have included much of contemporary Alabama and Mississippi.

This generosity seemed to many congressmen a dishonorable, back-handed way to treat Spain, an ally of France and a semi-ally of the United States, whose soldiers had done some effective fighting against the British in Louisiana and West Florida in the months before Yorktown. The solons had no idea of the virulent anti-Spanish feelings that John Jay had communicated to Benjamin Franklin and John Adams.

Madison reported in his notes on the debates (and clearly agreed) that Congress found the secret article "most offensive." It was "inconsistent with the spirit of the alliance and a dishonorable departure from the candor, rectitude and plain dealing professed by Cong[ress]." For the delegates, the dilemma posed by the secret article was personal; all of them knew and many liked the French ambassador, the Chevalier de la Luzerne. He had entertained them in his Philadelphia mansion and feasted the city's elite at his magnificent celebration of the birth of the Dauphin in July.

Should they show the secret article to Luzerne? Even more unsettling were the journals of the negotiations that the peace commissioners had enclosed with the treaty. These included frank accounts of John Jay telling the British of his antipathy to France and numerous anti-French remarks by John Adams. Wouldn't reading these and the secret article destroy "all confidence" in the Americans? Madison found wide disapproval of the way the commissioners, "particularly Mr. Jay," had refused to make allowances for France's "delicate situation" between Spain and the United States and instead had "joined with the enemy [England] to take advantage of it." They had made "the safety of their country depend on the sincerity of Ld Shelburne"—something that was "suspected by the whole world and even by themselves."[3]

Ambassador de la Luzerne contributed to Congress's uneasiness by telling Secretary of Foreign Affairs Robert Livingston and numerous delegates that Foreign Minister Vergennes was very unhappy with the way the Americans had shut him out of their negotiations. Even more disturbing was Luzerne's report that King Louis XVI had expressed "great indignation" when he was informed of the separate treaty and said "he did not know he had such allies to deal with."[4]

At the same time Madison and most of the delegates admitted that the treaty's terms were bound to be popular with the American people. Within a few days, this popularity became a political fact. A member of Congress (reportedly Thomas Mifflin of Pennsylvania) had given a copy of the treaty to the newspapers. Several congressmen asked the secretary of the French legation, Francois Barbe-Marbois, whether France was going to make a formal complaint to Congress. Barbe-Marbois replied that "great powers" never complained but they "felt and remembered."

The episode was a vivid example of how thoroughly Ambassador de la Luzerne had persuaded—and occasionally bribed—Congress into believing that America's survival depended on France's friendship. Congress's seemingly permanent bankruptcy had not a little to do with this almost cringing sense of dependence. Once more the Atlantic Ocean shielded the Americans from the worst effects of this possibly ruinous perception. Their negotiators in Europe were not exposed to Superintendent of Finance Morris's predictions of imminent doom—or the blandishments of Chevalier de la Luzerne.[5]

II

In New York, a wild mixture of despair and frantic, improbable hope pervaded the ranks of the loyalists when news of the king's speech from the throne conceding America's independence appeared in James Rivington's *Royal Gazette*. Judge William Smith continued to be General Sir Guy Carleton's advisor and confidant. He and the British commander in chief conferred endlessly on major and minor matters.

The seething mixture of white loyalist refugees, British and German soldiers, and fugitive slaves in the streets of New York was sowing rage and violence in many minds and hearts. Scarcely a week passed without a woman—probably a prostitute—found robbed and murdered in an alley. Smith advised General Carleton to promulgate tough new laws that would give the police power to deal with the "great depravation of manners in the city and the alarming multiplication of crimes."

The Royal Navy was another problem; while the army had been forbidden to fight unless attacked, the sailors continued their ruthless blockade of the American coast. Smith recorded in his diary Admiral Digby's angry denunciation of the government's decision to abandon offensive warfare. No one apparently had the courage to tell the sailors that a blockade looked like offensive warfare from an American point of view. The sailors' chief motivation was money, not patriotism. They made whacking profits selling their captured prizes.

The seadogs even extended their profit-seeking campaign by commissioning a fleet of whaleboats that ravaged the waters and shores of Chesapeake Bay. Maryland had sent a strenuous complaint to General Washington about the depredations of these mini-privateers. Smith convinced Carleton that he had the authority to stop this piratical warfare.[6]

Much of the time, Smith and Carleton discussed their continuing hopes for reuniting America and England. The general had written to Lord Shelburne, reminding him that he had not yet received the promised powers to negotiate with Congress and reach an understanding that would restore harmony with the mother country. Carleton still believed this was more than a possibility, thanks to the information he kept getting about the disagreements inside Congress, the army's discontents, and the rebels' looming bankruptcy.

Even after the king's speech reached New York, Smith managed to convince himself that George III did not mean what he said about independence. The judge published an article in the *Royal Gazette* with "conjectures" on the impact of the speech. He thought it would stir distrust among the rebels, who were divided into moderates in favor of reunion and "violent independents."

On March 26, 1783, these erratic flights of hope crashed to earth with a thud that ran through the entire city of New York. Smith somberly described it in his diary: "Letters came to Sir G. Carleton from Philadelphia importing that the preliminaries of a general peace were signed 21 January to take place in Europe 20 February and here 20 March. Sir Guy Carleton much affected at the dishonorable terms and the whole town credited the report."

III

The news of the general peace had arrived in Philadelphia aboard the French sloop of war *Triomphe,* sent from Cadiz by the Marquis de Lafayette. America's favorite Frenchman had swiftly recovered from the abrupt deflation of his hopes of becoming the rescuer of America as well as the conqueror of Canada. His natural ebullience made it easy for the Marquis to embrace the news of a victorious peace—and the pleasure of being the first to announce it to his American friends. Written in Lafayette's inimitable version of English, his letters to the new president of Congress, Elias Boudinot, to Secretary of Foreign Affairs Livingston, and to General Washington were a torrent of delight and excitement at this chance to play a historic role.

To Livingston the Marquis explained why he had not come to America to deliver the news personally. He was about to sail aboard the *Triomphe* when he received a letter from William Carmichael, the American whom John Jay had left in Madrid as charge d'affaires, lamenting that he had yet to be recognized in any official capacity by Spain. Lafayette decided his duty required an immediate trip to Madrid, wearing the uniform of an American major general, to change this deplorable situation. "I readily give up my personal gratifications," he told Livingston, although he doubted that he would succeed. "Among the Spaniards, we [Americans] have but few well wishers. And as they at the bottom hate cordially the French, our alliance, tho a political, is not a sentimental consideration."

Lafayette's letter to Washington was a boisterous combination of personal and public emotions. He told him if he were Julius Caesar or Frederick the Great of Prussia, he would almost regret sending the news that meant Washington's dramatic role at the center of a "great tragedy" was over. But with his "dear General" he could rejoice "at the blessings of peace where our noble ends have been secured." They would never forget "our Valley Forge times" and other "dangers and labours"—the memories would only make them "more pleased with our present comfortable situation."

As Washington prepared to enjoy the "ease and quiet" of civilian life, Lafayette proposed a plan to benefit "the black part of mankind" and remove from America's public reputation a moral stain that had long troubled him: slavery. He wanted Washington to join him in buying "a small estate" on which "we may try the experiment to free the Negroes." Washington's example might help make it "a general practice" in America. If that happened, Lafayette was prepared to spend more money to make it "fascionable" in the West Indies. "It may be a wild scheme," Lafayette admitted. But he would "rather be mad that way than thought wise on the other tack."

Finally, there was a favor Lafayette hoped Washington could obtain for him. When Congress ratified the treaty of peace, they would send an official to London to present the document to George III and his ministers. Lafayette yearned to be the man who performed this delicious task. It would be "the most flattering circumstance in my life" if this "honorary commission" could be worked out. Beneath the Marquis' American ebullience lay centuries of French antipathy to Perfidious Albion.[7]

Washington responded to Lafayette's letter with equally deep emotion. When he read the news of peace, his mind was "assailed by a thousand ideas" but none could compete with his gratitude to France. He told the Marquis that he had no doubt that the "armament" Lafayette had helped to gather at Cadiz had a great deal to do with persuading the British to opt for peace.

As for Lafayette's proposal to "encourage the emancipation of the black people," Washington declared he would be "happy to join you in so laudable a work." They would discuss it when Lafayette returned to America in a few months.[8]

Washington immediately wrote to Secretary of Foreign Affairs Livingston about making Lafayette the envoy who would bring the ratified treaty of peace to London. He admitted a certain uneasiness about giving this responsibility to a "foreigner," but if no one objected, he hoped the idea would meet with Congress's approval. Livingston replied that congressional distrust of France was now so widespread among the delegates, the foreign secretary feared proposing Lafayette would stir an uproar. Livingston also worried that the British would construe it as a deliberate insult. Washington accepted this verdict; there was "no man on earth" he was more ready to please than Lafayette—but not if it endangered America's "dignity or interest."[9]

In the meantime, hoping to prove himself worthy of the treaty assignment, Lafayette rushed to Madrid and made pompous Foreign Minister Floridablanca eat his words that American independence was a "misfortune." The Marquis wrote a letter to William Carmichael, knowing it would be read by Spain's secret police, declaring that if the envoy were not officially recognized, France would "stand a mediator" (intervene and perhaps get Floridablanca dismissed). In Madrid Lafayette obtained an audience with King Charles III, then escorted Carmichael around the capital, introducing him to high-ranking officials; the French ambassador, the Comte de Montmorin, often accompanied them. Floridablanca's opposition crumpled; he accepted Carmichael's credentials and presented him to King Charles III. A delighted Carmichael gave Lafayette all the credit for "my first public appearance at the court of Spain."[10]

The Atlantic Ocean disconnect between Europe and America made this achievement more or less meaningless for Lafayette. His chances of representing the United States as a diplomat were further soured by a scathing letter from John Adams. Depressed at being forced to share credit for the peace with Franklin and Jay, Adams lashed out at the prospect of Lafayette as an American diplomat. He denounced Congress for appointing Lafayette as "a go-between" with the Comte de Vergennes. The American commissioners had not needed him as a negotiator and they had even less need of him now. Lafayette's "mongrel character" as both a French and American patriot was ridiculous and dangerous. Americans should be more than ever on their guard against "the politicks of the French Court" and their desire to "break our union."[11]

IV

In Philadelphia Congress debated whether they should ratify the treaty of peace with Britain. Some delegates noted that it was called a provisional or preliminary agreement. A hasty ratification might be interpreted by the English as a sign of America's weakness and lead to attempts to impose tougher terms in later negotiations. But the arrival of Lafayette's letters with the news of the peace treaty among the European powers inclined most members to ratification.

In early April, a British officer arrived from New York with news that settled any lingering doubts. London had sent Sir Guy Carleton official word of a general peace, including a proclamation from George III ending hostilities. In their agreement with Lord Shelburne, Spain obtained both Floridas; this made moot the Americans' worries about the too-generous West Florida boundary their negotiators had offered the British. Congress ratified the treaty and officially proclaimed the war was over on April 11, 1783. Philadelphia celebrated exuberantly. President of Congress Elias Boudinot wrote to General Washington: "You can only judge from your own feelings on this occasion with what peculiar joy I congratulate Your Excellency and the army."[12]

At Newburgh, a copy of Congress's proclamation arrived on April 17, 1783, and produced little but anxiety and unrest. The proclamation had come with nothing but Boudinot's cheerful covering letter. There was not a word about what Congress was planning to do next as far as the army was concerned.

The commander in chief was all too aware that rumors and reports of peace had been rampaging through the New Windsor camp since February. As he explained the problem to President Boudinot in a tense letter, the troops had begun to suspect that the war had ended but the fact was being concealed from them. Well over half the army had enlisted for the duration of the war. These "war men," as Washington began calling them, made no distinction between an end of hostilities and a definite declaration of peace. They wanted to go home and it was going to be difficult to stop them.[13]

Stopping them might soon be the least of Washington's worries. The commander in chief had already received a petition from the soldiers of the New Jersey brigade, asking for an exemption from paying taxes as civilians. They wanted this stated clearly in their discharges. The sergeants of the Connecticut Line were readying another petition, demanding half pay for life or commutation to a lump sum, like the officers were supposedly getting.

At first, Washington considered withholding the proclamation of peace. He called a meeting of his general officers to discuss this possibility. The generals unanimously advised the commander in chief that it was "impractical as well as impolitic" to try to conceal it, even for a day. They recommended publishing it in the next day's orders. Washington did so, congratulating the men for winning a victory that had rescued "millions from the hand of oppression and laying the foundation of a great empire." All that remained now was for them to preserve a "perfect . . . consistency of character through the very last act." They must wait patiently for Congress to release them with "every mark of distinction and honor." To make it clear that he thought this would happen soon, Washington told Quartermaster General Pickering to prepare discharges for all the men enlisted for the duration of the war. He also ordered an extra ration of rum for "*every* man" the next day, when Congress's proclamation would be read aloud.[14]

At noon on April 19, eight years to the day after the first shots were fired on Lexington Green, soldiers and officers from regiments on duty gathered in front of the Temple, the scene of Washington's confrontation with the officers a month ago. A field officer read the proclamation, an Army chaplain recited a prayer, and the soldiers gave three cheers and sang "Independence," by New England's favorite musician, William Billings.

Washington made the ceremony as low-keyed as possible. There was no army-wide celebration. The general rode off to New Jersey to confer with Secretary of War Benjamin Lincoln on when and how to release British prisoners captured at Saratoga and Yorktown.[15]

Washington was trying to keep the army's emotions under control. This was not easy, because his own feelings were intense. He could not bear the thought that Congress might welch on its promises to the officers. Immediately after the confrontation in the Temple, he had warned Congress that if they failed to compensate the officers, "Then shall I have learned what ingratitude is, then shall I have realized a tale, which will embitter every moment of my future life."[16]

Now, Washington urged Congress to let the enlisted "war men" who would soon be departing take their guns and cartridge boxes with them. It was a small gesture, he knew, but it would stir "pleasing sensations" in the minds of the soldiers. Their weapons would be "handed down to their children as honorable badges of bravery and military merit." Whatever Congress thought of this suggestion, Washington urged speed to "make arrangements" on how to deal with the war men or they would be faced with "disagreeable consequences."[17]

V

At West Point, where General Henry Knox was in immediate command, the artillery commander brooded over the near catastrophe in The Temple and the army's ongoing disappointments. He began thinking about a way to perpetuate the army's military experience, not only to obtain justice and support a stronger federal government, but also to retain some of the camaraderie and pride that Washington evoked when he called them a band of brothers. Knox envisioned a national organization of retired officers who had served a minimum of three years in the Continental Army. It would be called The Society of the Cincinnati, and would have chapters in each state. Each year in Philadelphia or New York they would hold a convention which would speak to the nation with a strong and influential voice.

The hero they would emulate was Lucius Quintus Cincinnatus, who twice became a victorious general (in 458 and 439 BC) wielding dictatorial powers granted him by the Roman senate. When these wars ended, Cincinnatus put aside his sword and returned to the life of a humble farmer. This seemed the perfect model for an organization of retired American officers, most of whose members would soon do something similar.

General Knox conferred with General Friedrich von Steuben, who warmly endorsed the idea. From the German volunteer may have come the idea that The Society of the Cincinnati should be hereditary, with membership passed down through the generations to eldest sons. It would also collect money from the members to create a charitable fund for those who might need financial help in the coming years. As a badge of honor and brotherhood, each member would wear a gold medal on a deep blue ribbon edged with white, "descriptive of the union with France."

Soon Knox had drafts of the Cincinnati's constitution circulating among the regiments at West Point and New Windsor, where it met a warm reception. On May 13, 1783, after some revisions of the original proposal, including a decision to invite French officers to join, delegates from the regiments met at General von Steuben's headquarters in Fishkill and agreed to launch the venture. To no one's surprise, General Washington was asked to be the Cincinnati's first president-general. General Knox reported he was "warmly in favor" of the society.[18]

None of these earnest soldiers had the slightest idea that they would be ferociously attacked for creating a menace to the liberty and safety of the newly independent United States of America.

VI

Since the proclamation of peace, thousands of rebels who had fled in 1776 were pouring into New York City to assert their ownership of houses that the British and loyalists had used—and often abused—for seven years. Also in the chaotic picture were dozens of slave owners and hired slave catchers who were seeking to regain blacks who had fled to the British lines. A group of Virginians had agents in New York who claimed that at least three hundred blacks from their state should be returned to their owners, according to the stipulation that Henry Laurens had inserted in the treaty of peace just before it was signed.

The situation was complicated by the large number of slaves that the British had seized from rebel plantation owners in the South as loot. In 1781, in a typical foray, a royal navy sloop had come up the Potomac and taken seventeen blacks from Mount Vernon. Virginia Congressman Theodorick Bland and Governor Benjamin Harrison had lost dozens of slaves in similar fashion. A planter named John Willoughby had lost ninety. These were the blacks Henry Laurens thought should be returned—or if that were not possible, "a future claim" for the value of the slaves should be established against the British government. In his hasty amendment to the peace treaty, the former president of Congress had not considered the status of slaves who had sought their freedom voluntarily. Neither had John Adams, John Jay, or Benjamin Franklin.[19]

General Washington suggested a meeting with General Carleton to discuss these problems. He was seconded by Governor George Clinton, who was eager to reestablish his state's jurisdiction over occupied New York, Staten Island, and Long Island. On May 9, General Carleton, his loyalist advisor Judge William Smith, and two military aides came up the Hudson River in a royal navy frigate. They met Washington, Clinton, and their staffs in the De Wint house in Tappan, some three miles west of the Hudson opposite Dobbs Ferry. Washington had used the Dutch brick-and-sandstone house as a headquarters in earlier years.

At first the meeting was almost cordial. Governor Clinton had once been Judge Smith's law clerk. General Carleton said he was eager to evacuate New York but did not know when he could do so. A great deal depended on available shipping. He was being inundated by an unexpected number of loyalists who had decided flight was preferable to reconciliation with their rebel cousins.

Several statements had been issued by political agitators in New York and other states, declaring an intention to seek vengeance against the supporters of the king. During the meeting with Carleton, John Morin Scott, one of Governor Clinton's council, truculently declaimed that Americans would not tolerate anyone who had "waged war against them"—a remark that was not likely to reduce the number of loyalists choosing flight.

As for the blacks, Carleton insisted that he could not return any exslave who had fled to British lines and been promised freedom. Britain's "national honor" had been pledged to these men and women long before the peace treaty was signed. He added that not a few former slaves had already sailed to Nova Scotia. At this news Washington expressed surprise. It seemed to him a violation of the peace treaty.

General Carleton replied that he was keeping very careful records of each departing individual. If American owners could prove their blacks had not come to New York voluntarily, they could file a claim for payment from the British government. General Washington expressed doubts about how such a claim could ever be proven. The slave could easily change his name or give the name of a fictitious master. No one had time to check any records before the blacks went aboard the departing ships.

General Carleton testily insisted he was not going to change his mind. His system was already functioning. A brigadier general was holding daily hearings, at which blacks testified and if they were deemed qualified, received certificates entitling them to embark. The Americans could send commissioners to observe the proceedings.

Judge William Smith noted that during this exchange General Washington spoke "without animation, with great slowness and in a low tone of voice." He clearly had no enthusiasm for this task. He had already told Governor Benjamin Harrison that he had "little expectation" that many slaves would be returned. Washington had made clear to Lafayette, John Laurens, and others his dislike of slavery and his desire to at least begin its elimination from America. Nevertheless, the general went through the motions of cooperating with Carleton. On May 10, he sent a three-man committee to New York to superintend the registry of ex-slaves.[20]

VII

In Philadelphia, Congress acted swiftly on Washington's suggestion to let the departing soldiers retain their muskets. But many delegates balked at discharging the "war men" while there was a large British army still in New York. After much debate, they decided the answer was furloughs. Washington would send these men home on indefinite leaves, which would become permanent when and if a final peace treaty was signed. It was a clever but meaningless compromise. Only a British invasion of their home states would have persuaded most of these soldiers to return to the ranks. Moreover, these fake furloughs made many officers feel they were being tricked into going home without any of their grievances satisfied.[21]

Washington tried to find some money to give the men before they departed. The need became pressing on May 26, 1783, when Congress, trying to reduce expenses, ordered Washington to furlough all the war men as soon as possible. To give them three months back pay—a necessity in Washington's opinion—would cost $750 thousand. Superintendent of Finance Morris reported there was not a cent in the national treasury. Nor could the Bank of North America, the nation's only major financial institution, come up with that much cash.

There was only one answer. The men would have to accept "Morris notes"—certificates payable in six months—which had been passing as currency since the Superintendent took office. Morris was taking on a personal debt of over $1 million, including the interest on the notes. It was a noble gesture, but in the turmoil not many people appreciated it. Everyone knew the penniless soldiers would have to sell these pieces of paper to wealthy speculators as soon as they reached home—possibly before they got there. But it was the best Congress could do to reward the army for its hardships—an objective, the financier wryly remarked, "which all affect to have so much at heart." Morris was expressing his disgust at the emasculated impost bill Congress had recently passed.[22]

Each note had to be signed personally by Morris, which took weeks. On June 2, an almost frantic Washington sent a messenger to Morris from Newburgh, warning him that the "worst consequences may be expected" if the notes did not arrive soon. He begged the financier not to delay "a single instant" in giving the messenger the notes already signed. Washington "lamented" that Congress had been unable to give the men at least a month's pay in hard money. He could only hope the notes would avert "the most alarming consequences."[23]

On June 5, a committee of officers asked Washington to suspend the furloughs. In a letter signed by Major General William Heath of Massachusetts, they said they viewed the furloughs "with a mixture of astonishment and chagrin." The army was being disbanded without even one of their demands for justice met. They were being sent home without the means to "support and comfort their families," and liable to arrest for the debts they had contracted in the service. They asked Washington to "insist" that no officer should be sent home without being paid in full, including the commutation of their half pay, and a gift of $80 to each enlisted man.[24]

Washington's reply was labored, polite—and unsatisfactory. He said he was "only a servant of the public" and had no power to alter the furlough policy. There simply was no money to pay the cost of keeping the army together. He reiterated that he was sure Congress "entertain[ed] the best disposition towards the army" and would eventually meet their demands. In the meantime, he would send their letter of protest to Philadelphia. It was clear from this answer that nothing would be done and most men decided to go home without waiting for their Morris notes.

There were no farewell parades or ceremonies. The regiments of the victorious American army simply marched off one by one toward their homes. Among the officers, disgust with Congress—and with General Washington—was widespread. In a letter to General Horatio Gates, who was in Virginia at the bedside of his sick wife, Colonel Walter Stewart noted with unconcealed glee that the departing officers had cancelled a dinner at which they had planned to make General Washington the guest of honor.[25]

VIII

Joseph Plumb Martin of Connecticut, a corporal in the sappers and miners corps, left one of the few eyewitness accounts of the war men's departure. He portrayed the condition of himself and his fellow soldiers as "appalling in the extreme." They were all "starved, ragged and meager" without "a cent to help themselves." On June 11, their captain came into Martin's hut, which he shared with seven other men, and ordered them to empty their cartridge boxes on the floor. Then he told them they could keep the cartridges if they needed them. Every man stuffed the wads of paper and powder into his box. The captain handed them their discharges—"or rather furloughs" Martin added sarcastically. "In our present pitiful forlorn condition," an outright discharge might have caused "some difficulties."

Many of the soldiers "went off for home the same day that their fetters were knocked off," Martin continued. "Others stayed and got their final settlement certificates" for three months back pay. Most of them sold these Morris notes to speculators before they left camp "to enable them to pass decently through the country and to appear something like themselves when they arrived among their friends." Martin was one of those who waited to get his note. When he finally departed, he was surprised to discover there was "as much sorrow and joy" in his heart. He realized how much he was going to miss men with whom he had lived "as a family of brothers" for so many years. "Ah!" he concluded with a sigh. "It was a serious time."[26]

IX

In Philadelphia, hot-tempered Major John Armstrong was expressing the fury many officers felt at the failure to pay them as Congress had promised. The young incendiary told General Horatio Gates that Alexander McDougall had left Philadelphia for Newburgh, convinced that he had been representing "fools and rascals." The combative New York general was dismayed by the failure of the Newburgh addresses.

Meanwhile, Armstrong told Gates, unrest was stirring among five hundred Continental Army troops stationed in Philadelphia. If there were more of them and if "Mad Anthony" [Wayne] were in command, Armstrong thought they could right the wrongs being inflicted on them. "They feel like men" and if they could be brought to "think like politicians," they "might do some good."

The infuriated young major enclosed an appeal to the states that Congress had written, pleading for ratification of the new impost legislation to enable them to pay the cost of commuting half pay for life for the officers. The politicians included Washington's speech to the officers in Newburgh to underscore the gravity of the situation. The solons seemed to think that the officers' rejection of the Newburgh addresses would win admiration everywhere. They would soon learn this presumption was disastrously wrong.

Armstrong referred to the general's speech as "something to admire from the great Ilustrissimo of the age." Of all Washington's "illustrious foibles," the major added, "the affectation of zeal in a cause he strove to damn, is the most ridiculous." Armstrong denounced the furloughs with equal vehemence. "The[ir] meaning is evident—wrest the means of redress from the hands of the officers—by removing the old soldiers."[27]

There is no clear-cut evidence that Major Armstrong had anything to do with what happened next. But if he was sending opinions like this through the mail, it seems reasonable to suppose he was also expressing them in Philadelphia's taverns and coffee houses. His father was one of the most distinguished soldiers in Pennsylvania, the commander of the state's militia. The son had begun working as secretary to the state's executive council, the closest thing Pennsylvania had to a senate.

Another letter to Gates suggests that the major was in close touch with the discontented Philadelphia garrison. "The little corps at this place" had reacted to the furloughs "very spiritedly," Armstrong wrote. They had sent a message to Congress. "We will not accept your furloughs and demand a settlement."[28]

In Newburgh, General Washington, unaware of the names he was being called in Philadelphia, labored on a long circular letter to the governors of the states, seeing it as a sort of farewell address. He urged them to support the creation of an "indissoluble union" and to maintain a "sacred regard for public justice." This was readily translated as: pay your debts, to the army above all, and to the other public creditors. He also recommended the creation of a small peacetime "military establishment." He sent this long political sermon to President of Congress Elias Boudinot, who mailed it to the governors with a warm letter of approval.

X

The next day, June 21, 1783, an agitated President Boudinot sent Washington news that threatened to undo the general's earnest effort to raise money to pay the soldiers. Several hundred Continental Army enlisted men had surrounded the Pennsylvania state house and were threatening Congress with fixed bayonets. Some of the troublemakers had marched from Lancaster under the command of truculent sergeants and inflamed the combustible Philadelphia garrison. They wanted money and they did not want it in Morris notes. They also demanded the right to elect their own officers, claiming that their regular officers "had forsaken them."

Someone found Major General Arthur St. Clair, the soldiers' immediate commander; he tried talking to them. They told him to go away. Superintendent of Finance Morris also visited them and was similarly dismissed. A frantic Elias Boudinot begged Washington to send some "dependable" troops to Philadelphia as soon as possible. The president of Congress had been roughed up by three of the mutineers when he tried to pass through their cordon. General Washington had only 1,500 soldiers left in New Windsor. He put them on the road to Philadelphia under the command of Major General Robert Howe of North Carolina.[29]

In Philadelphia, the standoff with the mutineers persisted, while President Boudinot and other congressional leaders conferred with Pennsylvania President John Dickinson and his council. Dickinson was a badly frightened man. Before the mutineers surrounded the state house, they had sent a tough-talking sergeant named Nagle with another man to Dickinson's house, where they forced the trembling state leader to sign a document, promising them their back pay.

The congressmen urged Dickinson and his council to call out the city's militia to disperse the bayonet wielders. The Pennsylvanians waffled and finally refused, claiming that the militia, if they turned out, would be likely to support the soldiers. This was probably correct. Dickinson tried to defend the militia by claiming they would act if the mutineers committed a clear-cut act of violence. Apparently terrorizing the president of Pennsylvania in his house and grabbing the president of Congress by the scruff of his neck did not qualify as violence.

The Newburgh addresses and Washington's speech to the officers had been printed in the newspapers along with Congress's appeal to the states for funds to pay the soldiers. In Philadelphia and elsewhere the story had turned public opinion against Congress. People felt the federal legislators had crumpled under military pressure. Evidence of this dislike was visible from the state house windows; people were applauding the mutineers and giving them liquor from nearby taverns. Several times, when a drunken mutineer saw a congressman peering out, he would playfully aim his musket at him. The new nation's rulers were not amused.[30]

At 3:30 p.m., the usual hour of adjournment, the congressmen left the state house. They walked past the mutineers, who made mock attempts to block them and shouted obscene insults in the lingua franca of the barracks. It was a huge shock to these politicians, who had recently proclaimed peace in language that could easily have come from the lips of George III. "It is our will and pleasure," they declared at one point. "We hereby charge and command all our . . . subjects," began another sentence. Now these subjects were bringing the nation's spokesmen down to American earth in the rudest imaginable way.[31]

XI

The mutineers went back to their barracks, where they circulated various rumors. One judged highly probable was a plan to attack the Bank of North America. Another was a determination to seize the city's gunpowder magazine and arsenals full of muskets to distribute to civilian supporters. A third purported to be a plot to seize several congressmen and hold them as hostages until the mutineers got their money. In fact the soldiers did little more than drink heavily and curse the politicians.[32]

Congress refused to make any concessions to the mutineers. They reiterated to the officials of Pennsylvania that it was their responsibility to keep order in Philadelphia. Dickinson and his advisors still declined to call out the militia. Congressman Alexander Hamilton, who did some of the negotiating with the Pennsylvanians, called their conduct "to the last degree weak & disgusting." In a rump session convened that night, Congress passed a resolution, declaring their intention to move to New Jersey.

Almost instantly, the mutiny collapsed. The soldiers in the barracks, perhaps sober for the first time in days, threw themselves on the mercy of Pennsylvania and claimed they were led astray by two hotheaded officers, who promptly fled to Chester and boarded a ship bound for England. Congress, still affronted and frightened, decided to go to New Jersey anyway.[33]

According to Major John Armstrong, Philadelphia was glad to see them go. "The Grand Sanhederin of the nation, with all their solemnity and emptiness, has removed to Princeton . . . a consequence not unacceptable to many people here," he told General Gates. In Armstrong's opinion, Congress had "left a state where their wisdom has long been questioned, their virtue suspected, and their dignity a jest." While allowance must be made for Armstrong's fondness for extreme language, the mutiny and Congress's flight were not likely to raise the national or international standing of the rulers of the newly independent United States of America.[34]

XII

In London, the British Parliament was also behaving badly and the city seethed with several varieties of political unrest. For seven weeks after First Minister Lord Shelburne resigned, there was no government in the usual sense. George III repeatedly rejected the idea of a ministry that combined the conservative followers of Lord North and the radical supporters of Charles James Fox.

As His Majesty again threatened abdication, the government came close to breakdown. The stock market plunged, public credit wavered. Soldiers and sailors waiting for back pay or discharges or both mutinied not unlike the bayonet wielders in Philadelphia. Fortunately, the military demonstrated in distant ports and garrisons far from the politicians and the stubborn king. But they were additional symptoms that the nation was starting to unravel.[35]

After canvassing every possible member of Parliament with even the semblance of a following to form a ministry, George III was reduced to crying he would take a nobody like William Pitt's cousin, Thomas Pitt, or "Mr. Thomas Anybody" rather than swallow Lord North and Charles James Fox. But no one had the courage to challenge the solid majority that Boreas and Reynard could muster in the House of Commons.

Only the threat that further delay might "materially affect . . . the public finances" persuaded His Majesty to yield. But he vowed this "unnatural combination" would have neither "my favor nor my confidence."[36]

Behind the king's detestation of Fox, a far more important drama was in progress. Fox, urged on by Burke, demanded the right to form a ministry without submitting any names for His Majesty's approval. The demand for this privilege had incensed George III when it came from Lord Rockingham; from Fox it was intolerable. In a frantic letter to his son and heir, the Prince of Wales, His Majesty said he feared becoming "a kind of slave." The letter was proof of the king's mounting hysteria. The prince was one of Charles James Fox's most ardent admirers.[37]

On April 1, 1783, George III capitulated. Lord North became secretary of state for the colonies and Charles James Fox the foreign secretary. The Duke of Portland, a colorless yes-man, became first lord of the treasury and the titular first minister. Everyone knew Fox was running things but he had to share some of the patronage with North, who controlled more votes in the House of Commons. That left some Fox followers with sullen doubts about the coalition.

Fox dismissed Richard Oswald and Lord Shelburne's other negotiators in Paris and appointed Benjamin Franklin's old friend, David Hartley, as his peacemaker. The new leader was equally ruthless in replacing other Shelburne appointees, prompting Edmund Burke, who had again become paymaster of the forces, to remark: "One great man is not in good humor, some friends are a little wrong-headed, and the people who are out are violent."[38]

XIII

In Paris, Franklin welcomed David Hartley as an old friend and soon had him sending messages to Foreign Minister Fox urging a treaty of commerce which would have made the Americans the legal equivalents of Englishmen in all parts of the empire. There was even talk of dual citizenship. The bespectacled English liberal urged Franklin's favorite idea, ceding Canada, to salve the wounds of the war. Hartley also endorsed two other Franklin ideas, aimed at making war less savage. The final treaty should include a ban on seizing ships carrying cargoes that were not war materiel, and should also prohibit privateering, which was little more than legalized piracy.

Hartley was soon the most dismayed diplomat in Europe. Fox's replies to his liberal excursions were scorching negatives. George III's conviction that the Americans were a collection of renegades known chiefly for knavery was seeping through Parliament on the lips of Lord North's followers, all of them the king's men. Also in the game was a surge of protest from conservative British merchants who wanted the monopolistic rules of the prewar empire's Navigation Acts to remain intact. At the roots of this uproar was a morbid fear that American ships would seize an unacceptable share of British overseas commerce, destroying the nation's "nursery of seamen" that was the foundation of her worldwide naval power.[39]

Abandoning the sympathy and support he had showered on the Americans during the war, Foreign Minister Fox decided to make good on his claim that he could negotiate a better peace by giving the ex-rebels less than Lord Shelburne had promised them. By June of 1783, Fox was raging to the British ambassador in Paris that if Hartley let himself "be taken in by Franklin, he will disgrace both himself and us."

Before the negotiations stumbled to a close, Shelburne's vision of an era of reconciliation and free trade between America and England was a shambles. American ships were virtually banned from the profitable West Indies trade and they were forbidden to carry American manufactured goods to Great Britain. Only raw materials would be acceptable. Fox had wholeheartedly joined the naysayers in control of Parliament, who were determined to restrict the growth of American commerce wherever possible.[40]

Weeks passed without Hartley hearing a word from Fox. "When will your answers come? What makes the delay?" the envoy wrote plaintively. Fox did not even bother to inform the bewildered Hartley of the British decision to ban American ships from the West Indies. He learned of this Order in Council from Franklin and his fellow commissioners. Hartley could only gasp that it had "thrown our whole negotiation into confusion."[41]

Finally, on August 4, 1783, Fox wrote a curt note, telling Hartley to forget the treaty of commerce and all other gestures of reconciliation. Instead, he ordered the envoy to sign a definitive peace treaty as soon as the final agreement with France and Spain was concluded. It would consist of the already signed preliminary articles and nothing else.

On September 3, 1783, Franklin, Adams, and Jay went to Hartley's rooms in the Hotel d'Yorke and joined him in signing what is now known as the Treaty of Paris. The spirit of true peacemaking that Franklin had attempted to launch and Shelburne had supported in his oblique, tentative style was dead. The future of British-American relations would be marked by rivalry and often sneering hostility, leading to another war in 1812.

XIV

Around this time, Ambassador Franklin received a letter from an old Boston friend, the Reverend Samuel Cooper. The clergyman told him that friends of John Adams were filling ears in Boston and elsewhere with a vicious attack on Franklin as a man who was a virtual slave to France and tried to sell out American interests in the peace negotiations. He was blocked by the vigilance and diplomatic skills of Mr. Adams and his friend, Mr. Jay.

These tale-bearers also claimed that the French had done everything in their power to hamper Adams's negotiations with the Dutch for a loan and recognition of American independence. As a sincere (and well paid) client of the Chevalier de la Luzerne, Cooper thought that someone should refute such slanders against the American ambassador and the French alliance.[42]

Franklin was aware that Adams, waiting around for a definitive treaty of peace, had grown almost hysterical on the subject of France and Franklin. The ambassador had warned Robert R. Livingston that he hoped "the ravings of a certain mischievous madman" would not damage the alliance. Franklin would not have been surprised to learn that on the very day they signed the definitive treaty, Adams had denounced him as a man with an uncontrollable passion for women. This had put him at the mercy of French spies and made him a "tool of the most profligate of the human race."

Franklin sent the pertinent part of Dr. Cooper's letter, with the clergyman's name excised, to Mr. Jay and Mr. Adams, saying that he had no desire to "dispute any share of the honor of the treaty" but he could not tolerate "an accusation that falls little short of treason to my country." John Jay promptly replied with a testimonial to Franklin's "warm and steady" support of the entire treaty, including the disputed rights to fish off Newfoundland and the Mississippi boundary. It took John Adams three days to curtly acknowledge that Franklin had been "able and useful" throughout the negotiations.[43]

XV

The definitive treaties between Great Britain and France and Spain were signed in Versailles on the same day, September 3, 1783, that the Americans signed in Paris. These agreements represented another political defeat for Charles James Fox as well as the collapse of the friendship and cooperation between the great powers that Lord Shelburne had envisioned with Gerard de Rayneval in 1782. Instead, France and Britain immediately voted huge sums for formidable armies and expanded navies. Congressman James Madison wryly described it as "arming for peace."[44]

Foreign Minister Fox obtained only a few minor changes in the French right to fish off Newfoundland and the area in which the British could cut wood in Honduras. One member of Parliament mockingly wondered if the "aggregate merits" of Fox's "concessions, or rather alterations" deserved much in the way of "encomium." William Pitt, who already had his eye on Fox's job, attacked the coalition for delaying so long to sign the definitive treaties, when they contained "little or nothing" in the way of changes.[45]

The stage was set for the ruin of the faux peacemakers, Boreas and Reynard. As part of the reform of the British Empire that Edmund Burke saw as his destined task, he had persuaded Fox to introduce a bill to overhaul the British East India Company. A board of commissioners appointed by Parliament would try to restrain if not stop the officers of "the honorable company" from mulcting millions of pounds while ruthlessly ruling—and often impoverishing—their unwilling subjects in the huge swath of India they controlled.

George III decided this was his moment to pounce. He let the House of Commons approve the India bill and sent a secret message to the House of Lords, urging them to reject it. "Whoever voted for it," His Majesty declared, "was not only not his friend but would be considered his enemy." The Lords naysayed the bill, 95-76. Whereupon George III announced the time had come to prevent the House of Commons from pretending it was the only government of England.[46]

The flabbergasted coalition's leaders did not know what to do next. Debates in the House of Commons were desultory and uncertain. Boreas and Reynard watched each other closely, wondering who would be the first to cut a deal with the king. Each underestimated His Majesty's determination to get rid of both of them.

Well after midnight on December 19, 1783, a royal messenger stalked into Lord North's bedroom with a dispatch from George III. It ordered North to deliver the seals of his office to the courier and inform Mr. Fox to do likewise "this night." The king commented that he had chosen this method because "audiences on such occasions must be unpleasant."

The method, it should be added, was the most humiliating dismissal His Majesty could contrive. That same morning, twenty-four-year-old William Pitt became first minister. It was the third time the king had asked him to assume the role of rescuer. His acceptance this time revealed a cool political intelligence far in advance of his years.

Three months later, Pitt dissolved Parliament and called an election that gave him a solid majority. The nabobs of the East India Company played a not inconsiderable role in his success. In return for their support, Pitt reduced the import tax on tea to the vanishing point and did little or nothing to reform the company. George III was, of course, in thorough agreement with this move, which laid the foundation of the Second British Empire.

But His Majesty soon discovered that this "marvelous boy" was no more inclined to take orders from him than Charles James Fox had been. His Royal Highness's reign as the ruler of lords and commons was over. With this oblique crab-like progress, the American Revolution helped achieve at least one of Edmund Burke's noble goals for his perplexing country.[47]

XVI

In Paris, there was wry amusement and not a little satisfaction at London's political turmoil. By this time, the French government, disillusioned by Fox's inept peacemaking, had retreated into their traditional hostility to Great Britain. The Comte de Vergennes was mildly disappointed but not entirely surprised to learn that nothing would change in the barely civil relations between the two powers.

France's foreign minister turned his attention to the crisis in Eastern Europe and maneuvered Austria into staying out of the war that Russia was fighting with Turkey over the Crimea. With his usual backstairs skill, the Comte persuaded Prussia's King Frederick the Great, Austria's traditional enemy, to join him in applying pressure for an early peace. Although Turkey lost the Crimea, she was preserved from dismemberment and remained a client state whose trade provided a steady stream of profit for French merchants.

By and large, the French were satisfied with the peace terms, even if they were not as triumphant as optimists had envisioned in the months after Yorktown, when the West Indies and India seemed on the brink of capitulation. Vergennes had achieved his primary goal, the independence of America, which in his eyes and those of his fellow Europeans meant a tremendous loss of power and prestige for the British empire. He could—and did—refer to his early declaration that France sought no territorial gains from the war as justification for the final settlement.

In Versailles, the Comte emerged from the war as the most powerful man in France, after the king. Vergennes continued to display amazing dexterity at juggling the rivals and critics who swirled around him, above all Queen Marie Antoinette. He also appointed himself head of a committee on finance, taking on the most daunting problem facing the government—a reform of the nation's tax structure.

Here Vergennes was out of his depth and did little but change for the worse some of the reforms that his rival, Jacques Necker, had sought to make. The foreign minister unwittingly sowed the seeds of a tragic harvest for his royal master and his fellow aristocrats. The war for American Independence had cost France a billion livres—the equivalent of a billion and a half modern dollars. It was a burden that would soon overwhelm the already malfunctioning French tax system. Vergennes never admitted this menacing inevitability; he continually insisted financial collapse was on the English foot. In 1784, he assured Louis XVI that England was "bent under the weight of an enormous debt that was crushing her."[48]

Worn out by his endless eleven-hour days and the virulent political pressures that continued to confront him, Vergennes died in 1787 at the age of sixty-eight. Within a few months, national bankruptcy loomed and King Louis XVI, shorn of his steadiest and most devoted advisor, decided to convene the nation's Estates General, a parliament that had not met since the seventeenth century. A lethal mix of the ideas and ideals of the American Revolution and the far more radical theories of French intellectuals clashed with France's entrenched aristocracy, igniting a political conflagration that consumed the young monarch and his ambitious queen. In the last years of his life, as chaos and the guillotine loomed, Louis XVI said he never thought of the American Revolution "without regret."[49]

Chapter Eleven

George Washington's Tears

THE CONTINENTAL CONGRESS pretended to govern the independent United States from the village of Princeton. The delegates' flight from Philadelphia had aroused a swarm of critics. Some of them inveighed in the newspapers against the gutless president and council of Pennsylvania for their failure to call out the militia. But most commentators thought Congress had demonstrated a lamentable cowardice.

The editor of *The Philadelphia Gazetteer or Chronicle of Freedom* issued a summary judgment: Congress's decision to cut and run exhibited "neither dignity, fortitude nor perseverance." Newspapers throughout the nation repeated these animadversions and added to them. "The flight of Congress" became dinner-table conversation from Boston to Savannah.[1]

From Europe, before the end of the summer came more sneers. An American woman in England told a Philadelphia friend that everyone she met had magnified the story into "the annihilation of Congress and the utter destruction of the commonwealth." In London Henry Laurens struggled in vain to explain the story to prominent politicians. A worried Lafayette wrote from Paris that everyone saw the riot and flight as "a wane of disposition to the federal union." The peace commissioners, Messrs. Jay, Adams, and Franklin, chimed in with an anxious warning that the news had "diminished the admiration in which the people of America were held among the nations of Europe."

This diminution was especially evident in Holland, where Dutch bankers were advertising shares in the loan John Adams had negotiated, confident that 5 percent interest would attract buyers. Congress's flight sent sales plummeting from 195,000 florins in July to 10,000 in October. Who wanted to invest in a country that seemed to be disintegrating?[2]

With considerable reluctance, Congress assembled at Princeton in early July. The accommodations in the village of sixty houses were worse than inadequate. James Madison and Joseph Jones, both of whom had spent their lives in ample Virginia mansions, shared a single bed in a room so tiny, Madison complained there was barely space to "move my limbs" and no semblance of a desk on which to write. The diminutive Madison's plight was worsened by Jones's size—he was over six feet. Even President Elias Boudinot, who was living in Morven, the handsome mansion belonging to his widowed sister, Annis Stockton, complained of crowding.

But some congressmen decided they preferred the peace and quiet of the village to Philadelphia. They were influenced by Arthur Lee and his fellow Franklin and Morris hater, Ralph Izard of South Carolina, who still saw the city as a malevolent influence on Congress's political purity.[3]

On the delegates' collective mind was an issue that the flight to Princeton made urgent. Where should Congress settle as a permanent residence? President Boudinot fervently hoped it would be New Jersey. He had said as much to his brother in a letter as Congress decamped across the Delaware. Congressman Alexander Hamilton had written to Governor George Clinton of New York, suggesting he carve out a district on the Hudson, perhaps near Kingston. Maryland's delegates proposed Annapolis. Arthur Lee eagerly favored his home state and so did his fellow Virginians.[4]

Meanwhile, General Robert Howe and his 1,500 troops arrived in Princeton. Their condition did little to reassure the politicians that the soldiers could guarantee their security in Philadelphia. The forced march from New Windsor in the summer heat had left many men sick and almost all of them barefoot. A worried Howe wrote to Washington, urging him to send every available doctor still in the service to treat the invalids. Congress told Howe to march all the men he could muster to Philadelphia but declined to follow him.[5]

Alexander Hamilton made several attempts to persuade Congress to regain its dignity and return to Philadelphia. All his motions were voted down and the delegates approved a statement by Ralph Izard and an equally small-minded Massachusetts ally, Stephen Higginson, that until Congress received "assurances of protection" from the Pennsylvania government, it was neither "safe nor honorable" for them to go back to the City of Brotherly Love.

A disgusted Hamilton resigned from Congress and wrote a lamentation to John Jay, warning him that in spite of the independence Jay had helped to win, "our prospects are not flattering." In a last despairing gesture, Hamilton toiled on a lengthy resolution to call a convention to amend the Articles of Confederation. After talking it over with James Madison and others with similar opinions, Hamilton decided it was not worth the trouble of introducing and defending it. He wrote on it: "Abandoned for want of support," stuffed it into his baggage, and headed back to New York to practice law.[6]

II

In Newburgh, General Washington found himself with nothing to do for the first time in eight years. Congress relieved his tedium by inviting him to Princeton to discuss the creation of a peacetime army. Opposing this idea with the same passion with which he had fought the federal impost was David Howell of Rhode Island. At one point, he had forced a vote on a resolution which invited Washington but eliminated any mention of the army. Massachusetts, led by Stephen Higginson, was the only state that backed Howell, but the argument intimated the peacetime army was already in trouble.

Washington brought with him a military escort of some twelve dragoons, two of his aides, and his wife Martha. Congress arranged for him to stay at nearby Rocky Hill in a handsome twenty-room house that the patriotic owner had named Rockingham. The general saw at a glance that he might be wasting his time. Congress seldom had more than twenty-two members in attendance. Numerous delegates had gone home like Alexander Hamilton; their states had not yet persuaded anyone to replace them.

Washington gave a dinner for Congress under a marquee tent captured from the British. Rhode Island's David Howell portrayed the general as a man in a cheerful mood, thanks to the approach of peace. His face,

Howell told the governor of Rhode Island, was "uncommonly open and pleasant, the contracted pensive phiz, betokening deep thought and much care . . . is done away and sparkling vivacity of wit and humor succeeds." This was typical of Howell's ability to twist reality to his political advantage. He had never seen Washington's "contracted pensive phiz" during the war. That would have required service in the army, something Howell had avoided. It is unlikely that Washington was "open and pleasant" to the man who was sneering at the general's advice about a peacetime army and had destroyed the federal impost, which would have paid the Continental Army's officers and men some of the money owed to them.[7]

When President Boudinot remarked that Superintendent of Finance Morris had his hands full, the general growled: "I wish he had his pockets full." Morris was staying in Philadelphia, where he was more or less immune to Arthur Lee's barbs. The bitter financier would soon resign with a farewell blast at Lee and his ilk. Morris told Governor Benjamin Harrison of Virginia that Congress's "disposition to traduce and vilify" made him wonder if any "prudent man" would risk his reputation by accepting an important public office from them.[8]

In his disgust with Congress, Morris had discontinued his employment of Tom Paine as a public persuader. Washington heard that Paine was drifting around Philadelphia and its environs, depressed and close to penniless. The general invited him to Rockingham for a few days. Paine had recently published the last of his public essays, "Crisis No. 13," declaring that "the times that tried men's souls" were over. But the "new creation," the independent United States, faced serious dangers. They had to strengthen their federal union. "On this our great national character depends."

These were sentiments that Washington endorsed, and he welcomed Paine's visit with the hope that Congress might listen to the agitator. He also suggested Paine might remind Congress of his services to the Revolution and persuade them to vote him a pension. Neither hope materialized. Paine remained so broke that when a servant stole his overcoat, Washington gave him one of his own, which he wore for years.[9]

It gradually became apparent that Congress was eager to shower compliments on General Washington and discuss their plan to build a gigantic equestrian statue of him dressed as a Roman hero. But they had little interest in his recommendations for a peacetime army. David Howell, Stephen Higginson, and Ralph Izard persuaded most congressmen to back Arthur Lee's assertion that it was better for Congress to remain "a rope of sand than a rod of iron."[10]

III

In New York, the loyalist embarkation proceeded with confusion, acrimony, and bizarre spurts of hope swirling through the war's losers. Part of the reason was the three-month disconnect between events in London and Paris. After the meeting with Generals Washington and Carleton, William Smith wondered if the American commander was part of a plot which included a "party in Congress and American agents in Europe to bring about a reunion."

Another inflation of Smith's hopes was produced by an intercepted letter from Congressman Stephen Higginson, who ranted about how happy he was with Congress in Princeton. The "great man"—Robert Morris—did not have as much influence there, nor did Chevalier de la Luzerne, the French ambassador, who also spent most of his time in Philadelphia. Higginson denounced the "insidious conduct" of France and declared himself committed to "the union of the interests of Britain and America."[11]

General Carleton told Smith that it might serve "good purposes" if he could keep "12 or 14,000 men in New York this winter." The general sent Lord Shelburne's former secretary, Maurice Morgann, back to England to push this idea with the North-Fox ministry. Morgann had barely sailed when Carleton received orders from London to evacuate the city as soon as possible. Foreign Minister Fox had decided to sign the definitive treaty and write *finis* to the war with America.

IV

Along with thousands of rebel Americans streaming into the city came broadsides aimed at extinguishing any hopes the loyalists might have of reconciliation. One from Poughkeepsie, signed "Brutus," promised that "all adherents of the British government . . . commonly called Tories" would experience extremely unpleasant "horrors" if they tried to stay in America. Another broadside, equally menacing, was aimed at specific loyalist leaders such as William Smith. It warned him not to rely on "his numerous and wealthy connexions in the country" to protect him from retribution. Smith claimed he felt nothing but "contempt for such menaces" but he started listening to General Carleton's advice to go "home"—to England.[12]

The embarkation of the Negroes continued to cause turmoil. In July, the committee that Washington had appointed to share the supervision of the process resigned in protest. They were echoing the mood of Congress, who repeatedly expressed its fury at Carleton's decision to embark blacks who could prove—or claim—they had fled to New York voluntarily. Virginians, who had lost hundreds of slaves, led the angry chorus. James Madison called Carleton's policy "a shameful evasion" of the peace treaty.[13]

Theordick Bland proposed refusing to repatriate prisoners of war. Cooler heads decided the issue was not worth endangering the peace treaty. But it had not a little influence on the widespread hostility to the loyalists and a refusal even to consider compensating any of them for their losses.[14]

When Alexander Hamilton returned to New York in August of 1783, he was appalled by how many loyalists were leaving, even though they had not borne arms against the United States. He warned Robert R. Livingston, who had resigned as foreign secretary and was now chancellor of New York, that not a few of these loyalists were merchants who would each carry away about ten thousand pounds. He predicted "our state will feel for twenty years at least" the loss of these men. Hamilton deplored the "popular phrenzy" that was creating this exodus. In the next few years he would devote much time and energy to defending loyalists who chose to stay in New York.[15]

V

In October, Washington was still at Rocky Hill, trying to persuade Congress to create a peacetime army with no sign of success. Debates on the topic were interrupted by the arrival of the Dutch ambassador, Peter John Van Berckel, pensionary (mayor) of the city of Rotterdam. His brother had been pensionary of Amsterdam and had played a role in encouraging the draft treaty with the United States written by William Lee that had been the pretext for Britain declaring war on the Netherlands. Like his brother, Peter John had been an early enthusiast for American independence.

Ambassador Van Berckel was more than a little shocked to find Congress was not in Philadelphia. No one had bothered to find a residence for him in the city, much less greet him in the style he had expected. The ambassador brought with him another installment on the loan that John Adams had negotiated, making his neglect doubly inappropriate.

Mr. Van Berckel was forced to board at the City Tavern and send a letter to Princeton announcing his arrival. The letter took five days to reach Congress. A diplomatic contretemps was in the making, but President Boudinot rushed his secretary to Philadelphia with apologies and the ambassador decided not to get on his ship and go home. Mr. Van Berckel finally arrived in Princeton in his private coach and was greeted by Washington's cavalry escort and sundry dignitaries.

On the same day, October 31, 1783, and virtually the same hour, former Colonel Mathias Ogden arrived in Princeton from New York with news from England, where he had gone on a private business venture. The British had signed the definitive treaties of peace with the United States, and with France and Spain. The war was officially over. This news added considerably to the smiles and cheers that greeted Ambassador Van Berckel.

The news only made Congressman James Madison even more dissatisfied with Princeton. Still determined to see America act like a genuine nation, he remarked acidly on the "charming situation in which Congress found itself," forced to greet this foreign diplomat in a country village. The unreality of Princeton as a national capital was an ironic complement to the air of celebration with which Congress welcomed Ambassador Van Berckel. Shielded by the Atlantic's vast gulf, the Americans were oblivious to Holland's harsh fate in the peace negotiations. The Dutch had been ignored by the French and treated with contempt by the English, who rejected all their proposals.

Not until May 20, 1784—seven months after Van Berckel's arrival—did the Dutch sign a definitive treaty of peace with Britain. It stripped the Netherlands of important possessions in the Far East, such as Ceylon, which had been captured by the British navy, and gave British merchant ships access to trading posts in the East Indies, ruining the profitable Dutch monopoly in these islands. In a final humiliation, Dutch ships were required to salute the British flag whenever they encountered it on the high seas. The Dutch saw themselves, in the words of one of their historians, as "the real and only victims of the American Revolution." This bitter conclusion left the Netherlands torn by political strife that would eventually trigger a revolution.[16]

VI

One Princeton diversion General Washington found especially pleasant was a visit with Nathanael Greene. The Quaker general had said farewell to his army soon after Congress proclaimed that peace had arrived. The two generals undoubtedly lamented Congress's lack of power and money and its sinking reputation. If anything, Greene was probably more vehement on the dangers confronting the union, having experienced them face to face in independent-minded South Carolina.

General Greene also had a personal reason for lamenting Congress's bankruptcy. He was being pursued by the creditors of John Banks, the merchant whose promissory notes Greene had cosigned to feed the southern army, for some 30,000 pounds owed to them. Greene was enormously distressed by this looming financial cloud. At one point he told his wife, Caty: "I seem to be doomed to a life of slavery."[17]

The general had some consolations along with his worries. The Southern states had testified to their gratitude to the man who rescued them from returning to the British Empire. North Carolina had voted Greene twenty-five thousand acres of land and South Carolina and Georgia had each given him a valuable plantation confiscated from a wealthy loyalist. Greene would soon decide to settle in the South and become the master of the Georgia plantation Mulberry Grove.

Here, for a little while, the Rhode Islander seemed to enjoy an idyllic existence with his beautiful wife and children. But he was haunted by the debt he owed to the creditors of John Banks. Congress ignored his pleas to pay the money as a justifiable war expenditure. Mean-spirited critics, who had disapproved of Greene's partnerships with army suppliers when he was quartermaster general, claimed he was a secret partner of Banks and deserved to be saddled with the huge sum, the equivalent of a half-million dollars in modern money. In 1786, Greene died suddenly of what his doctor called sunstroke. But many friends suspected the continual anxiety over this debt was the real cause.[18]

VII

Instead of working out plans for a peacetime army, Congress ordered Washington to discharge the remaining regiments in the service, retaining only token garrisons at Fort Pitt to guard the western frontier and

West Point, where the army's artillery and ammunition were stored. This was an extremely unwise decision; the British had yet to turn over the northern and western forts they had promised to evacuate under the terms of the peace treaty.

Washington had sent Major General Friedrich von Steuben to Canada to confer with the British commander there, General Sir Frederick Haldimand, about a schedule for surrendering the forts. Haldimand had curtly rebuffed the German volunteer, telling him he had received no orders from London to give up any of the forts. With no army to make the British think twice about ignoring the peace treaty's terms, the forts would remain in enemy hands for another decade, enabling His Majesty's soldiers to retain strongholds from which London could continue to tempt Vermont and arm the Indians—doing their best to sabotage the American union.

General Washington decided to make the discharge of the rest of the Continental Army an occasion for a final goodbye, not only to men being sent home but to all the soldiers who had served in the long war "however widely dispersed" they might now be. He entitled the message "Farewell Orders to the Armies of United States."

Before the general took his "final leave of those he holds most dear," he asked their permission to make a "slight review of the past." Their victory should inspire in every heart and mind "astonishment and gratitude." Recalling their frequently "feeble condition," he attributed their triumph to "the singular interpositions" of Providence and the "unparalleled perseverance of the armies of the U. States through almost every possible suffering and discouragement." Their achievement against such daunting odds was "little short of a standing miracle." Men from all parts of the continent had become "one patriotic band of brothers."

Washington claimed he was sure they could make the transition from soldiers to citizens by maintaining the "steady and decent . . . behavior" that had distinguished their military character. As they parted, Washington wanted to profess one more time his "inviolable attachment and friendship." He hoped their country would do "ample justice" to them. For his part, he could only reiterate his recommendations to pay them what they deserved. No one else had secured by their courage and devotion such "innumerable blessings for others."[19]

VIII

At West Point, Washington discovered that his farewell had not mollified the army's remaining officers. They decided to write him a reply. They appointed a committee consisting of Generals Knox and McDougall and Quartermaster General Pickering to prepare a draft. By this time the officers had learned that the state of New York had voted to reject the new impost proposed by Congress, dooming all hope of the fighting men redeeming their Morris notes in hard money or winning their commutation of half pay. Pickering volunteered to do the writing. McDougall and Knox agreed the address should not be stuffed "with fulsome adulation," suggesting that at least one of them—probably McDougall—shared the quartermaster general's negative opinion of General Washington.

To no one's surprise, Pickering's praise of Washington was minimal. He exonerated him from letting Congress defraud the officers. "Causes" not in the general's "power to control" had led to the failure to obtain for the army "the just, the promised rewards of their long, severe and dangerous services." The quartermaster general spent the next two pages indicting Congress and the states for this continental malfeasance. One historian has described the text as "a snarl of self pity and defiant outrage." The officers did not bother to present this less-than-fulsome farewell to General Washington personally; they mailed it.[20]

IX

Only a hard-hearted anti-militarist would begrudge these departing officers the right to belabor a Congress and a nation that was reneging on the solemn promise of half pay they had made to these men when the United States was in desperate need of them. Unfortunately, the officers' anger only fueled a growing mood—even a movement—to denigrate the Continental Army.

In August, Brigadier General Ebenezer Huntington of Connecticut, who had worked closely with General Knox to create The Society of the Cincinnati, told his brother that newspapers were calling the officers "the harpies and locusts" of the country. In his home state, and throughout the rest of New England and satellite states such as New Jersey, half pay was seen as an attempt to create a privileged class in America; commutation was equally reprehensible.

The Massachusetts legislature, in a scorching reply to Congress's letter urging the impost and using the officers' rejection of the Newburgh addresses as proof of their patriotism, called commutation an attempt to "exalt some citizens to wealth and granduer [*sic*] to the injury and oppression of others." They warned if Congress persisted, the Bay State would secede from the Union.

Connecticut was even more hostile. Town meetings addressed the legislature, reminding them that America had revolted against Great Britain in no small part because the mother country sought tax money to support swarms of pensioners. Some Connecticutians carried this swelling prejudice to extremes. One ex-captain who lived near Litchfield reported that he had become "obnoxious to the mass of the people." When he fell ill, his neighbors told him they hoped he would die. One man said they planned to skin his corpse for a drumhead and "drum other officers out of town." Feeding this wrath were newspaper stories on the formation of The Society of the Cincinnati. For many people this organization increased their suspicion that the officers planned to establish themselves as aristocratic rulers of the independent nation.[21]

In October, Judge Aedanus Burke of South Carolina, one of the leading voices in rejecting Colonel John Laurens's proposal to enlist blacks in the Continental Army, crystallized this hostility to the Cincinnati. In a ferocious pamphlet, Burke claimed the officers planned to use the Society to create not only a pensioned class, but a hereditary nobility which would number as many as thirty thousand arrogant patricians with pretensions to running the country. Widely reprinted, Burke's diatribe convinced many people that the Society was a menace.

Before long, this anger mutated into a dislike of the entire Continental Army. A Washington County, Virginia, official reported, "Some how there is a general disgust taken place for what bears the name of a regular."[22]

X

In Princeton, not long after Washington's departure, Congress adjourned without making any decision on a peacetime army or any other pressing matter, such as Vermont. Ethan Allen and his Green Mountain Boys would remain an independent republic until 1791. The only item of importance that the solons settled was their place of residence.

The prospect of spending a snowbound winter in Princeton did not appeal to them.

James Madison thought their experience had already proved that "any small place" involved "degrading impositions" on the delegates. Madison predicted they would go back to Philadelphia. But resistance to that city among the Morris haters, who now included most of the New England delegates, remained intense. After more debate, the solons finally settled for a site on the Delaware River near Trenton.

The capital of New Jersey was not much bigger than Princeton and a great deal of new building would be needed to establish a federal city in its vicinity. Winter was coming on rapidly. The southerners returned to the attack and proposed two capitals, Annapolis and Trenton, to be used alternately in the cold and warm months. This compromise attracted enough votes to win agreement, and Congress announced it was adjourning to reassemble in Annapolis in mid-November.

President Elias Boudinot, who had lobbied for the New Jersey site as the sole capital, was disgusted. He told former Secretary of Foreign Affairs Robert R. Livingston that he could hardly wait to leave office. "Our public affairs are in a truly disagreeable situation," he moaned, and the two-capital solution was a perfect example of Congress's inability to make a sensible decision about anything. He predicted "great evil from this measure," which would turn members of Congress into "wandering stars."[23]

The solution inspired Philadelphia's leading poet and composer, Francis Hopkinson, to indulge his fondness for satire. He reported on an imaginary follow-up congressional debate in which the members considered where to build their huge statue of George Washington on horseback. It was supposed to be erected wherever Congress decided to settle. According to Hopkinson, the solons now decided the only solution was mounting it on wheels.

A brilliant delegate in the satire proposed making the statue big enough "to transport the members themselves, with their books, papers, &c from one federal town to the other." Yet another deep-thinking delegate had an even better idea—to save money, why not build the entire federal city on wheels, so it could be dragged back and forth, and "the business of the house might be going on whilst the house is going on?"[24]

A more realistic but equally sardonic view of Congress appeared in Philadelphia's *Independent Gazetteer* not long after the two-capital decision became public. "Simeon Woodenleg, an old soldier, presents his best respects to the honourable Congress and begs that before they fall to building their two federal towns . . . they would pay him the 45 pounds, 15 shillings and 10 pence they have owed him these past two years." The whole capital debate was absurd. Without the impost, Congress would not have enough money to build a shanty.[25]

XI

General Washington spent most of November at West Point, waiting for General Carleton to set a date for the final withdrawal from New York. The general was a commander in chief with only the ghost of an army—about eight hundred men. He was harassed by Governor George Clinton, who was anxious to make it clear that New York state, not that bankrupt entity, the Continental Congress, was taking possession of New York City and its environs. Having wrecked Congress's hopes of revenue by voting down the impost, Clinton was acting more and more like the head of an independent state. Washington had to reassure the impatient governor (whom he liked personally) that he would send him "by express the first notice I receive" of the exact date for Carleton's departure.[26]

General Washington's mostly symbolic presence did not prevent him from being harried by a familiar problem: no money. He asked his friend Governor Clinton to loan the Continentals $2,000 to march to New York and remain there a few days without starving. The embarrassed governor was forced to confess the state did not have that much money in its treasury. Quartermaster General Pickering sent an urgent appeal to Robert Morris in Philadelphia for anything that could pass as cash.[27]

Whatever the financier managed to scrape together was hastily dispatched and Washington began exchanging polite letters with General Carleton about the exact date of his departure. Toward the end of November, the British commander warned Washington that looting and mayhem seemed likely to break out as the last British troops withdrew. The thousands of former rebels who had streamed into New York were apparently preparing to wreak vengeance on anyone who had failed to meet their standard of patriotism. Carleton had stationed soldiers on every block in the city to keep order. Washington replied that he would do his best to make sure this upheaval did not occur.

Finally, on November 24, a letter from General Carleton reported that he would depart the following day. By this time, General Washington and Governor Clinton and the Continental troops had advanced to Harlem. November 25 was a clear, cold day with a brisk northwest wind. The 800-man column swung down the Boston Post Road and halted at a barrier on Bowery Lane, where a detachment of British troops stood guard. They soon withdrew; from Fort George at the tip of Manhattan came the boom of cannon, meaning the last British soldiers had departed. The American regiments, led by General Knox, marched into the city to keep order.

General Knox returned to report there was no sign of misbehavior. Rejoicing, not vengeance, was the emotion of the moment. Americans inside the city had already planned a triumphal parade. With General Washington and Governor Clinton side by side at its head, the procession began. Civilians dominated the marchers. Horsemen escorting Washington and Clinton were militia from Westchester, without uniforms. Behind the two leaders marched ranks of more civilians, many of them state officials and followers of Governor Clinton. Then came Washington's officers. It was another indication of the way civilians wanted to de-emphasize the Continental Army's role in the victory.

Along the packed sidewalks, New Yorkers cheered and wept. Around them, buildings were worn and shabby. Deprived of the commerce that had been its lifeblood, the city was a kind of civic corpse. Along the Hudson River, the charred ruins of the warehouses, churches, and homes burned by the great fire of 1776 were even more painful witnesses of the seven years of war. There was not a tree left standing on any city street, nor anywhere else on Manhattan Island. All had been cut down for firewood; this added to the city's barren look.

At Fort George on the Battery, everyone expected to see the American flag soar skyward in the crisp sunshine. But the enemy had added a touch of departing malice to frustrate this ceremony. They had cut the halyards and greased the pole. In the harbor British sailors leaned on the oars of the boats ferrying the last soldiers to their transports, enjoying the spectacle.

American ingenuity swiftly solved the problem. Sailors grabbed tools and nails from a nearby ironmonger's shop and fashioned cleats which enabled one of them to climb the pole, restore the halyards, and raise Old Glory to its proper place. The fort's cannon, now in the hands of General Knox's artillerymen, boomed a thirteen-gun salute. With a final cheer, the crowd dispersed.[28]

XII

Out in the harbor, disconsolate loyalists took a last look at their native shores. Over twenty-nine thousand of the king's supporters had departed from New York, including three thousand loyal blacks. In the cabin of the frigate HMS *Ceres*, Judge William Smith wrote to his wife, Janet, whom he was leaving behind to protect his property. He reported that he had a comfortable stateroom. His friend General Carleton had equally good quarters nearby.

Smith would spend three miserable years in England, frequently insulted by royal officials who rejected his claims for compensation for his services to George III. He finally settled for an appointment as chief justice of Canada. His admiring patron, General Carleton, had not a little to do with this royal benevolence. Sir Guy became Canada's governor general. Smith's only postwar consolation was the modicum of kindness displayed by his former law clerk, Governor Clinton. Unlike most loyalists, Smith's New York property was never confiscated.[29]

The vast majority of the departing New York loyalists accepted the British government's offer of land in Nova Scotia. New York's newspapers had been telling people that the province had mild weather and excellent soil and taxes were minimal. Another story claimed it was warmer in the summer than New York. General Carleton buoyed their hopes by promising 500 to 600 acres of land per family.

The unexpected flood of refugees in the final months of the occupation, spurred by threats in newspapers and sometimes by curses hurled in their faces by returning rebels, overwhelmed the authorities in the thinly populated colony. (The mocking rebels called it with more accuracy "Nova Scarcity.") Some earlier arrivals had found houses built, land grants surveyed; the late arrivals found nothing but a wilderness, with winter coming on.

One woman, the daughter of an Albany loyalist who had joined the British army and served in the ranks for seven years, told of landing in St. Johns to find the ground covered with snow. They had to live in tents and survive on government rations—moldy bread and salt pork. Many mornings they awoke in bitter cold to find their beds soaked by melting snow and rain. The woman's mother developed rheumatism that made her a near invalid for the rest of her life. They finally moved to a house her father built; it had neither a floor nor windows, but it was shelter.[30]

Edward Winslow of Connecticut, formerly mustermaster general of loyalist troops in New York, was given the thankless task of getting the refugees settled in what became the province of New Brunswick. He was soon in a state of near hysteria. "What in the world are you about?" he wrote to his former deputy, who was supposed to be forwarding food and other necessities from New York. "37,000 people crying for provisions . . . that's the situation of the country at present."[31]

Filer Dibblee, once a prosperous lawyer from Connecticut, could not bear the humiliating poverty to which his wife and five children were reduced. He lay down on the bed in their crude cabin and cut his throat. In one small town, three thousand loyalists were crammed into the church, the courthouse, and stores. They moved to tents and nearly four hundred died in a violent storm. One resident predicted "disease, disappointment, poverty and chagrin, will finish the course of many more."

The three thousand black refugees had an especially hard time. Edward Winslow described them as begging him "for Christ's sake that Masser would give 'em a little provision if it's only for one week." Many of the ex-slaves were settled in a place they called Birchtown, after the British general who had supervised granting their certificates to leave New York. It was a satellite of a much larger town, Shelburne, where some blacks also lived. Jobs were scarce and food was often scarcer.

White ex-soldiers accused the blacks of depriving them of jobs because "they labour cheaper." A race riot destroyed the houses of more than twenty blacks. The rioters drove all the free blacks out of Shelburne to Birchtown. A white man who visited the place in 1788 described it as "beyond description wretched." Even more infuriating, the blacks were denied the right to vote. A few years later, a thousand decided to return to Africa.[32]

XIII

In New York, General Washington spent most of the week after the British evacuation attending dinners and receptions where he was bombarded with fulsome tributes to his fame. He might be persona non grata to many of the Continental Army's embittered officers, but he was a national hero to everyone else.

The general responded by treating New Yorkers to the most spectacular display of fireworks they had ever seen, courtesy of General Knox's artillerymen. One barrage of rockets produced an immense dove with an olive branch of peace in its beak; another blast created two full-rigged ships. A final fusillade sent a hundred red, white, and blue rockets crisscrossing the night sky.

General Washington also found time to attend to some unfinished business. Throughout the war, several spy rings operated inside New York. These agents pretended to be loyalists, which earned them the enmity of those who thirsted for vengeance on the supporters of George III. Major Benjamin Tallmadge, who ran some of these espionage operations, told Washington that a big jovial tailor, Hercules Mulligan, was on the list of those to be abused. Mulligan had obtained valuable information while outfitting British army and navy officers in new uniforms. Washington made a point of visiting his shop and publicly declaring Mulligan was a friend of the country.

Another pretend loyalist in even more danger of a beating was James Rivington, the publisher of the *New York Royal Gazette*. The dandyish Rivington had decided early that the British war effort was a muddled mess and began leaking useful information to the Americans. Among his thefts were the secret signals of the British fleet, which may have been useful when Admiral de Grasse fought his battle with Admirals Graves and Hood in their attempt to rescue Lord Cornwallis from Yorktown.

Washington paid Rivington a public visit; witnesses reported that friendly compliments were exchanged and some Madeira drunk. Then Washington and Rivington adjourned to a back room and the clink of hard money became audible—a payoff for the newsman's treachery. In the eight and one-half years of the war, Washington spent over $55 thousand for such "secret intelligence."[33]

XIV

At the end of the festive week, the last British ships found the wind promising and left New York harbor on December 4. Washington immediately prepared to depart. He had promised Martha he would be home by Christmas. But there was one more task to perform. He invited the army officers in the city to join him for a farewell meeting at Fraunces Tavern.

At noon the officers assembled on the second floor of this familiar building on the corner of Broad and Pearl Streets. A cold collation and bottles of wine and brandy awaited them on long tables. Only three major generals (Knox, von Steuben, and McDougall) were on hand, one brigadier general, and one colonel. The rest were lower ranks. Conspicuously absent was Colonel Alexander Hamilton, who had moved to a house on nearby Wall Street to begin the practice of law the previous week.

Various theories have been advanced to explain Hamilton's non-attendance. A likely explanation is the rift between Washington and the army's officers that had developed since the Newburgh confrontation. The general was aware of Hamilton's role in the upheaval that had triggered this alienation. He came close to blaming him as well as Robert Morris when he warned that an army was a "dangerous instrument to play with." Hamilton expended a lot of ink claiming he was not guilty of any incitement that could be called dangerous.[34]

Precisely at noon, General Washington strode into Fraunces Tavern's second-floor room, accompanied by three aides. It took only a glance for everyone to see he was struggling with deep emotions. The conventional explanation is sentimental—the surging memories of eight years of comradeship and shared danger. But few if any of these officers were known personally to Washington, except for Generals Knox, von Steuben, and McDougall. The anger of the entire officer corps, all too evident in Quartermaster General Pickering's West Point response to his farewell letter, and the abuse the whole army was receiving in the newspapers, were a far more probable factor in the general's turbulent feelings. Would these men blame him for their misfortunes? Did the words he had written to Congress, warning them against failing to compensate the officers, flicker through Washington's mind? *Then shall I have learned what ingratitude is, then shall I have realized a tale, which will embitter every moment of my future life.*

The general poured himself a glass of wine and raised it to his lips with a shaking hand. The other officers passed decanters and quickly filled their glasses. Washington picked at the food on the table but he obviously had no interest in eating. He gazed at the men, his lips trembling. He wanted—even needed—to break through the disaffection and disappointment that was troubling many of them. He wanted to speak to this small cluster of guarded faces—and reach the whole officers corps.

Slowly, Washington raised his glass and said: "With a heart full of love and gratitude, I now take leave of you. I most devoutly wish that your latter days may be as prosperous and happy as your former ones have been glorious and honorable."

"In almost breathless silence," one officer recalled, they watched him drink. They raised their glasses in a mostly silent but equally emotional response. Tears began to stream down Washington's cheeks. The officers' anger at this man—if not at Congress—dissolved in the several meanings of the general's grief. They understood that parting was only one reason for those tears. A larger reason was regret. He had not only failed to get them the money they needed and deserved, their attempts to obtain this just reward had earned them widespread public obloquy.

"I cannot come to each of you," Washington said in a choked voice. "But [I] shall feel obliged if each of you will come and take me by the hand."

A tearful General Knox, standing closest to Washington, extended his meaty artilleryman's palm. Washington embraced him and kissed him on both cheeks. Next came Baron von Steuben and then General McDougall, the spokesman for the army's anger. Each was embraced; they were followed by the other officers, in rough order of rank, to receive a handshake and an occasional embrace. "In the same affectionate manner," recalled Major Benjamin Tallmadge, "every officer in the room . . . parted with his general in chief."[35]

Without another word, Washington walked to the door, raised his arm in a silent farewell, and left the room. Outside, Governor Clinton, his councillors, and other distinguished civilians awaited the general. The officers joined them and Washington walked past an honor guard of light infantrymen to the waterfront, where he boarded a waiting barge. "A prodigious crowd," recalled Major Tallmadge, watched what another observer called the "mute and solemn procession." The latter memoirist called the prevailing mood a "delicious melancholy." They all thought they would never see George Washington again. No one imagined he would return to New York in six years as the country's first elected president.

Three aides and General von Steuben, who was travelling with Washington to Philadelphia, followed the general aboard the barge. Washington removed his tricorn hat in a final gesture of goodbye. All the spectators on the docks did likewise as the barge's seventeen-man crew hauled on their oars. Ignoring the December cold, the spectators stood there, bareheaded, until the barge became a blur against the New Jersey shore.[36]

XV

General Washington must have wondered if he would reach home by Christmas when it took him four days to cross New Jersey. The citizens of town after town along his route bedecked their houses with flags and bunting, presented him and his party a fulsome address, and treated them to a banquet. The climax came in Trenton, where Governor William Livingston introduced him to the New Jersey legislature by recalling the wonder of his Christmas night 1776 foray across the ice-choked Delaware River that had rescued the Revolution from collapse. In his response to these tributes, Washington preferred to look forward rather than back: he urged everyone to give Congress the power it needed to govern the country.[37]

Philadelphia celebrated Washington's arrival with festivities that lasted for days. Crowds thronged the streets to catch a glimpse of him. Newspapers published odes to his greatness. In large type he was again called THE SAVIOR OF HIS COUNTRY. At every banquet, thirteen toasts were drunk and Washington responded with gracious thanks and an appeal for more power for Congress. No one booed, of course, but there was little enthusiasm for the federal legislature in the city they had deserted. The splendid clothes adorning both gentlemen and ladies in the latest London and Paris modes made it clear that Philadelphia was forsaking politics and concentrating on what it did best: making money.

Washington's particular friend Superintendent of Finance Robert Morris invited him to stay in his mansion, The Hills, on the outskirts of the city, while the two men went over the general's accounts. His personal expenses came to $64,335.30—not a bad price to pay for the services of a lieutenant general for eight and one-half years. Much of the money had already been repaid. The only large expenditure they discussed came from Quartermaster General Pickering—$5,500 for the reoccupation of New York. Morris had already spent every florin of the Dutch loan, but he juggled some other payments and sent Pickering a warrant (an eighteenth-century version of a check) for the round sum, hoping it would not bounce.[38]

XVI

With this last look at the federal government's bankruptcy, General Washington resumed his southward journey. He dismissed the small cavalry escort that had accompanied him from West Point and retained only two of his aides, Benjamin Walker and David Humphreys. With stops in Wilmington and Baltimore for the usual round of dinners and public addresses thick with praise, they reached Annapolis, the current capital of the United States, on December 19.

Cannon boomed thirteen rounds and the stylishly dressed citizens of this opulent town of five hundred houses swarmed into the streets. Among the greeters was an unexpected face—General Washington's enemy from Valley Forge and Newburgh conspiracy days, General Horatio Gates. He got a warm handshake. Washington saw no point in holding wartime grudges.

The next day, Washington wrote to the president of Congress, informing him of his desire to resign his commission as commander in chief. Here was more irony. The president was suave, handsome Thomas Mifflin of Pennsylvania. He had been the brains—and money—behind the plot to humiliate Washington into resigning at Valley Forge. Washington had eased him out of the army when Henry Laurens, then Congress's president, charged Mifflin with gross malfeasance during his career as quartermaster general. Mifflin's Pennsylvania and New England friends, backers of Gates, protected him from a serious investigation of the charges and he managed to stay in politics.

Neither President Mifflin nor General Washington wanted to recall this ugly clash. The president read Washington's letter to Congress and they responded with plans for a public dinner on December 22 and an "audience" for the resignation ceremony on December 23. Mifflin put a committee headed by a new delegate from Virginia, Thomas Jefferson, in charge of working out the details. Jefferson obtained a copy of the statement Washington planned to make and wrote a reply for President Mifflin.

The dinner was described by one guest as "the most extraordinary feast I ever attended." There were between two and three hundred gentlemen in the ballroom of the Maryland state house and the "cheerful voices" blended with the "clangor of knives and forks" to make a "delightful" din. Even more extraordinary, "not a soul got drunk although there was wine in plenty." This relative sobriety was worth noting because the diners drank the usual thirteen toasts to those who had helped achieve the glorious victory. General Washington rose to offer one more toast, by far the most important: "Competent powers to Congress for general purposes!"[39]

XVII

At noon on the following day, Washington walked to the state house, where Congress was meeting. He took a designated seat in the assembly chamber, and his two aides sat down beside him. The three soldiers wore their blue and buff Continental Army uniforms. The doors of the assem-

bly room were opened and Maryland's governor and the members of the
state's legislature crowded into the chamber, along with, in the words of
one eyewitness, "the principal ladies and gentlemen of the city." Other
ladies filled every seat in a small gallery above the chamber.

President Mifflin began the proceedings: "Sir, the United States in
Congress assembled are prepared to receive your communications."

Washington stood up and bowed. The members of Congress briefly
took off their hats in response to the general's bow. The rulers of the
United States numbered only twenty delegates from seven states. For the
preceding weeks in Annapolis, they had had trouble doing any business.
So few delegates showed up, they had lacked a quorum. Not until January, when delegates from two more states arrived, were they able to ratify
the definitive treaty of peace.

Having spent almost a week with Robert Morris in Philadelphia,
General Washington knew he was face to face with bankrupt politicians
who had accomplished nothing since Yorktown. They had ignored his
advice for a peacetime army. They had sent his officers home penniless,
embittered and disgusted with their country. Nevertheless, Washington
understood the significance of what he was doing. He—and Congress—
were both testifying to the vital importance of a federal government for
the fragile American union.

The general drew his speech out of his coat pocket and unfolded it
with hands that trembled with emotion. "Mr. President," he began in a
low strained voice. "The great events on which my resignation depended
having at length taken place; I now have the honor of offering my sincere congratulations to Congress and of presenting myself before them to
surrender into their hands the trust committed to me, and to claim the
indulgence of retiring from the service of my country."

His former aide, Dr. James McHenry, had changed his mind about
serving in Congress. He was sitting as a delegate from Maryland.
McHenry recalled that at this point, Washington's voice "faultered and
sunk . . . [and] the whole house felt his agitation." But he recovered his
composure and "proceeded . . . in the most penetrating manner."

"Happy in the confirmation of our independence and sovereignty, and
pleased with the opportunity afforded the United States of becoming a
respectable nation, I resign with satisfaction the appointment I accepted
with diffidence." The general went on to express his gratitude for the support of "my countrymen" and the "army in general."

Next Washington hoped Congress would do something special to acknowledge the "distinguished merits" of "the gentlemen who have been attached to my person during the war"—his aides. In particular the two young men who sat beside him.

This reference to his officers ignited some of the painful emotions Washington had felt at Fraunces Tavern. The feelings were still so intense, he had to grip the speech with both hands to keep it steady. He continued: "I consider it an indispensable duty to close this last solemn act of my official life by commending the interests of our dearest country to the protection of Almighty God and those who have the superintendence of them, to his holy keeping."

For a long moment, Washington could not say another word. Tears streamed down his cheeks. These words touched a vein of religious faith in his inmost soul, born of battlefield experiences in the French and Indian War that had convinced him of the existence of a caring God. The words also ignited the feelings of regret and frustration he had experienced in trying to persuade his opinionated countrymen to give Congress the power it needed to create a meaningful union. He could only hope that this caring God would eventually send Americans the wisdom they so badly needed, in His own mysterious way.

The deeply moved spectators "all wept," Congressman McHenry recalled. "And there was hardly a member of Congress who did not drop tears." Former aide McHenry was probably among the tearful. He knew how much the general cared about his army—and his country. He understood the depth of his sadness—and the anguish of his hope.

General Washington drew from his coat a parchment copy of his appointment as commander in chief, dated June 15, 1775. "Having now finished the work assigned me, I retire from the great theater of action and bidding farewell to this august body under whom I have long acted, I here offer my commission and take leave of all the employments of public life." Stepping forward, Washington handed the document to President Mifflin.[40]

This was—is—the most important moment in American history. The man who could have been King George I of America, or President General for Life after dispersing a feckless Congress and obtaining for himself and his officers riches worthy of their courage, was renouncing absolute power to become a private citizen, at the mercy of politicians over whom he had no control. This visible incontrovertible act did more to affirm America's faith in the government of the people than a thousand declarations by legislatures and treatises by philosophers. No one put it better than Thomas Jefferson, who was an eyewitness: "The moderation and virtue of a single character probably prevented this revolution from being closed, as most others have been, by a subversion of that liberty it was intended to establish."[41]

In Europe, Washington's resignation restored America's battered prestige. It was reported with awe and amazement in newspapers from London to Vienna. The Connecticut painter John Trumbull, studying in England, wrote that it had earned the "astonishment and admiration of this part of the world." No one was more surprised than George III. When he heard about it, His Majesty stuttered disbelievingly: "If he d-d-does that, he will become the g-g-greatest m-m-man in the world!"[42]

XVIII

President Thomas Mifflin now read the reply Thomas Jefferson had prepared for him. He did so "without any show of feeling," according to one spectator. The observation is all too plausible. Mifflin had too many negative memories of George Washington to be comfortable with the words Jefferson had written, assuring the general of "our warmest prayers" that his days "may be as happy as they have been illustrious."

Washington shook hands with each member of Congress and not a few of the spectators before departing. Meanwhile, his aides were bringing their horses and baggage wagons from nearby Mann's Hotel. They had left orders for everything to be packed and ready for an immediate departure. By two o'clock they were on the road to the ferry over the South River, below Annapolis. The next morning, after an overnight stop at a tavern, they crossed the Potomac River below Alexandria and rode at a steady pace toward Mount Vernon. The December wind was cold and cutting but Washington was warmed by anticipation of what was awaiting him.

Finally, as twilight shrouded the winter sky, Mount Vernon came into view beside the Potomac. Past bare trees and wintry fields the three horsemen trotted toward the white pillared porch and the green shuttered windows, aglow with candlelight. It was Christmas Eve. Ex-General Washington—and The United States of America—had survived the perils of peace.

Abbreviations for Notes

LMCC   *Letters of Members of the Continental Congress,* Edmund C. Burnett, ed. (Gloucester, Mass., 1963, reprint)

LDC   *Letters of Delegates to the Continental Congress,* Paul H. Smith, ed. (Washington, D.C., 1991)

PJM   *Papers of James Madison,* William T. Hutchinson and William M. E. Rachal, eds. (Chicago, 1969)

PAH   *The Papers of Alexander Hamilton,* Harold C. Syrett et al., eds. (New York, 1961)

PNG   *The Papers of Nathanael Greene,* Daniel M. Conrad et al., eds. (Chapel Hill, N.C., 1997)

PHL   *The Papers of Henry Laurens,* David R. Chesnutt and C. James Taylor, eds. (Columbia, S.C., 2003)

PJA   *Papers of John Adams,* Gregg L. Lint et al., eds. (Cambridge, Mass., 2003)

PBF   *The Papers of Benjamin Franklin,* Barbara M. Oberg, ed. (New Haven, 1999)

PRM   *The Papers of Robert Morris,* James Catanzariti and E. James Ferguson, eds. (Pittsburgh, Pa., 1984)

WGW   *The Writings of George Washington,* John C, Fitzpatrick, ed. (Washington, D.C., 1937)

Notes

CHAPTER 1: A POTENTIALLY RUINOUS VICTORY

1. Lee Kennett, *The French Forces in America, 1780–1783* (Westport, Conn., 1977), 149–151. Frank Moore, ed., *Diary of the American Revolution,* vol. 2 (New York, 1859), 508, note.
2. Harlow Giles Unger, *The Unexpected George Washington: His Private Life* (New York, 2006), 167.
3. Joseph T. Glatthaar and James Kirby Martin, *Forgotten Allies: The Oneida Indians and the American Revolution* (New York, 2006), 279–80. Alan Taylor, *The Divided Ground: Indians, Settlers and the Northern Borderland of the American Revolution* (New York, 2006), 100–101.
4. P. J. Marshall, ed., *The Oxford History of the British Empire,* vol. 2, The Eighteenth Century (New York, 1998), 81–82, 100–101.
5. John C. Fitzpatrick, ed., *The Writings of George Washington* (hereafter *WGW*) (Washington, D.C., 1937), vol. 19, 211. Here the size of Rochambeau's army is estimated to be 5,000 men. Kennett, *The French Forces in America,* 112–13, argues that by the time they reached Yorktown, the army had dwindled to 3,000 men. At least 400 men were left behind to garrison Newport and another 700 were detached to help man the French fleet.
6. Donald Jackson, ed., *The Diaries of George Washington,* vol. 3, 1771–75, 1780–81 (Charlottesville, Va. 1978), 356–57.
7. Ibid., 356.
8. *WGW,* vol. 22, 176.
9. Orville Theodore Murphy, "Contemporary French Opinion of the American Revolutionary Army," PhD diss., University of Minnesota, 1957, 222, 223. Evelyn M. Acomb, trans. and ed., *The Revolutionary Journal of Baron Ludwig Von Closen* (Chapel Hill, N.C., 1958), 89. "Letters of Fersen, Written to His Father in Sweden, 1781–1782," *Magazine of American History* 3 (May–July, 1879), 371.

10. Kennett, *The French Forces in America,* 127–39. Stephen Bonsal, *When the French Were Here* (New York, 1945), 77ff. Howard C. Rice Jr. and Anne S. K. Brown, trans. and eds., *The American Campaigns of Rochambeau's Army,* vol. 1, Journal of Sublieutenant Jean Baptiste-Antoine de Verger (Princeton, N.J., 1972), 133–38.

11. Acomb, *Baron Ludwig Von Closen,* 153. James Thacher, M.D., *A Military Journal During the American Revolutionary War, from 1775–1883* (Boston, 1837), 288–90. *The Journal of William Feltman of the First Pennsylvania Regiment, 1781–82, including the March into Virginia and the Siege of Yorktown* (Philadelphia, 1853), 12, 22–24.

12. Robert D. Bass, *The Green Dragoon, the Lives of Banastre Tarleton and Mary Robinson* (New York, 1957), 4–5.

13. Kennett, *The French Forces in America,* 150–51.

14. John McCauley Palmer, *General von Steuben* (New Haven, 1939), 295.

15. Harold C. Syrett et al., eds., *The Papers of Alexander Hamilton* (hereafter PAH), vol. 2, 1779–1781 (New York, 1961), 679–82. This is Hamilton's report of the assault to his immediate commander, Marquis de Lafayette. Also on page 682 is a letter to his wife, Elizabeth, urging her to read the details of the attack in the Philadelphia papers.

    For the preceding clash with Washington, one of the best accounts is Broadus Mitchell, *Alexander Hamilton, The Revolutionary Years* (New York, 1970), 223–46.

16. *WGW,* vol. 23, 297. This October 29, 1781, letter to the president of Congress warns against "a relaxation that will put us in a disreputable situation" in 1782.

17. *WGW,* vol. 23, 247–50.

18. Ibid.

19. Henry Wiener, *An Imperfect God: George Washington, His Slaves and the Creation of America* (New York, 2003), 248, 251. George Scheer, ed., *Private Yankee Doodle, Being a Narrative of Some of the Adventures, Dangers and Sufferings of a Revolutionary Soldier,* by Joseph Plumb Martin (Boston, 1962), 241–42. For Monticello slaves, see Gary B. Nash, *The Unknown American Revolution: The Unruly Birth of Democracy and the Struggle to Create America* (New York, 2005), 339.

20. Arthur S. Lefkowitz, *George Washington's Indispensable Men: The 32 Aides-De-Camp Who Helped Win American Independence* (Mechanicsburg, Pa., 2003), 233, 251.

21. Douglas Southall Freeman, *George Washington, Vol. V, Victory with the Help of France* (New York, 1952), 393. *WGW,* vol. 23, 241–44.

22. L. G. Shreve, *Tench Tilghman, the Life and Times of Washington's Aide de Camp* (Centreville, Md., 1982), 158–64.

23. Ibid., 165–67.

24. Ibid., 164–66. Paul H. Smith, ed., *Letters of Delegates to the Continental Congress* (hereafter *LDC*), (Washington, D.C., 1991) vol. 18, 165.

25. *LDC,* 164–65, note.

26. Judith L. Van Buskirk, "They Didn't Join the Band: Disaffected Women in Revolutionary Philadelphia," *Pennsylvania History,* vol. 62, no. 3 (Summer 1995), 320–21.

27. *LDC,* vol. 18, 165–66.

28. John Keane, *Tom Paine, a Political Life* (New York, 1995), 208–16.

29. Ellen Gibson Wilson, *The Loyal Blacks* (New York, 1976), 62.

30. Judith L. Van Buskirk, *Generous Enemies: Patriots and Loyalists in Revolutionary New York* (Philadelphia, 2002), 25.

31. Ibid., 31–32.

32. William H. W. Sabine, ed., *Historical Memoirs of William Smith,* vol. 2, from 26 August 1778 to 12 November 1783 (New York, 1956), 447ff.

33. Ibid., vol. 1, Introduction, viiff.

34. Thomas Fleming, *The Forgotten Victory* (New York, 1973), 34–36, 44–45, 189–96 passim.
35. Sabine, *Smith Memoirs,* vol. 2, 447–49. Also see Philip Ziegler, *King William IV* (New York, 1973), 35–39. The author describes the future king's visit in less emotional terms.
36. Sabine, *Smith Memoirs,* vol. 2, 455.
37. Ibid., 458–61.
38. William H. Mariboe, "The Life of William Franklin, 1730(1)–1813, 'Pro Rege et Patria,'" PhD diss., University of Pennsylvania, 1962, 527–28.
39. William B. Willcox, *Portrait of a General: Sir Henry Clinton in the War for Independence* (New York, 1962), 438–39.
40. Charles Ross, ed., *Correspondence of Charles, First Marquis Cornwallis,* vol. 2 (London, 1859), 124. Alan Valentine, *Lord North,* vol. 2 (Norman, Okla., 1962), 295.
41. Burke Davis, *The Campaign That Won America: The Story of Yorktown* (New York, 1970), 284. Also Freeman, *George Washington,* vol. 5, 400, note. For Cornwallis's final letter, see William B. Willcox, ed., *The American Rebellion: Sir Henry Clinton's Narrative of His Campaigns, 1775–1782, with an appendix of original documents* (New Haven, Conn., 1954), 583–87.
42. Daniel M. Conrad et al., eds., *The Papers of Nathanael Greene* (hereafter PNG), vol. 9 (Chapel Hill, N.C., 1997), 428, 505.
43. Ibid.
44. Patricia Brady, *Martha Washington, An American Life* (New York, 2005), 139–40.
45. *WGW,* vol. 23, 351–52, 359–60.
46. *WGW,* vol. 23, 340–42.
47. Howard Swiggett, *War Out of Niagara: Walter Butler and the Tory Rangers* (New York, 1933), 231–43.
48. *WGW,* vol. 23, 361–62.
49. Shreve, *Tilghman,* 168.
50. Harry M. Ward, *George Washington's Enforcers: Policing the Continental Army* (Carbondale, Ill., 2006), 69. John Jackson, "Washington in Philadelphia," *Pennsylvania Magazine of Biography and History,* vol. 56, 134–35.
51. James Thomas Flexner, *George Washington in the American Revolution* (Boston, 1968), 474.

CHAPTER 2: DIPLOMATS IN DISTRESS

1. *WGW,* vol. 23, 253–54.
2. Ibid., 252.
3. Ibid., 297.
4. Barbara M. Oberg, ed, *The Papers of Benjamin Franklin* (hereafter *PBF*) (New Haven, Conn., 1999), vol. 35, 616–19, 643.
5. Ross J. S. Hoffman, *The Marquis: A Study of Lord Rockingham, 1730–1782* (New York, 1973), 341.
6. Alfred Owen Aldridge, *Franklin and His French Contemporaries* (New York, 1957), 43.
7. Coy Hilton James, *Silas Deane, Patriot or Traitor?* (East Lansing, Mich., 1975), 104–05.
8. Louis W. Potts, *Arthur Lee, A Virtuous Revolutionary* (Baton Rouge, La., 1981), 161.
9. J. Kent McCaughey, *Richard Henry Lee* (Lanham, Md., 2004), 142.

10. James, *Silas Deane*, 20.

11. Robert Middlekauf, *Benjamin Franklin and His Enemies* (Los Angeles, 1996), 151.

12. Potts, *Arthur Lee*, 83.

13. McCaughey, *Richard Henry Lee*, 128. There was considerable antagonism between Richard Henry Lee and Robert Morris before Arthur Lee's appointment. They represented opposing groups claiming vast acreage in the Ohio River Valley. See 126–27.

14. Potts, *Arthur Lee*, 186.

15. Ibid., 182.

16. Ibid., 186.

17. Orville T. Murphy, "Charles Gravier de Vergennes, Portrait of an Old Regime Diplomat," *Political Science Quarterly*, vol. 83, 1968, 415.

18. Orville T. Murphy, *Charles Gravier, Comte de Vergennes: French Diplomacy in the Age of Revolution* (Albany, N.Y., 1982), 207.

19. Ibid., 206.

20. Ibid., 254–55.

21. Ibid., 256–58.

22. Potts, *Arthur Lee*, 199.

23. James, *Silas Deane*, 69.

24. *WGW*, vol. 11, 413. Edmund Cody Burnett, ed., *Letters of Members of the Continental Congress* (hereafter LMCC) (Gloucester, Mass., 1963, reprint), 260. *LDC*, vol. 9, 650–51. Also see Glenn A. Phelps, "The Republican General," 165-197, in Don Higginbotham, ed., *George Washington Reconsidered* (Charlottesville, Va., 2001). H. James Henderson, *Party Politics in the Continental Congress* (New York, 1974), 120–24.

25. James, *Silas Deane*, 70–75.

26. Richard Morris, *The Peacemakers: The Great Powers and American Independence* (New York, 1965), 21.

27. Potts, *Arthur Lee*, 214.

28. James, *Silas Deane*, 77.

29. Henderson, *Party Politics in the Continental Congress*, 195.

30. Ibid., 194.

31. Keane, *Tom Paine*, 176.

32. Ibid., 178–80.

33. Potts, *Arthur Lee*, 216.

34. Ronald J. Hoffman and Peter J. Albert, eds., *Diplomacy and Revolution: The Franco-American Alliance of 1778* (Charlottesville, Va., 1981), 135–38.

35. T. H. Butterfield, ed., *The Adams Papers, Diary & Autobiography of John Adams*, vol. 4 (New York, 1964), 67.

36. Ibid., 346–47.

37. Ibid. Also see Peter Shaw, *The Character of John Adams* (Chapel Hill, N.C., 1976), 117–21.

38. Butterfield, ed., *Adams Papers*, vol. II, 345, 346–50.

39. Potts, *Arthur Lee*, 221. Butterfield, *Adams Papers*, vol. 2, 353.

40. Potts, *Arthur Lee*, 224.

41. Mary A. Giunta, ed., *The Emerging Nation: A Documentary History of the Foreign Relations of the United States Under the Articles of Confederation*, vol. 2 (Washington, D.C., 1996), 159–60. Henderson, *Party Politics in the Continental Congress*, 198–213.

42. *PBF*, vol. 32, 186.

43. James Grant, *John Adams, Party of One* (New York, 2005), 244.

44. *PBF*, vol. 33, 162–63.
45. Shaw, *The Character of John Adams*, 143. The seventy-six-year-old Adams denounced Franklin's letter as "this dark transaction to posterity."
46. James, *Silas Deane*, 90.
47. Ibid., 99.
48. Stacy Schiff, *A Great Improvisation: Franklin, France and the Birth of America* (New York, 2005), 261. Potts, *Arthur Lee*, 245.
49. *PBF*, vol. 34, 371–73.
50. *PBF*, vol. 34, 443–48.
51. Keane, *Tom Paine*, 84.
52. Gregory D. Massey, *John Laurens and the American Revolution* (Columbia, S.C., 2000), 183.
53. Ibid., 188.
54. John Hardman, *Louis XVI* (New Haven, Conn., 1993), 64–67.
55. Samuel Flagg Bemis, *The Diplomacy of the American Revolution* (Bloomington, Ind., 1957), 181–82.
56. Grant, *John Adams*, 262.
57. Ibid., 263.
58. Gregg L. Lint et al., eds., *Papers of John Adams* (hereafter PJA), vol. 11 (Cambridge, Mass., 2003), 232, 317–18. *PBF*, vol. 35, 407–8.
59. *PBF*, vol. 35, 629.
60. *PBF*, vol. 36, (Diary of Elkanah Watson) 72–75.
61. *PBF*, vol. 36, 79.

CHAPTER 3: AN EMPIRE ON THE BRINK

1. Jacob M. Price, "The Imperial Economy," in P. J. Marshall, ed., *The Oxford History of the British Empire*, vol. 2, The Eighteenth Century (New York, 1998), 78–104.
2. H. Butterfield, *George III, Lord North and the People, 1779–1780* (London, 1949), 373–82. Alan Valentine, *Lord North* (Norman, Okla., 1967), vol. 2, 115–16.
3. Stanley Ayling, *George the Third* (New York, 1972), 95.
4. E. A. Reitan, "The Civil List in Eighteenth Century British Politics: Parliamentary Supremacy versus the Independence of the Crown," *Historical Journal*, vol. 9, 1966, 318–27.
5. Ayling, *George the Third*, 254–55.
6. G. R. Barnes and J. H. Owen, eds., *The Private Papers of John, Earl of Sandwich, First Lord of the Admiralty, 1771–1782*, vol. 1 (London 1932–38), 63.
7. Valentine, *Lord North*, vol. 2, 103.
8. Ibid., 103.
9. Conor Cruse O'Brien, *The Great Melody: A Thematic Biography of Edmund Burke* (Chicago, 1991), 194. Valentine, *Lord North*, vol. 2, 150–51.
10. Valentine, *Lord North*, vol. 2, 158.
11. John Brewer, *The Sinews of Power: War, Money and the English State, 1688–1783* (Cambridge, Mass., 1990), xvi, 42.
12. Ibid., 103.
13. O'Brien, *The Great Melody*, 3–4.
14. Ibid., 211–12.
15. Butterworth, *George III, Lord North and the People*, 329–32.
16. Hoffman, *The Marquis*, 178–79.

17. O'Brien, *The Great Melody*, 163.

18. Ibid., 164.

19. Andrew Stockley, *Britain and France at the Birth of America: The European Powers and the Peace Negotiations, 1782–1783* (Exeter, U.K., 2001), 23–25. When Denmark told the British ambassador that their merchant ships would be escorted by Danish men-of-war, the ambassador reportedly sneered: "And who will escort the Danish men of war?"

20. Friederich Edler, *The Dutch Republic and the American Revolution*, 1971 reprint of 1911 edition (New York, 1971), 59, 65–66, 148–50. Captain W. M. James, *The British Navy in Adversity: A Study of the War of American Independence*, reprint (Cranbury, N.J., 2005), 310–11. G. J. Marcus, *A Naval History of England*, vol. 1, *The Formative Centuries* (Boston, 1961), 432.

21. John Keay, *The Honourable Company: A History of The English East India Company* (New York, 1991), 411–12. Also see Marshall, ed., *Oxford History of the British Empire*, vol. 2, The Eighteenth Century, 100–101.

22. Marshall, ed., *Oxford History of the British Empire*, 101.

23. Ian R. Christie, *The End of North's Ministry, 1780–1782* (New York, 1958), 268.

24. Ibid., 269.

25. O'Brien, *The Great Melody*, 160.

26. Nathanael Wraxhall, *Historical Memoirs of My Own Time* (London, 1815), 138–39.

27. Valentine, *Lord North*, vol. 2, 174.

28. Ayling, *George the Third*, 287. Valentine, *Lord North*, vol. 2, 274–75.

29. Willcox, *Portrait of a General*, 456. Solomon Lutnick, *The American Revolution and the British Press* (Columbia, Mo., 1967), 188–89.

30. O'Brien, *The Great Melody*, 220.

31. Ibid. Also see Stanley Weintraub, *Iron Tears: America's Battle for Freedom, Britain's Quagmire, 1775–1783* (New York, 2005), 306.

32. O'Brien, *The Great Melody*, 221.

33. Valentine, *Lord North*, vol. 2, 276–77.

CHAPTER 4: THE ART OF MAKING SOMETHING OUT OF NOTHING

1. *WGW*, vol. 23, 380–81.

2. *LDC*, vol. 18, 227. Oliver Wolcott of Connecticut reported only nine states were represented on Dec. 3, 1781.

3. Ibid., 189–90, note.

4. *LDC*, vol. 18, 201–2.

5. *WGW*, vol. 23, 444–45.

6. Richard Buel Jr., *In Irons: Britain's Naval Supremacy and the American Revolutionary Economy* (New Haven, Conn., 1998), 31–40. In one six-month period, entering vessels owned by Philadelphians declined from 7,708 tons to 460 tons.

7. Nash, *The Unknown American Revolution*, 310.

8. Steven Rosswurm, *Arms, Country, and Class: The Philadelphia Militia and the Lower Sort During the American Revolution* (New Brunswick, N.J., 1969), 211–17.

9. Ibid., 220–22, 242–43. Also see *LMCC*, vol. 6, 83; Nash, *The Unknown American Revolution*, 364.

10. Rosswurm, *Arms, Country, Class*, 243–44.

11. *LMCC*, vol. 1, 433.

12. *LMCC*, vol. 2, 183–84. E. James Ferguson, *The Power of the Purse, A History of American Public Finance* (Chapel Hill, N.C., 1961), 118.

13. John N. Rackove, *The Beginnings of National Politics: An Interpretive History of the Continental Congress* (New York, 1979), 300.

14. Clarence L. Ver Steeg, *Robert Morris, Revolutionary Financier* (New York, 1976), 63. Morris never sent this letter. He may have learned of Necker's resignation on May 19, 1781, and decided not to mail it.

15. Ferguson, *Power of the Purse*, 128–29, 179–80 for foreign and domestic debts.

16. Ver Steeg, *Robert Morris*, 61–62.

17. Ferguson, *Power of the Purse*, 134.

18. Ibid., 119.

19. *LMCC*, vol. 6, 20.

20. Irving Brant, *James Madison, 1780–1787*, vol. 2, *The Nationalist* (New York, 1948), 20.

21. Ferguson, *Power of the Purse*, 180.

22. James Catanzariti and E. James Ferguson, eds., *The Papers of Robert Morris* (hereafter *PRM*) (Pittsburgh, Pa., 1984), vol. 4, 191.

23. Ver Steeg, *Robert Morris*, 133.

24. *PRM*, 201, 327–28.

25. Ibid., 205–13. Also see Edmund Cody Burnett, *The Continental Congress* (New York, 1941), 527.

26. *PNG*, vol. 10, 3–5.

27. Ibid., 20–22.

28. Ibid., 468–69.

29. Ibid., 468–70.

30. Patrick O'Kelley, *Nothing But Blood and Slaughter: The Revolutionary War in the Carolinas*, vol. 3, 1781 (Booklocker.com), 384ff. Edward McReady, *The History of South Carolina in the Revolution* (New York, 1902), 467ff. John S. Pancake, *This Destructive War: The British Campaign in the Carolinas, 1780–82* (Tuscaloosa, Al., 1985), 87–88. Robert S. Lambert, *South Carolina Loyalists in the American Revolution* (Columbia S.C., 1987), 206ff. PNG, vol. 9, Col. Leroy Hammond to Greene, Dec. 2, 1781, 651–52.

31. Massey, *John Laurens*, 86–106. Wiener, *An Imperfect God*, 223–24.

32. Wiener, *An Imperfect God*, 230–32.

33. Ibid., 233.

34. *PNG*, vol. 10, 5–6.

35. Ibid., 20–23.

36. Massey, *John Laurens*, 202–3.

37. *PNG*, vol. 10, 206–7, 242–44. Also see Massey, *John Laurens*, 203–6.

38. *PNG*, vol. 10, 228–29.

39. *WGW*, vol. 24, 33.

40. *PNG*, vol. 10, note, 229–30.

41. *WGW*, vol. 24, 421. Also see Wiener, *An Imperfect God*, 231.

42. Paul David Nelson, *Anthony Wayne, Soldier of the Republic* (Bloomington, Ind., 1985), 144–45, 163–64.

43. *PNG*, vol. 10, 173–75.

44. Ibid., 174, note; 176, note.

45. Wilson, *The Loyal Blacks*, 30.

46. *PNG*, vol. 10, 143, note, 340–41.

47. Nelson, *Wayne,* 167.
48. *PNG,* vol. 10, 423.
49. Ibid. For Cornell description, 301–2.
50. *LDC,* vol. 18, 345.
51. *WGW,* vol. 24, 2.
52. *PRM,* vol. 4, 256–59.
53. David Freeman Hawke, *Paine* (New York, 1974), 124–25.
54. Ellis Paxson Oberholtzer, *Robert Morris: Patriot and Financier* (New York, 1903), 125.
55. Rakove, *The Beginnings of National Politics,* 309.
56. *LDC,* vol. 18, 618.
57. Oberholtzer, *Robert Morris,* 125.

CHAPTER 5: UNCROWNING A KING

1. Piers Mackesy, *The War for America 1773–1783* (Cambridge, Mass., 1964), 461–62. Alan Valentine, *Lord George Germain* (London, 1962), 448–49.
2. Christie, *The End of North's Ministry,* 272–73.
3. O'Brien, *The Great Melody,* 222.
4. Valentine, *Lord North,* vol. 2, 280–81.
5. Ibid., 283–84.
6. Christie, *The End of North's Ministry,* 276–83.
7. Ibid., 273–74.
8. Mackesy, *The War for America,* 463.
9. Christie, *The End of North's Ministry,* 322.
10. Mackesy, *The War for America,* 446–50. Marcus, *A Naval History of England,* 446.
11. Marshall, *History of the British Empire,* vol 2., Rajat Kanta Ray, *vol. 2, Indian Society and British Supremacy,* 518–20. Mackesy, *The War for America,* 494–95.
12. *PBF,* vol. 36, 359–64.
13. Ibid., 435–38.
14. *PBF,* vol. 37, 141–42.
15. Christie, *The End of North's Ministry,* 292. Valentine, *Lord North,* vol. 2, 288.
16. Valentine, *Lord North,* vol. 2, 298.
17. Ibid., 299–300.
18. Mackesy, *The War for America,* 467.
19. Valentine, *Lord North,* vol. 2, 293–95.
20. Christie, *The End of North's Ministry,* 299–303.
21. Ibid., 314.
22. Valentine, *Lord North,* vol. 2, 304–5.
23. Mackesy, *The War for America,* 468.
24. Butterfield, *George III, Lord North and the People,* 315–33.
25. *PBF,* vol. 36, 621–22.
26. Weintraub, *Iron Tears,* 317.
27. Valentine, *Lord North,* vol. 2, 305. Christie, *The End of North's Ministry,* 339.
28. Valentine, *Lord North,* vol. 2, 306.
29. Mackesy, *The War for America,* 468.
30. Christie, *The End of North's Ministry,* 342–43.
31. Valentine, *Lord North,* vol. 2, 307.
32. O'Brien, *The Great Melody,* 224–25. Christie, *The End of North's Ministry,* 346–47.

33. Christie, *The End of North's Ministry*, 350.

34. O'Brien, *The Great Melody*, 225–26.

35. Valentine, *Lord North*, vol. 2, 312–13.

36. Ibid., 314.

37. Ibid., 315–16. Christie, *The End of North's Ministry*, 368–69.

38. O'Brien, *The Great Melody*, 226–27.

39. Hoffman, *The Marquis*, 378–79.

40. Ayling, *George the Third*, 290–93.

41. Mackesy, *The War for America*, 456-57. Marcus, *A Naval History of England*, 446.

42. James, *The British Navy in Adversity*, 339–40.

43. Marcus, *A Naval History of England*, 448–49.

44. James, *The British Navy in Adversity*, 347. Also see A. T. Mahan, *The Major Operations of the Navies in the War of American Independence* (Boston, 1913), 207–25. British losses were only 243 killed and 846 wounded in their 36-ship fleet. French losses were far heavier. More than 300 were killed aboard the *Ville de Paris*, de Grasse's flagship. Six French captains were killed against two British.

45. *PBF*, vol. 37, note 2, 314. News of Rodney's victory reached London on May 18 and was published in the newspapers on May 20.

CHAPTER 6: MEN TALK PEACE BUT
THERE IS NO PEACE

1. *PBF*, vol. 36, 645.

2. Ibid., 674.

3. Ibid., 672.

4. Ibid., 630.

5. Ibid., 20, 644, 647.

6. *PBF*, vol. 37, 87–89.

7. Ibid., 24.

8. Ronald Hoffman and Peter J. Albert, *Peace and the Peacemakers, The Treaty of 1783* (Charlottesville, Va., 1986), 79–80.

9. Bemis, *Diplomacy of the American Revolution*, 202, note 36.

10. *PBF*, vol. 37, 102–4.

11. Ibid., 166, note 5.

12. Ibid., 165–67.

13. Ibid., 291–96.

14. Ibid., 263–65.

15. Ibid., 198.

16. Ibid., 235, note 2; 282, note 8; and Franklin letter to John Adams, discussing Oswald's reticence; 281–82.

17. Ibid., 281–82.

18. Hoffman, *The Marquis*, 380–81.

19. *PBF*, vol. 37, 303–4 (BF Journal of the Peace Negotiations).

20. Ibid., 307–8. Also see note 7, 308–9.

21. Brian Gardner, *The East India Company* (New York, 1971), 118–19. Coote died in Madras after suffering a stroke during the follow-up battles.

22. *PBF*, vol. 37, 320 (BF Journal of the Peace Negotiations).

23. O'Brien, *The Great Melody*, 232. *PBF*, vol. 37, 341 (BF Journal of the Peace Negotiations).

24. *PBF,* vol. 37, 331 (BF Journal of the Peace Negotiations).
25. Ibid., 342.
26. Ibid., 344.
27. C. R. Ritcheson, "The Earl of Shelbourne and Peace with America, 1782–1783, Vision and Reality," *The International History Review,* vol. 3 (Aug. 1983), 337.
28. Hoffman, *The Marquis,* 382. *PBF,* vol. 37, 598, note 6.
29. O'Brien, *The Great Melody,* 231.

CHAPTER 7: LOOSE CANNONS FRONT AND CENTER

1. *PAH,* vol. 3, 89–91.
2. Robert Hendrickson, *Alexander Hamilton,* vol. 1 (New York, 1976), 360–61.
3. Ibid., 363–64.
4. *PAH,* vol. 3, 137–39.
5. Ibid., 368–69. McHenry's service in the Maryland state senate, about which he corresponded with Washington, obviously did not take up much of his time.
6. Ibid., 368–69.
7. Hendrickson, *Hamilton,* 364–65.
8. Ver Steeg, *Robert Morris,* 98–99.
9. Henderson, *Party Politics in the Continental Congress,* 294.
10. Brant, *Madison,* vol. 2, 212.
11. A. Elwood Corning, *Washington at Temple Hill* (Mewburgh, N.Y., 1932), 88–89.
12. E. Wayne Carp, *To Starve the Army at Pleasure* (Chapel Hill N.C., 1984), 214–15. Freeman, *George Washington,* vol. 5, 412.
13. Flexner, *George Washington,* vol. 2, 476.
14. *LDC,* vol. 18, 518–19, including note. *WGW,* vol. 24, 175–77.
15. Roger J. Champagne, *Alexander McDougall and the American Revolution in New York* (Schenectady, N.Y., 1975), 174–80.
16. Flexner, *George Washington,* vol. 2, 477, 484.
17. David J. Fowler, "Egregious Killers, Wood Rangers and London Traders—the Pine Robber Phenomenon in New Jersey During the Revolution," PhD diss., Rutgers University, 1987, 30.
18. Freeman, *Washington,* vol. 5, 412–14.
19. Bemis, *Diplomacy of the Revolution,* 201–2.
20. Ibid., 202.
21. *LDC,* vol. 18, 509ff has many letters from Madison and other congressmen expressing great concern about Carleton's diplomacy. Mingled with this was the impact of the news of Rodney's victory in the West Indies.
22. Sabine, *Smith Memoirs,* vol. 2, 503–4.
23. William Heath, *Memoirs of Major General Heath* (Boston, 1798), 316–17.
24. Sabine, *Smith Memoirs,* 504–5.
25. Ibid., 505.
26. Freeman, *George Washington,* vol. 5, 415–16. LDC, vol. 18, 619.
27. *PAH,* vol. 3, 119. WGW, vol. 24, 315.
28. L. H. Butterfield, ed., *Letters of Benjamin Rush* (Princeton, N.J., 1951), vol. 1, 278–82. Keane, *Tom Paine,* 228–29.
29. *WGW,* vol. 24, 273–74, including note.
30. *PNG,* vol. 10, 590–91.
31. *PNG,* vol. 11, 87–88, note 2.

32. Ibid., 93–94, 97–98.
33. Ibid., 474. Also see George Washington Greene, *The Life of Nathanael Greene*, vol. 3 (Freeport, N.Y., 1972) (reprint), 457.
34. *PNG*, vol. 11, 227–29, including note 1 on latter page.
35. Ibid., 275.
36. Nelson, *Anthony Wayne*, 170.
37. *PNG* vol. 11, 241–45. Nelson, *Anthony Wayne*, 170–71.
38. *PNG*, vol. 11, 365–67, including notes.
39. Ibid., 439.
40. Nelson, *Anthony Wayne*, 177. PNG, vol. 11, 440–41.
41. *PNG*, vol. 11, 183, note. The information came from a British informant in Charleston.
42. Sabine, *Smith Memoirs*, vol. 2, 528–41.
43. Giunta, ed., *The Emerging Nation*, 421–26.
44. Sabine, *Smith Memoirs*, 541–42.
45. Mackesy, *The War for America*, 492.
46. Giunta, *The Emerging Nation*, 425.
47. Sabine, *Smith Memoirs*, 543.
48. *PNG*, vol. 11, 91.
49. *PBF*, vol. 36, 59–60. Massey, *John Laurens*, 214–15.
50. *PNG*, vol. 11, 90–91.
51. Massey, *John Laurens*, 216–17.
52. *PNG*, vol. 11, 295. Massey, *John Laurens*, 230.
53. Massey, *John Laurens*, 213–14. Mrs. Clitherall gave Laurens the information about the withdrawal of 1,051 men from the Charleston garrison to defend Jamaica.
54. *PAH*, vol. 3, 144–45.
55. Massey, *John Laurens*, 226–27.
56. *LDC*, vol. 18, 440–41.
57. *LDC*, vol. 18, 623–24. Potts, *Arthur Lee*, 260.
58. *LDC*, vol. 18, 618.
59. Brant, *Madison*, vol. 2, 196.
60. Potts, *Arthur Lee*, 256.
61. *LDC*, vol. 18, 662–63. Brant, *Madison*, vol. 2, 194.
62. Brant, *Madison*, vol. 2, 200.

CHAPTER 8: A PEACE THAT SURPASSES UNDERSTANDING

1. Morris, *The Peacemakers*, 290. O'Brien, *The Great Melody*, 239.
2. John Norris, *Shelburne and Reform* (New York, 1963), 4–5. Shelburne's second wife was the sister of Richard Fitzpatrick, one of Fox's closest friends. But intimate contact only seems to have increased Fox's detestation.
3. *PBF*, vol. 37, 598, note 8.
4. Ritcheson, *The Earl of Shelbourne and Peace With America*, 339–40. Stockley, *Britain and France at the Birth of America*, 39.
5. Giunta, *The Emerging Nation*, 450–51.
6. *PBF*, vol. 37, 566.
7. Ibid., 599–601 (note).
8. Ibid., 621–22.
9. Giunta, *The Emerging Nation*, 470–71.

10. Ronald Hoffman and Peter J. Albert, *Peace and the Peacemakers, the Treaty of 1783* (Charlottesville, Va., 1986), 81–82.

11. Giunta, *The Emerging Nation,* 479–80.

12. Morris, *The Peacemakers,* 306–7. Walter Stahr, *John Jay, Founding Father* (New York, 2005), 150–55.

13. Stahr, *John Jay,* 152.

14. *PRM,* vol. 5, 261–63.

15. Morris, *The Peacemakers,* 309–10. Stahr, *John Jay,* 153.

16. Jonathan R. Dull, *The French Navy and American Independence: A Study of Arms and Diplomacy* (Princeton, N.J., 1975), 279–80, 297–98, 345–50. Also see Dull, "France and the American Revolution as Tragedy," in Hoffman and Albert, *Diplomacy and Revolution,* 101–2.

17. Morris, *The Peacemakers,* 308–9.

18. Murphy, *Charles Gravier, Comte de Vergennes,* 333–35.

19. Morris, *The Peacemakers,* 52.

20. Stahr, *John Jay,* 154–55.

21. Morris, *The Peacemakers,* 313.

22. Stockley, *Britain and France at the Birth of America,* 70–71.

23. Stahr, *John Jay,* 158–59.

24. Giunta, *The Emerging Nation,* Charles Thomson's Notes of Debates (in Congress), 512–13.

25. Ibid., 515.

26. Brant, *Madison,* 199. Potts, *Arthur Lee,* 257–59.

27. Dull, *The French Navy and American Independence,* 307–9. Marcus, *A Naval History of England,* 437–38.

28. Butterfield, *Adams Papers,* vol. 3, 38, 46–47.

29. Shaw, *The Character of John Adams,* 167–69. "Matthew Ridley's Diary During the Peace Negotiations of 1782," ed. Herbert E. Klingelhofer, *William and Mary Quarterly,* 3rd Ser., vol. 20, no. 1, Jan. 1963, 95–133.

30. Butterfield, *Adams Papers,* vol. 3, 47–50. "Matthew Ridley's Diary," 122–23.

31. Butterfield, *Adams Papers,* vol. 3, 82.

32. Dull, *The French Navy and American Independence,* 316. Also see Jonathan R. Dull, *A Diplomatic History of the American Revolution* (New Haven, Conn., 1985), 153. For the number of British seamen in 1783, see Stephen Conway, *The British Isles and the War for American Independence* (New York, 2000), 17–18.

33. Dull, *The French Navy and American Independence,* 317–20. Vergennes told Montmorin that France could raise enough money for a 1783 campaign but "I will not answer for the one following." Also see Harlow Giles Unger, *Lafayette* (New York, 2002), 170, and "Matthew Ridley's Diary," 122–23, in which he notes that Vergennes and his supporters were under attack from the French comptroller of finance, Joly de Fleury.

34. Morris, *The Peacemakers,* 331. Dull, *The French Navy,* 307.

35. Stahr, *John Jay,* 164. "Matthew Ridley's Diary," 123. Clever is used here to mean smoothly or dexterously.

36. Grant, *John Adams,* 282.

37. Stahr, *John Jay,* 167, 190.

38. "Matthew Ridley's Diary," 131. Morris, *The Peacemakers,* 375. Stahr, *John Jay,* 359–60.

39. Wilson, *The Loyal Blacks,* 48–49. David R. Chesnutt and C. James Taylor, eds., *The Papers of Henry Laurens* (hereafter *PHL*) (Columbia, S.C., 2003), vol. 16, 78–80.

40. Morris, *The Peacemakers*, 382.

41. Murphy, *Charles Gravier, Comte de Vergennes*, 393.

42. Giunta, *The Emerging Nation*, 720.

43. Ibid., 721–22.

44. Carl Van Doren, *Benjamin Franklin* (New York, 1941), 697.

45. Ayling, *George the Third*, 295.

46. Stockley, *Britain and France at the Birth of America*, 141–43. Morris, *The Peacemakers*, 411–12.

47. Valentine, *Lord North*, vol. 2, 338–39.

48. Morris, *The Peacemakers*, 413–14.

49. Ibid., 414–15.

50. Stockley, *Britain and France at the Birth of America*, 98–103. Murphy, *Charles Gravier, Comte de Vergennes*, 361–69.

51. Stockley, *Britain and France at the Birth of America*, 107–9, 119–24. Morris, *The Peacemakers*, 406–8.

52. Mohibbul Hasan, "The French in the Second Anglo-Mysore War," 34–45 in Marshall, *Oxford History of the British Empire*, vol. 2, *The Eighteenth Century*. Also see Dull, *The French Navy and American Independence*, 334. Keay, *The Honourable Company*, 414–15. Gardner, *The East India Company*, 120–21.

53. Dull, *The French Navy and American Independence*, 333, note.

54. Ibid., 334–35.

55. *PHL*, vol. 15, 514–15.

56. Mariboe, "Life of William Franklin," 556.

57. Mackesy, *The War for America*, 509. Morris, *The Peacemakers*, 421.

58. Valentine, *Lord North*, 350–51.

59. Norris, *Shelburne and Reform*, 266. Morris, *The Peacemakers*, 422. Solomon Lutnick, *The American Revolution and the British Press* (Colombia, Mo., 1967), 205–6.

60. Holden Farber, ed., *The Correspondence of Edmund Burke*, vol. 5, July 1782–June 1789 (Chicago, 1965), 71–72.

CHAPTER 9: WILL IT BE PEACE—OR CIVIL WAR?

1. Rakove, *The Beginnings of National Politics*, 316.

2. Charles Rappleye, *Sons of Providence: The Brown Brothers, the Slave Trade and the American Revolution* (New York, 2006), 217–18.

3. William T. Hutchinson and William M. E. Rachal, eds., *Papers of James Madison* (hereafter *PJM*) (Chicago, 1969), vol. 6, 11–12, note 3. Also see Rackove, *Beginnings of National Politics*, 316.

4. Keane, *Tom Paine*, 239–40. Rappleye, *Sons of Providence*, 220–22.

5. Catherine S. Crary, *The Price of Loyalty: Tory Writings from the Revolutionary Era* (New York, 1973), 293.

6. Wilson, *The Loyal Blacks*, 46–47.

7. *PNG*, vol. 12, 291–92.

8. Ibid., 364. O'Kelley, *Nothing but Blood and Slaughter*, vol. 3, 119.

9. *PNG*, vol. 12, 308–9.

10. *PNG*, vol. 12, 574–94. There were numerous overheated letters from both sides. Greene apologized to the British officer, describing Governor Guerard as an ignoramus who did not understand "the law of nations." For South Carolina's withdrawal

of its approval of the impost, see ibid., 383, note, and 494–95, Greene's letter to Gov.
Guerard, advising against the decision.

11. Ibid., 656.
12. Edward Countryman, *A People in Revolution: The American Revolution and Political Society in New York, 1760–1790* (Baltimore, Md., 1981), 154–58, 211.
13. Thomas Jones, *History of New York in the Revolutionary War* (New York, 1879), 210–12. John P. Kaminski, *George Clinton, Yeoman Politician of the New Republic* (Madison, Wisc., 1993), 63–77. Daniel M. Friedenberg, *Life, Liberty and Pursuit of Land* (Buffalo, N.Y., 1992), 311–18.
14. Flexner, *George Washington,* vol. 2, 484.
15. Carp, *To Starve the Army at Pleasure,* 216.
16. Acomb, *Journal of Baron von Closen,* 257–59.
17. Minor Meyers Jr., *Liberty Without Anarchy: A History of the Society of the Cincinnati* (Charlottesville, Va., 1983), 4-9.
18. Richard H. Kohn, "The Inside History of the Newburgh Conspiracy, America and the Coup d'etat," *The William and Mary Quarterly,* vol. 28, 1972, 187–220. Richard Buel Jr., *Dear Liberty: Connecticut's Mobilization for the Revolutionary War* (Middletown, Ct., 1980), 301. Champagne, *Alexander McDougall,* 185–86.
19. Kohn, "The Newburgh Conspiracy," 192.
20. *PJM,* vol. 6, 20–21.
21. Ibid., 31–34. Madison's notes on the Grand Committee's "audience to the deputies from the army."
22. Ibid., 40.
23. Ibid., 119–21. Madison's notes on debates, Jan. 24, 1783.
24. Kohn, "The Newburgh Conspiracy," 195.
25. *PAH,* vol. 3, 246.
26. Ibid., note 3, 246. Kohn, "The Newburgh Conspiracy," 196.
27. Kohn, "The Newburgh Conspiracy," 197. "Brutus" was the name McDougall had used when he wrote incendiary newspaper articles denouncing British rule before the Revolution.
28. *PAH,* vol. 3, 253–55.
29. Freeman, *George Washington,* vol. 5, 428.
30. *PAH,* vol. 3, 277–79.
31. Ibid., 256.
32. Kohn, "The Newburgh Conspiracy," 203.
33. Ibid., 196, 204.
34. Ibid., 306, note 62.
35. Ibid., 207.
36. *PAH,* vol. 3, 287. LMCC, 7, 61.
37. Kohn, "The Newburgh Conspiracy," 208–9.
38. *WGW,* vol. 26, 222–27.
39. Kohn, "The Newburgh Conspiracy," 209–11. Also Flexner, *George Washington,* 505–8.
40. Kohn, "The Newburgh Conspiracy," 212–13. Also see: *LDG,* vol. 20, 171–75. Eliphalet Dyer rants and fumes in a letter to Governor Trumbull of Connecticut and finally collapses.
41. Meyers, *Liberty Without Anarchy,* 11.
42. *PAH,* vol. 3, 307–8.
43. Ibid., 315–16.

CHAPTER 10: A RUNAWAY CONGRESS VS.
A BERSERK PARLIAMENT

1. *PJM*, vol. 6, 348.
2. Ibid., 328–29.
3. Ibid.
4. Ibid., 329.
5. Ibid., 329–30.
6. Sabine, *Smith Memoirs*, vol. 2, 560.
7. Stanley J. Idzerda and Robert Rhodes Clout, eds., *Lafayette in the Age of the American Revolution, Selected Letters and Papers, 1776–1790* (Ithaca, N.Y., 1983), vol. 5, 90–93.
8. Ibid., 119–21.
9. Ibid., 93, note. *WGW*, vol. 26, 297–301.
10. Unger, *Lafayette*, 17–75.
11. Ibid., 176.
12. *LMCC*, vol. 7, 135.
13. *WGW*, vol. 26, 330–34.
14. Ibid., 334–37.
15. Ibid., 337, note.
16. Ibid., 332.
17. Ibid., 330–32.
18. Meyers, *Liberty Without Anarchy*, 24–29.
19. *PHL*, vol. 16, 79–80. In this letter to the South Carolina delegates to Congress, Henry Laurens wrote: "I urged an addition to the later part of Article 7 prohibiting the carrying away Negroes and other property which I hope will lay a foundation for a future claim." The wording suggests he had little hope of regaining the slaves in a literal sense.
20. Sabine, *Smith Memoirs*, vol. 2, 586–88. *WGW*, vol. 26, 369–70.
21. *PJM*, vol. 6, Notes on Debates, 486.
22. Ver Steeg, *Robert Morris*, 178–79.
23. *WGW*, vol. 26, 466–67.
24. Heath, *Memoirs*, 344–46.
25. Flexner, *George Washington*, vol. 2, 514.
26. Scheer, *Private Yankee Doodle*, 279–81. Congress did not have the money to redeem back-pay certificates until the mid-1790s. By that time almost all had been sold to speculators. In 1828, Congress voted pensions for the comparative handful of surviving veterans. Don Higginbotham, *The War of American Independence* (New York, 1971), 412.
27. *LMCC*, vol. 7, 175, note 3.
28. Meyers, *Liberty Without Anarchy*, 35.
29. *LMCC*, vol. 7, 192–93. Helen E. Royer, "The Role of the Continental Congress in Prosecuting the Revolution in Pennsylvania," PhD diss., Pennsylvania State University, 1960, 339–41. Varnum Lansing Collins, *The Continental Congress at Princeton* (Princeton, N.J., 1908), 19–21.
30. Collins, *The Continental Congress at Princeton*, 22.
31. *PJM*, vol. 6, 451–52, note 4.
32. Collins, *The Continental Congress at Princeton*, 22.
33. *PJM*, vol. 7, 176–79, including notes 6 and 7.
34. *LMCC*, vol. 7, 199–200.

35. Ayling, *George the Third*, 298.
36. Ibid., 300–301.
37. Valentine, *Lord North*, vol. 2, 363.
38. Ibid., 367.
39. Morris, *The Peacemakers*, 430.
40. Stockley, *Britain and France at the Birth of America*, 179.
41. Ibid., 180.
42. Charles W. Akers, *The Divine Politician: Samuel Cooper and the American Revolution in Boston* (Boston, 1982), 344–46.
43. Ibid., 346.
44. *LMCC*, vol. 7, 276.
45. Stockley, *Britain and France at the Birth of America*, 198.
46. Ayling, *George the Third*, 305, 308.
47. Valentine, *Lord North*, vol. 2, 390–92.
48. Orville T. Murphy, "The View From Versailles," in Hoffman and Albert, *Diplomacy and Revolution*, 149.
49. Murphy, *Charles Gravier, Comte de Vergennes*, 252.

CHAPTER 11: GEORGE WASHINGTON'S TEARS

1. Collins, *The Continental Congress at Princeton*, 33–35.
2. Ibid., 248–49.
3. Potts, *Arthur Lee*, 265.
4. *PJM*, vol. 7, 207–9, including note 4.
5. Collins, *The Continental Congress at Princeton*, 61–62.
6. *PAH*, vol. 3, 416–17, 420–26.
7. *LMCC*, vol. 7, 291–92. For Boudinot lament, *LMCC*, vol. 7, 279.
8. Collins, *The Continental Congress at Princeton*, 80.
9. Hawke, *Paine*, 141.
10. Potts, *Arthur Lee*, 262.
11. *LMCC*, vol. 7, 251–52.
12. Van Buskirk, *Generous Enemies*, 165–66. Sabine, *Smith Memoirs*, vol. 2, 599.
13. *PJM*, vol. 7, 42.
14. Wilson, *The Loyal Blacks*, 55.
15. *PAH*, vol. 3, 431.
16. Collins, *The Continental Congress at Princeton*, 216–36. Edler, *The Dutch Republic and the American Revolution*, 244–46.
17. Terry Golway, *Washington's General: General Nathanael Greene and the Triumph of the American Revolution* (New York, 2004), 309.
18. Ibid., 312–14.
19. *WGW*, vol. 27, 222–27.
20. Gerard R. Clarfield, *Timothy Pickering and the American Republic* (Pittsburgh, Pa., 1980), 83–84. Flexner, *George Washington*, vol. 2, 522.
21. Buel, *Dear Liberty*, 302–13. Meyers, *Liberty Without Anarchy*, 49. Charles Royster, *A Revolutionary People at War: The Continental Army and the American Character, 1775–1783* (Chapel Hill, N.C., 1979), 349.
22. Royster, *A Revolutionary People at War*, 358.
23. Collins, *The Continental Congress in Princeton*, 167–88.
24. Ibid., 191–92.

25. Ibid., 190.

26. *WGW*, vol. 27, 228.

27. Freeman, *George Washington*, vol. 5, 458.

28. Ibid., 460–64. Van Buskirk, *Generous Enemies*, 180–81.

29. Sabine, *Smith Memoirs*, vol. 2, 612–14. Van Buskirk, *Generous Enemies*, 180, 194.

30. Crary, *The Price of Loyalty*, 402–3.

31. Ibid., 404.

32. Wallace Brown, *The Good Americans: The Loyalists in the American Revolution* (New York, 1969), 140–41, 203. Crary, *The Price of Loyalty*, 404–5. Wilson, *The Loyal Blacks*, 92–94.

33. John Bakeless, *Traitors, Turncoats and Heroes* (New York, 1959), 228, 290, 358. Stanley Weintraub, *George Washington's Christmas Farewell: A Mount Vernon Homecoming* (New York, 2003), 73.

34. *PAH*, 317–21.

35. Benjamin Tallmadge, *Memoir of Benjamin Tallmadge* (New York, 1904), 96–98.

36. Freeman, *George Washington*, vol. 5, 466–68.

37. *WGW*, vol. 27, 260–62.

38. *PRM*, vol. 8, edited by Elizabeth M. Nuxoll and Mary A. Gallagher, 809–10, including note 1. Also see Freeman, *George Washington*, vol. 5, 470–71, and John C. Fitzpatrick, *George Washington Himself* (Indianapolis, 1933), 442.

39. *LDC*, vol. 21, 232–33. *WGW*, vol. 27, 285–86, note. Freeman, *George Washington*, 472–74.

40. *WGW*, vol. 27, 284–85. Also see *LDC*, vol. 20, 221–22 (James McHenry's letter to his fiancée, Margaret Caldwell).

41. Julian P. Boyd, ed., *The Papers of Thomas Jefferson*, vol. 7, March 1784–Feb. 1785 (Princeton, N.J., 1953), 105–8.

42. Robert C. Alberts, *Benjamin West, A Biography* (New York, 1978), 123.

Index

BOOKS BY THOMAS FLEMING

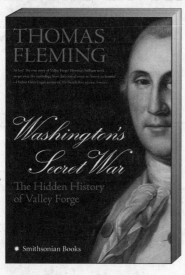

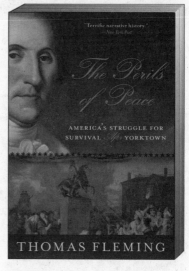

ISBN 978-0-06-087293-9 (paperback)
ISBN 978-0-06-082962-9 (hardcover)

ISBN 978-0-06-113911-6 (paperback)
ISBN 978-0-06-113910-9 (hardcover)

"[A] significant contribution to this history of the American Revolution . . . Fleming renders a satisfyingly sensible portrait of Washington's survival of the most frustrating winter of his discontent."

—Willard Sterne Randall, *Newsday*

"Fleming enhances his position as a leading general-audience historian of the American Revolution . . . [His] lively prose helps keep the complicated political maneuvers easy to follow."

—*Publishers Weekly* (starred review)

On October 19, 1781, Great Britain's best army surrendered to General George Washington at Yorktown. But the future of the 13 former colonies was far from clear. In this dramatic look at the Revolution after the last battle had been won, Thomas Fleming moves elegantly between the key players in this drama and shows that the outcome we take for granted was far from certain.

"Terrific narrative history."
—Terry Golway, *New York Post*

"A captivating account."
—*Kirkus Reviews*

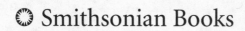 Smithsonian Books    COLLINS
An Imprint of HarperCollins*Publishers*
www.harpercollins.com